We would like to dedicate this book to
all the animation pioneers before us.
We are but fleas on the shoulders of giants.

The Magic of Animation

The theater was pitch-black as we made our way to our seats. I held my mother's hand because I couldn't see a thing in front of me. Once in our seats, I looked up at the towering screen and saw something I'll never forget. This was no ordinary movie, and the images on the screen were clearly not real. Yet they were hyper-real in a unique kind of way. The motion picture being screened that afternoon was Walt Disney's *Bambi*, and it was the first animated cartoon feature I had ever seen. Keep in mind, this was the 1940s, and television had not yet invaded our lives. The only way one saw an animated film was in a theater.

Floyd Norman,
Animator and Story Guy

Though only a small child, I knew the images I was watching were colored drawings. Yet these amazing drawings moved with life, had personality, and spoke clever dialogue. What kind of magic was this, I wondered? Whatever it was, this was something I wanted to do. This was something I had to do. That desire to bring life to pencil drawings has never left me. From my first animated scribbles in junior high school to viewing my early test footage at the Walt Disney studio, I continually remain in awe of moving drawings.

Over the years, I've been privileged to work with and learn from the best in the business. Masters whose work I enjoyed as a child were generous enough to share their years of experience with me. Yet knowledge can come from the most unlikely of places, so I've learned from kids as well as codgers. That's because we all shared the same passion, and continually searched for ways to improve our art.

This book continues that search, and you'll find yourself a better animation artist because of it. That blank sheet of pegged paper on your animation desk needn't engender fear or trepidation, because it's an incredible challenge. It is the opportunity to create, for lack of a better word, magic.

—Floyd Norman (www.afrokids.com/floydsbio.html)

This book has been lovingly crafted by two talented animators who enjoy their work and recognize the value of knowing the history, the art, and the craft of animation.

Jamie and Angie have pooled the knowledge of some truly talented professionals to help them convey to the artist, animator, historian, or fan the combination of technology, art, discipline, and heart that it takes to succeed as a contemporary animator.

Richard Taylor, Director, Designer, and CG Pioneer

What a phenomenal time this is in the evolution of animation and film. We are surrounded daily by the most complex visual imagery that mankind has ever created; be it in print, movies, television, games, or on the Internet, our lives are bombarded daily by images of seemingly limitless complexity. Today literally any image that a filmmaker can imagine can be realized. True, some dreams cost more than others, but the fact is the tools now exist that allow the artist, the animator, and the filmmaker to create photo-real illusions, fantasy characters that entertain and amaze us in films such as *Titanic*, *The Incredibles*, *Shrek*, *Jurassic Park*, *King Kong*, *Lord of the Rings*, *Harry Potter*, *The Matrix*, *Alien*, *Terminator*, *Blade Runner*, *Star Wars*, and *Tron*. Films packed with astounding special effects pour out of the studios yearly and on TV weekly. The technological tools to create this imagery are logarithmically improving as they become faster, better, and cheaper annually.

Tron—interesting that I would mention that film. I was co-visual effects supervisor on the picture, which was released in 1982. *Tron* was the film that introduced the world to computer imaging. So I've been involved with computer animation since its first use in the film industry. I've watched as art and technology fused to create the most powerful and limitless visual tool in the history of man. Computer-generated imaging (CGI) is now the fundamental tool used in creating visual effects and animated features. If there's one thing I've learned over the years, it's that computers and software don't create these fantastic images. A computer is analogous to a Steinway piano—it's an instrument. It's the artist who plays the instrument who brings it to life.

So how does one become an animator who is adept at the latest technological advances, yet still creates with the spirit and freedom of traditional hand-drawn animation? This book deals directly with that query and should give you plenty of answers.

v

To begin with, production designers, directors, animators, and other artisans who are legendary in the film industry have several things in common. They know how to draw, they study art and the history of their craft, they hang out with their peers, they are objective, and they make an effort to learn something new every day. But the most essential thing they have in common is self-discipline. Successful artists in painting, photography, music, dance, or animation are joined in an endless dance with their art forms. They put energy into the process daily, and in return it teaches them something new. The more you work at an art process, the more it teaches you. This dance is the mother of happy mistakes and magical revelations.

For those who love the art of animation and would like to make animation their life's work, this book will reveal some basic skills and understandings. Lean to draw 2D animation. The nature of hand-drawn animation allows the animator to exaggerate the elasticity, the personality of a character. Drawing by hand creates a rhythm and flow that's difficult to achieve in 3D work. It's the human feeling, the personality, the heart of the animator that can be realized through drawing. Dedicated animators observe the world around them. They constantly watch the way things move; they analyze body language and know that certain gestures convey feelings and emotions. A true animator creates more than anthropomorphic characters; they can bring life, personality, humor, or emotion to anything, be it a teapot, a tree, a lamp, or a chair.

Drawing, I believe, is essential to all the arts, especially the art of animation. The structure, design, and composition of a scene, the gesture of a character, the angle of view, the location, the set, and the props are all created through drawing. Conceptual drawings, storyboard frames, and character studies all seem to start on a napkin or a scrap of paper when an artist quickly sketches an idea before it vanishes. I'm sure you've heard the expression, "A picture is worth a thousand words." In filmmaking and games, thousands of dollars is more like it.

Technology has always affected the arts. Advances in technology spike the creative juices of artists, so it's inevitable that new ideas, new images, and new animations evolve—images that I like to say "remind you of something you've never seen before."

If you really want to be an animator, then begin right now by reading this book. And from this moment on, begin to learn and practice the basic skills of animation and learn to observe and interpret the magic movements of life.

—Richard Taylor (www.richardtaylordesign.com)

Acknowledgments

Like most CG productions, this book required an army of people to be realized. First, we would like to personally thank every artist who took time out of his or her day to talk with us about this book. This book is truly a collaborative effort and wouldn't be possible without the contributing authors: Henry Anderson, Bernd Angerer, Carlos Baena, Chris Bailey, Tony Bancroft, Mark Behm, Dave Brewster, Tom Capizzi, Brian Dowrick, Cory Florimonte, Dan Fowler, Angie Glocka, Eric Goldberg, Ido Gondelman, Evan Gore, Scott Holmes, Cathlin Hidalgo-Polvani, Ed Hooks, Victor Huang, Ethan Hurd, Mark Koetsier, Bert Klein, Keith Lango, Laura McCreary, Darin McGowan, Cameron Miyasaki, Mike Murphy, Floyd Norman, Eddie Pittman, Mike Polvani, Fred Raimondi, Nik Ranieri, Leigh Rens, Keith Roberts, Troy Saliba, Joe Scott, Tom Sito, David Smith, Roberto Smith, Javier Solsona, Mike Surrey, Richard Taylor, Alfred Urrutia, Conrad Vernon, Roger Vizard, Don Waller, Larry Weinberg, Paul Wood, Bill Wright, and Dave Zaboski.

> "Any idiot that wants to make a couple of thousand drawings for a hundred feet of film is welcome to join the club."
> —*Winsor McCay*

We also owe big thanks to Dan Patterson for building the clown model of our mascot, REDD, for this book. Dan was kind enough to work out not just the model, but also the hair and textures for our clown. Dan is a patient man and showed infinite patience during our "nitpicky" adjustments to his model. Thank you to Paul Tanner for refining the facial and making the model work smoothly in CG. To the great Christopher "Elegance" Christman, thank you for your time spent on lighting ol' REDD. We are also eternally grateful to Javier Solsona for rigging the clown. Javier, you have been a great friend over the years, and we wish to thank you so much for your hard work on this very flexible and powerful rig.

A big debt of gratitude is due to our editor, Cathleen Snyder, for all of her efforts and dedication to make this book great, and to Kevin Harreld for all of his assistance and encouragement. Bill Hartman is a master layout artist, and he did an amazing job with all of the charts and the very detailed timeline. To Steve Weiss, we owe much appreciation for believing in this project and pushing us to write this book in the first place. Audrey Doyle was also a strong contributor in the initial editing phase with Steve. And Harriet "The Bulldog" Beck—what would we have done without you? By far, you are the best attorney a couple of animators could have. To Scott Holmes, you were our sounding board for how to approach some of the toughest issues in the text, you are a walking textbook of the history of animation, and we are deeply indebted to you…"Thanks buddy, now get that chopper on the road…your part is done!" To Brian Dowrick, Floyd Norman, Mike Polvani, Troy Saliba, Joe Scott, Mike "Utah" Warner, John Riggs, and Dave Zaboski, thanks for all of your cartoons, comics, sketches, and amazing artwork. You guys all outdid yourselves. Jerry Beck, Tom Sito, Richard Taylor, and Floyd Norman all assisted us with the historical information provided in this book, and we thank them for their extra efforts to ensure we got the facts straight, as well as Richard and Floyd's endorsements of this book—it means a lot to us.

With extra special appreciation to those who have inspired and supported this work, Angie and Jamie would like to recognize: Diego Angel, Eric Armstrong, Bobby Beck, Cris Blyth, Jeremy Cantor, Kevin Culhane, Neil Eskuri, Cory "Rocco" Florimonte, Dan Fowler, Dominic DiGiorgio, Paul Griffin, Jeannie Hunter, Lisa Karadjian, Lorne Lanning, Joe Mandia, Craig Maras, Shawn McInerney, Sherry McKenna, Jeb Milne, Jane Mullaney, Steven Olds, Caleb Owens, James Parris, Carlos Pedroza, Nicki Reiss, Eric Riel, Kenny Roy, Jeremy Sahlman, Allan Steele, Craig Talmy, Elizabeth Laura Taylor, and Matthias Wittmann. You are all an inspiration to us.

Finally, thanks to Angie's parents for "allowing" her to draw on the walls when she was little. Jamie would like to thank his wife and family for their love and support.

About the Authors

Angie Jones graduated from Atlanta College of Art in 1994. Her first introduction to animation was at a San Diego studio of more than 150 traditional animators called Lightspan. As a female animator, she was a novelty. Even rarer at this traditional studio was her willingness to create animation with a computer. Although she was trained at a fine art school, she wasn't afraid of the computer and for the past 12 years she has worked on numerous productions, including *Stuart Little 2*, Disney's 50th anniversary commercials, *Oddworld: Abe's Exoddus*, *Garfield*, *Dino Crisis 3*, *Scooby-Doo 2: Monsters Unleashed*, *X2: X-Men United*, *Pan's Labyrinth*, *National Treasure*, and *Freddy vs. Jason*. To find out more about her, go to http://www.spicycricket.com.

Jamie Oliff was trained in classical animation at Sheridan College of Art and Design. He has worked in the animation industry for more than 20 years. An award-winning director and long-time feature film animator, Jamie's credits include the first season of *The Ren & Stimpy Show*, and many feature-length animated pictures, such as *The Hunchback of Notre Dame*, *Mulan*, *Hercules*, *The Emperor's New Groove*, and CGI animation on titles ranging from *Kangaroo Jack* to *Scooby-Doo 2: Monsters Unleashed* and *National Treasure*. He lives in Burbank, California, with his wife and two children and a biplane project that he never finds enough time to finish.

Contents

Preface: When Worlds Collide xvi

Part I
Foundation 1

Chapter 1
Fleas on the Shoulders of Giants 3
The Evolution of the Art Form 3
    Aesthetic Appeal Changes 4
    Broadening the Audience for Animation 4
    Unappealing Storytelling in Traditional Animation 4
The Importance of History and Trends in Animation 5
Digital Artistry Begins 7
Times Are Changing: 1981–1994 8
Roger Rabbit Pushes 2D and CG Forward 12
Popularity of the CG Medium or Story? 13
Visual-Effects Movies Broaden the Audience 16
The 1990s Shift: CG Becomes a Player 18
A New Digital Artist Is Born 21
The Animated Movie Industry: Moving into the Millennium 24
The Best of Both Worlds 27

Chapter 2

Tell Me a Story **31**

Plot and Premise 32

Here Come the Talking Animals 36

Desire and Growth 37

Growth and Character Arcs 39

Orchestration and Back Story 40

Storyboards, Animatics, and Pre-Viz 43

    Intention and Essence 48

    Handling Cuts and Camera Staging 49

    Savor the Moment, but Not for Long! 52

    Storyboards for Television versus Film 54

Storytelling 57

Index 1: Storytelling Strengthening 58

Index 2: Storyboard Musts 58

Chapter 3

The Good, the Bad, and the Just Plain Annoying **61**

Memorable Characters 63

Inspiration from Your Own Experience 67

Flaws and Emotions 69

Character Bio 71

Stereotype versus Archetype 73

Believability and Credibility 74

Motivation 76

Show, Don't Tell 78

The Fine Art of Being a Bastard 80

Design 84

2D Drawings Translated into CG 86

Handling Textures in CG 90

The Rig Equals Solid Drawing 92

Index 3: Character Bio Questionnaire 94

Index 4: Character Development 95

Part II
Animation 97

Chapter 4
The Thursday Animator 99

Thinking and Planning 101

Using Reference and Acting It Out 103

Gesture Drawings and Thumbnails 109

Sharing 113

Ten Things to Think About 113

    Listen 114

    Subtext 115

    Experiment 116

    Rhythm 118

    Empathize 120

    Simplify 121

    Texture 123

    Honesty 126

    Eyes 126

    Commit 128

Index 5: Ten Things to Think About 129

Chapter 5
Every Frame Counts 131

Spliney, Gooey, Computery, and Watery Motion 133

The Graph Editor 138

Stepped, Linear, and Spline 140

Posing and Layering 142
Breaking the Rig 145
Using Breakdowns 147
Animating Frame by Frame or on the Twos 149
In-Betweening 149
Creating Overlap and Secondary Motion 150
Creating Principal and Secondary Characters 152
CG Tools 153
Pushing Your CG Animation to a Higher Level 156
    Weight 156
    Contrasts in Timing 159
    Reality versus Entertainment Exaggeration? 160
    Dialogue and Lip-Synch Styles 161
    Moving Holds 162
    Attention to Detail 164
    Motion Blur and Squash and Stretch 165
    Drawing Skills 167
    The Approval Process 169
    The Revision Process 171
    The Cleanup Process 173

Chapter 6
Acting the Moment Again and Again and Again 177
Motion Capture and Acting in CG Animation 178
Improv 182
Helpful Improv Tools for Animators 183
Charlie Chaplin, Empathy, and Acting 186
Get Inside the Character 189
Body Structure 192
Psychological Gesture and Subtext 192
Stay in the Moment 194

Index 6: Acting Tools for Animators 195
  Remotivating the Moment 195
  Improv 195
  Power Centers 195
  Status 195
  Space, Time, and Weight 195
  Chaplin 196
  Emotion 196
  Empathy 196
  Observation 196
  Body Structure 196
  Psychological Gesture 197
  Stay in the Moment 197

Part III
And Now a Word from the Producer 199

Chapter 7
When Push Comes to Stab **201**
Workflow 202
Dailies 203
Multiple Art Direction 204
Mentorship Lost 207
Competition 212
Pigeonholing 215
Core and Glitz Skills 216
Responsibility 216
Communication between Departments 219
Problem-Solving 223
Freelancing 223
Networking 225

Mass Production of CG Animation 226
Death, Taxes, and Outsourcing 227
Schedules and Production 229

Chapter 8
The End of the Beginning 235
Bridging the Gap 235

Part IV
Appendixes...239

Appendix A
Author Bios 241

Appendix B
Traditional and CG Productions 1994–2005 259

Appendix C
The Digital Age of Animation Begins 267

Appendix D
Animation Hall of Funny 283

Appendix E
Principles of Animation 289

Appendix F
Character Animation Terms 295

Appendix G
Computer Animation Terms 307

Appendix H
Further Reading 313

Appendix I
Rigging Blog 315

Appendix J
Timeline Bibliography 331

Index...335

Preface: When Worlds Collide

We came to computer-generated animation from very different backgrounds. Jamie is a classically trained animator who had to make a major career shift after investing 25 years in the medium of traditional animation. Angie is an animator trained in fine art and computers who wondered if it would be necessary to start over and learn the traditional ways of animation to survive shifts in the industry. In the end, both of us found a way to coexist and learn from each other in a medium that is ever-changing.

> **"You can only do something well if you are willing to do it again and again and again."**
> **—Angie Jones and Jamie Oliff**

This book is the first of its kind. We give the reader valuable advice and applied techniques from professionals on creating believable characters with a computer. Interviewing more than 40 animators, story people, supervisors, and directors, all working in CG animation today, has provided us with invaluable insight as to what it takes to survive in the volatile and quirky world of professional animation. The contributing authors come from a wide range of backgrounds, such as stop-motion, traditional animation, visual effects, and computer-generated animation.

Most current books intending to teach CG character animation instruct you on how to animate using particular software. This book is different. There are many books out there that teach you how to animate in "X" software, but none of them effectively teaches you how to "think" before you animate on a computer. This book explains these rules, with an emphasis on animating with the computer while still embracing everything that traditional animation did so well. In addition, there is a chapter concerning studio politics intended to guide those who may come across difficult situations. We sincerely believe that some of the examples we have provided may someday make it easier for others to overcome some prickly situations.

This book offers something for everyone. Animators of all levels and backgrounds should find some meat in the text to help them push their craft further. This book is for:

◆ Traditional animators hoping to cross over into the CG industry.

◆ CG animators who want to learn from traditional approaches.

◆ 2D/FX/Comp boutique studios that want to break into character animation.

◆ Overseas studios with the technical skill, but lacking the level of artistry to break into CG effectively.

◆ Those already working in animation, but with an interest in learning more.

Experienced animators will value the content for the times when they hit a roadblock on a shot. Less experienced animators will find unique and applied information from the experts. Novice animators and renegade filmmakers will value the content in this book for years to come because it is comprised of tried and true techniques used over the years in both 2D and CG media.

Finally, this is the first book to bridge the gap between what traditional artists and animators have developed over many years and how to apply those time-tested techniques to CG animation. We hope we have created something desirable and helpful that is also fun to read. With more than 40 top animators, supervisors, directors, and story people contributing their thoughts and ideas to this book, *Thinking Animation* will bridge a gap that has been apparent for the past 10 years. Two legends, Floyd Norman and Richard Taylor, also help us connect these two worlds with their forewords.

THINKING ANIMATION:
BRIDGING THE GAP BETWEEN 2D AND CG

PART I

Foundation

Chapter 1
Fleas on the Shoulders of Giants

Hey, traditional animator. Yeah, you! The Digital Age is here. No, seriously. Put down that pencil or you're fired. Face it, the box is here to stay. Every facet of life has been affected by the computer, and things will never be the same. The animation world is no different.

> "I miss my pencil."
> —*Troy Saliba*

Hey you! CG animator. Yeah, we're talking to you too! Things are changing for you as well. The steady flow of traditional animators into the computer-generated animation industry has created more demands on your position in this evolution. So listen up!

The Evolution of the Art Form

Animators find themselves in the midst of a momentous change in their industry. As in many other fields, the computer has made what is known as a disruptive impact on our art form. Think of the car and the horse, the cellular phone and the payphone, the CG feature and the 2D feature…. To illustrate how the evolution of the art form has transpired, let us contrast the traditional and computer-generated forms of animation. There are two fields of traditionally animated features—such as *The Lion King* and *Beauty and the Beast*, also referred to as 2D animation—and computer-generated animated features, such as *The Incredibles* and *Shrek*, which are often referred to as CG or 3D animation. The terms "2D" and "traditional animation," as well as "3D" and "CG animation," will be used interchangeably throughout this book to refer to the respective mediums. The introduction of the computer has changed an art form that had been, up until now, a pen and paper medium for upwards of 80 years. Three major shifts are responsible for the progression from pencil to mouse in feature animation. These shifts can be traced to changes in audience, technology, and storytelling.

1824

PERSISTENCE OF VISION:
Peter Roget presented "The Persistence of Vision with Regard to Moving Objects" to the British Royal Society.

1832

PHENAKISTOSCOPE: Dr. Joseph Plateau and Dr. Simon Ritter constructed the phenakistoscope, which produced an illusion of movement by allowing a viewer to gaze at a rotating disk containing small windows, viewing a sequence of images that created an animated effect.

1872

PHOTOGRAPHIC ANIMALS IN MOTION:
Eadweard Muybridge started his photographic gathering of animals in motion.

Aesthetic Appeal Changes

The first shift was fueled by the increased popularity of visual effects movies in the 1990s. Visual effects–driven movies brought audiences to their feet with higher levels of entertainment and reality than ever before. Movies such as *Independence Day*, *Twister*, *Titanic*, and *Men in Black* were bringing hundreds of thousands of people into the theater to see these new visual effects. We are not talking about story here, but sheer aesthetic appeal. This change in the audience's taste was just one of the contributors to traditional animation's demise. The audience began to view CG features as visually richer and more exciting based solely on the aesthetic they portrayed. Video games and music videos also had a hand in shaping this new interest in computer-generated eye candy, especially among young viewers. The sheer richness of 3D and its ability to move the camera around in this new world made traditional animation suddenly seem, quite literally, flat.

Broadening the Audience for Animation

The second factor involved broadening of the audience for feature animation. Before visual effects movies became popular, there was a great divide between content for a kid's movie and for mainstream movies. In the 1990s, both parents and kids went to see movies such as *Titanic*, *Men in Black*, and *Jurassic Park* in droves. Here there was content that appealed to audience members both young and old alike. What made these effects-driven films more appealing was the computer's ability to create photo-realistic creatures and effects that wowed audiences because of their unprecedented believability. In addition, these effects were seamlessly integrated into the films. The films had something for everyone.

Unappealing Storytelling in Traditional Animation

Finally, the third shift in the animation evolution resulted from what many see as traditional animation's changing approach to story. The box office returns in traditional features began to suffer in direct proportion to the rising popularity of visual effects movies. In turn, traditional studios tried to broaden their audience through more adult story themes, such as *Pocahontas*, *The Prince of Egypt*, and *The Quest for Camelot*. Instead of writing stories that would appeal to the kid in all of us, the new screenwriters created stories for adults and hoped kids would like them too. After *The Lion King* was released in 1994, makers of traditional features felt that in order to be a success, they had to follow suit and create features that were epic in scope. Every studio tried to follow *The Lion King* mold and make large-scale, epic musicals. Studios were chasing both visual effects dollars and *The Lion King* money. As animation became a profitable business, stories were overworked by myriad "creative executives" in their efforts to create a blockbuster. In turn, the traditional movies made after *The Lion King* found a smaller and smaller audience.

1889

KINETOSCOPE: Thomas Edison announced his creation of the kinetoscope, which projected a 50-foot length of film in approximately 13 seconds.

1892

THEATRE OPTIQUE: Emile Reynaud opened the Theatre Optique in the Musee Grevin. It displayed an animation of images painted on long strips of celluloid.

1906

FIRST ANIMATED FILM: J. Stuart Blackton made the first animated film, *Humorous Phases of Funny Faces*. To do so, he drew comical faces on a blackboard and filmed them.

THREE MAJOR SHIFTS THAT CAUSED THE ANIMATION EVOLUTION

The three major shifts causing the evolution of animation include:

◆ Changed aesthetic of audience by visual effects–driven movies

◆ Broadening of the audience for CG through visual effects–driven movies

◆ Poor stories in traditional feature animated films

The Importance of History and Trends in Animation

Trends and history reveal how evolution of an art form occurs. Paying close attention to the trends and growth of any field helps predict the future of that industry. It is important to recognize trends in filmmaking, storytelling, and technology for an animator to increase his or her chances of continued employment. This book will point out many trends from the past and provide a blueprint of the future. By observing and learning about these developments, we remain educated about the technology and the audience.

The art of classical film animation has been ever-evolving since its early days. Artists and the studios at which they work have strived to raise the bar visually through storytelling since the first crude attempts at putting moving images on the screen. And no, we are not talking about *He-Man and the Masters of the Universe* here. We are talking about classical animation and its evolution into computer-generated feature films—think *Steamboat Willie* and *The Incredibles*.

With improvements in animation came demands for richer backgrounds, more complex camera moves, and an ever-increasing level of believability all around. This increasing need for more impressive visuals also pushed the budgets of these pictures higher and higher. Walt Disney paved the way for most animated features in the beginning by always striving to find new ways to push the technology and budgets in order to make a richer and more appealing animated film. With rising costs came the inevitable call to streamline production and establish more economical ways in which to get the message to the screen. Most of the other studios at this time focused on how to make their films as inexpensively as they could and still garner some of the success Walt Disney was having. Recounting every technological advance in the art of animation in this chapter would be boring. (However, we do provide an interesting 2D/CG chronological timeline of events and advancements in the footer of this book that might prove very enlightening as you read this text.) Instead, we will introduce the shifts and trends in animation that pushed us into the digital age.

1910

FIRST PAPER CUTOUT ANIMATION: Emile Cohl made *En Route*, the first paper cutout animation. This technique saved time because the animator repositioned the paper instead of redrawing each new sketch.

1911

LITTLE NEMO ANIMATION: Winsor McCay produced an animation sequence using his comic strip character, Little Nemo.

1913

ANIMATION ASSEMBLY-LINE PRODUCTION INTRODUCED: J.R. Bray introduced the management principles of the assembly line to the production of animated films.

This chapter explains how the visual effects industry had a great impact on the popularity of animation and how that popularity changed the production of traditional and CG animation forever. We explore how the digital artist was born and how the hiring criteria changed as computer tools became easier to use and traditional artists made their way into the computer industry. We will illustrate how storylines and box-office profits clashed as the use of CG increased and 2D waned. We will also explore the reasons for the demise of traditional animation, as well as CG's and visual effects' rise through content, box-office profits, and changes in the audience. Finally, we will bridge the gap between the two media of CG and 2D animation.

Traditional animation is an art that has been, for the greater part of its existence, a pencil and paper medium. Sketch by Jamie Oliff and Angie Jones.

1914

SLASH AND TEAR AND PEG SYSTEMS DEVELOPED: Raoul Barré developed a slash and tear technique for doing levels in animation, and he also devised the peg system for registration.

1914

HAND-DRAWN *GERTIE, THE TRAINED DINOSAUR:* Winsor McCay produced a cartoon called *Gertie, The Trained Dinosaur,* which amazingly consisted of 10,000 drawings.

1915

TECHNOLOGICAL DEVELOPMENT USING CELS: The cel animation process was invented by Earl Hurd and John Bray in 1915.

Digital Artistry Begins

Digital tools have fundamentally changed an art that has been, for the greater part of its existence, a pencil and paper medium. Think about that for a second. Every animated feature film from the early 1900s to the late 1980s was a traditionally hand-drawn or stop-motion animated film. The tools used to make these films did not change significantly in almost 80 years.

To illustrate this more clearly, we begin with some CG history. In the mid '70s, incredible leaps in computer technology began to take place. New 3D software began to emerge. In 1980, IBM licensed DOS from Microsoft, marking the beginning of computers available to the masses. In 1983, the Macintosh followed. Computer Graphic Imaging (CGI) was in its infancy, and there were but a handful of companies creating images for film and television. Primarily there was New York Institute of Technology (NYIT); Magi Synthavision in Elmsford, New York; Information International Inc. (III) in Los Angeles; and Digital Effects (DE) in New York City. In 1981, Disney contracted III, MAGI, DE, and Robert Abel & Associates to create computer graphics for the movie *Tron*.[1]

The 1980s brought about events that moved technology forward, but it also brought events that would have lasting consequences for feature animated films. In the 1980s, Hanna-Barbera (the largest producer of animation in the U.S. at that time) began using computers in their animation process.[2] In the 1970s, Marc Levoy developed an early computer-assisted cartoon animation system, which was used by Hanna-Barbera

---

III, MAGI, AND DE: CG FOREFATHERS

The III graphics effort was founded as the Motion Pictures Product Group by John Whitney Jr. (son of John Whitney Sr.—"Father of Computer Graphics") and Gary Demos (with Art Durinski, Tom McMahon, and Karol Brandt) in 1978. Between 1978 and 1982, III's motion picture work included *Westworld, Futureworld, Looker,* and *Tron*. III hired Richard Taylor, the original art director at Robert Abel, to handle the creative direction. He later became the co-effects supervisor for *Tron*. Although they defined much of the early view of CGI, disputes regarding the computing power necessary to continue in the business prompted Whitney and Demos to leave to establish Digital Productions in 1982. They departed before *Tron* went into production. Richard Taylor divided the high-end raster graphic imagery between III and Magi. The Abel studio, which at the time worked only in vector graphic animation, handled the opening title sequence and the real-world-to-electronic-world transition. DE created the opening shot of the *Tron* character being formed and the animated bit character. When the film wrapped, Taylor became creative director at Magi Synthavision, and they opened a new West coast facility in Los Angeles.[3]

1915

ROTOSCOPING INTRODUCED: Max Fleischer and Dave Fleischer patented the rotoscope process.

1916

MORE PATENTS FROM BRAY: Bray established a patent monopoly for the animation process and tried to enforce the patents by requiring all animation studios using his patented process to buy a license and pay a fee.

1919

BRAY AND FLEISCHER UNITE: Using the rotoscope test they created in 1915, the Fleischer brothers secured a contract with the John R. Bray Studios in 1919 to produce their series, *Out of the Inkwell*.

Productions to produce *The Flintstones*, *Scooby-Doo*, and other shows.[4] The traditional animation skills of drawing and inking began to give way to digital manipulation to produce new forms of animation.

As Hanna-Barbera explored ways to make animation faster, the 1980s also marked a trying time for Disney Studios. Disney had made a name for itself in feature animation by 1980, but was also experiencing a 10-year slump. Roy Disney resigned as an executive in 1977 due to disagreements with his colleagues' decisions at the time, but he retained a seat on the board of directors for several years. His resignation from the board in 1984 occurred in the midst of a corporate takeover battle by CEO Ronald William Miller (married to Walt's daughter, Diane Marie Disney) and prevented the hostile takeover by installing Michael Eisner and Frank Wells to run the business. Roy soon returned to the company as vice-chairman of the board of directors and head of the animation department. During this corporate shuffling, Disney Studios considered abandoning the production of feature-length animated films at the initial advice of Eisner, but Roy Disney convinced him that he could make animation profitable again.

DISNEY ALMOST ABANDONS FEATURE PRODUCTION

"[Roy Disney] resigned from the board in 1984 to spearhead an effort to prevent a corporate takeover; he was later reinstated. He was instrumental in bringing Michael Eisner and Frank Wells to run the company, taking over from Ron Miller, Walt Disney's son-in-law. Roy Disney became chairman of Walt Disney Animation in 1984." Roy fought to keep his Uncle Walt's dream alive and keep Disney Features producing animation at a time when many wanted to sell the then unprofitable division off.[5]

Times Are Changing: 1981–1994

The years between 1981 and 1994 are considered the second Golden Age of Animation. Disney's spectacular box office success started with *The Little Mermaid* and ended with *The Lion King*. In 1981, Walt Disney's *The Fox and the Hound* premiered. The film was the last work of the Frank Thomas, Ollie Johnston, and Woolie Reitherman, three of the Disney's famous Nine Old Men.[6]

THE NINE OLD MEN

Walt Disney named his key animators in the early days of the studio the "Nine Old Men," coined after President Franklin D. Roosevelt's nickname for his Supreme Court. The original Nine Old Men were Les Clark, Marc Davis, Ollie Johnston, Milt Kahl, Ward Kimball, Eric Larsen, John Lounsbery, Wolfgang "Woolie" Reitherman, and Frank Thomas.

 1920

WALT AND UB ENTER ANIMATION: 19-year-old Walter Disney started working in animation at the Kansas City Slide Company, with his friend Ub Iwerks.

1920

FELIX THE CAT MERCHANDISING: *Felix the Cat* started as the *Feline Follies* from Pat Sullivan's studio. Otto Messmer created Felix and also wrote the stories and directed, producing one film every two weeks.

 1921

KOKO AND FLEISCHER STUDIOS: The *Out of the Inkwell* films made at Bray Studios became very successful and were centered on Max Fleischer as the creative cartoonist who would always have to keep Koko the Clown in check. In 1921, Fleischer Studios was born because of Koko's success.

While CG animation was in its infancy, traditional animation was experiencing the end of an age with the retirement of the Nine Old Men and the beginning of a new age. It is at this point in time that we see the introduction of young artists, such as Don Bluth, Glen Keane, Bill Kroyer, John Lasseter, Brad Bird, and Tim Burton. The second Golden Age of traditional animation did not really begin until the late 1980s. However, *The Fox and the Hound* and the 1982 film, *The Secret of NIMH*, really got the ball rolling. *The Black Cauldron* nearly stopped the ball in its tracks. As we mentioned earlier, Walt Disney Studios was going through serious reorganization efforts at this time and almost abandoned feature animation completely. When you view the *The Black Cauldron*, the reason why becomes painfully obvious. *The Black Cauldron* was an animated feature released by Disney in 1985. It was supposed to revitalize Disney's waning animated division, "which had produced only one significant motion picture, *The Fox and the Hound*, since 1977's *The Rescuers*." *The Black Cauldron* represented a noteworthy departure from previous Disney features because it was presented in 70mm, it used computer animation to augment the hand-drawn images, it did not feature any musical scenes, and it was rated PG. Despite all of this, or maybe because of it, *The Black Cauldron* was a box office disaster. No one went to see it. The film was out of theaters in several weeks, and its "financial ledger was smeared with red ink."[7]

Whether you can blame the failure of *The Black Cauldron* on unappealing characters or confusing storyline is inconsequential. The film bombed. Thankfully, Disney managed to regroup for the future, but not before losing one of its top talents, Don Bluth. Bluth, unhappy with what he felt was a lack of respect for the art at Disney, left and took a group of experienced animators to start a new studio. Bluth Studios was one of the first production houses to compete with Disney for a piece of the feature animation pie. Bluth's first movie, *The Secret of NIMH*, was pivotal because its success marked the very early beginnings of the second Golden Age. This second Golden Age of animation started a renewed interest in traditional features. As traditional studios went through restructuring in the '80s, January 20, 1984, brought the first computer-animated character—Sexy Robot—for a 30-second commercial ("Brilliance") created by the Robert Abel & Associates Studio that debuted at the Super Bowl. Randy Roberts directed the spot and Con Pederson was the technical director; together, they created a chrome female robotic character that was visually stunning. The effect this work had on the film community cannot be overstated.[8]

Also in 1984, John Lasseter left Disney to become a part of the newly formed computer graphics group at Industrial Light and Magic. This group combined George Lucas' special effects company with Lucasfilm Computer Graphics and Special Effects group and was headed by Ed Catmull. At Lucasfilm, Lasseter made *Andre and Wally B*, which was an animated short premiering at SIGGRAPH in March of that year. Continuing the introduction of computer-generated animation, 1985 brought us the first 100-percent digitally animated character in a theatrical release. This character took the form of a stained-glass knight in the movie *Young Sherlock Holmes,* thanks to the efforts of Lucasfilm and its computer visual effects crew. And interestingly,

1922

WALT STARTS LAUGH-O-GRAM FILMS: Walt Disney's first studio, Laugh-O-Gram Films, was formed in Kansas City and produced popular but unprofitable cartoons for mostly local audiences.

1923

DISNEY BROTHERS MOVE TO L.A.: Walt and Roy Disney moved to L.A. after Laugh-O-Gram went bankrupt and opened Disney Brothers Cartoon Studio. Margaret Winkler put Disney under contract for the *Alice Comedies* series, which combined live action and animation.

1924

ALICE GOES INTO DISTRIBUTION: Disney's *Alice* series goes into distribution. Animators included Ub Iwerks, Hugh Harman, Rudolf Ising, and Friz Freleng.

John Lasseter designed and animated the knight before starting his studio a few years later with Steve Jobs, called Pixar.[9]

The (Sexy Robot) "Brilliance" commercial, *The Adventures of André and Wally B.* animated short, and the knight in the movie *Young Sherlock Holmes* were three big moments in CG. They were also the first tiny steps for the infant (soon to become giant) called computer animation. It took many years, a lot of help from visual effects–driven movies, not to mention a funny little rabbit to really make that baby get up and run.

CG animation was in its infancy in the 1980s. Sketch by Angie Jones.

1925

WALTER LANTZ ENTERS THE SCENE: Walter Lantz began to rise to prominence at the John R. Bray Studios in New York and directed, animated, and starred in his first cartoon series, *Dinky Doodle*, in the animated live-action short, *The Magic Lamp*.

1925

THE LOST WORLD: Willis O'Brien produced *The Lost World*. Pioneering stop-motion special effects by Willis O'Brien were deemed "culturally significant" by the Library of Congress and selected for preservation in the United States National Film Registry.

Monster Mash: 2D, CG, and visual effects. Sketch by Floyd Norman.

THREE BIG MOMENTS FOR CG ANIMATION

◆ "Brilliance" commercial with the Sexy Robot by Randy Roberts at Robert Abel & Associates, 1984

◆ *The Adventures of André and Wally B.* animated short by Lucasfilm and John Lasseter, 1984

◆ *Young Sherlock Holmes*: CG Knight by Lucasfilm and John Lasseter, 1985

1926

FIRST FEATURE-LEGNTH ANIMATION: Lotte Reiniger created one of the first feature-length animation films in the world called (in English) *The Adventures of Prince Achmed.* The film used cutout animation—silhouettes cut from black paper to portray backlit people, animals, or objects.

1928

TALKIE CARTOONS: Walt Disney added sound to *Steamboat Willy* with the Powers sound system. It was not the first sound animated film; Paul Terry's *Dinner Time* was released two months earlier. But *Steamboat Willy* was the first successful sound animated film; it made Mickey an international star and launched the Disney studio of today.

Roger Rabbit Pushes 2D and CG Forward

Moving through the 1980s, visual effects gained momentum with *E.T. the Extra-Terrestrial* and the *Star Wars* first trilogy film franchise. 2D movies fell into a slump until a crazy rabbit came into the picture. *Who Framed Roger Rabbit* was the channel for 2D, CG, and visual effects to push the envelope in animation. By combining live action and 2D characters convincingly, *Roger Rabbit* busted that envelope wide open. *Roger Rabbit* was rarity for traditionally animated films in the 1980s because it was an original animated film that appealed to both children and adults and was a mainstream hit in the United States.

Animators didn't know it yet, but the rabbit was helping to open the door for future character-driven movies, from *Casper* to the *Lord of the Rings* franchise. These movies combine animated characters with live action in what is now one of the staples of Hollywood blockbusters. Not too shabby for a rabbit movie no one really believed in at the time. Walt Disney said we owe our history to a little mouse, but maybe we should also give the crazy rabbit some credit as well.

THE SECOND GOLDEN AGE OF TRADITIONAL ANIMATION

◆ *The Little Mermaid* made $84 million domestically.

◆ *Beauty and the Beast* made $145 million domestically.

◆ *Aladdin* made $217 million domestically.

◆ *The Lion King* made $317 million domestically.

After the release and success of *Who Framed Roger Rabbit*, the 1990s exploded with a stream of hugely successful animated films. This new time for traditional animation brought the movies *The Little Mermaid*, which made $84 million; *Beauty and the Beast*, which made $145 million; *Aladdin*, which made $217 million; and finally *The Lion King*, which made $317 million domestically. Studio executives got whiplash watching these numbers climb. The increasing figures made traditional animators' heads spin and their bank accounts soar with the highest salaries ever. In 1994, Jeffery Katzenberg left Disney, unbeknownst to him at the end of this Golden Age of traditional animation, and started DreamWorks Animation, hoping to get a piece of the pie for himself. Fox hired Don Bluth to head up their feature animation division as well at this time. But storm clouds were brewing.

The first little cloud on the horizon for traditional animation was a successful film called *Tin Toy*, which became the first computer-animated short film to win an Academy Award. The *Tin Toy* short created by John Lasseter and Pixar marked a pivotal point for CG animation. *Tin Toy* proved that a 100-percent computer-

1928

OSWALD THE LUCKY RABBIT LEAVES DISNEY:
Oswald was first introduced in 1927. In the spring of 1928, Disney asked for an increase in the budget of the successful cartoon and was instead told he had to take a 20% budget cut, so he quit. Carl Laemmle of Universal opted to have the Oswald cartoons produced on the Universal lot and selected Walter Lantz to produce the new series of shorts.

1929

SOUND AND IMAGE ADVANCES: The *Skeleton Dance* was the first *Silly Symphony*, in which the use of prerecorded music led to a tight synchronization of sound and picture, and set the standard in animation for using prerecorded sound.

generated short film could be produced and contain the same quality and standards for story and characters as a traditionally animated short. It also meant that CG could actually be produced in a longer format than the short sequences in earlier films, and in the same realm as traditional animation. In addition, *Who Framed Roger Rabbit* grossed more than $329 million worldwide in 1988[10] and proved that traditional animation, at least when combined with live action, was not limited to a children's audience.

> "There is a beauty and fullness to CG that traditional never had, as far as eye candy goes. It is the ultimate moving storybook, an animated painting. Kids love that stuff."
>
> —*Scott Holmes*

Both CG and traditional media continued to go through drastic changes throughout the late 1980s. Visual effects also continued to generate more revenue at the box office and create more realistic-looking animation. However, traditional animation still held the upper hand when it came to caricaturing reality at this time. So, what has transpired to create the current environment, in which 3D reigns supreme and traditional features have all but vanished? Will traditional animation make a comeback?

Popularity of the CG Medium or Story?

Most of the 2D animators we have spoken to do not have much confidence that the 2D medium will regain its foothold in the future. The introduction of computer-generated animation to the masses and the push of heavy visual-effects movies have fundamentally changed the audience's perception. The "wow factor" of CG animation has pushed computer-animated films to the forefront. Nik Ranieri explains how the audience's tastes have changed.

> I just don't believe and I don't think the studios believe that it's story as much as it is novelty right now. I think 2D may come back as a novelty, as in black-and-white films. I hate to say that, but it's just the way the audience is reacting to it now. Ah, I miss the '90s. Remember the '90s, when the highest-grossing animated film was a good movie? I swear, if *Lilo & Stitch* was in 3D, it would have made double the money, and if *A Bug's Life* or *Shrek* was in 2D, it wouldn't have made anything.

Nik makes an interesting point. Is it really the popularity of the medium? Or could it be the poor content in 2D films made recently? Most of the successful CG films today have solid stories. Traditionally drawn films today have not embraced the great storylines they did in the original Golden Age of Disney (from 1937 to

---

1929

KRAZY KAT: Charles Mintz left Universal after the Oswald fiasco and started a studio with *Krazy Kat* as a main series. Krazy Kat was like Mickey Mouse and usually engaged in slapstick adventures with his look-alike girlfriend and loyal dog.

1930

TWO-STRIP TECHNICOLOR PROCESS: *The King of Jazz*, a short animated sequence done by Walter Lantz for Universal, is the first animation done with the two-strip Technicolor process.

1930

WARNER BROS. IS BORN: The first Warner Bros. short was *Sinking in the Bathtub* with the character Bosko. Harman, Ising, and Friz Freleng started the studio with Leon Schlesinger as the producer. Each short had to contain a Warner's song, so the *Looney Tunes* series, a takeoff on Disney's *Silly Symphonies*, began.

1942). *The Lion King* became a double-edged sword because it made so much money. The money brought more management into the ranks, and what was previously a cottage industry (a huge one at that) became a corporate monster, with the artists more and more removed from the process. Disney began to strangle the goose that laid the golden egg. Traditional hand-drawn animated movies with poor, formulaic storylines had lost the art and craft of animation and storytelling. The successful computer-generated movies produced today make story the most important part of production and do not let the technology (or the suits) run the creative process.

After *The Lion King*, we saw a steady decline in the popularity of traditionally drawn films and a rise of computer-generated animation. Just looking at box office numbers this is apparent. *The Lion King* brought in more than $760 million worldwide, and, in contrast, the last six traditionally animated movies Disney made or acquired took in $712 million combined (worldwide). *The Incredibles*, a computer-animated film, brought in $630 million alone worldwide, which is more than Disney's last five movies combined. Table 1.1 breaks down the numbers.

The first little cloud of change had suddenly grown into a tempest. 2D animation was gradually becoming antiquated in the audience's eyes. CG productions, both visual effects–driven and character-driven, were getting more attention and money as they became popular. More people were flocking to see what this new

Table 1.1 Worldwide Box Office Profits: Last Six Traditional Disney Films versus *The Incredibles*[11]

2D Film	Worldwide Profit	CG	Worldwide Profit
Treasure Planet	$110 million		
The Jungle Book 2	$135 million		
Piglet's Big Movie	$60 million		
Brother Bear	$251 million		
Home on the Range	$104 million		
Pooh's Heffalump Movie	$52 million		
		The Incredibles	$630 million
Total	$712 million	Total	$630 million

Holson, Laura M. "Has the Sky Stopped Falling at Disney?" *New York Times*. September 18, 2005. http://select.nytimes.com/search/restricted/article?res=F70F13F735550C7B8DDDA00894DD404482.

1930

DEVELOPMENTS AT DISNEY: Ub Iwerks and Carl Stalling left the Disney studio. Roy signed a contract starting Disney merchandising. David Hand joined as Disney's fourth animator. The Pluto character was born in *The Picnic*.

1930

BETTY BOOP CHARACTER EMERGES: Fleischer introduced the character of Betty Boop in *Dizzy Dishes*. Grim Natwick developed and animated Betty.

1930

FIRST TERRYTOON: The first Terrytoon, *Caviar*, was released. It was directed by Paul Terry and Frank Mose; Paul Terry also produced.

medium was all about. Conrad Vernon shares his perspective regarding the hard road for 2D because of the popularity of CG:

> The future of 2D animation will be strictly independent, like *The Triplets of Belleville*. God bless the person that comes around with a great 2D film and does it independently and gets some money-person with a little bit of vision and trust in his talent to give him the money to do it. That 2D animator then works his ass off and the movie has to become huge. You are fighting Goliath with this thing.

Conrad has a point. As the CG medium becomes more of an identifiable art, 2D could be lost forever. But how could this happen after *The Lion King* made so much money? As of the writing of this book, DreamWorks and Disney, the two largest animation studios in Hollywood, have shut down their traditional animation units for theatrical release, no longer accept traditional portfolios, and have dedicated all of their efforts to making CG films. In the 10-year period between the unbelievable success of *The Lion King* and the

CG and 2D arm-wrestle for the audience, while visual effects–driven movies make more money than ever. Sketch by Floyd Norman.

1931

MGM'S FIRST SOUND CARTOON:
Ub Iwerks' *Flip the Frog* was MGM's first sound cartoon character. Under the advice of MGM, Flip the Frog changed to become less froglike and more human-looking. By the time the series ended, Flip the Frog looked more like a boy than a frog.

1931

MERRIE MELODIES INTRODUCED:
Warner Bros. introduced *Merrie Melodies* as one-shot shorts.

1931

DISNEY ART SCHOOL: Disney starts a studio school under the direction of Don Graham, a former engineering student at Stanford.

release of *Shrek 2*, 2D production has literally dwindled to nothing. A more profound illustration of the impact of the computer on our industry would be hard to find. As of 2005, the last 2D movie produced was *Pooh's Heffalump Movie*, which barely cleared $19 million domestically. CG and visual-effects films are neck and neck for the same billion-dollar box office profits, while 2D films' profits diminish, barely pulling in a few million each year.

But is it really the popularity of the medium? Or is it the stories being told? Or could it be both? Successful CG films continue to uphold old story formulas, while 2D production has practically stopped except for old franchises, such as *Winnie the Pooh*, and new TV stars, such as *SpongeBob SquarePants*. Eric Goldberg expands on these ideas as he explains how he feels the popularity of 2D and CG has changed for audiences:

> I think the last slew of hand-drawn animation suffered from mediocre content, characters, and storytelling. I think if it's appealing and engaging, kids don't have a problem. Whether it's produced in CG or whether it's produced in 2D doesn't really matter. Now the truth of the matter is a CG movie costs as much to make as a traditional movie, if you compare dollar for dollar. *Treasure Planet* cost the same amount of money as *Monsters, Inc*. It's a kind of thing where one medium is not less costly than the other. Rather, one is currently more fashionable than the other.

Eric tells us that mediocre content and stories hindered the advancement of 2D. He is also quick to point out that the two mediums do not cost more than one another to produce. However, the return on the dollar for CG films has been, up to this point, more profitable than that of 2D films in the past 10 years. Eric argues this is due to popularity of the medium and the storytelling choices on the traditional end. We think he is right, but there is another reason why 2D animation has declined to the degree it has.

Visual-Effects Movies Broaden the Audience

The popularity of the medium is not the only trend that led to the virtual end of 2D productions. The huge success of visual effects–based films played a big role in how traditional studios viewed what the audience wanted to see. Visual effects–driven movies had mass appeal to all ages. As 2D animation went through a spell of weak stories and even weaker attempts at trying to get a piece of the VFX market, CG-animated movies continued with the old formula of making great stories for kids with a wink at adults. Now the same kid who saw *Men in Black* looked at a film like *Quest for Camelot* in a completely different light, and he didn't like it. Obviously, there will be failures in the CG realm as studios seek to generate profits at the

1931

INVENTION OF THE STORY-BOARD: The story team at Walt Disney Feature Animation developed the first storyboard. Walt Disney and Webb Smith are credited as the inventors in the mid-1920s.

1932

FIRST ACADEMY AWARD FOR ANIMATED SHORT: *Flowers and Trees*, a *Silly Symphony* and the first full-color cartoon, won the award for Best Short Subject: Cartoons. This film was the first to use three-strip Technicolor in animation.

1932

GOOFY IS BORN: Disney's *Mickey's Revue* debuts and Goofy is born.

expense of good old-fashioned storytelling. CG is not the silver bullet that will cover up a weak storyline or make up for uninteresting characters.

Throughout the 1980s and 1990s, the sheer number of traditional films being released was almost double the number of visual-effects movies, but visual-effects movies were finding a larger audience and a bigger box office. VFX movies were getting more "bang for their buck," so to speak. In 1982, some of the highest grossing visual-effects movies were released. The movies up for an Oscar for visual effects in 1982 were *Blade Runner*, *E.T. The Extra-Terrestrial*, and *Poltergeist*. Other notable visual-effects movies that came out in 1982 were *Star Trek II: The Wrath of Khan*, *The Dark Crystal*, and *Tron*. Previously, studios used visual effects for horror and thriller movies primarily, and few children would ever see these films. Franchises such as the first *Star Wars* trilogy, *Superman*, *Terminator*, *Back to the Future*, *Batman*, and *Jurassic Park* broadened the visual-effects audience to both kids and adults during the '80s and '90s. The audience for visual effects–driven films also became more discriminating of the level of quality expected as the medium evolved.

In addition, visual effects movies and the influence of games changed the aesthetic of what kids (and adults) wanted to see on the screen. The traditional studios tried to keep up and put out a product that they thought would be successful and would support the craft of traditionally drawn animation. In their fight against the newness of CG, they thought maybe if they embraced the old styles and designs of early Disney days, they might compete. They were wrong. Tom Sito offers more perspective:

> On Mickey's *The Prince and the Pauper*, we tried really hard to make an old classic cartoon. We used the old film stock. We used the same paints. We went from an acrylic to a watercolor to make it look more like *Brave Little Tailor*. The art directors worked very hard to make Mickey's *The Prince and the Pauper* look like a classic Disney film. However, the audiences said, "That is an old cartoon! It is something you find in the vault and that is not new!" To a modern audience, where kids have Game Boys and they are hip to the street culture that is a sort of "Asian Kung Fu/black street" combo, there is no way that 3D is going to disappear. These computer-generated movies are films for our generation.

And so, even after Disney tried to push a classic cartoon out there, the popularity of CG and the influence visual effects had in broadening the audience for computer animation had secured CG animation as a medium for our generation. In addition, the poor content in traditionally drawn films of the past 10 years didn't help. CG is here to stay.

1933

OSCAR FOR *THE THREE LITTLE PIGS* (DISNEY): Disney's very successful short, *The Three Little Pigs*, wins the Academy Award for Best Short Subject: Cartoons. Among animation historians, it is considered to be the first cartoon in which the characters displayed unique personalities, as opposed to being simple "good guys" and "bad guys."

1933

CHANGES AT WARNER BROS.: Hugh Harman and Rudy Ising, best known for founding the Warner Bros. and MGM animation studios, left Warner Bros. over money issues and took the Bosko character to MGM. Back at Warner Bros., Friz Freleng became a head director, and Bob Clampett and Chuck Jones joined.

VISUAL EFFECTS BOOM AT THE BOX OFFICE

◆ The *Star Wars* first trilogy franchise made approximately $1 billion domestically.

◆ The *Batman* franchise made almost $1 billion domestically.

◆ The *Jurassic Park* franchise made almost $800 million domestically.

◆ The *Back to the Future* franchise made almost $400 million domestically.

◆ *E.T. the Extra-Terrestrial* made almost $400 million domestically.

◆ The *Terminator* franchise made almost $400 million domestically.

◆ The *Superman* franchise made approximately $300 million domestically.

The 1990s Shift: CG Becomes a Player

We talk about the history of the medium to encourage artists to pay attention and be aware of the trends and shifts in their chosen field of work. This evolution from 2D to CG did not happen overnight, but many 2D and CG artists (not to mention studios) were unprepared for the changes that were coming fast and furious. Reluctant at first to pick up the new tools, many masters of hand-drawn animation were understandably wary of giving up a craft that took years, if not decades, to become proficient at. At the same time, many CG artists were expected to raise the bar as far as the quality of their animation was concerned. Many of these artists were not even trained in animation. The term "digital artist" was almost nonexistent as recently as 20 years ago. The phenomenal growth of the CG industry, due in part to the massive increases in technology and the rapid influx of computer-based talent, contrasts markedly to the snail's pace of growth in 2D from the days of *Steamboat Willie* (1928) to *The Lion King*; this quick growth caught many off guard.

In the very early days of computer animation, people ran around with no idea of what digital artistry was all about. The field was so new that people were being hired with no experience. Worse yet, people were being hired who were unschooled in any aspect of cinema. Many people developing software for computers were not really filmmakers. You know, the "I have a neighbor who has a cousin who drew a picture once, built model airplanes when he was a kid, and now is a whiz on the computer" type of artist. Tom Sito explains the negative effects this had on the quality of CG animation in the early days:

1933

NIGHT ON BALD MOUNTAIN PIN-SCREEN TECHNIQUE: Alexander Alexeieff and Claire Parker are best known for their invention of a new technique in animation for their first film, *Night on Bald Mountain*, called the pinscreen (or pinboard) process.

1933

POPEYE THE SAILOR INTRODUCED: The Fleischer Brothers introduced Popeye from Elzie Segar's comic strip in the short film *Popeye the Sailor.* This short introduced Sammy Lerner's famous "I'm Popeye the Sailor Man" song.

1933

SAG FORMS: The Screen Actors Guild was formed in 1933.

The lowly gopher orderly sitting by the Xerox machine reading television manuals overnight became a producer. I think the big danger to the art of animation with the rush to 3D is the loss of technique. The problem we have with our business is everyone is in a rush to believe it's the computer that is doing it. All the emphasis in schools is on learning Maya and learning Shake, et cetera. The thing is, in a year or two everything is going to change. Suddenly everyone is going to throw all that software out and learn all the new programs, but in the meantime the skill sets of performance animation and acting and cinema are going by the boards. I am seeing films that are done by guys who learn everything in the games industry, and their idea of entertainment is running into a new room! These gamers say to themselves, "Let's run into this room and see what happens!" That is the extent of their knowledge of performance and cinematic storytelling.

Troy explains to Angie his feelings about animating in CG. Sketch by Troy Saliba.

 1934

OSCAR FOR *THE TORTOISE AND THE HARE* (DISNEY): Disney wins the Best Short Subject: Cartoons Academy Award for *The Tortoise and the Hare.*

1934

MULTI-PLANE CAMERA INVENTION: Ub Iwerks creates a revolutionary multi-plane camera from the remains of a Chevrolet automobile. This camera was capable of filming several separate layers of cels, giving the final frame a truly three-dimensional look.

1934

HAPPY HARMONIES INTRODUCED: *Happy Harmonies* was a series of animated cartoons distributed by MGM and produced by Harmand and Ising. Produced in Technicolor, these cartoons were similar to Walt Disney's *Silly Symphonies.*

For years in CG animation, the tools were so technical that one artist and one programmer equaled one digital artist, with each having entirely different mindsets and backgrounds. While CG artists tried to figure out how to work with this new medium, 2D artists had to face a "sink or swim" proposition with regard to the mouse and box and leaving behind their pencils.

As the '90s went on, 2D continued to embrace new shading approaches to make the characters look more real and three-dimensional, following the technological breakthroughs in visual effects and computer-generated movies. CG tools such as CAPS (*Computer Animation Production System*) were introduced to aid the production of 2D.

Roger Rabbit was the character that first used the new tool called CAPS, developed by Ed Catmull and his recruited team of talented computer scientists at the computer graphics lab of NYIT. For Roger Rabbit to fit better in the live-action sequences, CAPS was developed to raise the level of shading on the characters. The initial work of this group was focused on 2D animation, specifically creating tools to assist traditional animators. A system was developed to scan and then paint pencil-drawn artwork. Catmull and Pixar would later evolve this technology into Disney's Computer Animation Production System (CAPS).[12] Tom Sito shows us the importance the CAPS system had:

> "I miss my pencil. I miss the graphic control I had. I miss the fact that I didn't need an army of people to do my job. I was the guy with the answers, instead of the guy with the questions. I don't think the art form will disappear. I just don't think it will be around as any viable media to keep loads and loads of animators busy anymore. Nobody wants to invest in it, unfortunately."
> —*Troy Saliba*

Art direction is the real revolution when it comes to using computers in animation. Now you can art direct shot by shot in CG. When we started *The Rescuers Down Under* in 1990, they said that the ink-and-paint system gave us the color palette of *Pinocchio* to the ninth square to the ninth power. That is how many color tones you had. *The Rescuers* was the first movie using a computer animated production system (CAPS). They did not use traditional methods like cells or paint on that movie. *The Little Mermaid* was one of the last traditional films completed, and color is really basic. Ariel has daytime colors and nighttime colors, and that is it. Actually, the last scene in *The Little Mermaid* of everyone waving goodbye to the ship was the first CAPS shot. They tried it as an experiment. They colored all of the drawings with the computer for that last shot.

1934
DONALD DUCK APPEARS: Donald Duck's voice debuts on Mickey Mouse's NBC radio program and appears in Disney's *The Wise Little Hen.*

1934
FIRST *MERRIE MELODY* IN COLOR: Warner Bros. released its first *Merrie Melody* in color.

1934
SNOW WHITE IS A TWINKLE IN WALT'S EYE: Walt Disney lays out his vision for *Snow White* during a four-hour staff meeting.

As the art of animation continues to evolve, we cannot forget the foundation and principles of animation necessary to create great performances. Yes, the computer has a very remote nature not as tangible as a pencil, but it's here to stay so let's try to find a way to unite both the technical and artistic sides of the CG animation world. People in animation now say, "Let's make a new, more improved digital artist."

A New Digital Artist Is Born

In the late 1990s, CG continued to develop the tools to be easier for non-programmers to use. The years encompassing the last decade of the twentieth century are particularly meaningful because they represent the largest single change in the art of animation since its earliest days. Never before has a technology made a more radical impact on the way we animate. More selective hiring criteria for digital artists began in these years at visual-effects and CG studios. The industry had come full circle. The foundation of classical animation, created by the past masters including Disney's Nine Old Men, was beginning to have an impact on computer-generated animation. Digital artists in the 1990s had to have a good knowledge of the traditional principles of animation as well as an understanding of the computer tools.

As 2D productions dwindled, traditional animators began to cross over into CG. However, in the early 1990s, artists willing to work on a computer with traditional animation skills were still very rare. Not enough traditional animators were willing to make the crossover to the computer at this time. Many 2D artists were fighting the computer. The demand for these traditional

The digital animator is redefined. Sketch by Floyd Norman.

OSCAR FOR *THREE ORPHAN KITTENS* (DISNEY): Disney wins a Best Short Subject: Cartoons Academy Award for *Three Orphan Kittens*.

EXPERIMENTAL ANIMATION AND GPO FILM UNIT: The GPO, or General Post Office Film, unit was established in 1933. Norman McLaren joined GPO Film unit in 1935 and produced 60 experimental animated films in a stunning range of styles and techniques, collecting more than 200 international awards and world recognition.

artists in CG was high, and the supply was low. As the traditional artists weighed the choice to cross over to the computer, CG artists trained as animators on the computer for years were frustrated with the idea that they might have to go back to school to learn traditional animation just to compete with the traditional artists making the leap. Ironically, at this time, CG animators were facing the same fears as 2D animators, thinking, "I spent years on a career I love, and now I might have to go back to school just to get a job!"

The introduction of more 2D animators in CG continued to push the boundaries of what computer animation was capable of and what animators demanded of the tools. Animation artists began to force programmers to develop tools that would enable them to realize their vision outside of what most thought a computer could do. Everything moved to a higher level because traditional animation stars began to enter CG. By now, the public and the industry had much higher expectations. Even people who did not work in the industry had their opinions. Exposure to quality changes your taste. Anyone who has experienced a fine wine or Egyptian 900 thread–count sheets has experienced this, and the same applies to animation. Conrad Vernon explains how even his brother's untrained eye was able to identify bad animation:

> My brother, who knows nothing about animation and doesn't know how to draw at all, went to see *Pokemon* and said, "God, the animation was bad in that, and it was so boring!" I think people are getting to a point where if the movie doesn't have good animation, people won't become as invested because the characters can't act as well, the characters can't emote as well, and the characters won't be able to carry a good story as well.

Understanding the basics and fundamentals of the profession is now equally as important as the software. By 2001, the 2D boom was in the past, and the success of *Shrek* was central to changing the face of animation. *Shrek*, *Toy Story,* and other CG films proved that grounding yourself equally in the arts and in computer sciences was the key to staying employed in the 1990s. Nik Ranieri tells a story of a friend who went to work at Pixar:

> I remember one of my friends, a story guy, who was about to go up to Pixar and live and work. He said to me, "Why don't you come up?" I said, "I don't know anything about the computer and all that." He said, "You don't have to know anything. They don't want people who know the computer. You can learn that. It's easy to learn. The animation aspect, that's the hard part." This was in the mid-1990s, when computer animation was still young.

1935

TERMITE TERRACE: Tex Avery joins the Leon Schlesinger/Warner Bros. studio. Bob Clampett joined Tex Avery's unit the same year, and the two soon developed an irreverent style of animation that would set Warner Bros. apart. They worked apart from the other animators in a termite-infested building dubbed Termite Terrace, a name used by fans and historians to describe the entire studio.

1935

PORKY PIG DEBUTS: *I Haven't Got a Hat,* a Warner Bros. cartoon short, introduced Beans the Cat, Little Kitty, Porky Pig, Oliver Owl, Ham, and Ex. Porky stole the show with his mixed-up attempt to recite "The Ride of Paul Revere."

This new perspective was devastating to many computer animators. CG animators who had spent years honing their skills on the computer and felt they were approaching their own version of *The Lion King* boom suddenly had doors shut in their faces. Traditional animators were being hired in place of those who had been animating on a computer for years.

Nineteen-ninety-five proved to be another big year in animation history. *Toy Story* made more money than any other animated film in '95, grossing $191 million domestically. Multiple patents were awarded to Pixar for compositing software, volume data solutions, and various application techniques used in *Toy Story*. The movie *Babe* was nominated and won an Academy Award for the use of live action and computer-animated effects, expanding further what the audience believed special effects films could achieve. Movies such as *Casper* and *Jumanji* were hanging in there with higher box-office sales than most visual effects movies had seen in years. This was the year DreamWorks Feature Animation was formed, and the year many important figures in animation died, including John Whitney Sr., the "father of CG animation"; Preston Blair, an animator on productions from *Fantasia* to *The Flintstones* and author of many great animation books that are still used; and Friz Freleng, whose career was one of the longest and most prolific at Warner Brothers. The computer software companies Wavefront and Alias merged, the Sony PlayStation was introduced, Sun introduced Java, and the MP3 standard format developed. Technology was now driving the art in new directions and from all angles. Animation was expanding on the Internet, in videogames, ride films, television, and feature films.

1995 HIGHLIGHTS

◆ *Toy Story* makes more money than any other animated film.

◆ *Babe* is nominated and wins an Academy Award for visual effects.

◆ DreamWorks Feature Animation is formed.

◆ John Whitney Sr., Preston Blair, and Friz Freleng die.

◆ Wavefront and Alias software merge.

◆ Sony PlayStation, Java, and the MP3 format are introduced.

1936

THE VOICE OF MEL BLANC: Mel Blanc joined Leon Schlesinger Studios and soon became noted for voicing a wide variety of cartoon characters, including Bugs Bunny, Tweety Bird, Porky Pig, and Daffy Duck.

1936

OSCAR FOR *THE COUNTRY COUSIN* (DISNEY): Disney wins a Best Short Subject: Cartoons Academy Award with *Country Cousin.*

The Animated Movie Industry: Moving into the Millennium

While Disney's new animated 1995 release, *Pocahontas*, made more than $346 million worldwide, the previous year *The Lion King* made more than $760 million worldwide.[13] In retrospect, these are tremendous figures. However, these numbers also show a downward spiral profit-wise for Disney. The second Golden

The audience for animated features changed. Sketch by Floyd Norman.

Age had peaked. As the first of its kind, the CG release *Toy Story* cost $30 million to make[14] and made $358 million worldwide after its release in 1995.[15] Before this film, the impression was that CG animation was too expensive to make a profit.

Box-office profits from 1997 to 1999 show the rise of CG and the fall of 2D specifically. The years 1997–1999 in Table 1.2 provide a snapshot of the greatest leaps in visual effects and CG movies and how they changed the audience for animated films. The 2D and 3D production index in Appendix B will take you on a more thorough journey of traditional, CG, and visual-effects movies made since 1994 to illustrate this point in depth. Table 1.2 identifies the reasons for this change in animation from both a financial and a social standpoint. Studios had been chasing after profits like those achieved by *The Lion King* for years. At the same time, the audience had changed. The audience for animated films was educated by the increased production of heavy visual-effects movies. 2D did not look expensive anymore, and 2D studios began to respond by changing how they marketed their product. This brings us back to the importance of story, and why a studio like Pixar was so successful. In addition to the importance of story and marketing, Table 1.2 reflects the changes effects-driven movies made in what the audience wanted to watch.

In the period from 1997 to 1999, nine traditional films made half the profits that nine visual-effects movies made. Although there were not as many productions made, CG-animated movies were holding their own against traditionally animated films during these years, making as much money or more. These numbers were not lost on the studios. Once *Shrek 2* was released in 2004, CG movie productions were making more money than some live-action blockbusters. The studios began to theorize that the answer was the medium and not the story. To quote Marshall McLuhan, "It's the medium, not the message." Tom Sito uses Fox as an example to show how studios can start thinking the medium is what is bringing the audience:

> Look at the experience at Fox. They spent 10 years bankrolling Don Bluth movies, culminating in one flop after another. *Titan AE* was really expensive, and nobody saw it. The first 3D film Fox supported after Bluth was *Ice Age*, and that movie made more money than *A Beautiful Mind*, the Best Picture winner of the year! The second movie—*Robots*—BOOM! It's another hit. Fox must think that CG is the answer then, instead of story.

1936

OSCAR FOR *THE OLD MILL* (DISNEY): Disney wins a Best Short Subject: Cartoons Academy Award for *The Old Mill*.

1937

SNOW WHITE AND THE SEVEN DWARFS RELEASED: At the 11th Academy Awards, Walt Disney was recognized with a special award for *Snow White* as a significant screen innovation that has charmed millions and pioneered a great new entertainment field for the motion picture cartoon.

1937

DAFFY DUCK APPEARS: *Porky's Duck Hunt* is an animated short film starring Porky Pig; it is notable for being the first appearance of Daffy Duck.

Table 1.2 1997–1999 Box Office Domestic Sales for Animated 2D, CG, and Visual-Effects Movies[16]

2D	$	CG	$	FX	$
1997					
Cats Don't Dance	$4 million			Titanic	$600 million
Anastasia	$58 million			Men in Black	$250 million
				The Lost World: Jurassic Park	$229 million
Traditional sales	$62 million	CG sales	0	EFX sales	$1.08 billion
1998					
Mulan	$120 million	A Bug's Life	$162 million	Armageddon	$201 million
The Prince of Egypt	$101 million	Antz	$90 million	Dr. Dolittle	$144 million
The Rugrats Movie	$100 million			Godzilla	$136 million
Quest for Camelot	$22 million				
Traditional sales	$343 million	CG sales	$252 million	EFX sales	$481 million
1999					
Tarzan	$171 million	Toy Story 2	$245 million	Star Wars: Episode 1 - The Phantom Menace	$431 million
The Iron Giant	$23 million	Stuart Little	$140 million	The Matrix	$171 million
Princess Mononoke	$2 million			Wild Wild West	$113 million
Traditional sales	$196 million	CG sales	$385 million	EFX sales	$715 million

1938

OSCAR FOR *FERDINAND THE BULL* (DISNEY): Disney's *Ferdinand the Bull* wins a Best Short Subject: Cartoons Academy Award.

1938

THE SCREEN CARTOONISTS GUILD ESTABLISHED: The Screen Cartoonists Guild Local #852 Hollywood chartered.

1939

OSCAR FOR *THE UGLY DUCKLING* (DISNEY): Disney's *The Ugly Duckling*, the last *Silly Symphony*, wins a Best Short Subject: Cartoons Academy Award.

The Best of Both Worlds

Initial bewilderment and punishing hand cramps slowly gave way to the realization that rather than giving up the craft 2D animators had struggled so long to perfect, all of the principles of traditional animation also applied directly to animation on a computer. Troy Saliba tells us of his experience transitioning from 2D to CG:

> When I was introduced to CG, I actually posed my animation out first on paper without doing any in-betweens. I just drew all my keys and my breakdowns. I said, "That's the scene." I still thank the guy who sat beside me through the whole CG process because it wasn't pretty. I created the same poses I had drawn on the computer and I used step curves. I Playblasted it, and I was happy to see that it worked. I could see the pose test there. I then (in another painful process) went in and did what I call the in-between part, working with the graph editor, which was very mysterious and scary to me. I was happy to find that the main principles as far as establishing poses, working on my timing with the blocking, and all that stuff just carried through. By the time I got to the graph editor, it was just a formality at that point. Before I worked through this process, I was really frightened. Once I did it, I said to myself, "Okay, there is obviously a lot of technical stuff I need to learn here, but it's a mountain I can climb now." It doesn't seem so scary and abstract.

Many animators that we have spoken with say they would never want to go back to traditional hand-drawn cartoons after discovering the advantages of CG. There are a few, however, for which the computer has no appeal. Unwilling or unable to make the transition, they have decided to have a go at staying with the art form that has provided them with a great deal of artistic satisfaction for many years. We truly hope there is room for both mediums and use *Spirited Away* as a great example. It should be encouraging, in light of the overwhelming popularity of CG, that a traditionally animated film with a fantastic story can win the Academy Award for Best Animated Picture in the new millennium.

In 2003, Disney made the decision to abandon the hand-drawn traditional approach for the new, popular CG medium. In April of that year, Glen Keane, a 31-year veteran who created the beast for *Beauty and the Beast* and Ariel for *The Little Mermaid*, gave a seminar called "The Best of Both Worlds" to a meeting of 50 animators. The subject of the seminar was a discussion of the pros and cons of each art form. Keane says he was confronted by Kevin Geiger, a computer animation supervisor, who said, "If you can do all this cool stuff that you are talking about—that you want to see in animation—but you have to give up the pencil to do it, are you in?" Keane says he hesitated, but answered, "I'm in." In this situation, did he really have a choice?[17]

1939

DISNEY MOVES THEIR STUDIO:
The new buildings in Burbank were designed around the animation process, with the large animation building in the center of the campus and adjacent buildings for related departments.

1940

OSCAR FOR *THE MILKY WAY* (MGM): *The Milky Way* won the Best Short Subject: Cartoons Academy Award.

1940

***PINOCCHIO* 2ND DISNEY FEATURE:** Based on the book *Pinocchio* by Carlo Collodi, the film was made in response to the enormous success of *Snow White and the Seven Dwarfs*.

Looking at the interesting turn of events in animation, many questions come to mind. What makes for a smooth transition? What has helped those who have made the jump? How much of the 2D art form is applicable to the digital realm? What have we gained and lost in the rise of CG? What is the impact of more 2D animators entering the CG industry? Without having drawing as a craft threshold, is there room for a new set of animation heroes in CG with a signature style like, say, Ward Kimball's? This is a relatively new art in the broader sense of the word, and we are all learning as we go. This book is meant to provide a connection between 2D and CG. We will learn from our past and build upon our future. We are but fleas on the shoulders of giants. Let us begin.

---

[1]*Tron*: Wayne Carlson, Advanced Center for Computing Arts and Design – Ohio State University. http://accad.osu.edu/~waynec/history/lesson6.html.

[2]Hanna Barbera Uses Computers: Wayne Carlson, Advanced Center for Computing Arts and Design – Ohio State University. http://accad.osu.edu/~waynec/history/timeline.html.

[3]III, MAGI and DE: Wayne Carlson, Advanced Center for Computing Arts and Design – Ohio State University. http://accad.osu.edu/~waynec/history/lesson6.html.

[4]"Marc Levoy Develops Cartoon Animation System." Computer Science at the University of Virginia. http://www.cs.virginia.edu/colloquia/oldcolloquia05.html.

[5]"Disney Biographical Sketch." The Associated Press. *LA Times*. December 1, 2003. http://www.latimes.com/business/investing/wire/sns-ap-disney-resignation-glance,1,3208262.story?coll=sns-ap-investing-headlines.

[6]Canemaker, John. *Walt Disney's Nine Old Men and the Art of Animation*. Disney Editions: 2001.

[7]*The Black Cauldron*. A Film Review by James Berardinelli. http://movie-reviews.colossus.net/movies/b/black_cauldron.html.

[8]Denslow, Philip: Sexy Robot. "Reaching for the Edge: A Conversation with Con Pederson." *Graffitti* magazine. January/February, 1986. http://www.denslow.com/articles/con.html.

[9]Stained Glass Knight: Wikipedia. Encyclopedia: Young Sherlock Holmes. Licensed under the GFDL. ©NationMaster.com 2003–5. All Rights Reserved. http://www.nationmaster.com/encyclopedia/Young-Sherlock-Holmes. Pixar. Company Information – Meet the Execs. John Lasseter Bio. http://www.pixar.com/companyinfo/aboutus/mte.html.

[10]Box office sales obtained from http://boxofficemojo.com.

[11]Box office sales obtained from http://boxofficemojo.com.

[12]McHugh, Michael P. "An Interview with Edwin Catmull." *Innerview*. http://www.usc.edu/isd/pubarchives/networker/97-98/Sep_Oct_97/innerview-catmull.html.

[13]Box office sales obtained from http://boxofficemojo.com.

1940

FANTASIA 3RD DISNEY FEATURE: *Fantasia*, a Walt Disney experiment in animation and music, consists of seven pieces of classical music. It is also notable for being the first major film released in stereophonic sound, using a process dubbed "Fantasound."

1940

BUGS BUNNY ENTERS ANIMATION: Tex Avery defines the character of Bugs Bunny in *A Wild Hare*. *A Wild Hare* is as also noteworthy for settling on the classic voice and appearance of Elmer Fudd. The design and character of Bugs Bunny would continue to be refined, but the general character was established in this cartoon.

[14]*Toy Story* production budget. http://www.the-numbers.com/movies/1995/0TYST.html.

[15]Box office sales obtained from http://boxofficemojo.com.

[16]Box office sales obtained from http://boxofficemojo.com.

[17]Holson, Laura M. "Has the Sky Stopped Falling at Disney?" *New York Times* online. September 18, 2005. http://select.nytimes.com/search/restricted/article?res=F70F13F735550C7B8DDDA00894DD404482.

1940

TOM AND JERRY ENTER THE SCENE:
MGM's *Puss Gets the Boot* showed us the first Tom and Jerry and was the first co-effort of Bill Hanna and Joe Barbera.

1940

WOODY WOODPECKER INTRODUCED:
Woody Woodpecker first appeared in the film *Knock Knock*. The Woody of *Knock Knock* is a truly deranged-looking animal, although his familiar color scheme of red head and blue body is already in place, as is his infamous laugh.

Chapter 2
Tell Me a Story

There are many books out there that talk specifically about how to write a good story. Here, we will touch upon some the important facets of telling a great story for animation. We talk about storyboards and their importance to the development of a visual medium such as filmmaking. In this chapter we tell you about the evolution of the storyboard into animatics, layout, workbook, pre-visualization, and choreography, and how these tools have made the story artist's job easier in some ways and a lot more complex in others. Each of these tools is used in animation to help refine the story and get to the heart of what the audience should be experiencing. The storyboard of traditional animation has evolved into a complex set of steps in CG to ensure that all the pieces of the puzzle fit.

> "What makes for a good plot? A giant monster, a pretty girl, and an obsessed scientist. Oh, and the scientist should smoke a pipe."
>
> —*Chris Bailey*

Sometimes time and budget constraints do not allow for all steps of the process to be used, but the desired story pipeline on a CG-animated feature goes from storyboards to animatic to a tool called *workbook*, and then on to layout, moving into pre-viz, and finally choreo. The boards are developed in the Story department using the animatic process. Animatics are the step where drawn boards are scanned into the computer and pacing is more fully worked out with the scratch track. The next step is to pass the animatic to layout. The Layout department's first pass is sometimes called *workbook*, where the boards are basically created in CG. During the workbook phase, no camera move, timing, or rough motion is created at all. The artist shoots out a frame for each major pose; or beginning and end frames for a talking head shot; or beginning, middle, and end frames for a camera move. This step is used to help locate the shots within the 3D set, to identify what elements need to be in the shots, and to make sure that things actually work in the 3D world.

At this point, the workbook is passed on to a "brain trust" where the leads of other departments identify what they will have to do for the shot—what elements need to be painted, what models were overlooked,

1941

OSCAR FOR *LEND A PAW* (DISNEY): Disney wins the Best Short Subject: Cartoons Academy Award for *Lend a Paw*.

1941

DUMBO 4TH DISNEY FEATURE: *Dumbo* was a deliberate exercise in simplicity and economy for the Disney studio, and is today considered one of its finest films.

1941

DISNEY STRIKE: The bitter 300-person animators' strike at Walt Disney Studio damaged Disney's standing with left-leaning intellectuals and destroyed the paternalistic relation between Disney and his animation staff, as well as cemented the studio's derogatory nickname of "the mouse factory."

what needs to be rigged differently, what FX need to be done, and so on. After that, it all goes to layout, where the real shot is generated with proper timing and a real camera move, if necessary. The layout camera is the actual camera that will travel down the pipeline to all departments and is adjusted if needed to fit animation in the final check before lighting. This step is called *layout finalling*. Some studios only use a few of these steps to get to the final product.

In the next step, animators take the final layout and pre-visualize the shot. The pre-viz step is a simple blocking of motion in the shot beyond what was done in layout. Typically the pre-viz animator will block out the motion and timing between extreme keys and have very rudimentary motion, similar to a stiff puppet. The pre-viz defines the composition of the movement on a simple level. As a final step before actual animation production, sometimes a choreography pass will be made depending on the director and how much he can visualize the motion thus far. This process in its entirety is the evolution of the storyboard in a CG production. So much for computers making things a lot simpler, eh? The storyboard was developed to assist in visually telling the story. Before we get into more on the storyboard and its role in storytelling, let's get into some of the building blocks of story.

Plot and Premise

The pressing question is: How do I write a good plot? The best plots are clear and simple. Remember the directive of the story. A premise helps solidify the plot and its intent. This directive or premise should be one or two lines that are the thread of meaning throughout the film. What is the point of the story you are trying to tell? If you remember this premise while developing the story, your ideas will be clear. The thrust should be reinforced in every acting choice and storytelling point. The situations you place onto your character should drive the storyline. Stick with the directive of what you want to say. Tack the premise onto the wall in front of you to remind you of what you are trying to say when you get stuck. *The Incredibles* is a perfect example of a story with a clear and simple premise, "A family of undercover superheroes, while trying to live the quiet suburban life, are forced into action to save the world."[18] Dave Zaboski talks about plot, character, and craft:

> A plot is the progression of the story to its conclusion. Plots can have many forms, but they must be clear. Boy meets girl, boy loses girl, boy gets girl is a standard linear plot. The point is, make it a compelling story; you can do anything you want to the plot. But, how do you make it a compelling story? The simple answer is, feel it. Does it move you? Does it move you down to your boots and your roots? Craft comes next, but story is first.

1941

SUPERMAN SERIES: Between 1941 and 1943, Paramount Pictures released a series of animated Technicolor cartoons based upon the comic-book character, Superman. These are seen as some of the finest, and certainly the most lavishly budgeted, animated cartoons produced during the Golden Age of animation.

1941

MISTER BUG GOES TO TOWN RELEASED: *Mister Bug Goes to Town* was a commercial flop and led to the bankruptcy and dissolution of the Fleischer Studio. Paramount fired the Fleischers and reorganized the company into Famous Studios, then re-released the film as *Hoppity Goes to Town*.

A compelling story depends on clarity and simplicity. Simplicity is a word that comes up again and again in this book. Simplicity is critical to any creative venture, especially one involving storytelling. The creative process is so open-ended that writing a story can easily result in a tale that wanders all over the place. It is up to you to keep your ideas clear. It's best to start a story when you know the beginning, the middle, and the end. These things will evolve as you write, but if you know the directive of the story, then you can keep the ideas simple. Write down the directive and hang it on the wall where you work. A directive or premise for the story about the shy man and his restaurant could be, "Even the blackest piece of coal can be polished into a diamond. Belief in yourself can take you far in this world, so don't let others' opinions get in the way." Every time you are stuck on the next idea for your story, look up at your directive and ask yourself: "If this is what my protagonist believes, then how would he react to the situations before him?" Don Waller explains how even the twists and surprises you provide in a story should support the directive you have set out for the character's growth:

> What makes a good plot is a story that one can follow and understand easily, without any effort to decipher what's happening and without it being so distorted or complicated that it's detracting from the film, rather than adding to it and making it an enjoyable film to watch! Not that a few surprises or twists in the story aren't good—as long as they help the story, rather than hinder it by being too off the wall.

There are many books out there that go into great detail about how to formulate a story. One of our favorites is *Art of Dramatic Writing: Its Basis in the Creative Interpretation of Human Motives* (Touchstone, 1972) by Lajos Egri. In this book, Egri helps you create your directive or premise for your story. The premise is the secret to simplicity. While writing you can always refer to the premise to stay on track and use all characters, plots, storylines, and arcs as supportive material to reinforce your premise. In this chapter we will just touch upon some of the important facets of story with respect to animation, but we do encourage Egri's book as a support text. Once you have your premise, you need to develop situations to place onto the character. This is the where experimentation comes into play.

> "Avoid putting characters into situations; put situations onto good characters."
>
> —*Darin McGowan*

When you are writing or storyboarding, your first ideas may be trite or cliché, and experimentation assists in thinking outside the box. Graphic designers are asked to do hundreds of thumbnails before committing to a design for a logo. The same is true for any creative venture, including writing a story or even animating.

1942
OSCAR FOR *MOCKING HITLER* (DISNEY): *Der Fuehrer's Face* won the 1943 Best Short Subject: Cartoons Academy Award.

1942
***BAMBI* 5TH DISNEY FEATURE:** *Bambi* was based on the 1923 book *Bambi: A Life in the Woods* by Felix Salten.

1942
***SPEAKING OF ANIMALS* AND TEX AVERY:** In 1941, Tex Avery quarreled with Leon Schlesinger over a series idea—comedy shorts featuring live-action animals with animated mouths dubbed onto their faces. Schlesinger suspended Avery from his job, during which time Avery sold the series to Paramount Pictures, where it ran for seven years and won an Academy Award.

When developing the performance for a scene, create an intention and be clear about it. Play the scene out in your head and figure out the best way to show what is going on inside the character's mind. Sometimes it helps to run around the room designing the most compelling and most emotional poses to clearly support the intention. If the intention for the scene is clear to you, the story will tell itself. Play around with different scenarios. Try to contrast ideas. If your character is big and strong, find his weakness or flaw and develop that to contrast his burly facade. Some of the best stories come out of stream of consciousness and experimenting. Larry Weinberg says to trust your own instincts:

> Trust yourself. If it moves you, give it a chance. Don't hold back. *Monty Python* had a great working principle. They went with any idea one of them had, even if others didn't like it. They gave anything a chance to live on. Sometimes this resulted in a failed skit. But other times, the results were completely unexpected and fantastic. If they had held back during early conceptualizing, they wouldn't have reached the unusual peaks they reached.

The best stories just feel right. These stories use good structure and solid characters effortlessly. When you are developing plot, each word you write makes sense and you see the end of the tunnel before you are even there. You already have a beginning, a middle, and an end in mind, and you can bridge those pieces easily. Whether your story path is linear or complex, your situations must still have a sense of believability.

Believability is also critical to a good story. The character actively drives the story through decisions. Those decisions must be supported by the character you develop. In animation, the terms "believability" and "convincing" are used more than "realism" because it's all about entertainment. If the story is entertaining and believable, then the audience will watch and believe the char-

> "I come from Old School, where the story artist was the writer. My complaint with current animation writers is they don't understand the medium and don't feel the need to. It's not that they can't write; it's just that they write poorly for animation. Their storytelling leans heavily on dialogue, and that's okay if you're doing live-action. What's lacking is the ability to tell a story visually, and that requires a visual sense."
>
> —*Floyd Norman*

1942

MIGHTY MOUSE IS INTRODUCED: Mighty Mouse was an animated superhero mouse character created by the Terrytoons studio. Originally, he was a superpowered housefly named "Superfly," but studio head Paul Terry changed him into a cartoon mouse instead. He first appeared in 1942 in a theatrical animated short entitled *The Mouse of Tomorrow*.

1942

FIRST ELECTRONIC COMPUTER INVENTED: The Atanasoff-Barry Computer (ABC) was the first electronic computer and was developed by physics and mathematics professor John Atanasoff and Clifford Barry. This computer used the binary system found in modern computers, and its method for storing data was quite similar to that of the modern computer.

Get used to criticism. Even the best of the great story artists got "hammered" by Walt.
Drawing by Floyd Norman.

acters and situations to be real. If it's realistic but not entertaining, the audience will leave the theater. Learn about your character and try walking in his shoes for a day. You can have a really good picture that is poorly animated but still successful, but you cannot have a brilliantly animated picture and a bad story because no one will care.

Animators share their work with other animators to get a fresh eye on the ideas being presented. The same goes for story. Story artists share their ideas with others they trust to get a better idea of what is working. Mark Koetsier explains how sharing ideas with other story people helps him narrow the scope of the story:

OSCAR FOR *YANKEE DOODLE MOUSE* (MGM):
Yankee Doodle Mouse won the 1943 Academy Award for Best Short Subject: Cartoons, making it the first of seven Tom and Jerry cartoons to receive this distinction.

SALUDOS AMIGOS 6TH DISNEY FEATURE:
Saludos Amigos was made up of four different segments; Donald Duck starred in two of them and Goofy starred in one. It garnered mixed reviews and was only reissued once, in 1949.

> On the movie I am doing right now, we do a lot of talking. Sometimes I sit there and work on an idea, and I will show it to someone and ask what they think, even if the other story artist isn't involved. We bounce ideas off each other. Sometimes we will pitch our rough storyboards in front of the story guys only (with no directors), and they will give their input. Then you can see where the problems are. If you are pitching to the director, the story guys are in there anyway. So what happens is, the director has the first say, and then the story guys will talk as well if they see a different idea. It just kind of helps to have other people's input. Just like animating, it helps to show someone else because you've got your blinders on and you are so focused on this one sequence.

When developing story, you should set the rules of character's world and abide by them. If you break the rules of your character's world and how he or she interacts in that world, you lose the believability. A prime example of breaking the rules for no purpose was in the movie *Chicken Little*. In one scene of this movie, Chicken Little and his father are watching *Raiders of the Lost Ark* (a live-action movie) at the theatre. There are no CG or live-action humans in the movie, so it makes no sense and adds nothing to the story. Make sure all characters you introduce and plotlines you raise have a reason for being there, and catapult your protagonist toward his or her goal. Set up ideas that can be relied on later in the story. Be creative and break rules, but not the rules you have applied to your world or your character.

We keep talking about rules. What are these rules or guides? Start with a character bio and background. How old is your character? Does he have a handicap? Does she drink? What is his profession? How does she feel about her family and friends? Once you establish who your character is, the story will begin to fall into place. Remember to follow the rules you made for your world, the atmosphere, the directive, and your characters, and the rest will write itself. Use the people around you to keep perspective and get a fresh eye.

Here Come the Talking Animals

Talking animals are the natural choice to present a story with moral or social concepts. It's easier to tell adult themes through the voices of talking animals, especially if the animals learning the lessons are young and childlike. It comes across as less preachy and more approachable to both kids and adults.

The Lion King story is reminiscent of the *Bambi* classic, in which a young animal deals with life and growing up much like a child does. This story is something both children and adults can relate to and appreciate, which is why it's so successful. The animals are voiced by both adults and children in these films, creating

1943

BILL TYTLA RESIGNS: Bill Tytla, one of the original Disney animators, resigns from Disney. Thought to be one of the best character animators during the Golden Age, Tytla is particularly noted for the animation of Grumpy in *Snow White* and Chernabog from *Fantasia*.

1943

JOHN WHITNEY MAKES HIS FIRST FILM: John and James Whitney's experimental first films were *Five Abstract Film Exercises*. Considered by many to be the "Father of Computer Graphics," John Whitney and the entire Whitney family have successfully linked musical composition with experimental film and computer imaging.

empathy with the audience. Movies geared toward adults with adult themes and adult voices can become preachy and judgmental in animation. In the act of trying to broaden the audience for animation, studios lost sight of what worked to get that audience in the first place, which is a good story with approachable, empathetic characters.

Specifically, one could argue that Disney lost their way with *Pocahontas*. DreamWorks lost their way right out of the gate with *The Prince of Egypt*. Also, Fox lost their way with *Anastasia*, again with their first animated feature. To a very large degree, the corporate structure of animated studios changed with the huge success of the pictures themselves. In essence, the massive success of the pictures was a double-edged sword. Increasingly, artistic decisions were being put through a filter of "creative managers," many of whom had backgrounds in business and not in art. This corporate approach to filmmaking and developing story was inherently dishonest because apparently its main goal was to generate massive amounts of money at the expense of good, honest storytelling.

From 1997 to 2004, almost every CG production had talking animals of one kind or another. During this time, movies such as *Toy Story*, *Chicken Run*, *Dinosaur*, *Stuart Little*, *Shrek*, *Ice Age*, *Scooby-Doo*, *Brother Bear*, *Finding Nemo*, and so on all used talking animals to tell their stories. Even the *Toy Story* franchise had a "toy" dog, a pig, a dinosaur, and a horse that talked. The talking animal theme continues in 2005, and every CG production incorporates talking animals, as Mark Koetsier explains:

> *The Lion King* had talking animals and made a huge amount of money. Now that we are getting into CG, almost all of the productions are talking animals. *Chicken Little*, *Over the Hedge*, *Madagascar*, *Open Season*, *The Wild*, *Flushed Away*, *Kung Fu Panda*...they are all talking animals. I think it's because it's a world beyond our own, yet you can make it similar—but you see a world from a different perspective.

By observing trends in storytelling, we can see what works and what doesn't when tackling tough subjects.

Desire and Growth

Emotion and empathy are the most important facets of storytelling in animation. Your animation must connect to the audience. To create empathy you must locate your character's desire and communicate it to the audience. What does the character want and—even better—need? Carlos Baena explains why the audience gets bored with story:

1943

DROOPY DOG IS CREATED BY TEX AVERY: Droopy first appeared in the MGM cartoon *Dumb-Hounded* and is considered by animation scholars to be one of Avery's best works.

1944

OSCAR FOR *MOUSE TROUBLE* (MGM): *Mouse Trouble* won the Best Short Subject: Cartoons Academy Award.

1944

HELL-BENT FOR ELECTION AND UPA: *Hell-Bent For Election* was a two-reel animated cartoon short and one of the first major films from UPA. It was created for the Democrats for the 1944 presidential election.

> There has to be some sort of connection between the characters on screen, and the audience watching what these characters are doing or are going through. If the audience doesn't relate to the characters, then they'll either get bored or will not believe what's happening.

Through developing the concept of desire for your character, you create growth for the individual. It's not fun to watch someone get what he wants easily. Life is rarely like that unless you are from Orange County or a member of the "Lucky Sperm Club." People have to work hard to get their hopes and dreams fulfilled. Those hopes and dreams have to be motivated from the character's background to be believable. In *Treasure Planet*, Jim Hawkins is frustrated and longs for adventure for no clear reason. He has hopes and dreams, but he comes across as annoying and whiny because those dreams aren't justified in his past. A kid who has everything can't just decide he is bored and go off to chase a dragon. The character must learn about himself as he strives toward his goals. Growth toward these goals is necessary to creating a believable story. The same things we have happen to us in real life should crop up as obstacles for your animated characters. Conrad Vernon talks about growth with the story of *Shrek*:

> One rule we always had on *Shrek 2* is that we do not lay back on another quest story. If we were to have Shrek go on a quest for this different thing, where he and Donkey go out on a new pursuit, Shrek doesn't grow or learn anything at all. Shrek has to find something, but he is not there to get a princess and bring her back; he is there looking for something much deeper. It's the easiest and the hardest thing in the world at the same time. Shrek and Fiona get married; now where do you logically go? They go to meet the families. How do we make it realistic to everybody, and how do we make it fun and interesting enough that it doesn't become a drag? That is the thing. That is the balancing act. What is the natural course from there? Shrek makes his own family. After that, Shrek has to deal with his daughters bringing boys home or his boys bringing girls home. Letting go of your kids is the next thing. It's just life.

Remember, your characters are human (or bats, chickens, mollusks, or one of the myriad lower primates that are so popular these days). Your characters are living, breathing people (mollusks) who have lived lives and experienced things (possibly under water), and these experiences have formed their personality. Their personas will determine their reactions to things like getting married, meeting the mollusk in-laws, and having a family. Growth caused by desire is necessary for your storytelling to be interesting and believable (even as a mollusk).

1944

SCHLESINGER STUDIO SOLD TO WARNER BROS: Schlesinger's studio was sold to Warner Bros. in 1944.

1944

YOSEMITE SAM IS INTRODUCED: *Hare Trigger*, a *Merrie Melodies* cartoon short starring Bugs Bunny, marks the first appearance of Yosemite Sam, who appears as a train robber.

1945

OSCAR FOR *QUIET PLEASE* (MGM): *Quiet, Please!* won the 1945 Academy Award for Best Short Subject: Cartoons.

Growth and Character Arcs

Growth creates an arc for your character. Character arcs have a beginning, middle, and an end. Without meaningful change in the characters, there is no story. How you decide to reveal the arcs will determine the pacing of the story. Your character must go through a process of change throughout the story in order to be interesting. What lesson does he learn? How does the journey change him? Are the hurdles that your character has to negotiate interesting and entertaining?

A good story has an organic flow that dynamically presents obstacles to your heroes and your villains. Laura McCreary sees the conflict or obstacle as something that can link the antagonist's and the protagonist's goals:

> Often the hurdle can involve the antagonist's goal being different than the protagonist's.

If the antagonist's goal is in direct conflict with the protagonist's, then you already have a solid struggle built into the plot. Growth means change. The character needs to change internally. A great example of change and growth in a character would be Stitch in the movie *Lilo & Stitch*. The charm of the little Hawaiian girl turns Stitch from an evil guy from space to a loving creature. Your plot needs to propel this growth through obstacles faced by the protagonist. The goal of the character is to overcome something and grow from that journey. Scott Holmes explains character growth using *Dumbo* as an example:

> Essentially, the plot should show the growth or development of the main character. A good plot can reveal that growth in an interesting, natural way. For example, in *Dumbo*, the realization that his ears are a special gift instead of a curse is one aspect of his growth as a character. In order to do this, he has to overcome ridicule and gain self-confidence. Once he accepts and appreciates his gift, his character is fully realized and triumphant. The main idea in *Dumbo* is accepting one's unique qualities, and the plot reinforces this as it unfolds, albeit in a natural and subtle way.

Let's go through a hypothetical plotline to show growth in a character. Let's say the character in question is a shy, introverted person because of his dominant parents and strict upbringing. This character must go through some process or challenge while pursuing his goal that changes him into a confident and poised person. Maybe this character has always wanted to run his own restaurant and is a very good cook, but his dominant parents have other ideas for him. He must break the ties with his parents to seek out his own

1945

PEPÉ LE PEW CHARACTER DEVELOPED: *Odor-able Kitty* introduced Pepé le Pew. Pepé creator Chuck Jones says Pepé was based loosely on the personality of his Termite Terrace colleague, writer Tedd Pierce, a self-styled "ladies' man."

1945

HARRY SMITH DRAWS DIRECTLY ON FILM: Smith's earliest films are his most geometrically abstract films. Number one was hand-drawn onto the film itself, avoiding any need for a camera.

1946

BOB CLAMPETT LEAVES WARNER BROS.: Clampett's big break came after Tex Avery left WB in 1941 and Clampett inherited Avery's former unit. Clampett was replaced as director by Arthur Davis.

A character's arcs is where the character grows and overcomes obstacles. Sketch by Jamie Oliff.

goal. Once he makes that break, he is successful beyond his imagination and has enough confidence to invite his parents to the restaurant. They come to see how he has turned his dream into reality and how his conviction and faith in himself has changed who he is. They in turn accept him and treat him with more respect. This is a good example of a simple, clear character arc. As an animator, this would be a great arc to work with because the character's transformation from a shy, quiet person to a self-assured, confident person is both clear and engaging. One way to achieve such a complex character arc is to work through back story.

Orchestration and Back Story

Back story is a historical account of the character's development prior to the story now being told. What area of the world did he grow up in? What were his parents like? Did he suffer some grievous psychological trauma (such as being de-boned or shaved of all of his fur)? A character's back story, or history, will determine his actions throughout the film. Use a character bio to figure out who your guy really is. (There is an example character bio questionnaire in the back of Chapter 3 as a reference; Chapter 3 goes into more depth on the character bio.) Story artists use back story to work out how the character would react in any given situation. The back story must remain implied, but its influence must be consistent.

1946

OSCAR FOR *THE CAT CONCERTO* (MGM): *The Cat Concerto* won the 1946 Academy Award for Best Short Subject: Cartoons.

1946

FOGHORN LEGHORN COMES ON THE SCENE: Foghorn Leghorn, a large, animated adult rooster, appeared in numerous Warner Bros. cartoons. He first appeared in *Walky Talky Hawky*. He is considered a significant *Looney Tunes* character.

1946

HECKLE AND JECKLE SERIES INTRODUCED: *Heckle and Jeckle* was a theatrical Terrytoons cartoon series featuring a pair of identical magpies who calmly outwit their foes in the manner of Bugs Bunny, while maintaining a mischievous streak.

It will color your character and add a depth to his personality that would be lacking if your character bio is not comprehensive.

Going back to our shy, reserved chef, maybe a bad argument with his parents has led him out into the world, leaving behind his sheltered life. This scene will provide the audience with all they need to know about the protagonist and his relationship with his parents. You don't need to go all the way back to when he was a child growing up. Unless you can go back in an interesting way to make your character believable, there isn't a need for lots of flashbacks. A simple setup to explain why a character is being introduced is all you need. Mark Koetsier talks about back story and how *The Incredibles* sets up scenes about the introduction of the villain early in the story:

> You have to set up your character in the beginning. *The Incredibles* does this successfully. They set up who the villain is in the first few minutes of the film. You don't think he is the villain until later, but you know who he is. Mr. Incredible stops to save the cat before he is on his way to his own wedding, and this kid shows up and wants to be like him. At this point you think the kid is harmless, a pest. You don't want to spend a lot of time on back story. You want to make it as simple as possible.

Orchestrate every event clearly and simply. Make sure there are no holes, no shortcuts, no copouts from conflicting events, and no loose ends. If you are having problems in the third act, it usually means the first and second acts have plot holes that need to be repaired. Arrange all events around the directive.

Every business venture can complicate the creative process. You will be given deadlines or you'll create self-imposed deadlines if it's your own short film—these will make the creative process strenuous. Many times you have to trust your own instincts as to when to introduce characters and orchestrate events. Remember the basic theories, but always listen to your gut.

There is an old story told by Milt Kahl that is from audio recordings made during the production of *The Rescuers*. Milt talks about how Walt handled story "by the seat of his pants." Milt was telling Walt during the production of *The Jungle Book* that he was worried about Sher Khan

> "Create a story that doesn't lose course and wander aimlessly. The best plot is propelled by the characters and moves the audience from point A to point B in the most efficient (although not predictable) way. In other words, trim the fat. Hitchcock was a master of this."
>
> —Eddie Pittman

1946

SONG OF THE SOUTH RELEASED: Disney's feature film, *Song of the South*, was based on the Uncle Remus cycle of stories by Joel Chandler Harris. It was one of Disney's earliest feature films to combine live-action footage with animation and was the first Disney feature film in which live actors were hired for lead roles. The film is often the subject of controversy, frequently accused of racism.

1947

OSCAR FOR *TWEETIE PIE* (WARNER BROS.): *Tweetie Pie* won the 1947 Academy Award for Best Short Subject: Cartoons.

and how he didn't make an appearance in the film until you were 40 minutes into it. You didn't see your villain for such a long time! Walt would say, "Don't worry about it." Walt was, as Milt Kahl put it, "an instinctive storyteller."[19] He did what he felt was right. In those days it was still up to him; it was one person who drove everybody else. If he needed money, what did he do? He went to his brother! There wasn't a business aspect there. He just said, "I need more money to finish my film," and Roy would go to all the banks and raise the money to finish the picture. It was a purely artistic and singular vision of Walt, who had final say on everything. He hired people and he let them do what they were good at.

Today, things are a bit more involved with multiple directors, writers, and story people. CG films being made today tend to have more people involved in the creative process, which sometimes can create a misguided or ambiguous vision. By always referring to the premise for the story, you can ensure your contribution will be heightening the story and reinforcing its themes. Remember, ultimately, if you follow the directive or premise of the story, your ideas will be successful.

Learn to love rejection. Most of what you do will be thrown away. It's part of the process of developing the story. Drawing by Floyd Norman.

1947

UCLA ANIMATION WORKSHOP FORMED: Bill Shull, a former Disney animator, created the Workshop in 1947. He established the Workshop's basic philosophy of "one person, one film" and a strong commitment to content and quality. The Workshop has been one of the top three animation programs for the past 47 years.

1947

COMMUNISTS IN ANIMATION BLACKLISTED: The House Committee on Un-American Activities (HUAC) sets up in Hollywood. Walt Disney testified the first week and denounced the leaders of the 1941 union strike as Communist-inspired.

Storyboards, Animatics, and Pre-Viz

The storyboard for animation was first developed by the story team at Walt Disney Feature Animation. Walt Disney and Webb Smith are credited as the inventors of the storyboard in the mid-1920s. Grim Natwick maintained that at the Hearst Studio in 1916, director Gregory LaCava was drawing his own storyboard on one piece of paper, then tearing off pieces as he handed off assignments to animators. But Walt and Webb Smith are still acknowledged as the first. The system of pinning up story drawings on corkboard has become universal in filmmaking.

Because animation is such a visual medium, the written word fell short when visually explaining the film and how to tell the story cinematically. The new approach of thumbnail drawings tacked across large boards in continuity helped explain story, shots, camera moves, and visually what is going on, all at the same time. A story team works together to develop the ideas for the scenes. Everyone usually has a voice while developing the story, but it's up to the head of story and the director to reign in the scope. The first step for a story artist, once he has the general direction for a shot, is to convey the story point in the clearest and most entertaining way possible. Because character and persona are so closely related to what is driving the scene, a voice or mannerism can make an idea for the story even richer.

"Storyboards, which I believe include the thumbnail-sketching process, are truly the first visual interpretation of the written story. Certainly a lot of story ideas come equipped with concept sketches to help sell the story with a visual aid, so to speak. But the storyboard is truly the first pass at visual storytelling and the first glimpse of potential animation to result from these panels. I've seen many storyboard panels so well thought out and laid out, and that nail a story beat so thoroughly, that the final animation of the scene was nothing less than an homage to that very panel. The hardest part of creating an effective storyboard would be to stay on message for a sequence. Don't stray from the beat; don't lose focus; don't get bored. Also, what is not drawn can be included by way of notation, i.e., camera move info, description of ancillary action, and timing poses. Every bit of information will help others interpret your ideas. In a sense, a good storyboard artist is effectively directing the story incrementally, panel by panel. This is especially true if the board artist and the director share a clear vision for what that particular part of the story is trying to convey."

—*Joe Scott*

1947

MOTION PICTURE SCREEN CARTOONIST/ANIMATION GUILD/IATSE FORMED: The Motion Picture Screen Cartoonists, I.A.T.S.E. Local 839, generally referred to as "The Animation Guild," was formed in 1947. This professional guild and union of animation artists was formed at a time when Disney and other studios were alleging Communist influence in labor unions.

1948

OSCAR FOR *THE LITTLE ORPHAN* (MGM): *The Little Orphan* won the 1948 Academy Award for Best Short Subject: Cartoons, this being the fifth Oscar (of seven) given to the cat and mouse team.

43

The voices for characters are developed as a scratch track by the story artists working on a sequence in order to sell the idea to the rest of the group and to fine-tune timing. Often, when the voice developed by that story artist is successful, it's kept as the final voice track for the character. Conrad Vernon explains the story process and how he developed the Gingerbread Man character and voice for the movie *Shrek*:

As a story team, we had just come up with the idea that the fairytale creatures were being dumped into Shrek's swamp as this "keep Dewlock free of freaks" idea. So, we all sat in a circle and spitballed ideas. We all just threw out names of fairytale creatures. Someone somewhere said the Gingerbread Man. We said that was a good one. It was put on a big list. Then they came up to me and said, "Here is the Gingerbread Man and here is the introduction to the evil guy—go." How do you use the Gingerbread Man in the introduction to the evil guy? So, I started thinking to myself torture, breaking off the legs, dipping in the milk. Then I remembered from when I was a kid I had the record and a filmstrip that played "Do You Know the Muffin Man?" I thought, okay, I can mix these two things. There weren't even script pages for it. It was up to the storyboard artists to be given a paragraph of what was to happen and then move forward with that scene. Of course, we did have a writer to help us figure out dialogue problems and story problems and make the thing flow properly, but the first eyes on it were always the story artists, and we would always have to pitch our ideas. When you pitch them, that is where the voice work comes from. Your job as a storyboard artist is to put the boards up and sell the idea, even if that means doing voices, music, and sound effects. Sell the jokes and make people laugh, get angry, and cry. So I did that little Gingerbread Man voice that me and a friend, Mike Mitchell, came up with for this little character called "Randall Candy Nancy Boy." He is just one of those little effeminate boys that you see. It's not that they are gay or anything; it's just they like mother's lotion and they like open-toed sandals and they like having their hair brushed by mother. They talk in this very effeminate way. It was just this tough guy with the fey voice of a "nancy boy." I thought it was funny.

The traditional way to present storyboards is for the story artist to use a pointer and go through each board, explaining the events to come using voices like Conrad did, to sell the idea. This way, everyone can see all the boards at once and can even jump ahead of you and your pitch. The jumping ahead part would sometimes give away the gag, however. The idea of an animatic arose with more computers on the scene and helped eliminate the ability for the audience to see the next panel before its time.

1948

ROBIN HOODLUM UPA'S FIRST THEATRICAL RELEASE: UPA moved to the crowded field of theatrical cartoons to sustain itself, and quickly won a contract with Columbia Pictures. *Robin Hoodlum*, the first UPA effort for Columbia, was so successful that it earned the studio an Academy Award nomination.

1948

JOHN WHITNEY SR. ENTERS EXPERIMENTAL FILM COMPETITION: John Whitney Sr. enters the First International Experimental Film Competition in Belgium.

Animatics involve scanning the hand-drawn boards into a computer program such as Premiere or Final Cut Pro, and these boards are played like a movie, in sequence. Each board panel hold for long enough to register how long each cut will be. However, the board artist often dictates the cuts, upsetting those in editorial. Soon enough, with the advent of computers, the story people found a way to pitch their boards, still have an element of surprise, and not tread on the feet of editorial. Mark Koetsier explains how they figured out the new presentation style with a computer:

> We were doing the same storyboarding process as it was in the 1920s. Giant boards pinning up these panels. They don't want us to step on editorial's toes with our cuts like animatics do, which inevitably we do because we time out our boards. So, one of the ideas is to just put it into a computer program and frame through it. We put all the panels into the program, where each shot is up for one frame, and you go through it by pressing the Next Frame button on the keyboard and pitch it that way. The interesting thing about that is people can't look ahead. The frames are cutting, and you see how it cuts, which we normally don't get to see. It's a simple animatic that is not timed out. Then you can get a sense of the timing by how long you stay on the panel.

Animatics help with understanding the pacing of your story and the beats of the cuts. If you keep the process of an animatic, as a story person you have to work well with the editor, who has final say on how the movie will be cut. If you want an action in there, you have to convince the editor that it works.

Live-action directors have a hard time transitioning to animation because the pipeline is so complex and needs to be predetermined through tight storyboards and pre-viz. CG animation takes a while to produce, and the quick, loose board drawings are much faster to create than actually animating it. A live-action director is used to an animatic of storyboards, and then shooting the footage and possibly changing his mind once he is on set. For CG and traditionally drawn films, this footage has to be

"Animatics are completely indispensable, for both fully animated films and effects flicks. They give the director and crew a common reference point to work from and a chance to check that the scripted action and timing work in 3D space. They're useful to people in every part of the entire film pipeline, from pre-production artists, D.P.s, and actors, all the way down to the editors."

—*Bill Wright*

1948

ROAD RUNNER IS INTRODUCED BY WARNER BROS.: *The Fast and Furry-ous*, a 1948 Warner Bros. *Looney Tunes* cartoon, was the first Warner Bros. cartoon short to feature Wile E. Coyote and Road Runner. It set the template for the series, in which Wile E. Coyote tries to catch Road Runner through many traps, plans, and products.

1949

OSCAR *FOR SCENT-IMENTAL REASONS* (WARNER BROS.): *For Scent-imental Reasons* won the 1949 Academy Award for Best Short Subject: Cartoons.

produced and dropped into the animatic as it is completed during actual production. This kind of work is expensive and takes time, so planning is significant, as Angie Glocka explains:

> You need an animatic to time the animation to the sound, and it also gives a stronger sense of how your story works. One of the hardest things when a live-action director shifts to animation is that everything has to be planned ahead of time. You can't just barf out 10 minutes of animation so the director can see how it looks, as you can with live action.

It's a great revelation to see the shots being dropped into the cut as they are completed. The movie comes alive. Some CG studios have gone as far as to pre-visualize the whole movie with the computer first. This is where animators block out the shots in a rough form with cameras and characters in the scenes. Nothing is lit; the pre-viz is simply for additional tightening of the story, timing of animation, and cuts. The pre-viz step in 100-percent CG animation features is important to really understanding how the whole thing will work with camera moves and characters interacting in the frame.

When working on a movie like *Kangaroo Jack* or *Stuart Little*, utilizing live-action plates, an animated character has to interact with a pre-shot character or scene. In this situation, the pre-viz step is equally important to making all the pieces correlate to one another. Sometimes a director will even have an animator on set to place the CG character into the scene interactively as the director shoots. This will help the director frame something that is not there on set, outside of using a stand-in or a mark of some kind.

If the pre-viz step is skipped in this circumstance, there will be much more time spent in the animation step staging and just trying to figure out where the character will be in the shot in relation to the plate, the set, and characters that have already been shot and are locked into that space. Sometimes, on the set there is a "stuffy"—a stuffed version of the character—used to help frame the shot and work out eye direction. Many live-action directors are frustrated later by footage that is not framed right for the character. The pre-viz step helps work out these issues and hookups with other shots.

Other studios working with live action and CG have gone as far as to "choreo" the shots. Choreo animators work out the pre-viz even further and are at times on set and animating with the footage as it is shot. This quick feedback enables the director to see whether the camera choices and cuts are working. "Choreo" means that all of the bits, even down to the fingers and facial features, have been touched, although in broad strokes. This approach is intense for the animators to produce quickly, but it works well with a smaller

1949

TEX AVERY DIRECTS *BAD LUCK BLACKIE*: Two things make this cartoon stand out. The first is that it's the classic cartoon to demonstrate the use of escalating variations on a repeated gag. Also, this cartoon is missing the scene where Spike sticks his head out of a pipe and appears with a Chinese face, showing sensitivity to racial slurs.

1949

BOB GODFREY ENTERS ANIMATION: Bob Godfrey enters the film world, later to be called "Master of the Absurd." Godfrey specialized in 2D media, often mixing techniques to produce fast-paced, sometimes racy films with a particular wit and sharpness.

46

budget. It also is closer to a traditional way of creating a pose test because the whole line of action is worked out down to fingers, toes, and appendages instead of layering in the animation. Tom Capizzi explains how once most of the movie has been dropped into the animatic, screenings can help the director see what the audience is responsive to:

> Moving animatics are being used more and more in feature animation. The hand-drawn animatics built from storyboard frames are constantly being updated with the latest animation cuts to get the editing and story tighter and tighter as production continues. By the time all of the animation is done, the animatic exists as a shaded (and sometimes partially rendered), fully animated reel. This can even be utilized for screening purposes and test marketing. Some features rely on part of the storyboard to be animated in pre-viz because the timing for that sequence has to be perfect before the sound is laid down.

The animatic and pre-viz steps are an evolution of the storyboard methods developed by Disney many years ago, and they are invaluable tools for the filmmaker today. Editing is where the story you developed is carved out, and animatics and pre-visualization help the whole team simplify and narrow the scope of the story and film. Don Waller illustrates how these tools are better than the Disney storyboard process for animation:

> I believe animatics are much more helpful than just the drawn boards, especially where fast-paced action is concerned. Much of the editing can be intricately worked out via the animatics, as a guide for the live-action shooting. And of course, for animation, the edits and timings can precisely be worked out down to the frame!

All of these additional steps (animatics, layout, workbook, pre-visualization, and choreography) have come about with the advent of digital filmmaking and were initially created to perfect the storytelling process. However, human nature being what it is, this has created a very complex system of approval using all of these steps. In the old days, an approved storyboard would go directly to layout and from there to animation. In short, the storyboarding process has evolved into a complicated set of steps in the hopes of making a better story. Drawing will never be replaced as the quickest way to visually tell a story. Computers just assist in seeing the timing, pacing, and edits of the film. And sometimes they make for a much longer approval process in the end.

1950

OSCAR FOR *GERALD MCBOING-BOING* (UPA):
Gerald McBoing-Boing won an Academy Award for Best Short Subject: Cartoons. It was meant to be an artistic attempt to break away from the ultra-realism in animation that had been developed and perfected by Walt Disney.

1950

MR. MAGOO'S FIRST APPEARANCE: Mr. Magoo's first appearance was in the theatrical short cartoon *The Ragtime Bear*. Audiences quickly realized that the real star was Magoo, one of the few "human" cartoon characters ever produced in Hollywood at the time.

We would like to make one final point about storyboarding before you even get to the presentation of the boards. Reinforce the premise. We cannot say it enough. The directive of the story is vital to creating simple and clear storyboards. Darin McGowan tells us how to make a strong storyboard:

> Good storyboarding is all about knowing and getting into the story. Shot flow, pacing, and cutting, et cetera will come naturally when you understand what has to happen and when you base the filmmaking on the story itself.

Follow the directive of the story and you will create solid boards.

Storyboard musts:

- ◆ Make sure your shots are clear.
- ◆ Have a good idea and a good story.
- ◆ Make enough panels for the business you are describing.
- ◆ Draw the atmosphere in the scene.
- ◆ Know what plot points to hit.
- ◆ Support the message of the story.
- ◆ Don't move the camera around unnecessarily.
- ◆ Savor the moment long enough for the audience to have empathy with your characters.
- ◆ Remember the importance of graphic awareness and staging in your whole frame.
- ◆ Effectively evaluate the pacing and timing.
- ◆ Draw the essence of a sequence.

> "Never confuse the audience with too many things going on in the sequences. Clarity should be up there in terms of priority because if a shot or a sequence is not presented clearly, then the audience misses a point within the story, and that'll hurt any film."
>
> —*Carlos Baena*

Intention and Essence

When working on boards you should go to the climax of the scene and work from there. For example, when telling a story about a guy who is taking a shower and the phone rings, do you show him in the shower, then grabbing a towel, stepping out and wrapping the towel around him, then walking to answer the phone? Or, do you show him answering the phone dripping wet in the towel!? Go to the heart of the matter and describe it simply and concisely.

1950

CRUSADER RABBIT IS FIRST CARTOON SERIES MADE FOR TV: Created by Alex Anderson, nephew of Paul Terry, *Crusader Rabbit* was the first cartoon series produced especially for television.

1950

CINDERELLA 12TH DISNEY FEATURE: *Cinderella* was adapted from the fairytale *Cinderella*, drawing primarily from the version by Charles Perrault.

1950

TREASURE ISLAND FIRST DISNEY LIVE-ACTION FEATURE FILM: *Treasure Island* was Walt Disney's first live-action feature film and first TV special.

Boards, animatics, and pre-viz should be so clear that no one should look around and ask, "What was that?" Action, continuity, and perspective or POV (*point of view*) should be so clear in each cut that you don't even need sound to know what is going on. Speaking of sound, sound and image should assist each other as the story plays out. Larry Weinberg talks about sound and image:

> Don't be strong with sound and image at the same time except in special circumstances. When the imagery is simple, let the sound play out. When the sound is strong, keep the imagery simple.

Sound and image should complement each other in the film. Now let's talk about cuts.

Handling Cuts and Camera Staging

Editors are well paid for a reason. They understand how to take raw footage and tell a story by editing out the irrelevant film. Live-action movies can leave a lot of film lying on the cutting room floor. Animation doesn't have the budget for this approach. It costs a lot to animate a film, whether it's CG or hand-drawn. You control where the audience's eye goes with your cuts. It's best to cut on action to keep the pacing interesting. Telling a story with the editing is very close to how you tell the story while animating, as Carlos Baena explains:

> I think of cuts, sequences, screen composition, and editing in similar ways to how I think of things in animation. Shots and sequences can be like animation shots. They have their own pace; they have their characters and language and their own personalities. Some sequences are slow and other sequences fast. It all depends on what's being told and how you want it to be told.

The best place to cut the camera to another angle is wherever action is happening. If you cut on a character that is emoting through the face but not moving his body, the cut will disrupt the moment. If the cut happens and the character hasn't moved, the cut can also feel dead and lifeless. We move while we talk and gesture and turn; if your animation doesn't reflect this, it will feel like Popsicle sticks with talking heads. Create your cuts when the character is gesturing or moving toward another character to keep the pacing alive.

1950

TV ARTS PRODUCTIONS CLOSES: TV Arts Productions originated the idea of an animated series made for television with animator Alex Anderson, who worked for Terrytoons Studios. Anderson approached Jay Ward for financing; Ward became business manager and producer and joined with Anderson to form Television Arts Productions.

1951

OSCAR FOR *THE TWO MOUSEKETEERS* (MGM): *The Two Mouseketeers* won the Best Short Subject: Cartoons Academy Award. It is the first in a series of Mouseketeer shorts, but was originally intended as a one-off.

"Cutting from one scene to the next ultimately should flow smoothly. There shouldn't be anything jarring or interruptive that distracts the viewer from taking in the story being told to them through (specifically) visual images. Ideally, make your cuts "invisible." There certainly should be a minimum of boredom. Overly repetitive shots will lose the viewer's attention. Another important trick is to try and keep the viewer's point of attention consistent from shot to shot. Maybe it's the character within the shot or it's a vanishing point or whatever, but try to keep the viewer's eye from having to search from cut to cut to find the information that the filmmaker wants them to see immediately. And for the love of God, refrain from centering anything smack in the middle of your scene. Give your composition just a touch of asymmetry; your viewers will thank you. Want a quick example of interesting shots? Look at just about any sequence of shots from Orson Welles' *The Third Man*. The tilted camera (Dutch angle) may seemingly be overplayed, but there is serious tension and deliberate disorientation created by these kind of shots. Exactly what the filmmaker was hoping for."

—*Joe Scott*

As an animator, it's best to work on several shots that link together. Unfortunately, the production schedule might not allow for this. So, if you are working on a sequence that cuts to another animator's shot, it's very important to communicate and make sure the continuity across these cuts is clear.

Many times in a 100-percent CG movie, you can change where the camera is and change the staging for the shot. This is one of the things about CG that can make CG-animated films more interesting than 2D and mixed CG/live-action films. However, the ability to move the camera around wherever you like can also be a double-edged sword. When a director doesn't understand the concept of playing up to the camera, he can go down an infinite path of camera choices. He might say to you, "Can I see that character from another angle?" They don't understand that you play up the entertainment value of the pose based on the camera chosen. All of a sudden, said director wants to see the character from a completely different angle, and your performance doesn't work anymore. In 2D, this is not even an option because changing the camera angle means having to draw every single frame for that sequence over again. CG mixed with live-action plates also does not have this flexibility of changing the staging of a camera. With mixed live-action and CG movies, you are locked into one angle for the shot. In a 100-percent live-action movie, the editor has minutes of footage

1951

COLOR TV INTRODUCED: Color TV was first introduced in 1951, with 15 million TV sets in the US. Animation for TV commercials was becoming an important segment of the industry.

1951

MOTION PICTURE SCREEN CARTOONISTS UNION: Motion Picture Screen Cartoonists Local #841 New York chartered.

1952

OSCAR FOR *JOHANN MOUSE* (MGM): *Johann Mouse* won the Academy Award for Best Short Subject: Cartoons. A cartoon in the Tom and Jerry series, it was inspired by the work of Viennese composer Johann Strauss II.

to edit from, and cuts can change drastically as the movie is edited. In animation, the storyboards are more specific, and the ability to slide cuts around is limited by header and footer tails. Most animated movies have between four and eight frames of header and footer designated as extra for the editor to play with if need be for the cut. It's best if the camera and staging are not toyed with too much in a tight sequence because that will affect all shots preceding and coming after the shot in question. Regardless of where your director wants the camera placed, cutting on action is the key. Chris Bailey explains how you can use staging and cutting on action to make a stronger shot:

> Construct your shots so that you are cutting on motion. Animators have great control over how their shots cut together. In live action, the actors take a step half into their shots so that the editor has motion to cut from and to. In animation, too often we cut from a static hold to another static hold for no reason. The continuity of pose is there, but the scene feels dead because the character completes his action within the shot and comes to a rest. That's why, whenever possible, I like animators to have a continuity of shots to work on, so that they can build a rhythm into their sequence. In general, my suggestion is to have 30 percent of an action (like a head turn, standing up from a chair, et cetera) on the B side of the first cut and carry 70 percent of that action onto the A side of the second cut.

Knowing where the camera is in relation to your shot and characters is so important. You must be clear about where the camera is in relation to the set and the character's action in your storyboards. If you are not clear, not only will you lose the audience, but the animators will have a hard time creating continuity. If your camera cuts are not clear, the story will be convoluted and difficult to follow. There is a cinematic rule called the *180-degree rule* that Larry Weinberg explains to help you keep your cuts clear:

> Always remember the 180-degree rule when planning your cuts. There is always an imaginary line of action in a scene. The camera should not cross this line into the next shot. It feels wrong. You can go on the line in a shot, and then across in the next, but don't cross it in one cut.

We are only briefly touching upon basic rules of cinematography. We recommend as additional reading *The Five C's of Cinematography: Motion Picture Filming Techniques* (Silman-James Press, 1998) by Joseph V. Mascelli.

1952

IATSE (THE ANIMATION GUILD): Hollywood cartoonists vote to affiliate with the International Alliance of Theatrical and Screen Engineers (IATSE). The Motion Picture Screen Cartoonists Local #839 chartered. Charter signed by Milt Kahl, Les Clark, and John Hench.

1953

OSCAR FOR *TOOT, WHISTLE, PLUNK AND BOOM* (DISNEY): *Toot, Whistle, Plunk and Bloom* won the Academy Award for Best Short Subject: Cartoons. This film was a return to *Silly Symphonies* and created in a modern style.

1953

LAST MICKEY MOUSE FILM: *The Simple Things* was the final Mickey Mouse cartoon made during what has been called the "Classic Disney Cartoon Era."

Savor the Moment, but Not for Long!

If the shots are cut together in the rapid-fire style of a music video, you will lose some of the best chances to really illustrate performance. There are times, of course, when quick cutting will enhance dramatic action sequences, but be careful where you use this. Sometimes you really want to slow down and just savor the moment. Savoring the moment is lingering on a subject long enough to get the point of the shot across to the audience. In high-action movies, some of this will be decided for you by the length of the live-action plate edited. But if you have control in the storyboards over how long a shot should be, act it out if you can, so you make sure you are not squeezing too much action into too short of a cut. You don't have to cut up a feature like a music video, because you have the time to tell the story. Embrace this! Angie Glocka tells us how she observes cuts in action films that are too fast:

> For animation, it's important to make sure you give the character enough time to actualize the scene and not look weird; for instance, I see a lot of flying superheroes that look way too fast and artificial because no one times out how long it would take to jump, fly, and land. So the action gets squeezed in the flying part, and it looks way wrong, whereas with live action the editor has the real-live footage that he/she is forced to work with.

In contrast to holding a shot long enough, you can also make the error of holding a shot for too long. Pacing is key to telling a story well. Savor that moment, but not for too long! If you hold the camera still for a really long time on a performance that is not moving a lot, the audience will be bored. Listen to the dialogue for the shot and try to imagine where your eye would naturally go if you were there in that shot. Try to mimic this with your cuts. You have control over where the audience will be looking, so take the wheel and steer it in the right direction at the right time. Tom Capizzi has more on how to make your cut decisions clear and strong:

> Cuts should be made to allow the audience to move easily from shot to shot. Basically, when there is enough time for the audience to look at their watches, you have already waited too long to make a cut. There is time required to make sure that the audience can breathe and recover from emotional sequences or action sequences, but long camera moves to show off the environment are only useful if they support the story. Avoid long pauses unless there is a specific reason to pause—otherwise, cut!

1953

PETER PAN 14TH DISNEY FEATURE: *Peter Pan* was the final Disney animated feature released through RKO; Disney established his own distribution company, Buena Vista Distribution, by the end of 1953.

1953

DUCK AMUCK BRINGS RECOGNIZABLE PER-SONALITY: *Duck Amuck* was a surreal 1953 animated cartoon produced by Warner Bros. and starring Daffy Duck. According to director Chuck Jones, this film demonstrated for the first time that animation can create characters with a recognizable personality.

As you choose the timing of your cuts, you must also be aware of how the shot is staged. The staging of the shot will reinforce the mindset of your character and will direct the viewer's eye to where you want it to be. A camera from above will make the character look meek and small. A camera choice from below will make a character seem empowered and menacing. The best choice for camera placement to create empathy is at eye level with your character. When the camera is on the same level as us, we associate with their plight.

Entertain! Don't forget, we're in the entertainment business. Don't bore your audience.
Drawing by Floyd Norman.

1954

OSCAR FOR *WHEN MAGOO FLEW* (UPA): The first Magoo cartoon in CinemaScope won the Academy Award for Best Short Subject: Cartoons.

1954

ANIMATED SHORTS ARE SOLD FOR TELEVISION: The major studios started selling their animated shorts to TV for syndication.

1954

TASMANIAN DEVIL APPEARS: The Tasmanian Devil makes his first appearance in Robert McKimson's 1954 *Devil May Hare*, in which he squabbles with Bugs Bunny.

A final thought on savoring the moment and deciding the length of your cuts: As an animator and as the story artist, it is up to you to find the best way to make that moment entertaining. Sometimes an exasperating situation is funnier when dealt with in a quiet moment. Humor is important. It's great to get jokes in there, but don't tell the same joke over and over because it gets old. Troy Saliba has a story about a scene he found to be funnier by using a quiet beat to savor the moment:

> One of the funniest bits of animation I have ever seen done was actually at Disney Australia. There was a scene where Goofy's neighbor, the fat, overbearing guy, is in this truck, and they had just driven over a cliff. They cut to a shot where it's a close-up looking in through the windshield with Goofy and the guy driving. It's a held cel of Goofy looking at the driver. The guy driving is looking really disgusted. The driver blinks and reaches over to turn a switch, and you see the windshield wipers stop, and the car disappears over the cliff. It's pretty much a held cel. It's great cinematic storytelling because you don't see a cut of the guy reaching to turn the switch. He is just there. He blinks. The windshield wipers stop. Then, an audio cue for the switch—"click"—and the car disappears. The storyboard called for all this Goofy-frantic stuff going on. Either it was comic brilliance or the animator said to himself, "I gotta get another 10 feet out this week." He decided to do it simply. It's the funniest damn thing I ever have seen in my life. I laughed for 10 minutes after I saw it.

Remember that entertainment will be heightened by how you choose to present it. The length of the shots and how you create performance will create the entertainment for your story.

Storyboards for Television versus Film

When you are developing storyboard for TV and film, there are several differences. The first difference is that television doesn't usually have time for as much action, unless the show is about superheroes. Television tends to be more dialogue-driven. This is where the "savor the moment" rule is so important. You don't want the show to feel like it's full of talking heads, so explore how you can create action to cut on. Features tend to open up the ability for even more cinematic storytelling through actual time allotted for each shot as well as format. Joe Scott elaborates more on how the approach to storyboards differs between TV and feature films:

1954

ANIMAL FARM IS FIRST BRITISH ANIMATED FEATURE: Britain's first full-length animated movie was based on Orwell's novel of the same name.

1955

OSCAR FOR *SPEEDY GONZALES* (WARNER BROS.): *Speedy Gonzales* won the 1955 Academy Award for Best Short Subject: Cartoons.

1955

DISNEY PHASES OUT SHORTS AND DISNEYLAND OPENS: Disney started phasing out shorts because costs had risen to $75,000 each. Disneyland also opened this year.

Feature offers a more cinematic approach in staging; longer, more realized story beats; and generally much more time to flesh out individual panels. Feature storyboard artists generally work on sequences, or even sequences within sequences. There isn't that sort of episodic mind frame when it comes to blocking out a section. Any good storyboard artist will have read the entire script and familiarized themselves with the entire story front to back. Then they must concentrate on their bit of the overall puzzle, always considering how it fits into the story as a whole. CGI animation is allowing storyboard artists to think more ambitiously than ever in regard to complicated camera actions, which should ultimately increase their ambition to expand their storytelling techniques.

Another big difference between creating storyboards for film versus television is size. Aspect ratios can greatly affect how a shot is composed. Film offers a wider aspect ratio and more room to play with how you stage the performance. Wide shots are used less often in television for storytelling purposes. Film also offers more time to tell the story by the nature of its longer format. The epic quality of film is sacrificed for the television medium, but the storytelling is more concentrated in both cinematic and script choices. Even though both mediums offer different problems, David Smith explains why the best storyboard artists work well in both:

Aspect ratios directly affect composition. In TV you may have to settle for illustrating [an idea] with a strong graphic representation to simulate that idea. The difference between the two experiences of TV and cinema is obvious. The time one has to tell a story—i.e., a 22-minute episode as opposed to feature length—is vastly different. The latter certainly has the time for more depth and how a character might think, act, and feel, and subsequently that would have to be reflected in what you physically draw and stage. It's important to know that each medium presents a terrific, enjoyable, and worthwhile task. Our industry has sometimes been known to give way to a prestige issue of film over television. The best storyboard talent is secure in both.

1955

GUMBY FIRST APPEARS:
Gumby had its genesis in a 1955 theatrical short called *Gumbasia*, which featured similar claymation characters. Gumby appeared on *The Howdy Doody Show* in 1956 and was given his own NBC series in 1957.

1955

TERRYTOONS SOLD TO CBS: Paul Terry sold Terrytoons to CBS for $3,500,000 and retired. 20th Century Fox continued to release the films.

1955

TEX AVERY RETURNS TO THE WALTER LANTZ STUDIO: Avery's return to the Walter Lantz studio did not last long. He directed four cartoons in 1954–1955, and although two were nominated for Oscars, Avery left over a salary dispute, effectively ending his career in theatrical animation.

Television animation is one thing, but commercials are an even more concentrated format. Going from 22 minutes to either a 60- or 30-second spot means storytelling in your storyboards must be concise and clear. Commercial storyboards are usually more advanced, showing color and more defined drawing. Commercial storyboards are much more detailed and well thought-out because the budgets are smaller and the schedule is shorter. There has to be a very clear vision. Commercials can involve many parties for approval, so the boards are part of the selling of the concept. In a commercial, you have the director, the client, the agency, an editorial shop, and the studio providing special effects or animation; all are involved in the process. Okay, let's pause here to state that there is no more frustrating and demanding job in filmmaking than storyboarding. Most storyboard artists require long sessions of therapy after their careers are over. And, sadly, those involved in storyboarding for commercials lose their sanity long before their careers are over. A final difference between developing storyboards for television versus film is schedules, plain and simple. Overall, storyboards for any medium should not be limited or overextended by the medium. However, the schedules for television are much tighter and challenge the storyboard artist more greatly, as Joe Scott explains:

> Good storytelling can't be limited by format. That being said, let me now disqualify that. A big difference is in schedule, obviously, which can hinder the amount of time spent and attention given to individual story panels. Certainly a feature schedule will allow more time to fully realize visually the look of your idea on paper, but any idea worth boarding out can and should be tailored to work within the given timeframe. TV schedules are brutal and ruthless at times. Three weeks is not an uncommon deadline to storyboard 10 to 15 pages of script. That is a *lot* of work. But the savvy board artist will know how to economize his output and make sure to get in the essential story information and sacrifice the extraneous stuff to make a deadline. This is the reality of a TV production schedule. Does it sacrifice quality of storytelling? Absolutely not. You learn to work your same story magic using an abbreviated shorthand-style of boarding. Or as many board artists do, you can stay up all night to complete your 22-minute masterpiece.

That said, the demands placed upon the television board artist can be overwhelming at times because the demands of overseas production and cost trimming have meant that the story artist must now draw into his boards things that were previously done by a (now nonexistent) layout and animation-pose crew. Format, aspect ratio, schedule, technology, and money all affect how storyboards are developed for both mediums. By recognizing the differences between TV and feature storyboards, we can utilize the advantages of both to tell our story in a more effective way.

1955

INTRODUCING MICHIGAN J. FROG: Warner Bros. released *One Froggy Evening*, a six-minute Technicolor animated short film, in 1955 as part of its *Merrie Melodies* series. Chuck Jones later dubbed the nameless frog Michigan J. Frog, after the original song for the short. Michigan later became the mascot of the WB network.

1956

STORYBOARD STUDIOS FOUNDED: John Hubley and Faith Elliot started Storyboard Studios. Hubley was forced to leave UPA in 1952 when he refused to appear before the House Committee on Un-American Activities. He founded Storyboard Studios the next year and worked on commercials, but was forced to turn down more exciting projects because his name was still blacklisted.

Storytelling

No matter whether you are developing a story for film, television, commercials, or a short, the same rules apply. Keep your plot clear in your head and see the beginning, middle, and end clearly, and you will write a solid story. Entertainment reinforces believability and is more interesting than realism. Foregrounding desire, growth, and character arcs is how you make the story real. Remember back story, but don't feel the need to put all of it into your writing. Back story will help you as you write about what is important, reinforcing who your characters are and what they want and need. Follow the directive of the story as you write. Keep your ideas clear. Stage the shots so that they reinforce the premise. Use storyboarding to narrow the focus of the story and tell it cinematically. Remember the importance of graphic awareness and staging in your whole frame. Lead the viewer to watch what you want them to see. Don't move the camera around unnecessarily, and be sure to savor the moment long enough for the audience to have empathy with your characters. Gratuitous camera moves will pull your audience out of the story. In CG, animatics, pre-viz, and choreo will save you a lot of time in the animation stage by solving any cutting or continuity problems before they arise.

As an animator, storytelling is the nitty-gritty of your everyday life. That said, many animators have been heard saying, "I'm an animator, not a writer. Why do I need to know about story?" Understanding the components of creating a good story will help you as an animator, plus heighten any scene. If you think about story while animating, it will give your performance a richness not found in the works of others who are just trying to fulfill the basic needs of a scene. You will be walking in the character's shoes while you animate. You are telling the story through your character's actions. In order for your scene to fit properly into the story, you must understand the character and his or her drive and needs. You also must empathize with the character and those needs, even if you are animating the villain. Justify those needs in your head, and you will get to the core of the situation at hand. The character is flesh and blood and needs to feel real to the audience. Understanding how to tell a good story will help your animation immensely. Ultimately, the story is defined by the character and what the character desires. Guess what? You are a "character" animator.

---

[18]http://imdb.com/title/tt0317705/plotsummary.

[19]Kahl, Milt. *On Animation*. 1979. Track 06. Kahl talks about Walt Disney and story. http://www.dazland.com/sewardmirror/miltcd%20-%2006%20-%20disney%20and%20story.mp3; http://www.dazland.com/sewardmirror/miltkahl_tracks.htm; http://jrhull.typepad.com/seward_street/multimedia/index.html.

1956

OSCAR FOR *MAGOO'S PUDDLE JUMPER* (UPA): *Magoo's Puddle Jumper* won the 1956 Academy Award for Best Short Subject: Cartoons.

1956

FIRST PRIMETIME ANIMATED TV SHOW, *GERALD MCBOING-BOING* (UPA): *The Gerald McBoing-Boing Show* was an animated television series that aired for one season. The program proved too expensive and lasted only three months. The episodes were repeated in the summer of 1957 and, as a result, it became the first cartoon series to air regularly during primetime.

Index 1: Storytelling Strengthening

◆ Keep your plot clear.

◆ Entertainment reinforces believability.

◆ Remember desire, growth, and character arcs.

◆ Back story reinforces who your characters are.

◆ Follow the directive of the story as you write.

◆ Use storyboarding to narrow the focus.

Index 2: Storyboard Musts

◆ Make sure your shots are clear.

◆ Have a good idea and a good story.

◆ Make enough panels for the business you are describing.

◆ Draw the atmosphere in the scene.

◆ Know what plot points to hit.

◆ Support the message of the story, not just the story.

◆ Make sure you have the right amount of drawings.

◆ Don't move the camera around unnecessarily.

◆ Savor the moment long enough for the audience to have empathy with your characters.

◆ Remember the importance of graphic awareness and staging in your whole frame.

◆ Effectively evaluate the pacing and timing.

◆ Draw the essence of a sequence.

1956

ANNECY, THE FIRST INTERNATIONAL ANIMATED FILM FESTIVAL: In Annecy, France, the first major international animation festival begins within the framework of the Cannes Festival. In 1960 this became an independent festival at Annecy under the sponsorship of the Association Francaise pour la Diffusion du Cinema.

1957

OSCAR FOR *BIRDS ANONYMOUS* (WARNER BROS.): *Birds Anonymous* won the 1957 Academy Award for Best Short Subject: Cartoons.

1957

THE RUFF AND REDDY SHOW: Hanna and Barbera were asked to leave MGM; with George Sidney, they started Hanna-Barbera studios. *The Ruff and Reddy Show* was their first TV series.

1957

WHAT'S OPERA DOC? CHUCK JONES' MASTER-PIECE: *What's Opera, Doc?* is a short animated cartoon in which Elmer Fudd chases Bugs Bunny through a six-minute oper-atic production of Wagner's "Der Ring des Nibelungen." This marks one of the few times that Fudd actually succeeds in beat-ing Bugs Bunny.

59

Chapter 3
The Good, the Bad, and the Just Plain Annoying

Who our favorite characters are has to do with empathy and identifying with the personality and plight of a character. We root for the underdog or the hero because we see something in that character that we see in ourselves. We polled people in the industry for reasons why they feel empathy with a particular cartoon character; on the next page are some of the results we got.

> "Charlie Brown is my favorite because everybody hates him, and he knows it."
> —Darin McGowan

This list could go on and on, but the point is that it's a character's personality that makes people identify with him. It is because they see something in the character that they see in themselves. So, what is it about these characters that makes them so memorable? Evan Gore offers some great advice on why a character becomes memorable:

You are not in control of your or your character's legacy. Trying to force a character to be memorable is, to me, like trying to make yourself memorable—people will think you're a pretentious sap. You can make your characters lovable by having them give love to others, by showing them trying their hardest, and by struggling against their own limitations. Be sure to give them limitations. You can make them funny, quirky, unique, et cetera, with superficial means like a catchphrase or physical tic, but even better, by basing them on real-life people you know and tossing out the elements you are copying from someone else's work. Don't force. Tell the truth, and the truth will be funny.

1957

***TOM TERRIFIC* SHOW ON *CAPTAIN KANGAROO* (CBS):** *Tom Terrific* ran in a series of five-minute cartoons on *Captain Kangaroo* and has occasionally been rerun since. The Tom character also appeared in a comic book for six issues in 1957, with some stories drawn by Ralph Bakshi.

1957

ASIFA FOUNDED: ASIFA (Association Internationale Du Film D'animation) was founded in France and chartered under UNESCO in 1960 as a membership organization devoted to the encouragement and dissemination of film animation as an art and communication form. It has grown to more than 1,700 members in 55 countries.

"Wyle E. Coyote. He is obsessed. Me too. Cracks me up."

—*Ed Hooks*

"Marvin the Martian. I find his wry, under-stated character to be the perfect antagonist for Bugs Bunny."

—*Angie Glocka*

"Daffy Duck. For his lessons in self-esteem and perseverance."

—*David Smith*

"As far as a favorite character, I'd have to say that Bugs would be the one. He's just so friggin' irreverent, and there's so much that you can do with his body language. We look for ourselves in animated characters, and I see a lot of Bugs in me. And no, I don't dress as a woman. Well, not that often anyway."

—*Fred Raimondi*

"Bugs Bunny. I loved the animation on him and I love his character. Bugs has always been well ani-mated. He also has a personality that anyone can relate to. He's the underdog. Making Bugs look stupid and inept is just too far out of character for him. He's always in control, even if he's losing."

—*Brian Dowrick*

"Donald Duck; it's always entertaining to watch him react. It's effortless, really. Put a Donald cartoon on, and he shows up; doesn't matter what the situation, place, time, whatever—you know something's going to get at him and he's going to go into a fit. I've always found misguided actions the best source of humor. We couldn't stop this big blue ball of spit spinning we call Earth even if we tried, but I'm sure Donald would try it without a thought. Not to mention he has the best cartoon voice out there."

—*Leigh Rens*

1958

OSCAR FOR *KNIGHTY KNIGHT BUGS* (WARNER BROS.): Warner Bros.' *Knighty Knight Bugs*, a 1958 *Looney Tunes* cartoon directed by Friz Freleng and released by Warner Bros. Pictures, features a medieval Bugs Bunny trading blows with Yosemite Sam (as the Black Knight) and his fire-breathing dragon. *Knighty Knight Bugs* won the 1958 Academy Award for Best Short Subject: Cartoons.

1958

***THE LITTLE ISLAND* RELEASED BY RICHARD WILLIAMS:** *The Little Island* was Richard Williams' first animated film. Self-financed, it was a half-hour philosophical argu-ment without words that won several international awards.

The main objectives when creating unforgettable characters are to draw from your own experiences, stay true and honest to who the characters are and what they desire, and make sure the characters evolve.

Memorable Characters

Memorable characters are a mix of traits we relate to and find appealing. A character must have some kind of appeal—both physical (good design) and emotional (strong personality type)—the audience identifies with and roots for. Even villains should have this kind of appeal. As much as the audience wants the hero to get what he is after, you are quietly rooting for an unbeaten villain to get his, too. A fully developed character stands out on the screen as acting humanlike. Many times this is based simply on survival. What your villain believes he needs to survive is different than what your hero needs. Audiences respond to these humanlike characters more naturally because they reflect human traits.

Stereotype and archetype are a couple tools you can use to create a fully developed character the audience will identify with immediately. The *Merriam-Webster* dictionary defines stereotype as "a standardized mental picture that is held in common by members of a group and that represents an oversimplified opinion, prejudiced attitude, or uncritical judgment." In other words, a stereotype adds someone's opinion to the topic or character at hand based on past experience. It gives the situation or character baggage that may not apply depending on your own experiences. The *Merriam-Webster* dictionary defines archetype as "the original pattern or model of which all things of the same type are representations or copies" or "a perfect example." So an archetype is still something people would identify with, but it doesn't hold the cultural baggage a stereotype does.

Stereotypes and clichés are easy ways to get across ideas people will quickly understand. You can develop your character with a stereotype, but you must develop beyond that to make a three-dimensional character. Archetype is a better way to start without being offensive because it lacks societal judgment. Is he the boy next door, the

> "Archetype is collective consciousness as to who the person is and why they act the way that they do. Stereotype is societal judgment, which is also collective consciousness. Don't try to create an identifiable character archetype. It's never been done with that intention. Be true to your observations and don't try to tap into the collective consciousness. If you are true, you already have created a memorable character."
>
> —*Dave Zaboski*

1958

JAY WARD PRODUCTIONS OPENS: Jay Ward Productions, an animated cartoon studio, was best known for producing *Rocky and His Friends* and many other films and series. The company also designed trademark characters and made numerous commercials for such products as Cap'n Crunch, Quisp, and Quake breakfast cereals.

1958

HUCKLEBERRY HOUND INTRODUCED: Huckleberry Hound, created by Hanna-Barbera, was the star of the animated *Huckleberry Hound Show*. The show made Hanna-Barbera a household name, thanks to Huckleberry and the two supporting segments of the show: Yogi Bear and his sidekick, Boo Boo; and Pixie and Dixie, two mice who found myriad ways to outwit Mr. Jinks the cat.

immigrant who runs the 7-11 down the street, or the street hood on the corner? Stereotypes tend to be insulting to the audience. A stereotype is not grounded in reality, but by a social label.

Stereotypes are not honest caricatures and are not noteworthy or unique.

Go beyond the stereotype to get three-dimensional characters. Sketch by Floyd Norman.

1959

OSCAR FOR *MOONBIRD* (HUBLEY STUDIO):
Moonbird won the 1959 Academy Award for Best Short Subject: Cartoons. It was a production of John Hubley and his wife, Faith, whose shorts were nominated for seven Academy Awards, of which they won four.

1959

UPA CLOSES ITS DOORS: The HUAC commission hearings on Communism in Hollywood took a heavy toll on UPA; the *Mr. Magoo* series sunk to an embarrassing level. Henry G. Saperstein kept UPA afloat in the 1960s and beyond by abandoning animation production completely and selling off UPA's library of cartoons, but no new productions were made after 1959.

The intention is to be true to a personal observation. Be true to your observations, and don't try to tap into the collective consciousness. If you are true, you will portray good characters that are three-dimensional, as David Smith points out:

> Three-dimensional beings have thoughts, actions, and emotions. If you put one above the other, the character is shortchanged and becomes stereotypical.
> Superhero = one-dimensional.
> Superhero + perhaps past his prime and in midlife crisis + now with family/deep emotional paternal love (that which many can relate to) = three-dimensional or Mr. Incredible.

Character design for Major Damage by Chris Bailey.

1959

***THE ROCKY AND BULLWINKLE SHOW* AIRS:**
This is the collective name of an animated series that originally aired from 1959 to 1964. Much of the success of the series was because it appealed to children and, using its clever puns and topical references, also to adults.

1959

FIRST ANALOG COMPUTER GRAPHICS BY JOHN WHITNEY: John Whitney Sr. created analog computer graphics. By 1959, John began his pioneering work in the development of mechanical analog systems, which founded the principles and techniques of "incremental drift" and "slit-scan." Whitney's first analog computer was made from an M-5 Antiaircraft Gun Director and later with modifications from an M-7.

Stereotypes can work sometimes, as in the case of clichés, because they quickly get to a personality that the audience is aware of. Archetypal characters are based on stereotype but add some bit of reality that makes them more approachable. Stereotype is one-dimensional; however, if you put a twist on the idea of the stereotype to make the character have enough depth to be interesting, it can work. Examples of this could be a "big man on campus" who has an eating disorder or a neighborhood bully who is only three feet tall. These are twists that break through the stereotype and make your character more appealing. Chris Bailey talks about using stereotype effectively:

> I think you have to rely on archetypes because they communicate immediately. You can play against type and get some comedy from that too, like the geeky hero coming to the rescue as if he's Arnold Schwarzenegger. The key is to avoid negative stereotypes that demean people.

You can take the archetype and develop it over the course of the story. It's a great hook to give the audience something to latch onto in the beginning of the movie. This gets them involved in the character's deeper emotional stories as the movie progresses.

"Never treat a character as filler or mere mechanism to advance your plot. No 'Hmm, I think I need an old lady on roller skates to get my hero Gerald the Flea from Pasadena to the Kansas City dog show in time to save his trapeze-artist girlfriend, FiFi the Poodle, from the Bayone Barbequed Dog Cartel.' Somebody in the audience is gonna wonder why an old woman suddenly shows up, out of the blue, on a pair of roller skates."

—Bill Wright

You must make the character relatable. Create a character that you really know—someone who is not exactly you, yet you can visualize clearly. This will enable you to really get inside the character so you can write about him. Give the audience a reason to get behind the character. Characters who are shallow and dumb are boring. Archetypes are something that you can start with and develop. If your character has depth and honesty, he will avoid the pitfalls of a stereotype. Don't build a character who lacks motivation and simply serves as a protagonist to move your plot forward. You will lose believability, and your audience will lose interest.

1960

OSCAR FOR *MUNRO* (REMBRANDT FILMS): *Munro* won the Academy Award for Best Short Subject: Cartoons.

1960

THE FLINTSTONES, 2ND PRIME TIME TV SERIES: Hanna-Barbera's *The Flintstones* is one of the most successful animated television series of all time, originally running in prime time for six seasons.

1960

COMPUTER GRAPHICS COINED: The term "computer graphics" was coined by William Fetter of Boeing.

Character design lineup by Troy Saliba and Angie Jones.

Inspiration from Your Own Experience

Character is the core of what we do as animators. We are character animators. Animated characters emote, just like live-action actors. The animator needs to create a connection with the audience through her character. The animator needs to infuse the character with life to create this connection. The personality, mannerisms, conversations, and desires are what drive the character to be different from others in the movie. Each and every one of us reacts to things differently because of our past experiences. We all have idiosyncrasies due to our upbringing, the area of town we grew up in, whether our big brother was nice to us, as well as countless other factors. These are the little things that make us all act in a singular and significant

1961

OSCAR FOR *ERSATZ (THE SUBSTITUTE)* (ZAGREB FILM): *Ersatz (The Substitute)* won the Academy Award for Best Animated Short Subject: Cartoons.

1961

DO-IT-YOURSELF CARTOON KIT **ANIMATED SHORT BY BOB GODFREY:** The *Do-It-Yourself Cartoon Kit* sends up the myth of the lone animator who spends hundreds of hours on a brief sequence, only to see it cut from the final film. Crude but energetic, the film sets the tone for the ways in which Godfrey was seeking to reinvent the cartoon outside the American tradition, and at the same time poke fun at orthodoxy and establishment thinking.

way. The connection you feel to the character will come through clearly in his performance when you use your memories and experiences. Fred Raimondi expands on this idea:

> Most of the time when I direct a character's action, I try (if I'm physically able) to do the action for the animator. Sometimes I'll videotape myself doing the action. I also try to anthropomorphize the character because I feel that what we really want to see when we're watching animated characters is ourselves. This may sound weird, but I think that's the same reason people like to watch monkeys. They remind us of us. I'm also constantly looking for characters in everyday life to apply to animated characters. For instance, when I see Goofy, I don't see Goofy—I see Kramer from the *Seinfeld* show.

Character design lineup by Troy Saliba and Angie Jones.

Empathy is crucial to creating a performance that the audience will find believable. If you can create empathy with your audience through your characters, you will have a scene that stands apart from the rest and adds immeasurably to the story. When you approach your characters from an honest and true place, they will reflect that in their performances. Your unique nature is significant to creating an original performance, and the extra time you spend making the character act truthfully to who he is, while still moving and react-

---

1961

TETSUWAN ATOMU FIRST JAPANESE ANIMATED TV SERIES: Japan's first television animation series begins. *Astro Boy* is the American title for the Japanese animated series, *Tetsuwan Atomu.*

1961

START OF THE "NINE OLD MEN" ERA AT DISNEY: Disney's Nine Old Men were the core animators (some of whom later became directors) who created the Disney Studios' most famous work. Walt Disney jokingly called this group of animators his "Nine Old Men," referring to what FDR called the nine judges of the US Supreme Court. The original "Nine Old Men" were Les Clark, Marc Davis, Ollie Johnston , Milt Kahl, Ward Kimball, Eric Larsen, John Lounsbery, Wolfgang "Woolie" Reitherman, and Frank Thomas.

ing a little differently than your average person, will make your character stand apart. Scott Holmes uses Marlon Brando as an example of performance that is honest and yet original:

> The best way to create empathy is to treat your characters honestly. Great performances are born from good actors that give an honest performance that is unique to that character. Brando in *A Street Car Named Desire* is so powerful and honest in that role that audiences feel for him and feel like they know him even though they have little to do with being a drunken dockworker. The same is true of animation. If the animator can get into the character's head and give a true, honest performance and avoid clichés or animation tricks, he can take that character to a more true performance, thus affecting the audience in an emotional way.

If you find inspiration in these little nuances, your characters will appear honest. These ideas are most believable when they come from your own experiences. You cannot fake that kind of understanding. Your own life experiences are rich with character. Your imagination will heighten the memory of the characters you portray. It's these memories and experiences that will create the emotional bond between your audience and the character.

Flaws and Emotions

Character flaws are the best place to start with creating an original character. A villain is an example of a person with a deadly character flaw. Cruella De Vil's "little" flaw was her preference for animal-fur coats, especially those made of Dalmatian fur. Hannibal Lecter is a likeable guy who just so happens to eat people. These are extreme cases of flaws in villains, but the rule applies. Who wants to watch a perfect character who does nothing wrong, gets everything he wants easily, and never struggles to do so? Flaws create chinks in the armor that make up who the character is and reveal humanity. Humans are flawed in countless ways. Finding those flaws and exploiting them will add dimension to your characters.

Survival is the core of human nature. Flaws are those traits that will get in the way of our achieving the goal of survival. What we each believe we need to survive is different and based on our past experiences. Emotions arise out of the need to survive, and all characters have a different idea of what they need to get along in this world. Many times a character's flaw is his inability to control his emotions in certain situations. Most people can identify with this one. Emotions and flaws are the two greatest obstacles to your characters

---

1961

YOGI BEAR GETS HIS OWN SHOW: Yogi Bear became popular on *The Huckleberry Hound Show*, and in 1961 was given his own show.

1961

101 DALMATIANS RELEASED: *101 Dalmatians* was based on the novel of the same name by Dodie Smith and was Disney's 17th animated release.

1961

FIRST COMPUTER-ANIMATED FILM: E. E. Zajac created the first computer-animated film, called *Simulation of a Two-Giro Gravity Attitude Control System*. In this CG film, Zajac showed how the attitude of a satellite could be altered as it orbits the Earth. He created the animation on an IBM 7090 mainframe computer.

getting what they believe they need to survive. Ed Hooks explains how empathy is created through a character's survival instincts:

> Humans act to survive. Emotions, or automatic value responses, are the light beacons we send to one another. We empathize only with emotion, not with thinking. An audience puts up with thinking in order to get to the emotion.

Depending on whether you are working on your own short or someone else's film, your ability to exploit a character's flaws may be limited. The rules set forth by the story will set boundaries for your character and how he will act in any given situation. Remember to incorporate flaws in your characters as obstacles between them and their desires, and you will create a performance that is original and has depth. Maybe the flaws you create grow into a strength the character never thought he had. It's all about perception. Your character's perception of the world and his own place in it inspire empathy from the audience. Scott Holmes offers more on how a flawed character is stronger than a perfect one:

> Start with a flawed character. If our character has something wrong with him, either emotionally or physically, he has a journey to take. Dumbo had his ears. Mr. Incredible had his loss of status as a superhero. The Beast was a beast. Hercules... well, he was perfect, and that's kind of why that movie didn't work. He had no journey to take. He was a demi-god, not really a good foundation for a change in character. Every good hero takes a journey of growth and discovery, but before they begin the journey, they have to have a need to take one. The arc is the natural progression from flawed individual to one who has grown through his experiences.

What Scott tells us is that the flaws are key to making the character human and credible in his actions. Not only was Hercules perfect, he was also naive. There isn't much you can do with that because naiveté just isn't a strong enough flaw; in fact, it can almost become a compliment in some situations. The flaws you give your character need to have a direct contrast to what the character wants to achieve in life and how he perceives himself. A perfectly naive demi-god with no real arc isn't the strongest character to start with for your story. In contrast, take a young elephant with big ears who is shunned by his own kind and desperately wants to belong, and you have a flawed character with wants and desires we can all relate to. A character bio will help you deepen who your character is and make his idiosyncrasies more apparent.

 1961

FIRST COMPUTER ANIMATION LANGUAGE DEVELOPED: The first computer animation language (MACS) was developed by Larry Breed of Stanford University.

1962

OSCAR FOR *THE HOLE* (STORYBOARD FILMS/HUBLEY STUDIO): *The Hole* won Best Animated Short Subject: Cartoons.

 1963

WARNER BROS. CLOSES STUDIO: The studio briefly reopened in 1967 before shutting down for good in 1969, when Warner Bros. ceased production on all its short subjects.

Character Bio

A character bio is a history of the character devised to develop who the character is and what drives him. Animators can make use of a character bio when deciding on performance for their shots. The audience might never see this kind of back story, but if the animator uses it well, this bio will season the performance. The bio helps story people stay on track while developing the plot. The character bio also prevents you from treating the character like a one-dimensional stereotype. It reveals where the character comes from, his education, his financial status, and his cultural background. The bio can go into back story—for example, if parents are still alive or if some tragedy befell them. The most important part of the bio will be what the character's goals and desires are. Following is a typical character bio list that will help you get to know who your character is and why he is that way. These questions will help you break out of stereotype and create a more memorable character.

Age	How old is the character now? Is he much different than he was when he was young?
Ethnicity	What is the origin of the character's roots? How does he feel about where he comes from?
Height	How tall is the character? How does that affect how he views his place in the world?
Weight	How much does the character weigh? How do others treat him because of his weight, if it is out of the normal range?
Sex/reproduction	How does the character propagate? Does he have sex? Is he a virgin? How does this change his demeanor?
Gender	What sex is the character? How does this factor into his role and status in the world and within his family?
Health	Is the character handicapped? If so, was he born like that? Does he have asthma? How does his health affect him reaching his goals?
Intelligence	Is the character of average or below-average intelligence? Is he a genius? How does intelligence make him react to those around them?
Education	This is not to be confused with intelligence; you can have book smarts and have no common sense. Is the character someone who was brought up in the finest schools

1963

OSCAR FOR *THE CRITIC* (PINTOFF-CROSSBOW): The *Critic* won the Academy Award for Best Short Subject: Cartoons.

1963

THE SWORD AND THE STONE RELEASED: *The Sword in the Stone* is the 18th animated feature for Disney. It is loosely based on the novel *The Sword in the Stone* by T.H. White. This was the last animated feature released while Walt Disney was still alive.

1963

IVAN SUTHERLAND OPENS THE WAY TO COMPUTER ANIMATION: In computer animation, Ivan Sutherland's doctoral dissertation at MIT opened the way to interactive computer animation. He also created Sketchpad, which was the first extensive interactive drawing program.

or is he perhaps a high-school dropout? These things will have a great effect on how the character interacts with others who he feels are not in his league or who he could never live up to.

Evolutionary cycle	This is the character's lifespan. Obviously, if you are dealing with humans, you know the basic lifespan, but many times animation is working with aliens, animals, or even characters from another time when lifespans were much shorter.
Culture	This refers to the character's belief system. This weighs heavily on the character's mind even if he no longer believes in how he was brought up because it's the only thing the character knows—it's what he was taught since he was a child.
Food/eating	The food that your character eats can reveal how he regards himself and his body. Is he an athlete who can only eat certain things? Is he an out-of-work truck driver who loves chili dogs?
Nocturnal	Is the character a night owl? Does he like to stay up late?
Family	Values? Size? The family structure plays a heavy role in forming who your character is and how he perceives his place in the world. If he came from a big family, he might be loud and boisterous from trying to be heard. If he was an only child, he might be more introverted and shy, keeping to himself.
Money	Is the character wealthy? Poor? Destitute? Filthy rich?
Profession	What does the character do for a living? How does that contribute to his goals or hinder him from attaining them?
Body structure	This attribute totally affects how the character moves and how he is perceived by others. Is the character big and lanky? Does he walk funny? Is he tiny and does he go unnoticed?
Flaws (fatal)	We spoke of flaws earlier. Flaws are crucial to showing humanity. Flaws also can bring the demise of the character and be the obstacle between the protagonist and his goal.

1963

1964

1964

COMPUTER MOUSE IS INVENTED: The computer mouse was invented by Douglas Engelbart of Stanford Research Institute after extensive usability testing.

OSCAR FOR *THE PINK PHINK* (DEPATIE-FRELENG): *The Pink Phink* won the Academy Award for Best Short Subject: Cartoons. It was the first Pink Panther animated short released by United Artists.

BAKSHI DIRECTS *GADMOUSE THE APPRENTICE GOOD FAIRY:* The first cartoon Bakshi directed, this has been described by one cartoon buff as "probably about the best-designed Terrytoon since Gene Deitch left."

72

Idiosyncrasies	What makes the character different? This is how you create a memorable character. Does he smoke a pipe? Does he point at his head when he talks? Does he have a stutter? These are the juicy bits that will make your character, no matter which archetype you choose, different than the rest.
Atmosphere	How does a church versus car-wreck atmosphere influence the character? The character might have had experiences in which he reacted out of the norm because of his past. Maybe he had a mom who was in and out of hospitals all his life, so he just can't bear to go into one.
Goals	What does your character hope for? What does he desire more than anything? How can he make that happen? What does he need?
Dreams	What are your character's dreams? Dreams are lofty ambitions that we think about doing but that are just high enough that they might be out of reach. Unlike goals, dreams seem to be further into the future. Dreams and goals are similar because dreams soon become our goals as we get closer to making them happen.
Trauma	Has your character experienced trauma? Trauma is something that happened in the past that affects how the character acts. These adrenaline moments stay with us for a long time and make us think about what we want and what we believe in.
Talent	Does your character have a talent? What makes your character different than all the other characters in the story?
Addictions	Does your character drink? Smoke? Do drugs? Have an addiction to pain pills? These things can help or hinder your character from reaching his goal.

Stereotype versus Archetype

We talked about stereotype and archetype earlier in this chapter, but the basic idea is to use an archetype to establish a character we know of, and then use idiosyncrasies to humanize that ideal and make it have appeal.

By using the questions in the preceding list, you will greatly increase your chances of creating a character full of personality and humanity. Maybe you have a superhero who has irritable bowel syndrome and an

1964

THE ADVENTURES OF JONNY QUEST AIRS ON PRIME TIME: *Jonny Quest* was an animated sci-fi series produced by Hanna-Barbera and created and designed by comic book artist Doug Wildey. But prime-time animation was quickly proving to be a mere fad, and only 26 episodes were made.

1965

OSCAR FOR *THE DOT AND THE LINE* (MGM): *The Dot and the Line: A Romance in Lower Mathematics*, which Chuck Jones adapted from the book by Norton Juster, won an Academy Award for Best Short Subject: Cartoons.

overly devoted mother who seems to always show up to check on him at the weirdest times. Maybe the character is the sweet little girl next door who broke her leg when she was pushed on the swing set and now uses her crutch to bully the kids at school out of their lunch money. Play the stereotypes against the idiosyncrasies and exploit interesting facets of the personality to create engaging and unique personas.

Believability and Credibility

Because character and story are so closely related, we have to bring up believability again. Believability is not realism; it's the level of entertainment your character has in his personality while still holding true to the rules of that character. You make rules using the character bio and back story to establish who your character is. If you have the character do something that is out of character or doesn't follow these rules, you better have a convincing reason for doing so, or you will begin to lose the audience. Be sure that the character believes what he is saying and doing. Archetypes are a great way to start, but if the character doesn't have credibility, you are sunk. Ed Hooks has a humorous and succinct way of explaining this point:

> A character is what a character does. Don't worry about archetypes. Worry about credibility and story.

When you create your character, listen to who he is and what he wants. The character will tell you who he is and what he believes in. If you follow those rules, the character will act honestly through your writing and animation.

"**The motivation of each character has to be understood and believed by you for the audience to get it. To create drama, obstacles have to come between the character and the character's goals. Sometimes those obstacles have to come from the character itself. If a character has to make a bad decision for the sake of the story, the audience has to completely believe and understand why the character would make that decision when it so obviously is a bad idea; otherwise, it will detract from their empathy for the character and ultimately hurt the story.**"

—*Cory Florimonte*

1965

THUNDERBIRDS BRITISH TV SERIES AIRS: *Thunderbirds* was the fourth children's action-adventure series made by AP Films (APF), as well as its most popular. It used a form of puppetry called "Supermarionation."

1966

OSCAR FOR *HERB ALPERT AND THE TIJUANA BRASS DOUBLE FEATURE* (HUBLEY STUDIO): This animated film won the Academy Award for Best Short Subject: Cartoons. A prototype of modern music videos, it was set to the music of two popular tunes recorded by Herb Alpert and his Latin-flavored brass ensemble.

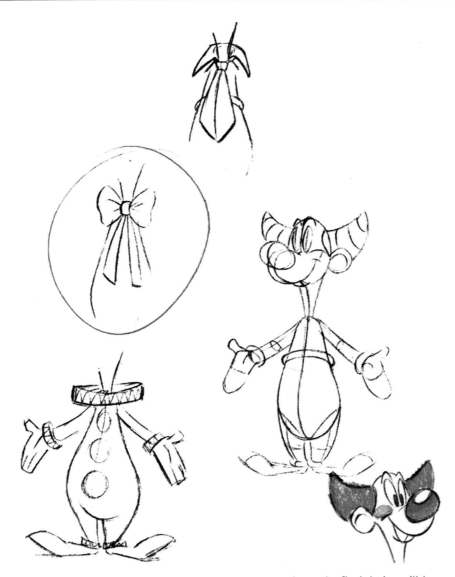

Go through many iterations when designing your character so you know the final design will be appealing and translate well to CG.

1966

**LAPIS MOTION CONTROL ANIMATION INTRODUCED
(JAMES WHITNEY):** *Lapis* is a mathematically precise early com-
puter-aided animated piece. James Whitney created it with analog
computer equipment (prototype of motion control camera) donated
by his brother, John Whitney, Sr. Three years in the making, the result
is an incredibly intricate and complex film.

1966

DISNEY DIES: Walter Elias Disney dies.

When you establish rules for how your character will react emotionally to the situations presented in the story, you must follow these rules at all times, or you will risk losing believability. All of us have experienced a sarcastic individual. If the sarcasm falls away too easily to create a character arc, we will not believe it. Breaking character will make the audience hate that character for contradicting who they believed him to be. In addition, the more you heighten the characteristics of your character, the funnier and more natural the scene will feel. If the character is sarcastic and just keeps being more and more sarcastic, it's funny. For example, if a sarcastic guy is sarcastic even when he has a gun to his head, it's more powerful than if he suddenly starts crying, although that's what one might expect. The audience will empathize with the character and desire what he desires if you remember the rules you discovered while creating the bio. Angie Glocka offers more on how you can create a contrived character if you do not follow his inner motivations and guiding principles:

> We need to have the characters believable in their emotional landscape. They need to express genuine feelings that we have all felt or imagined, even if it's a tin can that is feeling it. For instance, one of the things that used to drive me crazy in many old films is that women would become helplessly catatonic in the face of violence, an utterly abnormal animal behavior. The writers would ignore women's built-in defense reflexes in order to focus on the male action. This would make the female's emotional strata contrived, and I could no longer believe the rest of the story.

Remember that your audience is smarter than you give them credit for most days. The cheerleader is not going to fall for the bad boy in school unless he is on her social plane. Make the bad boy a jock, maybe the quarterback on the football team. Now we believe that the most popular girl in school would give the bad boy the time of day. Believability and credibility are also dependent on the character's motivation.

Motivation

We are all motivated to get up in the morning. Why? Usually money. The motivation for your character is critical to staying on track toward the goal. When you are given a scene in a movie, you must remember the goal of the character and reinforce it in even the most subtle ways. We all act to survive, and what each of us thinks we need to survive is vastly different from what another person believes. Some characters will find money and status the most important motivation because they grew up poor or they need independence. Others will see having a family as the only way to feel secure and comfortable. Some characters do not trust

1966

KIMBA THE WHITE LION ARRIVES FROM JAPAN: *Kimba the White Lion*, a Japanese animated series from the 1960s, was the first color TV animation series created in Japan.

1966

IT'S THE GREAT PUMPKIN, CHARLIE BROWN TV SPECIAL: *It's the Great Pumpkin, Charlie Brown*, an Emmy award–winning popular animated television special, was based on the comic strip "Peanuts" by Charles M. Schulz. Its initial broadcast took place on CBS in 1966; CBS re-aired the special annually through 2000, with ABC picking up the rights beginning in 2001.

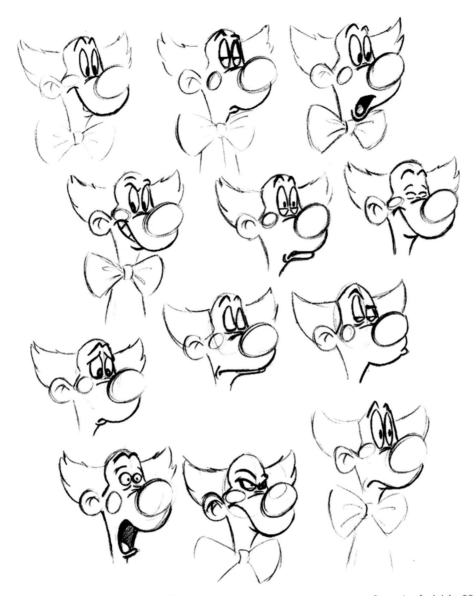

Face charts are the best way to illustrate to the modeler what you expect from the facial in CG.

1966

DR. SEUSS' HOW THE GRINCH STOLE CHRISTMAS: Dr.
Seuss' How the Grinch Stole Christmas was adapted to television by MGM as an animated TV special, directed by Seuss's friend and former colleague Chuck Jones. Jones served as director, character designer, and character layout artist and modified the appearance of the Grinch somewhat to fit the medium, rendering him in green and with a more elongated, froglike face.

1967

PERMUTATIONS BY JOHN WHITNEY:
Permutations was an early artistic film constructed entirely off the black-and-white monitor of a large computer system. Color was added by editing with an optical printer. It is an elegant, abstract work composed of architectures of color dots that develop a pattern while displaying a kinetic rhythm.

anyone, so they are motivated to stay closed up and never reveal themselves to anyone. Whatever the motivation is for your character, write it down on a piece of paper in front of you while you work, and it will keep your performance on track. Then write down the goal. Sometimes motivation and goal are in contrast with one another and sometimes they work together.

Dumbo is a great example of motivation and goal working together. This poor little elephant tries so hard to please with enthusiasm. His motivation is only to be accepted, and his goal is to be back with his mother, who has always accepted him as he is—big ears and all. Here the motivation and goal are the same, but Dumbo's obstacle is the acceptance of society. The introduction of the crow characters represents acceptance and social outcasts befriending another social outcast. While writing a story, it's best if the premise you create reinforces the motivations of your characters.

Show, Don't Tell

It's a creative choice to make a narrative story or a cinematic story. A narrative story is usually told by an omnipotent voice placed over the visual imagery. *Forrest Gump* is a great example of narrative storytelling. A cinematic approach uses more visuals and dialogue. *Crouching Tiger, Hidden Dragon* is a good example of cinematic storytelling. When it comes to character, it's always more interesting to show than to tell. Even the nightly news has an image over the anchor's shoulder, showing you what happened as the anchor reads you the story. In contrast, a narrative film such as Forrest Gump can offer an understanding that a cinematic film might not have by filling in the blanks of what the main character is thinking. David Smith explains more about how the narrative quality of Forrest Gump helped the movie along:

> Literary adaptations to film make good use of narrative because perhaps the book was written with a narrator-character point of view. Narration can offer necessary depth that might not be available in cinematic form. Forrest Gump was not always in the cinematic position of offering many words, and at times narrative supported the story well.

When designing a character for a story, decide whether you will be telling the story from a narrative or a cinematic point of view. This will help you figure out how much of the character will need to be revealed through acting or spoken words. As you get to know who your character is, learn whether he would be more likely to gesture a lot with his hands or to overreact with his body. As you develop these characteristics, you can keep them in mind for when you get to designing the character. Both body structure and persona go hand in hand. For example, the ladybug in *A Bug's Life* is always ticked off because everyone thinks

1967

OSCAR FOR *THE BOX* (MURAKAMI & WOLF): *The Box* won the Academy Award for Best Short Subject: Cartoons.

1967

FIRST COMPUTER-ANIMATED FILM – CIBERNETIC 5.3: This was the first computer-animated film at the UCLA Animation Workshop. It combined computer graphics with organic live-action photography to create a new reality. However, Stehura considerd the film only an "incidental test" in an ongoing experiment with computer graphics that occupied most of his time for more than nine years.

1967

SPEED RACER SERIES INTRODUCED: *Speed Racer* is the English adaptation of the Japanese anime *Mach Go Go Go* and is an early example of an anime becoming a successful franchise in America.

he is a *she*. You get this with just a glance at his body structure. You show it and don't necessarily have to *say* it. Pixar does this a lot with their characters. In *Toy Story*, Mr. Potato Head is always irritable. Well, his face keeps falling off! Wouldn't you be irritated? Using the body structure to reinforce the character is a great way to show and not tell the story. These subtle choices might not be read by the audience that deliberately, but they are absorbed as acting choices that tell you who the character is and why. Henry Anderson talks about how character can be developed by showing and not telling:

> When it comes to storytelling in animation, I really believe the old axiom that actions speak louder than words. Don't *tell* it if you can *show* it. Dialogue is an important part of character development, but seeing how a character reacts to a given situation—or to another character—can speak volumes. That's why stories usually get a huge lift as soon as they go from script to boards.

Remember that your character may have a lot to say, but he doesn't have to constantly verbalize it. There is a rule of threes when creating a character design. A successful character is based on voice, story, and animation. These three parts equal the whole, and you have to consider all three while designing and creating your characters. If the character is a mute, how do you handle the design differently than if he can talk? Nik Ranieri answers us, using his design of Meeko from *Pocahontas* as an example:

> It didn't rely on a voice; it was all pantomime. The reason why Meeko's my favorite is because there was no voice, and it was dependent on the animation and the story aspect. It was more me, the animators, the crew, and the gags from the story department. So, it was almost like animation got a 50-percent, if not higher, importance in that character.

"When I directed *Mulan* for Disney, I remember trying very hard to find visual storytelling moments. The scene where Mulan makes her decision to cut her hair and go off to war in her father's place comes to mind. Looking at that sequence, we used carved faces on her sword, the family beis, and the wardrobe to simulate the feeling of her ancestors (whom we meet later) watching her make this decision. It can be subtle but effective in using visual storytelling."

—Tony Bancroft

1967

THE JUNGLE BOOK 19TH DISNEY FEATURE: *The Jungle Book* was the last animated feature produced by Walt Disney, who died during its production. It was loosely based on the stories from *The Jungle Book* by Rudyard Kipling. The movie remains one of Disney's most popular.

1968

OSCAR FOR *WINNIE THE POOH AND THE BLUSTERY DAY* (DISNEY): *Winnie the Pooh and the Blustery Day* was the second *Winnie the Pooh* short and won the 1968 Academy Award for Best Short Subject: Cartoons.

1968

THE YELLOW SUBMARINE RELEASED: The Yellow Submarine is an animated film based on the music of the Beatles.

Pantomime and acting will always win the audience over as opposed to talking heads explaining what they are going to do. You can also use other graphic elements in clothing and atmosphere to reinforce a character and show his place in the story. In *Toy Story 2*, every time you see Emperor Zurg there are graphic Zs in the environment. There are Zs as shadows on the floor, the grating is in the shape of Zs, and there are Zs on his costume. This is just another way to show the story without telling and to reinforce the character's persona.

Use design, environment, style, and pantomime to create a "show, don't tell" approach to storytelling for your character.

The Fine Art of Being a Bastard

Good villains start like any memorable character—with humanity. A good villain is human with a fatal flaw. A movie doesn't necessarily have to have a villain, but a really good villain can make the movie so much more interesting. The success of a protagonist is dependent on the success of the antagonist and vice versa. What a villain brings to any feature is a clear and present threat. People relate to a villain the same way they relate to religion. People want to believe bad things will happen to you if you are a bad person. We also want to know why this character wants to do bad things. The audience wants to relate to the villain in a human way. If a character wants something that would be harmful to your hero, then you need to explain why that character should desire it so and humanize his evil nature. If the villain is just a bad guy for no reason, then his character will fall flat and not be convincing. As twisted as the character's actions might be perceived in a movie, the audience has to say to themselves, "I understand why he is doing it." Ed Hooks explains why we relate to villainous characters:

> A villain does not think he is a villain. Every character is a hero in his own life.

If the villain doesn't have humanity and a valid reason behind his evil, then the character becomes one-dimensional and unappealing. When developing who your villain is and why he is that way, walk a day in his shoes to understand why he would commit such wickedness.

1968

2001: A SPACE ODYSSEY RELEASED:
2001: A Space Odyssey is an influential sci-fi film notable for combining episodes contrasting high levels of scientific and technical realism with transcendental mysticism. It contained the first major use of motion control animation and won the Academy Award for visual effects.

1968

RAY TRACING IS BORN:
Ray tracing was invented. Arthur Appel of IBM developed hidden surface and shadow algorithms that were precursors to ray tracing.

1968

TERRYTOONS CLOSES:
CBS Terrytoons closes theatrical production.

What makes for a great villain? Sketch by Floyd Norman.

The same rules apply to villains as to any other character. There has to be some form of empathy for the villain, just as there is for the hero; otherwise, why do we care? Anthony Hopkins' Hannibal Lecter character from *The Silence of the Lambs* comes up again and again as the perfectly likeable villain. He is almost charming. If it wasn't for the fact that he dines on human flesh, you might even consider asking him to supper. A good villain is one you feel some sympathy for in his plight, one you may actually find oddly appealing.

1969

OSCAR FOR *IT'S TOUGH TO BE A BIRD* (DISNEY): *It's Tough to Be a Bird* won the Academy Award for Best Short Subject: Cartoons.

1969

SCOOBY DOO, WHERE ARE YOU TV SERIES: The debut on TV of *Scooby-Doo, Where Are You!* was the first incarnation of the long-running Hanna-Barbera Saturday morning cartoon *Scooby-Doo*. 25 episodes were ultimately produced.

1969

UNIX DEVELOPED: The UNIX operating system was developed by Thompson and Ritchie at Bell Labs (in PDP-7 assembly code).

The villain can be a simple obstacle instead of an actual character, but it is more fun when it's someone you can actually personify. A villain can be "the system," "the man," fate, or luck. A good way to approach a villain is to take a likable antagonist and place misfortune in front of him to explain why he wants revenge. This gives your villain the reason why he is the "hero in his own life," as Ed Hooks said before. This kind of energy behind the villain's intentions will justify his means for both himself and the audience. The villain is focused because of his own idea of heroism and will stop at nothing to achieve his goal. And if his goal is an obstacle to the protagonist, then you have a strong villain.

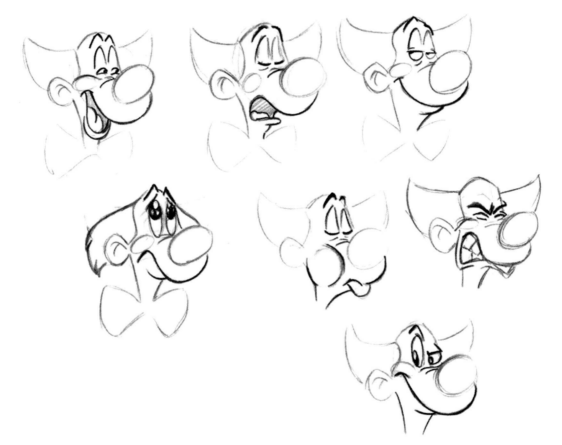

Be sure you stay on model when drawing face charts, and watch volume to see that it's even throughout the face. Otherwise, the shapes will look like his head is a balloon and someone just sucked all the air out.

1969

GUI DEVELOPED:
Graphical User Interface (GUI) developed by Xerox (Alan Kay).

1969

SIGGRAPH STARTED: SIG-GRAPH (Special Interest Group in GRAPHics) is the name of the annual conference on computer graphics convened by the ACM SIGGRAPH organization. The first SIGGRAPH conference was in 1974.

1970

OSCAR FOR *IS IT ALWAYS RIGHT TO BE RIGHT* (STEPHEN BOSUTOW):
Is it Always Right to Be Right won the Academy Award for Best Short Subject: Cartoons. A blend of still photography and very limited animation, it looks and feels like the old UPA cartoons from the 1950s.

Another great facet to a good villain is to create one who has a belief system that is completely in contrast to your own. It's easy to despise a villain who doesn't have any basic human morality. A villain has to have humanity to be three-dimensional, but his resistance to what we have been taught to value is interesting. If the villain has twisted what he thinks is good or bad into his own reality, it makes us want to find out how he got that way.

"Captain Hook is the most cold-blooded villain Disney ever had. He is a caricature, and he has his basis in the original *Peter Pan* stage productions, but there is a gag in *Peter Pan* that no one would ever do now, which I love. There is a guy up in the yardarm, singing badly, and Hook doesn't like the singing. Without even looking up, he takes his pistol and BANG, he fires and you just hear the splash. Then he goes back to what he was doing. That is the coldest thing I have ever seen in an animated film, and it's funny too. It just reveals so much about his character. He cares that little about human life that it's offhanded and over the shoulder, and he doesn't even have to look."

—*Eric Goldberg*

Even though the villain is most successful when defying our own morality, he still requires a definite motive to survive. That reason should drive his meaning of life and need for air to breathe. Scott Holmes has more on successful villains:

It helps if your villain has a reason to exist—then the villain is consumed with that reason. The witch in *Snow White* is obsessed with her beauty over all others. When Snow White becomes the most fair of all, the witch goes off on a binge to destroy the person in the way of her obsession. She is a well thought-out villain in that her evil is driven by a need or motive.

Remember, a good villain is human with a fatal flaw. The villain is a hero in his own world. His own obstacles should be just as relatable to the audience as the hero's obstacles. Finally, the villain's belief system will be different than our own, but we will understand it because of the human nature involved. This belief system is what drives the villain to do the things he does.

 1970

THE FURTHER ADVENTURES OF UNCLE SAM RELEASED: This film was an Annecy Grand Prize Winner and an original and sophisticated animated film with strong pop art and surreal influences.

1970

THE ARISTOCATS 20TH DISNEY FEATURE: *The Aristocats* is noted for being the last film to be approved by Walt Disney himself; he died while the film was still in early production.

 1971

OSCAR FOR *THE CRUNCH BIRD* (MAXWELL-PETOK-PETROVICH): *The Crunch Bird* won an Academy Award winner for Best Short Subject: Cartoons.

Design

Actual design of a character in general for CG or for 2D holds the same main objectives. There are basic rules handed down through the years, such as making the character readable from all angles. But one of the best ways to make a character who is unique and also memorable is the same way caricature artists work. They choose one single part of your face or body that is a little bigger or smaller or different-looking, and they make that part the focus. This is how your character will stand apart from the others. Dave Zaboski uses the genie from *Aladdin* as an example of good design:

> What do you want people to look at? It's the same when you meet someone. They might have a feature that you just can't take your eyes off of. What is it? Find that one feature and make it clear. The genie designed by Eric Goldberg is a good example. The eyes and nose had this relationship that was clear and recognizable. Then you could make him into anything and it was readable. He even became Jack Nicholson, and it was still the genie. That's brilliant design.

This kind of design and appeal can be an intangible thing that you have to create by drawing many iterations of a character. Does the design convey the intention of the character? A good design should also aid the needs of the character in the story. If the character needs to perform very physical tasks, you should probably not dress him up in elaborate, restrictive costumes. Design can also reinforce character if it goes in contrast to the character's personality. A villain can be extremely handsome. A hero can be an ogre. You can contrast an archetypal personality by using character design and body type. Keith Lango shows us how:

> Another design aspect is personifying the character in his shape. I'm a big believer that if you're going to animate something, you'd better have a good reason why. One of the biggest reasons is to form the actual design of your characters to accentuate their overriding character traits. You can even play games with it. A big, tough, muscular guy who's afraid of the dark is funny. His design can trick you into thinking one thing, and then we pull the cover off his character for something different. Design plays a huge role in understanding your character—or fooling you into thinking you do.

1971

FRITZ THE CAT RELEASED; X-RATED ANIMATION: Ralph Bakshi's *Fritz the Cat* was the first animated feature film to be rated X. The movie was a box-office hit, drawing in audiences as much for its shock value as for its appeal to the "love generation" of the 1960s.

1971

ROBERT ABEL & ASSOCIATES BEGAN: Robert Abel & Associates was founded by Bob Abel and Con Pederson. Abel joined Pederson to adapt the camera system used for *2001* to general film effects work. Abel & Assoc. was one of four companies contracted to do graphics for the Disney movie *Tron* in 1982.

This is where story, character, and design all come together. But how do we sustain the appeal when we move from a concept sketch to the computer? It takes both a great understanding of appeal in design with pencil and paper, and an understanding of how to apply the grace of drawing to a CG model. A modeler in CG is worth his weight in gold when he knows how to lay down the topology or little lines that describe the surface of the model effectively. Those little lines can make or break your character when it moves in 3D.

Draw as many emotive states as you can so that the rigger will understand what you expect out of the puppet he builds.

1971

UB IWERKS DIES: Ub Iwerks dies (1901–1971); he was considered one of the greatest animators ever. The first few Mickey Mouse cartoons were animated almost entirely by Iwerks. He spent most of his career with Disney and developed some of the most important technological advancements in animation. Later, he left Disney to start an animation studio under his own name.

1971

THE ANDROMEDA STRAIN USES COMPUTER ANIMATION IN FEATURE: The first film to make use of digital animation for special effects was The Andromeda Strain.

1971

THE POINT IS FIRST ANIMATED FILM TO AIR ON TV: The first hour-long animation film on US TV was The Point, first aired as a "movie of the week."

2D Drawings Translated into CG

The most difficult task in taking a hand-drawn character and bringing it into the world of CG is upholding the charm, warmth, and appeal that live in the sketch. It takes many revisions to keep that charm alive. A modeler with a keen sense of the aesthetic is vital to a successful crossover. Equally important in that modeler is the technical understanding of where the topology should lie to support clean deformations in tough areas such as shoulders, hips, and tight spaces within the joints. It's best to think about your character in parts when designing him in 2D. This will help the modeler and rigger understand how you expect him to move. We asked our rigger, Javier Solsona, to explain his approach to rigging our clown character, since we were so demanding of its construction and flexibility:

> I wanted to create a kind of freedom in the rig that would eliminate the restrictions that a CG artist has usually. This was a very interesting challenge, and the rig was built in a very different way than standard rigs. Having enough detail in the model is very important for this kind of rig so that it can be pushed to the limit. The model needs to be able to deform in ways that it normally wouldn't, and the detail needs to be there so that the character doesn't break. The process was divided into two parts: body and facial.

Just like in animation, simplicity is always the best rule. The more bits you add, the more complicated the model will be, and this will affect every part of production from there, including rigging, skinning, texturing, lighting, animation, and so on. Bernd Angerer has a good idea of how to keep a character simple in design for CG:

> I think it comes down to clearly recognizable shapes. In most cases, I'd also apply the rule that less is more.

1971

GOURAUD SHADING DEVELOPED: Intensity interpolated shading was developed by Henri Gouraud in '71. Gouraud shading is a method used in computer graphics to simulate the differing effects of light and colour across the surface of an object.

1971

MICROPROCESSOR CHIP DEVELOPED: One of the most important advancements to computer graphics appeared on the scene in 1971, the microprocessor. Using integrated circuit technology developed in 1959, the electronics of a computer processor were miniaturized down to a single chip, the microprocessor, sometimes called a CPU (*Central Processing Unit*).

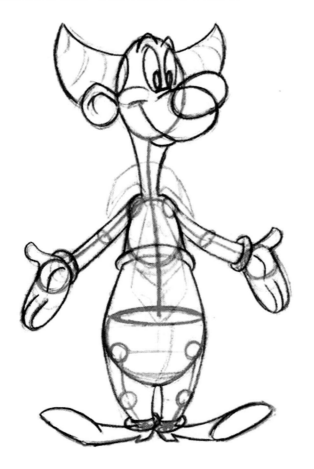

Create structural drawings so you know that simplicity is being applied and the rigger will understand where you intend joints to be located and places to be flexible.

"2D has a kind of freedom that is difficult to reproduce in CG. In 2D, the artist can draw what he/she wants. He can make use of squash and stretch techniques that are easy to draw in 2D but hard to duplicate in CG. In CG you are bound to physical restrictions. You can only work on an enclosed, controlled environment. Facial in a character is probably the hardest thing to duplicate in CG. In 2D, the artist usually deforms the face in ways that are physically impossible."

—*Javier Solsona*

1971

LUCASFILM BEGINS WITH
THX 1138: *THX 1138* was George Lucas' first feature-length movie. It was a feature-length version of an earlier student film by Lucas.

1972

OSCAR FOR *A CHRISTMAS CAROL* (RICHARD WILLIAMS): *A Christmas Carol*, an animated cartoon adaptation of Charles Dickens' venerable novella, won Best Short Subject: Animated Film.

1972

NELVANA IS FOUNDED:
Nelvana is a Canadian company that produces children's animation and other series. The company was founded in Toronto, Ontario by Michael Hirsh, Patrick Loubert, and Clive Smith.

Simplicity enables the animator to create a more clear performance as well. Simplicity will enable the model to work with the technology more easily. Work closely with your modeler to create a design that will work smoothly with the technology and not fight against it. Read the script and assess every possible type or extreme of movement that might come up.

If your character is an animal on all fours, but there is a possibility that it might have to get up and walk around convincingly on two legs, you must think about how to build the model to deal with this technicality, or it will look broken when animated. Many shows are told that a character will never walk upright, only later to hear from the guys upstairs, "Well, they want the kangaroo to do a break-dance thing now." You must build for this kind of growth. Brian Dowrick explains how a simple thing such as the position a character is built in for its neutral pose can really mess with how the character will be animated:

> I hate it when I get a character in the basic "T pose" (with the arms outstretched from the body), and the first thing they have us do is put his arms in front of him and rotate the hands 90 degrees. If it is a dog and is walking on all fours, then don't model him like he's a plane with the arms outstretched. Always model it with the idea that this more natural starting pose will be the neutral/middle pose (for the range of motion) for all the extreme things the limbs will be doing. So, if the front limbs will spend most of their time in front of the body, model them somewhere in front of the body, not sticking out the side or backward.

The old saying goes, "Design your characters to work from any angle."

We ran into many different issues while designing the clown character in CG, and we hope to offer a little insight when you try this yourself for the first time. It is crucial to provide the modeler and rigger with as many drawings as possible. Our rigger, Javier Solsona, explains why this helps him create the most powerful rig:

> It's great to be able to see what the character is supposed to look like and what kind of poses, expressions, et cetera it's supposed to hit. This provides a ground on which to base the model and ideas on how to build the rig.

1972

JAN SVANKMAJER BANNED FROM FILMMAKING: Jan Svankmajer is forced to begin a seven-year Czech government–imposed "silencing" during which he is not permitted to make films of any kind. He spent this period working as a special effects designer and coordinator. 1972 also saw the start of his lengthy series of Natural Science etchings and aquatints, all depicting a bizarre alternative universe.

1972

CARL STALLING DIES: Carl Stalling was a music director and composer who set the standards for animation music in the Golden Age of animation. He is most closely associated with the *Looney Tunes* shorts.

Clown turnaround for the modeler.

However, the artist using pencil and paper can easily go off model. It is crucial for the artist to maintain structural integrity when drawing the turnaround model sheets. If not, the modeler is subject to using creative license in deciding which drawing he should follow. You should provide the rigger and modeler everything in the following list for your character to successfully translate to CG:

◆ Emotive drawings showing extreme attitudes and gestures

◆ Structural drawings that illustrate where you intend flexibility and joints to be placed within the skin

◆ Face charts for the modeler to build the facial rig and blendshapes from

◆ Watch volume when you are drawing your face charts

The issues that arose during the building of our clown model mostly had to do with matching the drawings. If you are a modeler, it's best to drop the drawings into the view port as you create the shapes. This way, you will not detour from the design. Our first versions of the clown looked a little too "doglike" in CG simply because when you add dimension to the shapes, they tend to look longer. His nose looked really long even though it matched the drawing, so we shaved it down a bit. We also elongated the neck and placed it further

1972

FRANK TASHLIN DIES: Frank Tashlin (Tish-Tash) (1913–1972) joined Schlesinger's cartoon studio at Warner Bros. in 1936, where he brought a new understanding of camerawork to directors. Many of Tashlin's films have attained cult status.

1972

MAX FLEISCHER DIES: Max Fleischer (1883–1972) was an important pioneer in the development of the animated cartoon. He brought such characters as Betty Boop, Koko the Clown, Popeye, and Superman to the movie screen and was responsible for a number of technological innovations.

back on the head. In the drawings, Jamie was able to do this per pose, but in CG we needed the most neutral place for the head, and then could "cheat" poses from that point.

There is a term called "off model" used in traditional circles, and it refers to staying true to the size and volume relations of the character design. Traditional animators can go "off model" any time to add charm and warmth to their drawings. A subtle change in the arc in a pencil line can give a facial expression a completely different feel. In CG, you are always "on model." By virtue of the model being a tangible sculpture in space, the model will always be rendered at the correct size correlation to perspective unless you break it deliberately.

You can make cheats to get the same charm and go "off model" while animating, but it's best to get the most appealing and neutral model to start with before trying to cheat facial and skin shapes for the body. By "cheat," we mean playing the shape and form up to the camera. Sometimes the shapes you create to make your character appealing to the camera view must be cheated, and if you looked at your character from any other angle, he would look completely broken or crazy. For example, let's use a character that has an unusually large head, such as the mouse character in *Stuart Little*. Let's say Stuart must wipe something off his face for the scene. Say rose petals. How would you do that if his arms will not even stretch far enough to reach the tip of his nose or in front of his eyes? It's called a cheat. For a few frames, you will scale the arms to be three times as long as they normally would be. However, you can't create any of these cheats until you get a solid model in its most appealing and neutral pose.

The eyes on our clown were tricky as well, because eyes tend to look so dead when they are just two spheres in CG. We played with the shapes and their placement to get the most charm out of the model in its neutral pose.

Handling Textures in CG

When approaching textures for your characters, remember the style and atmosphere you hope to create. If you have to integrate the character with live action, you will need to lean toward something less stylized and more grounded in reality. The textures will have to be convincing in your environment. The textures for characters with live action also can have more depth and detail to them because they most likely will not squash and stretch as much as cartoon-styled characters to fit into this environment. If you are working in 100-percent CG, you can have a little more fun with it. If your animation is going to push the boundaries of naturalistic and cartoonish motion, then you have to be careful with things like bump maps, reflections, fur, cloth, and so on. These things in CG can break and reveal the cartoonish tricks and cheats. It's best to keep the textures simple, as Eric Goldberg explains:

1972

PONG IS DEVELOPED: Nolan Kay Bushnell and a friend formed Atari and then created a game called *Pong* in 1972. *Pong* was not the first video game, but it was the first video game that people were able to play without reading instructions, which made it widely successful.

1972

ED CATMULL CREATES ANIMATION LANGUAGE FOR SMOOTHING AT UNIVERSITY OF UTAH: Ed Catmull (U. of Utah) develops an animation scripting language and creates an animation of a smooth shaded hand.

1972

FRED PARKE CREATES THE FIRST CGI PHYSICALLY MODELED HUMAN FACE: Fred Parke (U. of Utah) creates first computer-generated facial animation.

My approach to textures with well-established, hand-drawn characters being transferred to CG is to be minimal, minimal, minimal. The less texture that is on them, the more fluidity and squash and stretch and distortion you can get in their movements. Then you are not watching fur distort. They did a very minimal fur texture on these Disney commercials at DD, and it was fine and very subtle. You play up the textures where necessary. We can see Goofy's sweater with more texture in it than there is on his skin. You texture the stuff that people can read without being overdone, and you minimize the texture on the stuff you want some fluidity on. Even on clothing you can't have burlap because it's such an obvious texture that it's really going to hamper certain distortions in the animation. However, you can, for example, have shiny, hard shoes on Goofy.

Color comps help everyone involved with the texturing for your character to know exactly what you hope the character will look like.

OSCAR FOR *FRANK FILM* (FRANK MORRIS USA): *Frank Film* won an Academy Award for Best Short Subject: Animated Films and has been selected for preservation in the United States National Film Registry.

BAKSHI'S *HEAVY TRAFFIC* RELEASED: Krantz/Bakshi's *Heavy Traffic* is a full-length animated film by Ralph Bakshi. Halfway into production, Bakshi got into a fight with producer Krantz and was fired from his own movie. Bakshi was re-hired later, and despite this disagreement, he stated that *Heavy Traffic* was the most enjoyable film to make.

Textures are clearly a way to make your character fit into the world better when working in CG. Just remember the other parts of production and how they affect the rest of the pipeline when you are developing how detailed the textures will be. The computer enables you to add almost unlimited amounts of detail and texture, but step carefully here. Do you really need it?

The Rig Equals Solid Drawing

One of the 12 principles developed by the "Nine Old Men"[20] was called *solid drawing*. This meant if you did not have a command of the craft of draftsmanship, you were going to have a hard time being a classical animator. This same principle can be applied to CG but with a twist. Instead of the pencil (although thumbnails and sketching are important), the one important tool you need to create good animation is your rig. The rig is the puppet you use to animate with on the computer. Animating on a computer can be much like stop-motion because one key frame will involve moving many parts on the puppet or rig. The rig should have the least number of controls with the most power and flexibility. When you grab the arm control, you should be able to access the hand translate, the wrist rotate, the finger and thumb controls, and maybe even a twist on the elbow. Simplicity is key. Your rig *is* your character, as far as ability to create skillful movement goes.

Working with your rigger, you can create the most powerful tool a CG animator can have—a solid puppet. With a clean and simple model design and a solid rig, you are on your way to creating a memorable character. When the modeler, designer, animator, and rigger are all communicating about what the expectations are for the character, the most solid foundation is established. The modeler must understand how the lines flow with the musculature and topology in the model, so it will deform properly. The rigger knows where the skeleton will lie inside that model, and this is usually a back-and-forth arrangement until both the riggers and the modelers are happy with the way the character is built. The modeling and rigging processes can take equal amounts of time, so your scheduling should take this into consideration. Javier Solsona requested that we add one more thing about riggers that you should be aware of:

> Riggers are the best people in the world—they are clever, handsome, and super cool. Not only that, but they also like cookies.

We hear the Famous Amos brand is most popular with riggers.

As more and more animators become involved in the design of characters for CG, the styles in design will be pushed further, and the art form will continue to evolve. Animators have to know the laws of creating strong characters in order to push their animation performances. The relationship between animator, modeler, and

1973

LONDON ANIMATION RENAISSANCE IN COMMERCIALS BEGINS: Richard Williams invited Hollywood animators such as Art Babbitt, Ken Harris, and Chuck Jones to train his London staff, sparking the London Commercial Renaissance.

1973

FIRST FILM TO USE 3D COMPUTER GRAPHICS (PIXILIZATION) - WESTWORLD: Seminal sci-fi movie Westworld debuts as the first significant entertainment film to employ computer animation.

1973

ROBIN HOOD 21ST FEATURE FOR DISNEY: *Robin Hood* recounts the traditional stories of Robin Hood with the characters cast as anthropomorphic animals.

rigger in CG is the most important factor in creating a solid design. Conrad Vernon explains how more animators being involved in design will push the styles and designs in CG today:

> A good, strong animator who has input into the design and style of the character would only help define new styles. That animator would know what he needed the character to do in order to fully emote. He would go to the rigger and say, "You have to put points here and here and here in order to move it correctly." Sometimes the modelers and the riggers think they have to put 10 billion points all over the place, and still the character can't do what you want it to do. An animator being part of that process and being able to design the character can say, "Well, let's have two points here so it will go up into the eyes, but when he smiles we will be able to scrunch his chin up here and drop the neck, et cetera." An animator can help these people design a character that moves correctly. Many times, even on *Shrek*, we would have the people rig and model a character, and as soon as it was time to animate it, it didn't look like the voice was coming out of there. The eyes were bulging or as soon as you moved that king's mouth, his teeth shot out (these *huge* teeth), and you would say, "Whoa! We need to remodel and re-rig it." If they had animator input from the beginning, this could have been avoided. Once you get these people into that realm of modeling and rigging and even helping in the design, then you are going to see their personalities come out in the look of the character, as well as the movement of the character. Just like Milt Kahl and the *The Aristocats* and *The Rescuers*, and then you look at *Pinocchio* and you think Frank Thomas and Ollie Johnston. You look at "Night on Bald Mountain" from *Fantasia*, you see Bill Tytla. Every time there was a beautiful woman on the screen, Mac Davis animated her impeccably. This is how those animators drew for me, and they designed the characters the way they drew. The animators are going to have to be involved in that stuff in CG, and the more they are involved in it, the more their personalities will come out in it.

So get more involved. Get to know your rigger and modeler. Take into consideration the limitations forced upon him by the studio system. A good working relationship with the people who are putting your character together is vital.

In the next chapter, we will show you how the "Thursday Animator" takes what we have learned so far and really begins to take performance to a higher level.

---

[20]Johnston, Ollie and Frank Thomas. *The Illusion of Life: Disney Animation*. Revised edition. New York: Disney Editions, 1995.

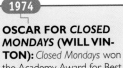

1974

OSCAR FOR *CLOSED MONDAYS* (WILL VINTON): *Closed Mondays* won the Academy Award for Best Short Subject: Animated Films.

1974

FIRST COMPUTER-ANIMATED FILM NOMINATED FOR AN OSCAR - *HUNGER* (NFB): Peter Foldès directed and animated this 11-minute short. Partially animated by computer, *Hunger* posits black-and-white animated illustrations against a colored backdrop, with surrealistic figures that fluidly bend, stretch, change shape, and ultimately take on new forms. This film featured Burtnyk and Wein interactive key framing techniques.

Index 3: Character Bio Questionnaire

- Age
- Ethnicity
- Height
- Weight
- Sex/reproduction: How does the character propagate? Does he or she have sex?
- Gender
- Health: Handicapped? From birth?
- Intelligence
- Education
- Evolutionary cycle: Lifespan
- Culture: Beliefs
- Food/eating habits
- Nocturnal
- Family: Values? Size?
- Money
- Profession
- Body structure: Totally affects how the character moves and how he/she is perceived by others
- Flaws (fatal)
- Idiosyncracies
- Atmosphere: How does a church vs. a car wreck influence the character?
- Goals
- Dreams
- Trauma: Something that happened that affects how the character acts
- Stereotype vs. archetype
- Talent
- Addictions

1974

Z-BUFFER AND TEXTURE MAPPING ON CURVED SURFACES DEVELOPED BY ED CATMULL: Ed Catmull (University of Utah) developed the Z-buffer and pioneered texture mapping on curved surfaces.

1974

FIRST SIGGRAPH CONFERENCE: SIGGRAPH 74 took place in Boulder, Colorado, and was a great success, with more than 600 people attending from around the world.

1974

III FORMS MOTION PICTURE GROUP: Information International Incorporated (a.k.a. III) formed the Motion Pictures Product Group with John Whitney, Jr. and Gary Demos. Between 1978 and 1982, III's motion-picture work included *Westworld, Futureworld, Looker,* and *Tron.*

Index 4: Character Development

◆ Empathy creates memorable characters

◆ Deepen archetype, rather than starting with stereotype

◆ Use your own life experience and memories

◆ A flawed character is more interesting

◆ Believability and credibility are dependent upon the character's actions

◆ Have defined motivations and goals

◆ Show/don't tell: Narrative vs. cinematic

◆ Good villains are human with a fatal flaw

◆ Focal point improves character design

◆ Less is more when designing a character

◆ Reinforce the style with texture in CG

◆ Your rig will make or break your character's ability to emote

1975

OSCAR FOR *GREAT* (ISAM-BARD KINGDOM BRUNEL): *Great* won an Academy Award for Best Short Subject: Animated Films.

1975

***2,000 YEAR OLD MAN* PREMIERES:** In this TV special, Mel Brooks played the oldest man in the world, interviewed by Carl Reiner in a series of comedy routines that appeared on television as well as being made into a collection of comedy records.

1975

ILM FORMED: Industrial Light & Magic (ILM) is a motion-picture special visual effects company founded by George Lucas and owned by Lucasfilm Ltd.

THINKING ANIMATION:
BRIDGING THE GAP BETWEEN 2D AND CG

PART II

Animation

Chapter 4
The Thursday Animator

Excitement! This is what you feel when you have been handed a really juicy scene to animate! So you're excited; what do you do? You turn on that computer and start animating. No! Idiot! Have you learned nothing? Don't you dare! This will only lead to a scene that is convoluted and hard to follow at best.

You must think about your scene and get inside the head of the character in the space and time of the story. Over the years animators have adopted many approaches to how they think about their scenes. This chapter will introduce and label some of these techniques. However, just like any creative undertaking, the journey can have forks in the road. You might go back and forth between all of the suggested methods as you develop your ideas. There is no formula. Using the practices in this chapter, you will create something that is original and unmistakably clear in performance. Dave Brewster says it best:

> "To just jump in and start animating so the director sees something, anything, is a waste of time. Think about what you want to do. Then, think about it again."
>
> —*Brian Dowrick*

I close my eyes and try and see the scene already done.

You should think about the following key strategies before animating:

- ◆ Think and plan.
- ◆ Create and/or find reference and act the scene out.
- ◆ Draw gestures and make thumbnails.
- ◆ Share your ideas with others.

1975

PHONG SHADING IS DEVELOPED:
Phong Bui-Tuong developed a specular illumination model and normal interpolation shading on a computer.

1975

BILL GATES STARTS MICROSOFT: Days after reading the January 1, 1975, issue of *Popular Electronics* that demonstrated the Altair 8800, Bill Gates called the creators of the new microcomputer, MITS (Micro Instrumentation and Telemetry Systems), offering to demonstrate an implementation of the BASIC programming language for the system. Gates left Harvard University, moved to Albuquerque, New Mexico, where MITS was located, and founded Microsoft there.

It's best to analyze for at least a day what the character's desire is and what the obstacle to that desire might be. There is an old title in animation known as the "Thursday Animator." This animator is handed a scene on Monday and spends until Thursday planning the animation or shopping, sleeping, going for long lunches, and generally appearing to be goofing off. Monday through Wednesday the animator is collecting all of the important data necessary to plan for a great performance. Thursday, the animator actually starts to animate.

As you plan for your shot, look for psychological gesture and subtext in the dialogue to add the seasoning and spice to the acting. Psychological gesture describes what the character is thinking. The subtext of acting choices is based in psychological gestures such as looking around the room, scratching the head, or using one of many other gestures that reveal what is going in the character's mind. Figure out how you would react in the same circumstances and then, without betraying the personality of the character, put a little of yourself into the shot. Using psychological gesture and subtext, you can give the performance more depth and play with the personality a bit by contrasting what the character might be saying with what the character might be thinking. However, do not clutter the acting with too many ideas.

Simplicity is the key to creating a clear idea. Until every idea for poses and acting is out of your system, these thoughts will continue to arise as you animate. This is when too many notes are usually added to the composition, and you may end up cluttering up a strong shot. When you take the time to really think about and absorb every possible solution to the planning of your scene, you will come up with thousands of ideas. Every new idea will help create a more pleasing and honest piece. Mark Behm clarifies this practice:

I sit down and plan it out completely, then throw away my first idea because it's probably too obvious and not terribly interesting. I'll try to get as many independent ideas out as I can to get through the bad ones. It's a struggle, but I try to see the whole shot in my head. If I can get to that point, I know I haven't glossed over anything and I've retained a clear core of the idea. I usually plan this for a full day and a half if I can get away with it. I ask myself "Am I *sure* this is the most interesting and the clearest possible way? Why this way and not another? Does the idea fit *this* character at *this* moment?" Am I just getting attached to the idea? Is my ego too involved with it? The hardest part of animating a shot for me is answering these questions. So many ideas seem to be good, but you know there's that one out there that will really make the character come alive and the shot shine. You have to relentlessly hunt it down.

Now! You are the hunter, seeking out the clearest and most interesting way to convey the acting and thoughts of your character in the shot. Go get 'em, tiger!

1975

CGI TEAPOT IS CREATED TO TEST RENDER-ING ALGORITHMS: Martin Newell (Utah) developed a CGI teapot. The Utah teapot was modeled by Martin Newell as a test object for many of the rendering algorithms, including bump mapping.

1975

JET PROPULSION LABORATORY OPENS A GRAPHICS LAB: Bob Holzman, a member of the JPL technical staff, thought it might be worthwhile for an artist to have access to a high-level computer graphics system, and that was the beginnings of the JPL graphics lab.

Thinking and Planning

Visualize what the core of the scene is. Is the character angry, happy, or possibly disturbed? Is there a character arc throughout the scene? What is really being said between the lines of the dialogue? What happened in the scenes previous to this shot, and what happens in those that follow? What significance does this scene have to the previous and later shots? No matter how short a scene is, there is always a beginning, middle, and an end.

Before touching the computer you must think about your scene. Thinking and planning are the answers to creating a solid performance. This is also the fun part of animation. It is between you and your scene, and it should be treated as an exciting opportunity to explore and experiment rather than a chore you have to tackle before you get to the fun of actual animation. This is about the only place your ideas will be untouched and pure. Great animation comes from the depth and feeling. These are moments that make you think. Stay critical of your work. If you do not think about the scene from beginning to end, the piece will be muddled and ideas will not be clear. Dave Zaboski explains how he starts a scene:

> I go over it in my head about a thousand times. I think about my scene all of the time. I don't even start to draw until I have every frame clear in my head. Especially when the pressure is on, I make it a rule to not even start to draw for the first day that I get a scene.

Planning helps any creative pursuit maintain focus and clarity. The creative process can have a meandering path at times. If you plan for the important ideas to be structured within the scene, the acting and motion will be clear and will prevent you from over-animating the character. Planning is one of the most important steps you can take. Cameron Miyasaki explains how he approaches planning for a shot:

> I typically spend a good amount of time planning what I want to accomplish in the scene before I actually start animating. I think about what the point of the scene is (how the scene fits into the plot of the movie), the characters' attitudes at this moment (what they are thinking and feeling, which may be different from what they are saying), and how I can communicate all of this clearly through my animation.

While you're visualizing the scene, use stream of consciousness notes to help narrow the scope. Only when you think about the demands of the scene will you begin to get to the heart of its story and understand how

1975

COONSKIN OPENS: One of the most controversial films ever made, Bakshi's _Coonskin_ is a violent portrayal of Harlem street life and the black condition of the 1970s. _Coonskin_ opened to much controversy and protests by the Congress of Racial Equality, leading Paramount Pictures to withdraw the film's release.

1976

COMPUTER GRAPHICS LABORATORY AT NYIT FOUNDED: The first computer graphics application NYIT focused on was 2D animation and creating tools to assist traditional animators. With Ed Catmull at the helm, they also developed a "tween tool" and a scan-and-paint system for pencil-drawn animation. This would later evolve into Disney's CAPS (_Computer Animation Production System_).

101

to tackle the poses and acting necessary to convey this to the audience. Spend some time discovering what the character's motivation is and how that can be revealed in the performance. These subtle nuances in acting and attitude are the cornerstones to creating a character who the audience will relate to and empathize with. Your goal is to create a character that moves you, not just moves to the dialogue.

If you have a soundtrack or dialogue for the scene, start there. Listen to the dialogue and observe the pauses and accented points that you might not catch when you are actually listening to what is being said. Find the words that have the biggest accent and play up to those beats with pauses and motion creating contrasts in timing. Mike Surrey thinks about his scenes by listening to the track. He says:

> "Many times I sit and think things through for hours. I get accused of sleeping at my desk from time to time, but I'm really animating. No lie. After working out a lot of the basic timing, I'll get up and act out what I was thinking. This gives me new ideas and some more stuff to think about regarding balance and timing."
>
> —Brian Dowrick

I'll close my eyes and have it playing on a loop and will just let it go. I'm sure if you came into my office it would look like I'm sleeping, but I'm listening, trying to envision the performance. This exciting step might go on for about an hour before I'll draw a single line.

Under intense deadlines you might think that this is a waste of time. To think about the scene for a whole day without actually working on the computer to block anything out sounds crazy, right? No! It's the sanest thing you can do before animating. This is because you *are* animating during this step. You are *Thinking Animation*. Once you know what your plan is for the shot, you are halfway there. Understand that the creative process is a complex and organic journey. You can veer from the plan as you discover new and better ways to animate the scene. Just start with a general plan for the scene so you have a foundation on which to build. As Keith Roberts puts it:

If you animate without a plan of what the scene needs to be, you will waste bucket-loads of time.

OSCAR FOR *LEISURE* (FILM AUS-TRALIA): *Leisure*, directed by Bruce Petty, one of Australia's best known political satirists and cartoonists, won Best Short Subject: Animated Films.

APPLE COMPUTER BEGINS: Apple Computer was founded in Mountain View, California, on April 1, 1976, by Steve Jobs, Steve Wozniak, and Ronald Wayne, to sell the Apple I personal computer kit for $666.66. They were hand-built in Jobs' parents' garage, and the Apple I was first shown to the public at the Homebrew Computer Club.

If the thinking and planning step is the blueprint for what you are going to do with your scene, then gathering reference and acting it out are the building blocks for actually implementing that plan.

Thinking and planning for a scene. Sketches by Dave Zaboski.

Using Reference and Acting It Out

One of the most important aspects of animation is observation. Through observation even the most uneducated eye knows whether movement is believable and acting is accurate. From the time we are born, we observe every nuance in the motions of those around us. Both mechanics of motion and acting in all living things are very specific. The animator must observe, catalog, and translate that observation clearly, or

1976

FUTUREWORLD **DIGITIZES PETER FONDA'S HEAD AND MATERIALIZES WARRIORS:** Peter Fonda's head was digitized and rendered by III for *Futureworld*, the sci-fi sequel to the film *Westworld* and the first film to use 3D computer graphics. In addition, robot Samurai warriors needed to materialize; to accomplish this, III digitized still photographs of the warriors, then used image-processing techniques to manipulate the digitized images and make the warriors materialize over the background.

1976

BLINN SHADER IS INTRODUCED: Jim Blinn introduces environmental mapping. Blinn was a pioneer of texture mapping and light reflection on curved surfaces.

believability will be lost. Mike Surrey has a story describing how reference footage helped him define a character in the movie *Tarzan*:

> The ability to create a pleasing design for me comes from studying the character I'm attempting to animate. I will start by looking at as much footage of the voice actor as possible, trying to find anything to exploit. For example, on *Tarzan* I had the pleasure of studying Rosie O'Donnell, who has a huge, square head with her facial features all pushed to the middle. I started by trying to do a caricature and pull the design of Terk off that drawing. It's a process that takes me multiple passes.

Reference is the one thing that will help your scene look convincing. If you can find reference of how the character should be moving through videotaping yourself or other animators, finding footage online that has a similar action, locating footage of the character animated previously and successfully, using footage from the dialogue recording of the voice talent, or using any other kind of reference, do it! An example of using the recording footage of the talent would be Melanie Griffith, who voiced the little bird, Margalo, in *Stuart Little 2*. Many times the talent will deliver a more genuine performance because they are not acting for a camera; they are acting for the microphone. Melanie has a little habit of clearing her throat after each line delivered. She makes a girlish expression as she does this. It added charm to the Margalo character when animators used this almost imperceptible gesture that you wouldn't have picked up had you not watched the video reference.

Trying to guess what you know in your head to be realistic motion and shapes never compares to actually viewing that action frame by frame. Eric Goldberg tells the story about his most difficult animation task ever because of his lack of reference while working at Richard Williams' Animation Studio in London:

> At Richard Williams I had to do a commercial with Superman in it, and the agency wanted a kind of Neal Adams Superman. That was tough because I hadn't done a lot of realistic animation and we had to draw it on cel with grease pencil. Fortunately, Dick set up the leica reel for me. There were some things I had to change, though. I did get the benefit of some of Dick's good drawings to start with. It was difficult to make convincing comic-book animation with no reference. At the time, it was the hardest thing I had ever done.

1976

EXHIBITORS ALLOWED AT SIGGRAPH: The ACM allowed exhibitors in the annual SIGGRAPH conference for the first time.

1977

OSCAR FOR *SAND CASTLE* (*CHATEAU DE SABLE* - NFB): This claymation short won 23 awards, including the Academy Award for Best Short Subject: Animated Films.

1977

SINGLE FRAME VIDEO TAPE TRANSFER SYSTEMS ARE DEVELOPED: Single frame video tape animation systems were introduced. Used for pencil testing, they were a major development in the production of animation.

Observing reference for motion or dialogue will help you more easily visualize what can be very complex movement and show the intent to the audience more clearly. Why not use every tool you possibly can to make your scene great? Reference helps you plan out what works for the scene and what doesn't. Reference material also helps you stay honest to the character's personality and design. It helps you with timing and ensures you haven't chosen too many poses for the time allotted. It can help you pre-edit your acting choices. Carlos Baena talks about the importance of reference in planning his animation:

> In terms of the characters to be animated in the scene, I prepare myself with as much reference material as I can regarding whatever I have to animate. If I'm animating a character, I look for things such as model sheets, animation tests of whatever has been done with the character previously, even things such as video/film reference of actions or characters that have similar things that I can use on my shots.

Inspirational things come out of reference footage for your scenes too! If you are acting out a scene yourself in front of a camera or a mirror, you will observe little things that happen that you would never have discovered otherwise. Don Waller has a great story from his days at ILM that illustrates this point:

> Acting out the action yourself can help a great deal. A video camera really comes in handy at times to capture certain actions. On *Jurassic Park*, a number of us went out into the parking lot at ILM and pretended we were a herd of Gallimimuses leaping over a log! The action was filmed, and it helped considerably in getting a feel for the energy of the herd, but one accident helped to incorporate an inspired bit of action into the sequence as well. One of ILM's artists, also recruited to play a Gallimimus, unfortunately fell and broke his arm that day. So we stuck a few stumbling dinos into the sequence, as an homage to this poor artist who performed above and beyond the call of duty! I believe it added a neat little detailed, realistic touch to the frenzy of the scene.

1977

VISUAL EFX CATEGORY ADDED TO THE ACADEMY AWARDS: The Academy of Motion Picture Arts and Sciences introduces a Visual Effects category for the Oscars.

1977

R/GREENEBRG FOUNDED: Founded in 1977 by brothers Richard and Robert Greenberg, whose pioneering achievements in computer-assisted filmmaking earned their company a technical Academy Award.

1977

THE MANY ADVENTURES OF WINNIE THE POOH 22ND FEATURE FOR DISNEY: *The Many Adventures of Winnie the Pooh* is a full-length animated film based upon the *Winnie the Pooh* books by A. A. Milne.

By acting out a performance, you can discover all kinds of nuances, like Don Waller tells us in his story about animators on *Jurassic Park*. Sketch by Floyd Norman.

Another great tool is to utilize those around you. You can act out your scene, but how would the guy next to you do it? If you have other people act out your scene too, you get even more ideas on how to solve the issues with the shot. You can direct that person because you're watching, not performing. You will get some of your best ideas from this technique. Look at the scenes around your shot as a point of reference, as well. Research is so important to making your choices believable. Tony Bancroft offers more insight on his first steps to animating a scene:

I look at the scenes around it to check for hookups. I ask myself, "What is the purpose of this scene in the movie?" That question always helps me to not overthink the acting.

1977

WIZARDS BY RALPH BAKSHI: *Wizards* was originally to be entirely cel-animated from scratch, but because of budget problems, Ralph Bakshi was unable to complete the battle sequences. As a result, he finished his film by paying out of his own pocket and using rotoscoping for the unfinished sequences. The art in this film is heavily influenced by Vaughn Bode's *Cheech Wizard* comics and has inspired many street and graffiti artists of today.

1977

PETE'S DRAGON RELEASED: *Pete's Dragon* is a live-action movie, but its title character, a dragon named Elliott, is animated. This was Don Bluth's biggest influence on a Disney film, and Ken Anderson designed the dragon.

The scenes leading up to and after your shot will give you a point of reference for the state of mind of your character. Now, play that moment out to understand the meaning behind the action. When acting out a scene, you begin to really feel what is going on physically and mentally. Acting it out for reference is the best way to observe how the scene feels and to try to live inside the head of your character. Victor Huang tells us why his new digital camera is his best friend:

> I picked up this [digital] camera that shoots full-motion video and copies MPEGs right to your computer. It's my new best friend when it comes to planning a scene. Acting an entire scene out lets you "animate" it 10 different ways without setting a single key frame. From there you can pick out your favorite performance. Acting is essential to my prep time before starting a scene.

Finally, acting out the scene as a form of reference will help you get all of the different ideas out of your system, concentrating more and more on the goal of the scene. Improv actors have many warm-up exercises they do before performing. These exercises help the improvisers get rid of all of the trite and used ideas in their head and start a more evolutionary and organic approach to their scenes. You need to have fun exploring your own interpretation of what the acting should be. If YOU were the character, how would you do it? Conrad Vernon offers his approach to providing reference for his animators on *Shrek*:

> On *Shrek*, when I was giving direction on a scene, I would get up and say, "Here is a suggestion for the acting the way I see it." I would get up there and literally act it out. They would sketch my poses every once in a while. I would give them ideas, and sometimes they filmed it. I would go to their desks and re-act it out for them because I knew what I wanted in my head. The animators will come up with such great stuff. You give them the raw materials, and they make it work. I get up and act it out, and I do the body language to it. They take an impression away with them. They don't film me and then literally match my every move. They are looking and they say to themselves, "Okay, I get it. I see what he is going for." It's never that literal, thank goodness. They do take an impression away, and what we see next is their interpretation, which is really, really great.

1977

THE RESCUERS 23RD FEATURE FOR DISNEY: *The Rescuers* was inspired by a series of children's novels by Margery Sharp.

1977

DEATH STAR SIM USING GRASS PROGRAMMING LANGUAGE: Larry Cuba produced Death Star simulation for *Star Wars* using Grass at UICC developed by Tom DeFanti at Ohio State. GRASS (Graphics Symbiosis System) was a programming language created to script visual animations in 2D.

1977

RAGGEDY ANN & ANDY: A MUSICAL ADVENTURE FIRST ANIMATED MOVIE BASED ON A TOY: *Raggedy Ann & Andy: A Musical Adventure* was directed by Richard Williams, who reluctantly took over after Abe Levitow's death.

107

Hard at work. Sketch by Dave Zaboski.

1977

**FRANK CROW CRE-
ATES ANTI-ALIASING:**
Frank Crow created innovations in anti-aliasing and
shading algorithms.

1978

**OSCAR FOR *SPECIAL DELIVERY*
(NFB):** *Special Delivery* won the Best
Short Subject: Animated Films Oscar
and numerous other international hon-
ors, including top prize at the Zagreb
Animation Festival in the former nation
of Yugoslavia.

1978

**DIGITAL EFFECTS (DE) IS
FOUNDED:** DE was the first CG house
in New York and was one of the first companies to establish itself as a contributor to
the film industry in a big way. They teamed
with Abel, MAGI, and III to contribute to
the motion picture *Tron*.

This is what acting out your scene does for you before actually animating. Whether you are using a pencil or a computer, this step is crucial. Don't worry about making a fool of yourself jumping around and acting out at your desk, because the animators around you understand what you are doing. If they are not animators, then just do what Corey Florimonte does, and they will stay far away from you and let you work (because they will think you are crazy):

> Before I start animating a scene, I like to think of how I would do the action myself. Generally, that gives me a great idea of what not to do with the animation because it is usually not broad enough. After that is established, I try to find the other extreme—to go completely overboard on the motion. This is where I like to start acting out the part in my cubicle or in the hallway, especially if there is running and jumping involved. Be careful, though—non-animators tend not to understand when you come flying around a corner and crash into them. If this happens, you should simply state, "This is gonna be great—you've really helped me nail down this character!" and run back to your desk, put your headphones on, and pretend you've been struck by the lightning bolt of inspiration until they stop staring at you. Generally you'll find the action you want somewhere within these two extremes.

Acting out a scene as a form of reference will help you escape stale and cliché ideas when posing your scenes and will tighten up the ideas you have for the shot. It's one of the most organic ways to really walk in your character's shoes. Video reference is a great tool to use when acting out your scenes because you can be "in the moment" and watch that recorded. If you use the reference footage loosely and stylize it into exaggerated moments, you will come up with some really creative performances.

Gesture Drawings and Thumbnails

What is a gesture drawing? What is a thumbnail? Animators have different ideas of what these two tools are and how they help create a plan for their animation. Essentially these steps are a visual shorthand. Gesture and thumnnail drawings are the first steps in creating a good performance.

You do not have to be the most amazing draftsman to make use of this step. Drawing a pose (even if it's a simple stick figure) helps you see the graphic intent behind its meaning. We all know that crossed arms

1978

FRANK THOMAS AND OLLIE JOHNSTON RETIRE FROM DISNEY: Frank Thomas and Ollie Johnston (two of the Nine Old Men) retired from Disney.

1978

AARDMAN ANIMATION ESTABLISHED: Peter Lord and Davis Sproxton established Aardman Animation in England. Aardman's first feature film, *Chicken Run*, was released in June 2000.

1978

JOHN BRAY DIES: John Randolph Bray (1879–1978) patented many of his improvements on the animation process. One of these innovations was the use of translucent paper to make it easier to position objects in successive drawings.

usually mean someone is closed off or steepled hands mean the character is judging. These are physical gestures that tell you what a character is thinking. Your gesture drawings are key to getting that attitude into your animation. Larry Weinberg says it best:

> You have to know what your character is doing and thinking, and you have to play it out in your mind. And even if you are doing your animation on the computer, you should draw it out on paper completely. Drawing makes you think deeply. I can't stress this enough.

Gesture drawings by Jamie Oliff.

VIDEO LASERDISC (LD) IS INVENTED: The laserdisc was the first commercial optical disc storage medium, and was used primarily for the presentation of movies. This technology provided a cleaner way for animators to do frame-by-frame study of animation, since video tape would have visual striations between frames, making it hard to read.

1978

BLINN INTRODUCES BUMP MAPPING: Blinn devised new methods to represent how objects and light interact in a three-dimensional virtual world, such as environment mapping and bump mapping.

110

The gesture-drawing step is one of the most organic parts of the process in planning for a scene of animation. A gesture drawing holds a lot of information because it's loose and shows a line of action and intent behind the pose. Chris Bailey says gesture drawings are his first attempt at laying out his thoughts about a scene:

> Think, then do a number of little gesture sketches. I'll do many of these before I even thumbnail a shot. It's generally a good idea to know where you're going before setting a single key frame.

In contrast to a gesture, which holds a lot of information, a thumbnail is more of a rough snapshot of an idea. It's a small, quick sketch that implies the framework of an acting choice or pose. Thumbnails are used in the development of storyboards and should be one of the many tools an animator has on his or her tool belt to create believable acting in animation.

Thumbnail drawings by Jamie Oliff.

1978

THE LORDS OF THE RINGS BY BAKSHI OPENS: This was the first successful attempt to film the epic novel. Much of the film used live-action footage, which was then rotoscoped to produce an animated look.

1979

THE BLACK HOLE USES CGI IN THE OPENING: Disney's 1979 sci-fi movie, The Black Hole, used CGI for the opening. The film was nominated for cinematography and visual effects Academy Awards. This first PG-rated Disney film led the company to experiment with more adult-oriented films, which would eventually lead to the creation of its Touchstone Pictures arm to handle films considered too mature to carry the Walt Disney label.

111

Thumbnails take the movement described in the gesture drawings and simplify these ideas into distinct poses to be used in the animation. Mike Surrey describes his use of gesture drawings and thumbnails when envisioning his scenes:

> I'll still listen to the track, but I'll concentrate on small chunks of the dialogue, stopping it periodically to draw out some ideas. These drawings are far from pretty. They are little gesture drawings to get the idea of the pose I want. Sometimes I'll write notes beside them to fill in any info the drawing doesn't have. A lot of times I will spend the first day with the scene doing nothing more than listening and thumbnailing. The pressures a production can put on you for footage make you feel like you're wasting time because you're not animating, but quite the opposite happens. You actually are saving time because you have created a blueprint for your scene and now can spend the rest of the week concentrating on just hitting the poses with your pencil or mouse.

Thumbnailing is the best way to narrow the scope of all those great ideas you had during the thinking process. This step simplifies the ideas and creates a clear and direct line to the heart of the scene. However, everyone has a different approach to how they use thumbnails and gestures while thinking about their animation. The creative process is a winding path, so find your own workflow. While Mike Surrey likes to rely heavily on stream-of-consciousness drawing of many thumbnails to get to the heart of the scene, Ethan Hurd likes to go straight to his first impression of what the heart of the scene is and develop that idea through thumbnails:

> I don't thumbnail in order—you know, pose one, two, three. Instead I'll thumbnail out first what's important to the shot. I may not even draw the whole body. I'll just draw the hands or the feet or something. Whatever I think is most important. I try a dozen different ways of doing an action to figure out what's best. Once I feel like I know where I'm going with the important stuff, I'll then start to thumbnail the surrounding poses—the poses that are important to get the idea across but less important than the main idea. Once I feel that I have thumbnailed enough that I've wrapped my brain around an action, I'll number the thumbnails in order and make sure they flow together.

1979

DAVE FLEISCHER DIES: David Fleischer (1894–1979) was a German-American animator, film director, and film producer, best known as a co-owner of Fleischer Studios with his older brother, Max Fleischer. From 1921 to 1942 Fleischer supervised Talkartoons, Betty Boop Cartoons, Popeye the Sailor, Color Classics, and several others.

1979

TURNKEY ANIMATION SYSTEMS DEVELOPED: The term "turnkey" is also often used in the technology industry, most commonly to describe pre-built computer "packages" in which everything needed to perform a certain type of task (e.g. video/audio editing) is put together by the supplier and sold as a bundle. This often includes a computer with preinstalled software, various types of hardware, and accessories.

Every animator has his or her own method for creating a great performance. Almost all great animators agree that designing the performance with some kind of sketches will keep your ideas simple and clear. The traditional methods of planning for a shot, which include reference and acting it out, as well as drawing gestures and thumbnails, drive CG animation forward as a more entertaining medium and art form. Instead of just sitting down at the computer and animating away, this is where you begin to *visually think animation*.

Sharing

Now you know what the scene is about and what ideas you want to present in the scene. Why not talk about it with your peers? A fresh eye or perspective can help you see things in your scene that you might not have alone. Just show it to a few animators and see what they think of your approach. For example, Mike Surrey shares his scenes in this way:

> Once I have explored as much as possible, I will show a fellow animator to get their opinion and even have them draw over my drawing to get their take. Seeing someone else drawing over your drawing provides a fountain of information and hopefully, with every pass you take on that design, it will improve.

On big shows, it's usually difficult to get much time with the supervisors outside of the short time you have with them in dailies. Be proactive about sharing your ideas and getting feedback from the people around you. Stay tight with the folks working on the shots on either side of your shot, too. Continuity will depend on your communication with these animators. The other animators on your show are sitting in dailies with you and might even be more familiar with the shots that are before and after yours. They might be able to provide more insight into the directive of your particular shot within the movie. Talking with the animators around you helps you reinforce the effectiveness of your own ideas and what works, as well as gives you a fresh impression of what the scene should be about.

Ten Things to Think About

Armed with the steps to thinking about your animation, what exactly do you start asking yourself, and what should you think about? Here are 10 ideas to think about and consider regarding the scene and your characters specifically. Consider these 10 concepts while designing the acting and movement of your character.

1979

OSCAR FOR *EVERY CHILD* (NFB): Winner of 12 awards, including the Academy Award for Best Short Subject: Animated Films, *Every Child* was produced at the invitation of the United Nations Organization to celebrate UNICEF's Declaration of Children's Rights.

1979

LUCASFILM GRAPHICS GROUP FORMED: George Lucas hires Ed Catmull, Ralph Guggenheim, and Alvy Ray Smith to form the Lucasfilm Computer Graphics and Special Effects Group. This new group worked with Lucasfilm artists and programmers to create the first 100-percent digitally animated character in a theatrical release, which was a stained-glass knight in the movie *Young Sherlock Holmes*.

Listen

Listening is a broad term. At the same time, listening is very specific to understanding the focus of the shot. First, listening to your supervisor will get you halfway there because he was prepped by the director and was told what the director expects to see in dailies. Directors work closely with the storyboard artist, so listen to how the boards present the reason for this shot to be in the film. Story is key, so listen to the story being presented in the previous and latter shots as well. Dave Zaboski says:

> There is no best way. Stories unfold themselves if we really listen. If you have time constraints, listen to the story. Detach yourself from the shiny parts and let the story tell you what is essential. Listen.

Listen to the dialogue. Ask yourself what is really being said in the words. Listen for arcs in the voice and acting choices you can make to reinforce the energy in the dialogue. Cameron Miyasaki says:

> If there is dialogue, I listen to the track repeatedly to find the little nuances of the delivery and changes in attitude that I can apply to my animation. Only after going through this process and feeling comfortable with my decisions do I begin animating.

Listen to the input you get from other animators and your supervisor. Even if you do not agree, if you commit to what they are telling you about the scene, you will produce a concise and clear idea—the idea the director is looking for in his film.

Remember the 10 concepts we have discussed and implement them into your thinking process before animating, and the result will be a clear and unique performance.

Equipped with these 10 ideas and your new planning process of sketching, acting it out, and sharing with other animators, you should know how to think before ever touching a computer to animate! You are there to communicate, not to impress, and thinking about your performance will help you communicate the idea more clearly. Now, let's talk about animating!

> **"Find the truth or meaning of the movements a character makes in a scene. Don't just move him to move him. If your character makes a gesture in accordance with some dialogue, it should help to express either what he is saying or what he is not."**
>
> **—Tony Bancroft**

1979

JOHN LASSETER GRADUATES CAL ARTS: John Lasseter graduated Cal Arts and went on to work for Disney Studios for five years, where he became inspired by computer animation in the film *Tron*.

1980

PDI FOUNDED: Pacific Data Images (PDI) was started by Carl Rosendahl, Glenn Entis, and Richard Chuang. PDI developed their own animation and graphics software environment, which included an animation scripting language, modeling, rendering, and motion design programs, all written in C. In 2000, DreamWorks SKG entered into an agreement to acquire the majority interest of PDI.

Subtext

Adding subtext is one of the best ways to get depth and dimension into your performance. Every piece of dialogue, no matter how simple, has a subtext. If your character made a statement earlier in the film and later makes another statement proving that he was lying earlier, this adds subtext to the line of dialogue. The audience doesn't necessarily need to know the character's long-term purpose, but that long-term purpose affects the character's short-term actions. Listening is the building block to finding the subtext in your character. Dave Brewster says:

> Human beings are multilevel creatures that are often far more than they seem. We can be saying one thing while completely meaning another. Oh, and what makes us interesting are our flaws. Perfection is totally boring to me.

Perfection is something that is easy to create with a computer. Subtext makes the computer-generated characters seem more real, and any animation express humanity. Humans have flaws. They lie. They get sick. They have ulterior motives. They are allergic to peanuts. They have been hurt by other people. Dig underneath and listen to what the character is *really* saying. Mike Murphy says:

> I always strive to consider the subtext of the scene. If the character is saying "I love you," what's he really saying? If he's saying it to his mom, it's different than sarcastically saying it to his brother or his enemy. That's subtext, and sometimes we say the opposite of what we feel.

"Subtext is all that's underneath the dialogue. The inner dialogue the character may be having with himself is subtext. I think it's a treat to any animator to have the opportunity to work on those kinds of shots where the character is not saying as much, where it's the actual thinking process that is doing the talking for the character. Also, acting doesn't have to be big or broad with big gestures and big actions. Sometimes smaller actions and subtlety are more effective and touch people even more."

—*Carlos Baena*

1980

OSCAR FOR *A LEGY (THE FLY)* (PANNONIA STUDIOS): *A Légy* won the Best Short Subject: Animated Films Oscar.

1980

FRED "TEX" AVERY DIES: There is a story that Disney did not want his animators to see Tex Avery films because they were too extreme in their humor and animation. Tex directed some of the most outrageously funny cartoons of the '40s and '50s. One of Avery's most famous characters was Red from *Red Hot Riding Hood* and other films. Tex was instrumental in the development of Bugs Bunny and Daffy Duck.

The character does not have to speak in order to demonstrate the subtext of the scene. Eye darts and avoidance of eye contact or any other little textural quality added to the quiet moments will add depth. Ask yourself what the character is thinking. How is the character feeling?

Subtext is the dialogue of the mind translated through actions. Picture this. You've got a loaf of banana bread and you taste it. You think to yourself, "Wow! This bread is really good!" What is that flavor that is making this bread so good? Subtext is that almost imperceptible ingredient baked into the heart of the scene that raises it from a good scene to one that is great.

Experiment

Experimenting is one of the more fun parts of the whole process. This is when you, as an animator, can try to break all of the formulas and rules you have learned to create something original. Try every possible idea that comes to you. Taking this time will give you options that will improve your initial ideas. Don't be afraid, be bold! This is the most creative part of animating, so see how far you can expand your ideas. Do not let the left side of your brain take over and start analyzing and tearing your ideas apart. Let your ideas flow and see where you go. You will end up with the most unique and interesting approaches. If your ideas support the directive of the scene as you expirement, they will be successful. By experimenting, you have the ability to make a heartfelt scene. You can explore like comedians and improvisers do to create something utterly hilarious and offbeat. Something different! Larry Weinberg says:

> Trust yourself. If it moves you, give it a chance. Don't hold back. *Monty Python* had a great working principle. They went with any idea one of them had, even if others didn't like it. They gave anything a chance to live on. Sometimes this resulted in a failed skit, but other times the results were completely unexpected and fantastic. If they had held back during early conceptualizing, they wouldn't have reached the unusual peaks they reached.

When you think about pushing the limits of the scene through experimentation, you can begin to embrace the concepts of caricature and exaggeration. These are the things animation can do that live action cannot. Welcome the idea of experimenting.

1980

DONKEY KONG INTRODUCED: *Donkey Kong* was introduced by Nintendo. Like many Nintendo franchises, *Donkey Kong* was created by Shigeru Miyamoto.

1980

HANNA-BARBERA STARTS USING COMPUTERS: In the 1970s, Marc Levoy developed an early computer-assisted cartoon animation system, which was used by Hanna-Barbera Productions to produce *The Flintstones*, *Scooby-Doo*, and other shows.

1980

QUANTEL INTRODUCES PAINTBOX: In 1981, Quantel released the Paintbox, an extremely advanced television graphics system for its time. Paintboxes are still in use today due to their image quality and versatility.

Dave Brewster says:

Animation is a caricature. The job is to capture the impression, not to imitate. Animation can play with time—compress or expand as well as push action to its limit.

Animators attending an animation lecture. Sketch by Dave Zaboski.

1981

OSCAR FOR *CRAC* (FREDERIC BACK): Frederic Back directed and animated the industrialization of Montreal, as seen from the point of view of a rocking chair, called *Crac*. In 1981, *Crac* won the Academy Award for Best Short Subject: Animated Films.

1981

STEVE BOSUSTOW DIES: Steve Bosustow (1912–1981) became head of UPA in the 1950s. He helped start a studio first known as United Film Production, where they were able to apply their ideas of animation. One cartoon they made was *Hell-Bent for Election*, a film made for the re-election campaign of FDR. With its sudden fame from the film, the studio renamed itself United Productions of America (UPA).

The best actors and comedians experiment and ad lib their scenes over and over. This might drive the director crazy using up loads of film in a day, but the final scenes they get from that kind of energy are more true and honest. Most directors of live-action films, especially comedy, have an open kind of ad-lib process in which actors will try a scene several times to really get to the heart of it and how the lines should be read and the performance should come across. This same experimentation applied to animation will push your scenes to create something new and exciting to watch.

Rhythm

Rhythm is a broad term that can be applied in very specific ways. First there is rhythm in timing. Just like music, animation has a rhythm that is important to the storytelling. Rhythm helps build excitement in a scene. There is a beginning, middle, and an end to most scenes and sequences. A great example of rhythm happening throughout a sequence would be in the short film *The Little Whirlwind*. This short begins with Mickey Mouse catching a whiff of Minnie Mouse's cake cooling in the window. He makes a deal with Minnie to clean up the yard to get a bite of her cake when it is done. The rhythm of the scene is bouncing along nicely with Mickey jumping around raking leaves in the yard until the little whirlwind enters the scene. The scene heightens with frenzied motion as the little whirlwind plays jokes on Mickey and messes up the leaves in the yard after he has cleaned them all. The antics between Mickey and the little whirlwind become more intense as the scene moves along, until papa whirlwind comes along and is a full-fledged tornado! Papa whirlwind tears the yard to shreds, so that when Minnie comes outside with the cake, the yard is worse than before and Mickey gets a cake in the face.

This is an example of rhythm throughout an entire short film, and how it flows and builds. Think about the rhythm within your scene and also how it plays out in the course of the whole sequence. An example of a great beat that happens within a shot inside of a building sequence would be in the movie *The Incredibles*. There is a moment when Mr. Incredible comes home from work and, as he gets out of the car, he slips on a skateboard in the driveway. Next, he bends the roof of the car with his hand as he tries to gain his balance, which in turn makes it impossible for him to close the door to the car. As he tries to close that door, the energy of the scene builds and builds until he finally loses his temper and slams the door with such force that the glass shatters. Now completely losing it, he picks the car up and lifts it over his head, ready to toss it, when he notices the neighborhood boy sitting on a tricycle in the driveway watching him. That moment—that shot of the little boy in awe of Mr. Incredible holding the car over his head—is priceless. It's a quiet beat that is so poignant in contrast with Mr. Incredible's outburst over the car.

1981

DIGITAL PRODUCTIONS FORMED: After *Tron*, Demos and Whitney left III to form a new computer graphics company called Digital Productions. They landed their first major film contract to create the special effects for *The Last Starfighter*. Digital Productions invested in a Cray X-MP supercomputer to help process the computer graphics frames. The effects were impressive and photorealistic, but the movie still didn't make Hollywood sit up and take notice of computer graphics.

1981

LOOKER IS FIRST FILM WITH CG SHADED GRAPHICS: *Looker* includes the virtual human character, Cindy. It is the first film with shaded graphics (III).

In music, this kind of beat is called a *caesura*, or a break in the flow of a rhythmic melody marking a point of division. The final end to this caesura is when the little boy's bubblegum pops across his face. This is not only a humorous moment, but it is timed perfectly to the rhythm of the scene. Dan Fowler explains more about the relationship between music and beats in dialogue:

> Before I begin blocking out my animation, I look for all of the hits, pacing, or where the important actions take place. I look for the rhythm of the animation. In my opinion, all animation and action are based on rhythm. I've been playing drums and music for 20 years, and the first thing I figured out about animation and production is 30 frames per second for TV and video and 24 fps for film. Time is segmented, and I have a way of precisely finding, or counting, frames to find where my action will land. It's very helpful for me to break everything down into frames and timings. Find where your hits, or beats, are in frames, and then it's easy to map out where everything will land.

Rhythm has a second application to animation. It can also be described in the poses you create. Once you know where the first pose will be, you must find a rhythm in breakdowns and poses that takes you to the next and the next. If the character is bent in one direction on one pose, the rhythm should flow to arc in an opposite way on the next pose. The force and the flow you apply to each pose are important in creating a rhythm to the motion. If your character is reaching for something and is making a kind of "C" shape to reach for it, the next pose should be a reversal of that "C" shape as he retrieves it, moving into a reverse "C" shape with the line of action.

This will create a clean flow and rhythm in your character's movement. Physics plays a part, but you determine what is driving the forces and physics of your scene to keep the flow of the lines clean.

> "There is directionality and flow to creating poses as a complete thing. You know which way you are going with reversal, et cetera. You are not a slave to the physics. You are manipulating the physics to the point where they still work but everything is contributing to your pose."
>
> —*Troy Saliba*

1981

THE FOX AND THE HOUND 24TH FEATURE FOR DISNEY: *The Fox and the Hound* was the last work of three of Disney's original Nine Old Men: Frank Thomas, Ollie Johnston, and Woolie Reitherman.

1981

CRANSTON/CSURI PRODUCTIONS FORMS: In 1981, Chuck Csuri approached an investor to transfer the computer animation technology created in the CGRG lab to the commercial world, and Cranston/Csuri Productions, Inc. was formed. During its seven-year life, CCP produced almost 800 animation projects for more than 400 clients worldwide.

Just like in music, rhythm can be a nebulous and intuitive part of animation. Feel the rhythm as you watch your poses. Ask yourself whether that pose flows to the next in a pleasing way. If there is a stutter or a jitter or a wacky change of timing in the rhythm, ask yourself whether it is called for in the scene much like it's called for in music.

Empathize

Empathy is the core element of acting. If the audience does not empathize with your character, all is lost. No matter how short the shot is, there must be empathy. Empathy takes place when the audience sees something in that character they have experienced. Empathy is also when the viewer wants for your character the same thing the character wants for himself. The viewer is rooting for the character! Carlos Baena explains why he roots for the characters that are engaging in a movie:

> If the audience doesn't relate to the characters, then they'll either get bored or will not believe what's happening. From personality traits to everyday situations, mannerisms, and conversations, I love it when I go, "I've been in that exact same situation!" Right there, a connection gets started.

Animators are observers of life. Many take mental notes of people in their lives. For example, the crazy uncle who likes to drink strawberry milkshakes and make shadow puppets on the wall. The sweet grandmother who makes scrapbooks of everything her grandchildren do. Remember the bully who beat you up every day in the school yard? These are the characters in your day-to-day life that you can pull from to add empathy to your scenes.

By using various people and the impressions they have made on you in life, you can add to your stockpile of experience. You did not have to have the experience yourself; however, by adding human elements to the character that you see in people you have met or are related to, you add that extra little something that makes the character seem more real. Remember when we talked about observation and reference earlier?

1981

AMERICAN POP RELEASED: *American Pop* was a 1981 Ralph Bakshi animated film. The primary animation technique used was rotoscoping, but the film also used a variety of other mixed media, including watercolors, computer graphics, live-action shots, and archival footage. The film was rediscovered after animation went through a Renaissance upon the release of *Who Framed Roger Rabbit*.

1982

OSCAR FOR *TANGO* (ZINGIER RYBCZYNSKI): *Tango* won the Academy Award for Best Animated Short Film. It had 36 characters from different stages of life—representations of different times—interact in one room, moving in loops, observed by a static camera. Zingier had to draw and paint about 16,000 cel-mattes and make several hundred thousand exposures on an optical printer.

Ethan Hurd says:

> I believe that the audience needs to identify with either the characters or the situation. This doesn't mean that the characters need to be like the audience or that the situation has to be familiar to something the audience has experienced. It just has to have that ring of truth to it. You could tell a story about a hardened coal miner. I'm sure none of the audience has ever mined coal before. But if you do your research, find out how these people live, what they eat, what they listen to, how they get along with their families, friends, et cetera, you can uncover enough truth to connect with the audience. If the situation feels believable and has that ring of truth to it, audiences will connect.

Empathy is one of the strongest elements to breathing life into your characters and the scene. Picture your character as a longtime friend or an actor you would work with on set and get to know his personality. Many animators see the characters they work on as a family friend, a relative, or even a famous movie star they always wanted to work with. It's like hanging out with old buddies. If you empathize with the character you are animating, even if he happens to be a villain, you will infuse that character with the personality that the audience will relate to as well. If you animate through feeling first without worrying about how it looks, you will create empathy. Once you find your own empathy with the character you are animating, the audience will follow.

Simplify

The old saying Keep It Simple Stupid, or K.I.S.S., has been around for years. Simplicity applies to every single part of your animation: simplicity in rhythm, simplicity in poses, simplicity in your ideas, and simplicity in acting. Too many poses and acting choices will not communicate clearly. Animation is a visual communication, as in any art form. Paul Wood says:

> A memorable character is created through strong and deliberate acting. Stay clear of character behavior that is not important to the development of that character. You don't want the character to appear wishy-washy or overly complicated.

1982

THE SECRET OF NIMH FROM BLUTH STUDIOS: *The Secret of NIMH* garnered critical acclaim for being one of the most vibrantly animated films ever made. This is surprising considering a handful of independent animators led by Don Bluth animated the entire film in a garage over the course of two years.

1982

TRON RELEASED WITH MORE THAN 15 MINUTES OF CG: *Tron* was one of the first movies to contain 15 minutes and 235 scenes of computer-generated images. Though the movie has been criticized for poor acting and incoherence of plot, it is celebrated as a milestone of computer animation.

Simplicity will give the viewer's eye time to rest and appreciate the moment. The eye follows what is moving the most. Make the most amplified motion mean something. Be clear about your ideas first and lay them out simply, and then add any seasoning and life to those poses after you have ensured the ideas are clear. Otherwise, you can get lost in the madness of too many notes in the composition. Follow the directive of the scene.

Bert Klein tells us how to keep simplicity in mind:

> I guess the trick is to be clear first, then add interest second. Clarity is the most important but overlooked aspect.

Also, when you have more than one character in a scene, keep the poses simple so viewers can concentrate on what they should be looking at. You have control over this! It's best to take charge of the more aggressive character first when two interact. Keep the motion simple when you want to draw the focus. The eye will look for movement. If the audience should be hearing the dialogue of one character but observing the reaction of another, simplicity will help you focus the eye on that moment.

"When supervising, the thing I do most often is have the animator simplify what they've done. Time and again, animators—especially on the computer—will have too many things in motion, with too many conflicting pulls on the eye. Keep it simple and in order. A viewer can really only follow one motion at a time comfortably, so you need to have all movements work into each other and together to draw focus to the one thing that matters."

—Larry Weinberg

In addition, a character can hold completely motionless and still show emotion. Remember Tony Fucile's scene of Mr. Incredible in the early teaser trailer when he is looking at his belt on the floor? When Tony handed over his animation file to be rendered and lit, the lighter freaked out, thinking he had lost all of the

1982

***STAR TREK II: THE WRATH OF KHAN* GENESIS EFX:** ILM's computer graphics division developed Genesis effects for *Star Trek II: The Wrath of Khan*. It was the second feature film based on the popular *Star Trek* science-fiction television series. It is widely regarded by fans as the best film of the series.

1982

***VINCENT* SHORT FILM BY TIM BURTON:** *Vincent* is a 1982 short film written, designed, and directed by Tim Burton. It is a stop-motion tale set to a poem written by Burton. There is currently no individual release of the film, although it can be found on *The Nightmare Before Christmas* DVD as an extra. The film was narrated by Vincent Price, a lifelong idol and inspiration for Burton.

animation in the file. In truth, there was only one key frame for the entire scene. Talk about simplicity. Motion does not always equal emotion. Troy Saliba explains the need for simplicity:

> When you first start, the tendency is, "I am going to animate the crap out of this thing! I am going to put blood, sweat, and tears into this scene. I am going to move everything, and everything is going to be offset, and there is going to be overlapping action on top of overlapping action." It's the hardest thing to sit back and go, "Sometimes I really need to see what is going on in his eyes in this scene." So, I have to keep things still. It's the hardest thing to just not move it sometimes. What is important in this scene? Is it a physical comedy scene? Or is it a moment where I need to keep things still and just focus on one subtle thing? It's hard.

Simplicity results when you have exhausted all the other steps. Once you have experimented to find the best ideas, really listened to all of the input you are given, and gathered to find the heart of the scene, simplicity will rise to the top and stare you straight in the face. Give simplicity a big ol' hug and dump all that extra nonsense.

Texture

Texture is another broad term that can be applied specifically to different parts of animation. There is texture in timing. There is texture in poses. There is texture in contrasting the motion of two characters against one another. There is also texture in acting choices.

Talking first about texture in acting choices, psychological gesture is one of the most powerful tools an animator is armed with. An example of psychological gesture would be when a flight attendant is going through her normal everyday routine of telling passengers to put their seats and tray tables in their upright position, and then she sniffles and wipes her nose or yawns and puts her hand in front of her mouth. These gestures add texture to the initial directive of the scene. The scene is about the flight attendant. However, you may have a previous scene in which it was apparent that she was going through a lot. You can show this through psychological gestures such as yawns. Or, maybe she scratches her head because it's her first day and she is

1982

JIM CLARK FOUNDS SILICON GRAPHICS: Silicon Graphics, Inc., commonly called SGI, began as a maker of graphics display terminals. SGI focused its resources on creating the highest-performance graphics computers available.

1982

SKELETON ANIMATION SYSTEM DEVELOPED: The Skeleton Animation System (SAS) was developed at CGRG at Ohio State. Dave Zeltzer developed goal-directed motion description capabilities for skeletal and creature animation. His system and the underlying theories are some of the most significant contributions to the area of autonomous legged motion description in the discipline.

unsure of herself. This also falls back on subtext or finding the underlying meanings to the scene. As Keith Lango explains, texture adds more life to your shots through psychological gestures and acting choices:

> I like to have my characters interact with themselves in natural and comfortable ways. Scratch an ear, sniff their noses, play with their lip, fuss with their clothes, et cetera. It can become noise if used too much, but a little touch of something here and there can really ground a character as a real, living person. And if characters are of an appropriate relationship, I'll have them be more comfortable about touching each other as well.

One of the best ways to illustrate the need for texture in timing is when developing a moving hold in CG. In traditional animation, a kind of life is added to a moving hold once the drawing has been drawn over and over again while trying to hold the pose. The moving line that the animator adds, trying to draw the same drawing over and over again in a moving hold, creates a lifelike energy, vibration, and texture. In CG this kind of texture is harder to achieve because drawing is not involved and replicating a pose on the computer is easy. Troy Saliba explains the need for texture on a moving hold in CG:

> Moving holds are a lot harder in 3D than they are in 2D. You can get away with doing two drawings and a really big timing chart, and just the fact that somebody has to trace it over and over the line gives it some kind of life. 3D, it's just too perfect—like, "Whoa! You gotta add some kind of nuances in there and randomness to it." In order to get the randomness, parts have to break and parts have to be perfect.

Texture is what adds life to your animation. It is what makes your motion have charm beyond what the computer creates as a sterile in-between. If you have texture in your animation, no one will accuse it of being mechanical or spliney-looking. Spliney motion is the enemy of the animator and makes the motion look as if it's under water. Nik Ranieri illustrates why every frame of the motion counts:

1982

MORPHING IS DEVELOPED: Tom Brigham of NYIT astounded the audience at the 1982 SIGGRAPH conference with video sequence showing a woman distorting and transforming herself into the shape of a lynx. Thus was born a new technique called *morphing*. In 1987, Lucasfilm used the technique for the movie *Willow*.

1982

SYMBOLICS GRAPHIC DIVISION FOUNDED: The first CEO, chairman, and founder of Symbolics, Inc. was Russell Notfsker. Symbolics designed and manufactured a line of Lisp machines, single-user computers optimized to run the Lisp programming language. The Lisp machine was the first commercially available workstation (although that word had not yet been coined).

One of things about 3D that bothers me in the studio is there are people who think that once they set the keys, you don't have to do anything else! Like, you don't have to break down the lip-synch shape. In 2D, you have to draw that in. In 3D, it's open and it's closed. So, they are lazy. When you run it, it's okay—it's there—but it doesn't have any life to it. It doesn't have any squash and stretch. It doesn't feel alive because you haven't gone through it frame by frame and added life to it. I guess it's like working in 2D on fours and, yeah, it moves. It doesn't move convincingly, but it moves. It's hard to find people who have the desire to make every frame useful. I think that is what a lot of the computer guys do. They aren't thinking well-rounded visuals. That is why things look computery and floaty—because they are not thinking about texture and overlapping to make it come off as convincing and believable.

Another way texture can be employed in animation simply and clearly is by contrasting two characters. If one character has a fast, hyped energy and the other has a slower, more lethargic energy, the characters of both are reinforced by their contrasting styles of movement. This is a very successful way to illustrate contrasts and texture in your characters. Imagine a big burly man and his four-year-old daughter walking through an amusement park. One should have slow, steady movement, and the other can be light, indirect, and airy. CG animation has a way to go to really push the ideas that have been used for years in traditional animation. Eric Goldberg offers his favorite example of this in a Tex Avery scene from *Little Rural Riding Hood*:

The city wolf and the country wolf enter a nightclub, and the city wolf is leading the hick wolf by the hand. The hick wolf is kind if all over the place, going, "Girls, girls, bring on the girls!" The city wolf continues to walk smoothly with his nose up in the air like Ronald Coleman. We still do not see this in CG animation yet, where the entire body and posture are used to telegraph who the character is.

By using texture in your timing, poses, and acting choices, the animation will begin to have life and personality. Concentrate on simplicity and rhythm when adding texture, and you will bring a sense of believability to the character.

1982

WHERE THE WILD THINGS ARE TEST BY MAGI:
One of the more interesting productions created at MAGI was a test for Disney for the film *Where the Wild Things Are*, which used 3D scenes, camera control, and 2D character animation. This test was supervised by John Lasseter and used digital compositing to combine CG backgrounds and traditional animation.

1982

AUTODESK FOUNDED AND AUTOCAD RELEASED: Autodesk, Inc., a design software and digital content company, was founded by John Walker and 12 other cofounders in 1982. In 2006, Autodesk acquired Alias for $197 million, along with its 3D animation package, Maya. It is currently headquartered in San Rafael, California.

Honesty

Staying honest to the character is fundamental to your audience believing in your scene. A shy character would never just jump out front and center and do a dance. An angry character wouldn't act sympathetically to others. Of course, subtext can fly in the face of this idea, but those cases are very specific to acting outside of character. Brian Dowrick offers how Bugs Bunny stayed true and honest to his character:

> Making Bugs look stupid and inept is just too far out of character for him. He's always in control, even if he's losing.

If your character is sarcastic, dry, and unmotivated, the acting will typically remain simple and low key. If the character is wacky, hyper, and high-strung, the character would, in all likelihood, never become nonchalant about the things that happen to him in a story. You must get inside the head of your character, and then walk in his shoes. Character traits become familiar to the audience, and they empathize with those traits. When characters act against who they are and what they believe in, it kills the illusion and makes the acting and story weak. Why is your character doing what he is doing, what is his motivation, and would you do that if you were in his shoes?

You are very much an actor in your role of animator, and you must stay honest to who your character is, even when the character is experiencing an arc and learning about himself. A villain is a great example in which honesty has to play out as to who the villain is and why he is doing these evil things. The best villains are the ones who are unpredictable but at the same time stay true to who they are and why they are doing these things. When a person reacts very differently than we would expect, he is betraying our belief system.

Eyes

Eyes are very important to animation and acting. The eyes are windows into the soul, and the soul is controlled by the mind. If the mind is driving the character, then the eyes tell the story. Eye darts and glances can tell more than any gesture of the body or hand when used in the right place in a scene. A good example of a great eye dart or rapid eye movement would be in the movie *Finding Nemo*. The character Dory from *Finding Nemo* made use of eye darts quite often when she couldn't remember things to show she was thinking about it. Eye darts show a thought process, whether afraid or anxious or simply thinking. When we think about something, we tend to look around. Angie Glocka says:

1982

LUCASARTS FORMED: Lucasfilm had its beginnings in May 1982 in the Games Group of Lucasfilm Ltd. Lucas wanted his company to branch out into other areas of entertainment, so he cooperated with Atari to produce video games. The first results of this collaboration were unique action games such as *Ballblazer* and *Rescue on Fractalus*.

1982

BAKSHI RELEASES *HEY GOOD LOOKIN':* Bakshi's *Hey Good Lookin'* was originally going to be a live-action movie with a few animated characters, similar to *Who Framed Roger Rabbit*. However, Warner executives told Bakshi that the idea of having live-action and animated characters in the same frame was too unbelievable, delaying the film's release and forcing Bakshi to go back and animate the live-action sequences in between making three other films.

If you look at live action, you'll see that the eyes are very alive. If they don't move, the character looks like it's in a trance. If you combine this with other facial animation, the character looks much more complex than a character whose eyes are stationary.

There is an old saying that there are only two times when eye contact is significant: love and hate. Eye contact is required when a character is going to kiss someone or hit someone. The eyes can translate intense emotions. Eyes can dilate to show pleasure or fear. The subtle motion of the eyes themselves can personify uneasiness, lying, or confusion. Conrad Vernon offers his experience with directing animation of CG eyes on *Shrek*:

In *Shrek 1* it didn't look like the character's eyes ever really connected because they are ping-pong balls with an iris and a pupil on the surface of a ping-pong ball. Then, the computer programmers went in and actually gave a lens, an iris, and a pupil that dilated, so you had a real eye. You could lock eyes and stare into each other's eyes. You saw moments where people didn't realize it, but they felt it twice as much because the characters were really looking into each other's eyes.

Desire is always described in the eyes, even when desire is being hidden through a subtext acting choice. Eye darts can show a character's frustration or fear. In other words, eye darts rarely happen when someone is evoking an honest emotion, such as love or hate. Some of the strongest acting comes from the eyes.

Remember to handle the eyes with great care. Eyes explain everything that is going on in that character's head.

> "My stuff always starts with the eyes. The acting always comes out in the eyes, and that's how you can really establish who the character is, how it acts, and what it wants. You establish all that, and character comes through."
>
> —*Darin McGowan*

1983

OSCAR FOR *SUNDAE IN NEW YORK* (MOTIONPICKER): *Sundae in New York* won the Academy Award for Best Animated Short Film.

1983

OTTO MESSMER DIES: Otto Messmer (1892–1983) was an American animator, best known for his work on the *Felix the Cat* cartoons and comic strip produced by the Pat Sullivan studio.

1983

HE-MAN AND THE MASTERS OF THE UNIVERSE: *He-Man and the Masters of the Universe* was an animated television series produced by Filmation and based on Mattel's successful toy line. The show was one of the most popular animated children's shows of the 1980s and has retained a heavy cult following to this day.

127

Commit

Now! You have slept, doodled, listened, jumped around, talked to other animators, gone shopping, played ping-pong and foosball, drawn thumbnails over and over, goofed off, watched DVDs, and played video games or Scrabble with your cubemate. You have done everything but animate the scene.

Congratulations! It's Thursday! You are now the "Thursday Animator," and you have a deadline. Committing is selling the idea you believe is the best for this scene. If you have a scene in which the character has to propose marriage and you forge ahead, half-confident with the ideas you are expressing, the scene will feel halfway done. Commit fully to what the character is feeling and really push it. That character is excited, anxious, hesitant, and reluctant all at the same time. Commit to those ideas completely! Troy Saliba explains his commitment to a scene:

> I don't need to worry about the mechanics of how I am going to get there. I will worry about that later. Again, the mechanical part is something that should be second nature to you by the time you call yourself an animator. There is a lot to be gained from being able to make premeditated decisions about, "I am going to be here at a certain time; I am committing to this."

1983

DRAGON'S LAIR VIDEO GAME: Cinematronics' *Dragon's Lair* was one of the first laserdisc video games. It featured polished Disney-like animation created by former Disney animator Don Bluth and his studio. For the first time, this video game allowed players to control a fully realized character, as opposed to a pixel-based sprite.

1983

PARTICLE SYSTEMS INTRODUCED: Bill Reeves at Lucasfilm published a paper on techniques for modeling particle systems. The paper also promoted motion blur.

Index 5: Ten Things to Think About

◆ **Listen:** Listen to your supervisor. Listen to the story. Listen to your character.

◆ **Subtext:** What is the character *really* saying in the scene or dialogue?

◆ **Experiment:** Do not be afraid to try new things.

◆ **Rhythm:** Move too fast and the viewer is confused—too slow and he is bored.

◆ **Empathize:** Find the one thing about your character that the audience will identify with, and grab it and squeeze every drop of that into what your character does.

◆ **Simplify:** Less is more. All the clichés apply. Give the audience a chance to rest and savor the moment you are trying to convey.

◆ **Texture:** Texture is what makes all living things look real.

◆ **Honesty:** Is your character really emoting his personality and how he sees themselves in the world?

◆ **Eyes:** Eye darts and glances can tell more than any gesture of the body or hand when used in the right places in a scene.

◆ **Commit:** Creating a believable, feeling character who will make your audience cry takes commitment to the ideas you decided on while thinking about your animation.

1983

FIRE AND ICE **RELEASED:** *Fire and Ice* was a collaboration between cult heroes Ralph Bakshi and Frank Frazetta. The animated feature was made using the process of roto-scoping. The film was neither financially nor critically successful, but later became a cult classic among fans of the film's two creators.

1984

OSCAR FOR *CHARADE* **(JOHN MINNIS):** *Charade* won the Academy Award for Best Animated Short.

1984

CG SEXY ROBOT FOR 30-SECOND COMMERCIAL: Robert Abel & Associates produced the first computer generated 30-second commercial, used for the Super Bowl. Together, Randy Roberts and Con Pederson created a chrome female robotic character that was visually stunning.

Chapter 5
Every Frame Counts

Whether you came from a stop-motion, 2D, or CG background, you've no doubt been frustrated by trying to animate with a computer at one time or another. The computer distances you from the final image. It has a remote nature that is not as tangible as 2D or stop-motion. There are literally thousands of controls that you can use when animating on a computer. You have to establish an efficient workflow to be successful in computer-generated animation. The tools can often be not only complicated, but sterile and mechanical, so you must develop a workflow that makes the process more approachable, streamlined, and natural to you.

> "Animating with a computer is like getting both hands cut off and trying to use robotic arms in one of those plastic containers used for handling toxic stuff."
>
> —*Nik Ranieri*

Then, once you finally start to get the hang of it, the software changes and you have to learn new tools! What is an animator to do? Nik Ranieri provided us with one of the best descriptions of the mechanical and remote nature of animating with a computer:

It's sort of like driving a car. When you first get into a car and you start to learn, it's like this machine and there are all these pulleys and there are all these things you have to do. Then, after a few years, you just get in and it just becomes part of you and you just go. You feel like you have the reaction time. You swerve, and it's almost like it's what you would do if you were just walking or running. You get comfortable with it. The only difference is, for the most part, cars change very little. They still have a few pedals and gears and all that stuff, whereas computers have new hot keys, et cetera. In 2D, whatever studio you go to, you sit down, they give you a desk, a piece of paper, and a pencil, and you just go. That's it. In CG you're basically going back to school every time you go to a different job.

1984

BOB CLAMPETT DIES: Robert Emerson "Bob" Clampett (1913–1984) was an animator, producer, director, and puppeteer best known for his work on the *Looney Tunes* series of cartoons from Warner Bros. and the television show *Beany and Cecil*. In 1935, he designed the studio's first major star, Porky Pig, who appeared in Friz Freleng's film *I Haven't Got a Hat*.

1984

WAVEFRONT TECHNOLOGY FIRST COMMERCIALLY AVAILABLE 3D SOFTWARE: Wavefront Technologies was the first commercially available 3D software package.

If you stop fighting the cold nature of the machine, you will recognize that, in time, you will learn how to drive it very easily. You will take the road with confidence soon enough. However, don't become a software jockey, because the tools and approaches in technology and software change rapidly, and you may be left behind. Cory Florimonte has a theory about computer animation software and the tools developed by the vendors:

> One thing I like to keep in mind is that most of the software we work with is not version 1.0. All the different software packages are competing with each other and evolving, always trying to be better in some aspects while making sure they keep up in others. With this in mind, I can figure that all software has a way to do just about everything I want it to do. The programmers wouldn't have left it out; it's just a matter of figuring out how *they* think I should do a certain thing. And usually if something (God forbid) *has* been left out, it's such a glaring hole that it's easy to find someone who is already bitching about it, thereby giving advance warning of the software's inability. This has made it easy for me to jump from package to package and still be able to function. I still get hot key–lag for a few weeks after switching, though.

Stay open to these changes because with each new version of software, your job as a computer animator will become easier. An open mind will also make your chances of continued employment much greater. Animating on a computer involves understanding the tools provided by the computer and following trends in technology that drive these tools. More important to the computer animator is how to creatively manipulate those tools to create believable performances.

This chapter will introduce computer animation tools, such as the graph editor, and explain their value in preventing your animation from becoming too robotic. The differences between 2D and CG approaches in animation will be explained, as well as how to apply the methods of traditional animators to the computer. Specifics regarding how to avoid the unconvincing movement and timing in much computer-generated animation are explained in depth, including weight, contrasts in timing, reality versus entertainment, staging, and the revision process. Techniques developed by CG animators to get more dynamic poses, such as breaking the rig, moving holds, and using motion-blur frames, are all discussed here. So let's get started.

1984

A-BUFFER HIDDEN SURFACE ALGO-RITHM CREATED: Loren Carpenter is a computer graphics researcher and developer, and co-founder and chief scientist of Pixar Animation Studios. One of his many inventions is the A-buffer hidden surface algorithm.

1984

THE MAGIC EGG PREMIERES AT SIGGRAPH: The *Magic Egg* is a wide-ranging collection of visual segments developed by 18 computer animation teams at various research institutes and universities across North America. These teams combined vector graphics, molecular modeling techniques, and simulated time-lapse photography with the mathematical calculations needed to pre-distort images for IMAX dome projection.

Do you take the mathematical path like a scientist, sculpting the curves of your animation? Or are you more comfortable with a more intuitive approach—knowing what each pose should be, placing the overlap and follow-through into the keys? It's up to you, but the best CG animators understand both approaches and use what works best for the shot. Sketch by Floyd Norman.

Spliney, Gooey, Computery, and Watery Motion

The biggest complaint many experienced animators have regarding CG animation is that it looks "spliney," "gooey," "mechanical," or "like it is moving under water." This is because the computer will naturally generate mathematically perfect in-betweens if you let it. The linear nature of the computer will never support the arcs that come naturally to motion in any organic, living being. You must learn to take it upon yourself to make sure that this underwater, slow, unnatural motion does not happen.

1984

NAUSICAA (KAZE NO TANI NO NAUSHIKA) RELEASED: Director Hayao Miyazaki would go on to become the Japanese Walt Disney, with a string of animated hits produced by his studio. The old US release titled *Warriors of the Wind* is a heavily edited version, thus creating an entirely different story.

1984

FIRST MACINTOSH INTRODUCED WITH CLIO-WINNING COMMERCIAL: During the Super Bowl, Apple Computer introduced the Macintosh computer with a 60-second Orwellian epic commercial called "1984," created by Chiat/Day. The spot launched a new computer technology, turned the Super Bowl into a major ad event, and began an era of advertising as news.

133

As the animator, you need to view the computer as a tool at your command. Don't take the lazy way out, setting keys and leaving it up to the mathematics of the machine to fill in the blanks. Cameron Miyasaki illustrates how to prevent the computery look in his animation:

Don't just set keys and let the computer interpolate the animation for you. Even though it's computer animation, the less you let the computer do, the better your animation will be. Make sure you understand what's going on behind the scenes (i.e., with your curves, slow-ins, and slow-outs) when you insert every key frame into your animation, and how that affects the character's movement on your screen.

Stay away from creating floaty motion when animating on a computer. Sketch by Floyd Norman.

1984

JOHN LASSETER LEAVES DISNEY FOR LUCASFILM: In 1984, a disappointed Lasseter left Disney after the studio passed on his proposed animation project, *The Brave Little Toaster*. Ed Catmull convinced Lasseter to come to Lucasfilm to experiment for just a month. Lasseter liked what he found and never left.

1984

DIGITAL PRODUCTIONS RECEIVES THE TECHNICAL ACHIEVEMENT AWARD FOR CGI SIM: Digital Productions (Whitney and Demos) received an Academy Technical Achievement Award for the practical simulation of motion picture photography by means of computer-generated images. In 1984 Digital Productions created the first photorealistic computer graphic images for a feature film, *The Last Starfighter*, using a Cray X-MP supercomputer.

All animators have had trouble with this aspect of animating on the computer. It's very easy to select the curves that define your motion and change their interpolation to a smoothed spline between two keys, and then not understand why it looks so slow and rubbery. The graph editor is your friend. Embrace what these curves represent and how you can add texture to your motion. This doesn't mean you need to add a million keys, either. CG animation lies somewhere between stop-motion and 2D. Avoid placing so many keys that the animation becomes choppy or is too complicated to revise easily.

The term "spliney" in animation usually refers to the "floaty" motion the computer generates when the graph editor has set the curves to interpolate each key frame as a spline, as opposed to keys that are stepped or clamped. Natural and organic creatures and characters do not move in that manner. Natural motion is full of strange and wonderful textures and rhythms. Look at Muybridge's books on human and animal motion, and you will see some incredible things happening. The animator must add life to the character when deciding how the character will move from one pose to another. Adjusting the timing in the graph editor as well as adjusting the spacing of your key frames will give clarity to the motion and add life. Dave Brewster elaborates on how to take charge and prevent the mathematically even timing the computer tends to generate:

> Control the scene. That means tweaking things you know are more specific and that the computer will inherently generalize.

Understanding how to change the tangency of each spline to sharpen the bias of a curve will give you the power to stop that floaty motion. The Bezier handles that describe the shape of your curve have a bias applied to them. If a curve is sharp, like a sharp turn in the road while driving that fancy car, then the bias is angled steeply. If the bias of the curve is meant to show a softer "hit," then the bias has a shallow incline. Think of the graph editor curves as a rollercoaster. If the bias is sharp, the motion will feel like coming around a sudden bend on the rollercoaster. If the bias is looser, then it will feel more like the rollercoaster is coming up to the top of a smooth incline.

Instead of setting a key on every frame to get a sharp bias to the motion, you can alter the weighted handles of a curve and keep your animation lighter with fewer keys. This makes revisions much easier because you are dealing with fewer keys to describe your motion or fewer notes in the composition. This also provides for an uncluttered graph editor. Do this step first to keep the keys simple and, if you still see a floaty motion, begin to add more keys or adjust the tension in the splines to sculpt the texture you need.

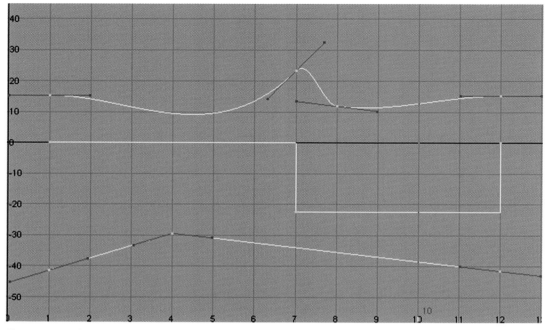

The top curve has the bias of the Bezier handles set at a sharp angle to make for quicker timing without resorting to multiple keys. The middle curve is set to stepped timing for blocking a scene. The bottom curve is set to linear timing. Learn how to manipulate your curves in the editor, and you will prevent the computer from animating the scene for you.

Another problem with CG animation is the animator's tendency to become overwhelmed by all the controls provided. Some CG animators forget to think about the whole pose when working on a computer because they have so many controls in front of them to animate. When you draw in animation, you are forced to think about the whole pose because each line must connect to the previous one.

On a computer, each key frame represents a single control you move in the viewport. You could have 100 keys that build up to one pose. A traditional animator refers to a "key" as an entire pose composed of one key frame. When CG animators use the term "key frame," they can be referring to the key of a wrist or a finger or the neck individually, or all of the above. When animating on a computer, you can have hundreds of controls that add up to one single key-frame pose. Larry Weinberg offers his experience at Sheridan College, where the animators were getting lazy in the face of so many controls:

1985

OSCAR FOR *ANNA AND BELLA* (RING BORGE): *Anna and Bella* are a pair of old ladies, living life vicariously through their memories. As they page through a photo album, the ladies conjure up images both sweet and sour of their past lives and loves. Directed by Ring Borge, *Anna and Bella* was the 1985 Best Short Subject, Animated Films Oscar winner.

1985

A COMPLETE CG CHARACTER IN YOUNG SHERLOCK HOLMES: The film Young *Sherlock Holmes*, directed by Barry Levinson and written by Chris Columbus, is notable for including the first computer-generated character, a knight composed of elements from a stained glass window. The effect was created for Lucasfilm by John Lasseter, who would go on to create *Toy Story* 10 years later.

I visited Sheridan College one year and was very impressed at how they trained people through traditional animation first before getting on the computer. What surprised me more than anything else was that the quality of animation dropped dramatically when individuals switched to the computer. They stopped thinking about the details. When you draw, you have to think about every finger, every limb, and every line on the face. When you are on the computer, you tend to lay down some simple things and let the computer do a quick in-between, and you fall in love with it without really looking closely. You can't get lazy with the computer. You need to discipline your eyes to look. If you can, draw it out on paper first until you are happy. Then do it on the computer.

One more reason CG gets that "floaty" look is because it is so easy to set keys with the same timing. It's natural in the beginning to set keys in an even manner to keep your ideas organized when working on a computer. This is a good way to start; however, you must massage that timing into something that is more natural by offsetting the motion. The best way to identify timing that is too even is to simply say to yourself when you watch your motion, "One-one thousand, two-one thousand," counting out the seconds. If the poses are all hitting at the same timing and all of the body parts are keyed on the same key frames, it will look robotic and unnatural.

Most experienced animators can see this right away just by watching the playback. The character starts to look like a member of a chorus line rather than a living, breathing, individual character. Try to walk across the room with even timing. It's hard to do because humans have organic motion that is affected by their mood, weight, sense of balance, physical condition, and so much more. Only a robot will have an even, mechanical sense of timing. Don Waller offers a great explanation of the need for offsets in timing to escape the floaty look:

The problem I see most of the time with this is that when CG animation has that computery look to it, it usually stems from the fact that everything is moving all at the same time and at the same speed! It's all much too even and usually slow in pace, having a languid feel to it, with no weight! For those artists with the necessary animation talent skills, they should really study and learn about overlapping action and the benefits obtained from it. The overlapping action, timing, illusion of weight, or lack thereof can make or break the animation. These sorts of timings and actions are not easy to achieve, and I feel they're the crux of the animator's art!

1985

COMMODORE LAUNCHES NEW AMIGA: Commodore's new 16-bit computer design, the Amiga 1000, was a flexible broadcast-quality personal computer and was a popular early animation system.

1985

MAX HEADROOM INTRODUCED: Max Headroom appeared as a stylized head on TV against harsh primary color backgrounds. Max's image was actually actor Matt Frewer in latex and foam rubber prosthetic makeup, superimposed over a moving geometric background. When these things were combined with clever editing, the appearance of a computer-generated human head was convincing to many. At first, the background was not computer graphics, but hand-drawn cel animation. Later, the US version generated graphics utilizing an Amiga computer.

137

In addition to even timing, the CG animator is prone to placing all of the keys on the same key frame. This also makes for mechanical motion. Try to bring your arm down to hit your fist on the table and make every single joint in your arm from the shoulder to the elbow to the wrist move and hit at the same time. It physically hurts to do this! As a CG animator, you must know which parts of a character would follow through on an initial motion after the main body of the action and be able to portray those timings convincingly. The two principles of secondary action and overlap, established in the book *The Illusion of Life: Disney Animation* by Ollie Johnston and Frank Thomas (Disney Editions, 1995),[21] should be a foundation of animation you already understand. If you are using the title of Animator, these principles should be second nature, and you should not get held up trying to figure out how these parts move.

Practice makes perfect. Simple animation tests such as jumping up and down, and run and walk cycles teach you these fundamental concepts. Sculpting this motion in the computer is up to you. As a CG animator, you are now the lead animator, breakdown artist, in-betweener, and cleanup artist all in one. This means you will create the broad strokes of animation with main keys, as well as the breakdowns and in-betweens that will describe the motion in an entertaining and convincing manner.

The Graph Editor

In this section, we will talk specifically about a computer tool that every animator working on the computer should come to know and utilize. No matter what software you are using, the graph/curve editor is one of your most valuable tools. It is a 2D representation of your motion, and is where you will pull the rabbit from the hat!

The graph editor is the tool you use to add weight, texture, and rhythm to your animation. Your problem-solving happens directly by manipulating the curves. The graph editor helps you adjust slow-ins and slow-outs, timing, and spacing. Finally, it helps you troubleshoot for errors such as gimbal lock or spikes in the motion. Most 2D animators who cross over to CG are fearful of this tool. The graph editor is a strange, complex, mathematical-looking series of curved lines that are understandably daunting at first. It just looks like spaghetti. The graph editor offers the same information as the timing chart does for a traditional animator. Some 2D animators try to get away with not using the graph editor, but they soon find that understanding the tool makes their lives much easier, as Nik Ranieri did:

1985

PIXAR IMAGE COMPUTER GOES TO MARKET: The Pixar Image Computer was a graphics-designing computer made by Pixar in May 1986, intended for the high-end visualization markets, such as medicine. The expensive system did not sell well, and by 1987 Pixar only had a handful of buyers. By 1988 Pixar had only sold 120 Pixar Image Computers, and they eventually sold the machine to Vicom for $2 million.

1985

PAPER ON CREATURE ANIMATION: Girard and Maciejewski at OSU published a paper describing the use of inverse kinematics and dynamics for animation. Their techniques were used in the animation "Eurythmy."

138

I use the graph editor more than I thought I would. When I first looked at the graph editor, I didn't understand it. Now I understand it. How can you animate without the graph editor? The problem with 3D is that if something is wrong, you are not sure what is affecting it. But if I go into the graph editor and see spikes, I know what to do. In the graph editor, the scene is flat. You see all of your curves at one time. I fix those curves and it works again. The graph editor, to me, is like seeing your scene in four dimensions, seeing all sides at the same time, as opposed to the camera view, where you have to keep rotating your scene to see anything. In the graph editor, you can see all the moves at the same time and see what you need to adjust.

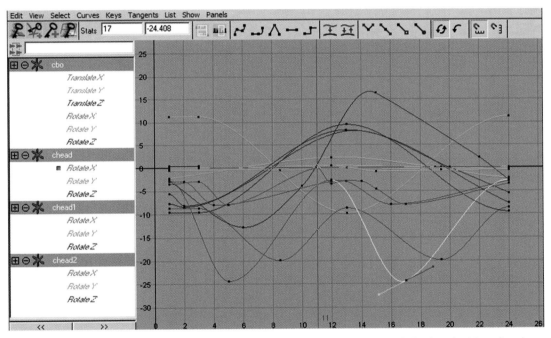

Curves in the graph editor manipulate the timing. By changing these curves and altering the bias of each tangent, you can get a sharper angle to your curve, making the motion less floaty.

1985

BOSS FILMS FOUNDED BY RICHARD ELUND: Boss Film Studio's founder and president is effects legend Richard Edlund, who has a list of credits unparalleled in the effects industry. After working with ILM on such films as *Raiders of the Lost Ark* and the *Star Wars* trilogy, Edlund put together Boss to complete effects for *Ghostbusters* and *2010*. Boss Film was one of the few houses in existence that could boast a pre-digital era. It ceased production on August 28, 1997.

1985

THE CARE BEARS MOVIE RELEASED (NELVANA): *The Care Bears Movie* was the first to feature the popular Care Bears toy characters. This movie has often been cited as being the first to be based on a toy line, but this is not really the case. The honor actually belongs to 1977's *Raggedy Ann & Andy: A Musical Adventure*.

Stepped, Linear, and Spline

To spline or not to spline: That is the question. All animators have different ways of approaching the animation process. Most have adopted the technique of working in a stepped mode first, then in a linear mode, and finally, in splined fashion as they work out the last 10 percent of cleanup. Stepped mode simulates what a traditional animator calls a *pose test*. It tells the computer to hold on a pose for as long as the animator wishes, and then pops to the next keyed pose. This presents the motion in a very clear manner, concentrating the viewer's eyes on the main poses of the scene. Each pose is defined as to how long it will linger, giving the viewer enough time to enjoy the moment. This method enables the animator to get motion, timing, and acting choices approved before committing to a lot of work on the shot. Most management in CG animation today understand what a stepped key pose test is.

The best structure for approval in CG animation is one in which the director, supervisor, and lead animator all embrace this stepped, linear, and then splined approach to animating with a computer. However, sometimes you will get a live-action director who cannot understand or even watch a stepped pose test. You also might work for a lead who subscribes to the layering method of animating, and you will have to adjust your workflow accordingly. We will talk more about this subject in Chapter 7. After you have completed the stepped pose test, the next step is to move to linear curves, which will not pop from pose to pose and will look very mechanical between each key. The linear curves enable you to see where you need to place the breakdowns to start sculpting a more natural motion.

By working in linear mode in the graph editor, you force yourself to carve the motion in the curves. If you don't set breakdown keys for your ins and outs, it will be apparent that you are letting the computer animate for you. The linear curve makes your motion look mechanical, and you may have to set more keys to avoid that look. Henry Anderson describes how he directs his animators to get around the computer look as they develop their animation:

> I have asked animators working on my projects to animate using stepped interpolation for the first few passes on a scene. It makes animating in the computer more like doing a pose test in drawn animation. Once the timing has been worked out, the animator will start doing the breakdown in-betweens, now working in linear mode. You continue working in smaller and smaller frame ranges until your animation is looking smoother, and only then do you go in and spline small segments of your data curves where you really need it. I used this approach when I was a CG animator, and I think that it gives the animator the most control over every key and in-between. It also keeps the animation snappy, which is something that I prefer.

1985

***THE BLACK CAULDRON* DISNEY'S 25TH FEATURE AND FIRST TRADITIONALLY ANIMATED FILM TO USE CGI:** The *Black Cauldron's* objects were animated on a computer before their outlines were printed onto cels. *The movie was* Disney Studios' attempt to reach out to teenage fans of fantasy novels, but the gamble proved unsuccessful. Critics blamed the film's lack of appeal on the atypical dark nature of the film. The film's failure at the box office, combined with its dark tone, led to Disney all but disowning the film for nearly 15 years.

1986

OSCAR FOR *A GREEK TRAGEDY* (NICOLE VAN GOETHEM): *A Greek Tragedy* won the Academy Award for Best Short Subject: Animated Films.

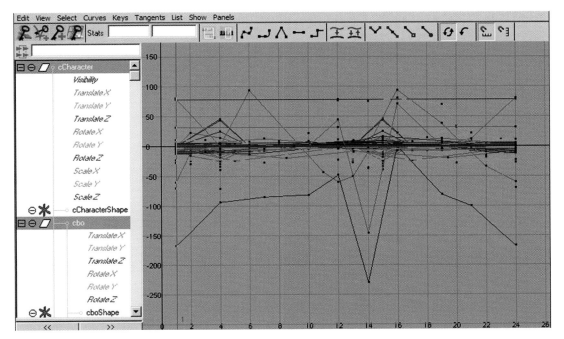

Linear curves in the graph editor.

Working in linear mode forces you to see only your key poses and how you will transition from one to the other without adding so many in-betweens that the motion becomes confusing. It is a good way to see exactly where the computer will make the animation look too spliney.

"I once worked with an animator who kept all of his splines linear until I had approved the direction of the shot, and then he would spend at least a day tweaking the splines to get the action clean and the motion supple and real. The guy was a genius! By working this way, 100 percent of his thought was put into his poses and broad timing until the shot was approved. Too many people worry about in-betweens when their shot isn't working. That's like frosting a cake that isn't done yet."

—*Chris Bailey*

 1986

IWERKS ENTERTAINMENT FOUNDED: Iwerks Entertainment was founded in 1985 by Stan Kinsey and Don Iwerks, two former Disney executives, and became well known through 1996 as a leading developer of special venue and virtual reality theaters throughout the world. The company was named to honor Don's father, Ub Iwerks.

1986

AN AMERICAN TAIL RELEASED: While all of the animal characters in *An American Tail* were animated from scratch, the human characters are portrayed using the rotoscoping technique. The movie became the highest-grossing animated feature in first release at the time.

Another advantage to working in linear mode is that it helps you keep things simple and clear and makes it much easier to make revisions. You can always switch back and forth between spline and linear to see how the animation is coming along, but it's important to wait on moving into spline mode until you have fixed every pose. Once you think you have completely worked out your timing in stepped and linear modes, you can begin to smooth things out in spline mode.

When bridging the gap between 2D and CG animation, you see the two disciplines are not all that different. You can take many of the tools traditional animators use to create hand-drawn animation and apply them to computer-generated animation with very minor differences in their application. It's best to take in all of the principles that the greats of traditional animation have developed and apply them to your CG animation. There are plenty of books and Web sites out there explaining the principles of animation. We provide a brief list of the principles, as defined by Frank Thomas and Ollie Johnston in their book *The Illusion of Life: Disney Animation* and paraphrased by Nataha Lightfoot, in Appendix E for reference.

This chapter probes deeper into how to apply traditional principles in animation to the computer. This chapter also illustrates how CG animators have found new applications for the principles while working on the computer. There are some differences between 2D and CG that every animator should think about, no matter what their background.

Posing and Layering

There are two schools of thought as to how to animate in both CG and traditional circles. One approach is to key the entire pose down to the fingers and small bits on the body. The second system is to layer in the motion starting with the big parts, and once the bigger motion is timed out, slowly add motion moving down to the smaller parts of the body. Sometimes these techniques are used interchangeably.

The first method entails posing everything on the character down to the digits. The facial elements, the fingers—everything is a part of the pose, forcing the animator to always think about the line of action and where that line will flow from pose to pose throughout the entire body. The offsets of motion are placed inside of each posed key frame. The silhouette already incorporates how the offsets will be happening throughout the hierarchal tree of the skeleton. Eric Goldberg explains how he likes to approach CG and ensure it contains all of what he loves in 2D animation:

1986

***THE GREAT MOUSE DETECTIVE*, DISNEY'S 26TH FEATURE, IS THE SECOND TRADITIONALLY ANIMATED FILM AIDED BY CG:** *The Great Mouse Detective* is notable for its early use of CGI. The film is sometimes cited as the first animated film to use CGI, but that honor actually goes to 1985's *The Black Cauldron*.

1986

TOPAS 3D SOFTWARE RELEASED: Crystal Graphics introduced TOPAS, one of the first high-quality 3D animation programs for personal computers. Over the years, Crystal Graphics would continue to be a major contender in the PC-based 3D animation field.

> I am always going to approach CG with a 2D sensibility. How can I make CG look the most like the animation that I admire, the animation that I love? It does require a different set of rules and a different way of thinking than normal CG. The whole idea of CG characters being blocked in first and then layering the limbs, facial, clothing, and finger poses on top is completely counter to the way I like to approach it. When I am drawing, everything is posed.

The fully posed method is used by both traditional animators and CG animators alike. Some animators will animate each pose completely and clean up each drawing until the ideas are pristine and clear. Then, they will use the second approach of layering action on top of that to get more secondary action into their breakdowns and work out things such as appendages, cloth, and hair that should have even more fluid action.

The second school of thought on how to pose out the animation on a computer deals more with the layering technique Eric described earlier. The hips are resolved first to get the weight figured out, and then the weight works out from the COG (*center of gravity*). Layering makes sense when using the computer to animate because the key frame on a computer is actually a collection of key frames set all over the hierarchy instead of one drawing. There are hundreds of controls, and some of those controls need only a few keys, while some at other levels need many keys to define the motion. By layering, it's easier to keep up with all of this data.

John Lasseter wrote a paper called "Tricks to Animating Characters with a Computer" for Course 1 at SIGGRAPH '94, "Animation Tricks,"[22] in which he describes his first attempts at animating on a computer. Under the section of the paper called "Key Frames," Lasseter explains how he learned to work down the hierarchy of the model. He used the layering technique to limit the amount of key frames necessary to create one whole pose on the computer. This way he could control the motion on many levels. Troy Saliba further explains how the layering approach isn't really second nature to a 2D animator's thought process, but can work:

> I was always surprised at the layering method some animators take on, especially when 2D animators embrace layering. It's not how 2D animators think. The first thing a CG animator moves is the COG for a walk, moving it up and down. To me, as a 2D-trained animator, this approach is completely alien. The layering technique requires shifting keys to create the offset instead of creating an offset with the pose itself. I understand the principle behind it, but in 2D you get the offset in the pose. One way isn't better or worse; I am just surprised when 2D people follow that path so easily. I know many very talented animators who use it very well and make it beautiful. Some animators are total scientists when they are animating.

1986

COMPUTER GRAPHICS DIVISION OF ILM SPLITS TO BECOME PIXAR: In 1986, Steve Jobs bought Lucasfilm's computer graphics division from George Lucas for $10 million and named the new computer animation studio Pixar. Part of the deal was that Lucasfilm would get continued access to Pixar's rendering technology. Pixar contracted with Disney to produce a number of computer-animated feature films, which Disney would co-finance and distribute. The first film produced by that partnership, *Toy Story*, brought fame and critical acclaim to the studio when it was released in 1995. Pixar continued to develop their rendering hardware, eventually turning it into RenderMan.

Animators who use the layering technique understand the computer curves and can create breakdowns and texture in their motion using their curves effectively. Layering involves animating one part of the body at a time. It's not a better technique; it's just a more mathematical one that embraces the fact that secondary motion is very easy to map out on a computer when you understand how to offset frames by sliding them.

The means you use to get there are not important. What is important is that you avoid letting the computer animate for you. Mike Surrey explains a little about his approach to layering:

> I work in layers. After blocking in the shot, I'll go back to the first frame and work through to the last frame, working on one part of the character, then going back to the beginning and picking another part and doing the same process until I've hit everything I need to get what I'm looking for.

Sometimes, by mixing the techniques, you can get the best of both worlds.

One last thought on layering. If you combine layering of animation on joints and then offset the timing for each joint, it can be a really powerful tool to get fluid secondary action quickly. This is something you can only do on a computer. For example, if you want a tail to wag and you approach this by layering, you would animate the first joint in the tail closest to the body and copy that curve to each joint down the tree. Then you could slide the curves ahead one frame for each joint. Each joint will be happening a frame later than the last. This will create a fluid wag for the tail quickly that can be adjusted with more varied timing to make it natural. Dave Zaboski offers his experience on *Stuart Little 2* applying this technique:

> I did a hawk flying in *Stuart Little 2*, and I animated it with the wings going up and down evenly, using the computer to help complete the in-betweens. Then when I had the rhythm down, I shifted the whole animation for one wing joint one frame up. It had the effect of seeming less mechanical and pretty natural.

Layering and offset by sliding keys can quickly generate some nice results on the computer.

No matter what method you choose, it all comes down to the pose. Both the 2D approach (applying the entire pose to a key) and the CG approach (getting that pose by layering) work well. However, sometimes you will need to be flexible when it comes to dealing with your supervisor or director. Depending on their background, they might want to see the whole pose. They might not understand the layering technique you

1986

SOFTIMAGE IS FOUNDED: Daniel Langlois founded Softimage in 1986. Then, in early 1987 he hired some engineers to help create his vision for a commercial 3D computer graphics program. The Softimage software was released at the 1988 SIGGRAPH show and became the animation standard in Europe, with more than 1,000 installations worldwide by 1993.

1986

TURNER WHITTED AND HIS FAMOUS FLOATING CHROME BALLS: Turner Whitted's SIGGRAPH paper with its famous image of balls floating above a checkerboard floor is widely regarded as the first modern description of ray tracing methods in computer graphics and won him the ACM SIGGRAPH Achievement Award.

plan on employing and why there are no finger poses or facial poses on the animation yet. Dealing properly with supervisors and differing opinions is crucial to your future in the business. This issue and others regarding playing well with others are covered in more depth in Chapter 7, "When Push Comes to Stab." It's best to be aware of both approaches and have them in your back pocket, ready to pull out at any time.

Breaking the Rig

Many times, you just want to break the constraints controlling that arm and put the arm where it needs to be, regardless of how an IK solution or other controllers are saying you can pose it. Do it! What is stopping you? If you get the pose that is in your head and in your thumbnails, then you will be creating animation that pushes the envelope! Do everything you can to get that dynamic pose. If you cheat a pose, you can push what the anatomy can do. This is how you get charm into the pose! As long as how you break the rig still makes the pose appealing, you will have a stronger performance because if it.

Successfully hiding the cheat is the key. If you want an arm to raise high in the air, you can hide the shoulder behind the head and stretch it above and beyond its natural state. The audience will never be the wiser. Your pose will look more dynamic and interesting. Eric Goldberg offers how he likes to break the rig to get the most dynamic pose he sees in his head:

> My approach to CG is, "What can I break?" I know what I am aiming for, and like it or not almost everything I have done in CG thus far has been to replicate something that already was established in 2D and translate it into the medium. There are a lot of things you have to do in order to achieve that. It basically comes down to cheats. When I say cheats, I mean poses the audience will never see as a cheat and will think are right.

Take great care in how you move from the cheated pose to a more natural pose to the rig. If you don't, the cheat will be revealed. If your character has fur or cloth or dynamics of some kind on the rig, the cheat could break these technical elements further down the pipe. If you hide where the cheat is happening, such as a shoulder pose behind a head to get the arm raised higher than the rig wants to allow, then you will be successful. Shadows will also factor into the final image, so take them into consideration when you are hiding the cheated pose. The fur, cloth, dynamics, and other technical solutions to the rig can be compromised to support your pose, but this is a delicate venture, and you should communicate what you are trying to do with the digital team.

1986

HENSON'S WALDO PROJECT INTRODUCES MOTION CAPTURE: Jim Henson of *Muppets* fame approached Brad DeGraf at Digital Productions with the idea of creating a digital puppet. Henson had brought with him a Waldo unit (the name of which was inspired by a 1940s sci-fi book by Robert A. Heinlein) that he had previously used to control one of his puppets remotely.

1987

OSCAR FOR *THE MAN WHO PLANTED TREES* (FREDERIC BACK): *L'homme qui plantait des arbres* (English title: *The Man Who Planted Trees*) was released to international critical acclaim and became one of the most award-winning animated shorts ever made. It won the Academy Award for Best Short Subject: Animated Films.

The relationship between the animation support team (those who build the tools/rigs for the animator) and the animator is occasionally strained, but can be handled with humor, like Mike Polvani did with this sketch.

Before you even consider breaking a rig, it's a good idea to run it by your rigger. The relationship between rigger and animator is the most important partnership you can have outside of your relationship with your supervisor. Both the relationship between animator and sup and the relationship between animator and rigger will ensure the success of your animation. You all need to make each other look good. Much like the craft of drawing is the foundation of being a 2D animator, the rigger and the rig are the foundation of how well you will be able to animate on a computer. Great rigs are extremely important to helping an animator

1986

OMNIBUS HOSTILE TAKEOVER OF DIGITAL PRODUCTIONS AND ROBERT ABEL: In 1986, the two largest computer graphics houses in the United States were bought out by Omnibus Computer Graphics Inc. in hostile takeovers, Digital Productions (in June) and Robert Abel & Associates Inc. (in October).

1986

LUXO JR. IS FIRST CG-ANIMATED FILM TO BE NOMINATED FOR AN OSCAR: Luxo Jr. was the first film produced in 1986 by Pixar Animation Studios, following its establishment as an independent film studio. Technically, the film demonstrates the use of shadow maps to simulate the shifting light and shadow given by the animated lamps featured in the film. Cinematically, it demonstrates a simple and entertaining story, including effectively expressive individual characters.

get his ideas across, and any limitations built into the rig will affect the range of motion you will be able to achieve. Nik Ranieri offers an experience he had with limited rigs:

> On *Chicken Little* there are all these background characters, and the rigs are terrible because they don't have enough controls. They're not as good as the main rigs. You're only as good as your rig. If you have a lousy rig, there's only so much you can do with it, you know. With some of those background character rigs on *Chicken Little*, you couldn't even raise the arm above the head, they were so limited. That's a bad thing.

Get to know the rigger and make nice because this relationship will make your job so much easier. It is human nature to want to please, so present to the rigger how the tools you are asking for will make the animation look better. Make sure how you break or cheat your poses isn't revealed in how the character enters and exits those frames, or your argument will be moot. Check the poses technically with your supervisor to ensure that they don't cause any problems further down the pipeline.

Using Breakdowns

Breakdowns are the best way to take control of the in-betweens and to prevent a computer look. Remember that breakdowns also define emotion. If the character points a finger with a lot of snap in the breakdown, it could mean something with a lot more energy, such as an angry emotion. If the breakdown makes the same move feel more like an aimless point, it could translate into nonchalance. The breakdown happens when you use two poses and twist another pose inside.

Breakdowns also help you define the intent behind the motion. Even when you're animating an eye blink, the eye shouldn't just close in a linear way. How you handle your breakdowns will define sleepiness, excitement, or disdain. Every frame counts. Nik Ranieri concludes:

> There are people who think that once they key it, you don't have to do anything else! You don't have to break down the lip-synch shape. In 2D, you have to draw that in. In 3D, it's open and it's closed. So they are lazy. When you play the animation, it's there and the eyelid closes, but it doesn't have any life to it. It doesn't have any squash and stretch. It doesn't feel alive because you haven't gone through it frame by frame and added life to it. It's hard to find people who have the desire to make every frame useful. I think that is what a lot of the computer guys do. They aren't thinking well-rounded visuals.

1987

THE SIMPSONS APPEARS ON THE TRACY ULLMAN SHOW: The *Simpsons* TV series is a spin-off of a series of animated shorts originally aired on *The Tracey Ullman* Show. It is the longest-running sitcom and longest-running animated program of all time. *The Simpsons* is the highest rated cartoon of all time, at one point averaging more than 25 million viewers.

1987

NORMAN MCLAREN DIES: Norman McLaren (1914–1987) was a Scottish animator and film director. In 1941 he was invited to Canada to work for the National Film Board, to open an animation studio and to train Canadian animators. During his work for the NFB, McLaren created his most famous film, *Neighbours* (1952), which has won various awards around the world, including the Canadian Film Award and the Academy Award.

"You have to think of what the character is reacting to. The character would think first—his look or eyes would change according to what he's thinking, then his body, then his shoulder, and then his arm, working out to point with finger. That's a lot of breakdowns. That is what you should not let the computer do. Never rely on the computer to 'fill,' or the performance will suffer."

—*David Smith*

Animators listening during a rigging demonstration. Sketch by Dave Zaboski.

 1987

JAPANESE ANIME BOOMS: In 1987, Japan produced 24 anime features, as well as 72 anime features for video release. Anime is a style of cartoon animation originating in Japan, with distinctive character and background stylings that visually set it apart from other forms of animation.

 1987

SIDE EFFECTS SOFTWARE ESTABLISHED: Established in 1987, Side Effects Software is a world leader in the development of advanced 3D animation and special effects software for use in film. It leads the field of procedural animation with its unique, award-winning Houdini technology.

Breakdowns are another tool in your collection that will help eliminate the computer look in your animation. Don't be lazy and let the computer define your breakdowns. Take control of every frame of animation, and you will be pleasantly surprised by the added punch it will give your work.

Animating Frame by Frame or on the Twos

Some traditional animators like to animate on twos, meaning placing a key every two frames. They keep all of their curves linear and sculpt the motion by placing a key on every two frames, much like the way traditional animation is created. This method is really helpful when dealing with tight timing and specific motion. Sometimes you have to animate at this level to get the motion to look right. However, if you animate an entire scene this way, there will be so many keys that the revision process will be extremely difficult and time consuming. As long as the final product looks right, your methods don't really matter. Just remember that the more keys you have, the more complicated the revision process will be. And there will always be revisions!

In-Betweening

In-betweens are the frames that happen in the middle of the breakdowns and key frames. In-betweens are the second level of adding life after you set the first level of main key frames. The in-betweening process is where you refine the timing of your poses. These spacing choices will define the intent behind the gesture. The breakdowns create purpose and eliminate the floaty CG look. The in-between further reinforces the impact of each pose and sets the timing and spacing for that movement. If you do not take control of your in-betweens, you run the risk of generating the computery motion we have been discussing. If the breakdowns are well thought-out with overlap already integrated into the pose, your in-betweens will flow fluidly.

> "Break up the timing in intuitive and spontaneous ways. The computer is exacting in the in-betweens. A human is not. Be organic."
>
> —*Tony Bancroft*

Some animators use a dry erase marker to draw out their arcs and shapes directly on their computer screen. This is a great way to map out your in-betweens and spacing. The graphic notes you make while drawing the arc directly on the screen ensure that no weirdness or spikes in animation are happening in

1987

OMNIBUS CLOSES: In March of 1987, Omnibus started defaulting on the $30 million it had borrowed from several major Canadian creditors. Some of the debts were the result of acquiring Digital Productions and Robert Abel & Associates the previous year. In May, Omnibus officially closed down and laid off all its employees.

1987

METROLIGHT STUDIOS FOUNDED: Metrolight Studios was founded by James Kristoff, Mits Kaneko, and Dobbie Schiff. They made a mark in feature film with 1989's *Total Recall.* The project required animating skeletons as characters passed through a futuristic security device capable of detecting anything from a weapon to a slipped disk. Metrolight won the Oscar for Visual Effects that year, the first for use of CG in a feature film.

your arcs and your spacing is placed where you know it should be. You can follow the arcs of your motion by choosing a point, such as the nose on a head, and placing a little dot on the screen for each frame. As you step through the animation, follow along the dot-to-dot pattern to see where the arc goes. You can also draw the arc you want the head to follow and step through the process of adjusting the head to follow that arc. When pressed for time on a shot, you can even work out thumbnails directly on the screen as you revise motion per the director's and supervisor's comments.

Some animators also watch live-action reference frame by frame to help them figure out what the next frame should look like while working on their in-betweening. Whatever it takes, pay attention to your in-betweens and do not let the computer do them for you. In 2D, the key animator draws the whole pose and the breakdown artists and in-betweeners follow your timing chart to figure out the in-between frames. In CG, you are in charge of *all* of the motion. This is sometimes even more difficult than 2D because much of traditional animation is drawn on twos, and you are now animating on ones. Remember, every frame counts!

Creating Overlap and Secondary Motion

Overlap is the technique of describing the mechanics of motion as weight throughout the character and any drapery that the character may be wearing. Overlap is one of the traditional principles of animation. If your character comes to a complete stop, various elements of its structure as well as drapery will come to a rest at different times. This is overlap. Different parts of the body will arrive at different rates, depending upon their relative weight. It's a subtle thing, but the viewer feels that motion. You must take great care when applying this traditional principle to computer animation. When you are using a computer to animate, it is easy to create overlap mathematically by offsetting frames, but it can become cyclical and stale if you do not tweak this motion outside of the mathematical solution the computer generates. As discussed previously, this layering and offsetting of keys method works well if you understand how to progressively break the joints in the hierarchy. Whether you use the layered, offsetting keys method or the posed overlap method, you must understand what you want the final motion to look like in your head. Otherwise, this motion will never move accurately. If you understand how to create overlapping motion in the poses you assign to the motion, you will most likely create the most realistic description of weight.

Nothing in a living, breathing character moves at the same rate. It's pretty easy to let the computer create the overlap for you, but you must remember that every frame counts. You must tell the computer how much overlap you want, thereby defining the weight. A character's ears can be as floppy as a rabbit's or as stiff as a

1987

DeGRAF/WAHRMAN IS FORMED: deGraf/Wahrman was founded by former Abel employee Michael Wahrman and former DP director Brad deGraf after the folding of DOA. In 1988, deGraf/Wahrman developed Mike the Talking Head for Silicon Graphics to show off the real-time capabilities of their new 4D machines. Mike was driven by a specially built controller that allowed a single puppeteer to control many parameters of the character's face, including mouth, eyes, expression, and head position.

1987

RHYTHM & HUES FOUNDED: Founded by former Abel & Associates employees and Omnibus' Larry Weinberg, R&H is one of the most reputable CG firms in the industry and a leading producer of character animation and visual effects for the entertainment industry.

cat's according to how much overlap you allow. The computer will only apply a mathematical approximation of how much these things move between each key frame you set. Don't rely on the computer to create the overlap for you. Mike Surrey explains applying this 2D approach to CG:

> I think the best success I've had is when I apply a 2D approach to the planning of a CG shot. I look at every control on a rig as a possible pencil stroke and keep in mind the basics of squash and stretch and, most importantly, overlap. Overlap, more than anything, gets overlooked, and animators will lean on the computer to do it for them when they need to get the scene done for production.

Using the computer to get halfway there by mathematically offsetting keys is fine when you are creating overlapping motion. However, you must understand how to add texture to that motion. We have talked about the floaty look that is caused by even timing and how to prevent that by adjusting the bias of curves in the graph editor as well as setting additional keys. Adding texture can be done by using both of these techniques. If you do not add texture to overlapping motion, it will appear stale and mechanical.

Utilizing variations in texture will lend your overlap personality. The cycle of overlap on a bouncing rabbit's ears can be created initially with even timing to get the basic motion looking right. Then the animator must add texture to a cycle to show shifts in weight or to make one ear lighter than the other. Many times living things favor one limb. For example, if you are right-handed and you walk in a desert with no compass, thinking you are walking in a straight line, you will actually be walking in a circle because you will be stronger on your right leg and take longer strides on that side. It's very easy to get a cycle of overlap going on a character jumping up and down. Bounce, bounce, bounce go the arms and ears at different rates but at cyclical timings. Nik Ranieri illustrates more about how he creates overlapping motion on the computer:

> Secondary motion takes just as much time as the primary animation, just trying to get that working. That's one good thing about 3D also—that the secondary animation is so much easier. I mean, you can get something going, a cycle, and you just repeat it and repeat it and then finesse it a bit.

1987

KLEISER/WALCZAK CONSTRUCTION CO. FORMED:
When Omnibus closed, Jeff Kleiser, a computer animator, joined Diana Walczak and formed a new company, Kleiser-Walczak Construction Company. Their new firm's specialty was human figure animation. In 1988 they produced a 3 1/2–minute music video with a computer-generated character named Dozo and used motion control to input all of her movements.

1987

ReZ.n8 FORMS IN LOS ANGELES:
Paul Sidlo worked as Creative Director for Cranston/Csuri Productions until he left to form his own computer graphics studio, ReZ.n8. Since then, ReZ.n8 has continued to be a leader in producing high-quality computer graphics.

151

The next step is to alter that cycle according to shifts in weight, such as a bum knee giving in, the character getting tired, simple differences in how the character takes off and lands, or whatever. Just like the walk in the desert, different things can affect how overlapping will describe weight. As long as you ensure that the timing is not the same for the motion, you will be in good shape.

Creating Principal and Secondary Characters

In traditional animation, the hierarchy of animators is very structured. On a hand-drawn movie the supervising animator is usually in charge of a character for the entire movie. This individual is the point person for that character and will handle most of the scenes with that character, even if there are other characters in the scene. Rarely does a traditional animator handle all characters in a scene. Occasionally, if there is a lot of interaction between two characters—if the characters are dancing or fighting, for instance—the supervising animator will let other animators handle all the characters, including the main character. In these cases, the supervising animator will sometimes provide rough drawings for size and position, or even a rough box for where the character will be placed.

In CG, it works best to have the CG animator handle all the characters. The introduction of the Z-axis in computer-generated animation makes it almost impossible not to have one animator working on multiple-character scenes with heavy interaction. In traditional animation, animators can lay pieces of paper with drawings on top of one another and animate to each other's motion. In CG, the characters physically touch each other in 3D space, and this method of having multiple animators doesn't always work. The important thing to remember when animating multiple characters is to contrast their actions in a complimentary way. A great example of this kind of contrast is with the Spike the Bulldog and Chester the Terrier characters in the Warner Bros.' *Looney Tunes* and *Merrie Melodies* series of cartoons.

Spike is a burly, gray bulldog, the bully in the neighborhood, who wears a perpetual scowl. Chester is just the opposite. Small and jumpy with yellow fur and brown, perky ears, Chester is very active, jumping up and down next to Spike as he plods along. Adding this element of contrast in character is very important when working on multiple-character scenes. Do not animate your character inside a vacuum. Make sure that your character relates well to both the background and other characters in the scene.

1987

PRINCIPLES OF TRADITIONAL ANIMATION APPLIED TO 3D COMPUTER ANIMATION: John Lasseter at Pixar published a paper describing traditional animation principles. Demos were *Andre and Wally B.* and *Luxo Jr.*

1988

***ALICE* IS JAN SVANKMAJER'S FIRST FILM – STOP-MOTION:** A memorably bizarre screen version of Lewis Carroll's novel *Alice in Wonderland*, mixing one live actor with a huge variety of sinister animated puppets, ranging from the complex to the incredibly simple. Jan Svankmajer is known for his surrealistic animations and features, which have greatly influenced many other artists.

CG Tools

With all this bashing of the box, is there anything that CG makes easier for the animator? Well, believe it or not, the computer does have some advantages. Workflow and ease of revisions are at the top of the list. It's been a long, hard road to get the kind of instant feedback that tools such as Playblast provide. Tools such as the Undo button also offer easy revisions compared to a pencil eraser. Bernd Angerer offers more on how CG has come far in its tools for the artist:

> I think the digital workflow offers an intriguing logistical advantage over traditional media, generally speaking. Undo is a wonderful invention. But having been in this industry since the late 1980s, I can also say that back then, CG animation was mostly a technical exercise, spending a lot of time trying to make the software do what it can't do. Today's software has generally figured out the basics and offers time to actually work artistically.

The feedback you get on the computer is pretty instant and helpful. To be able to see your moving poses within seconds in real time is a plus. In addition, to be able to delete something or go backward through steps with the Undo button is equally powerful. Not to mention the fact that you can view your action from various different angles, a feature never available in traditional animation. 2D animation has always required a lengthy approach to see exactly how drawings would play out in motion. Flipping pages was the fastest way to see how the action was working, but that was never completely accurate. Tom Sito provides an amusing example of what some 2D animators used to have to do to see what their drawings looked like in motion:

> In the 1930s, Max Fleischer was too cheap to do all the film developing. The animators between each desk had a bucket of developer. When they shot the test, they gave the animator the roll, and he yanked it out of the cartridge, dropped it in the bucket, and pulled it out and looked at it before it went black. It was insane! Who knows what kind of poison was absorbed into your skin from the developer?

In addition to faster feedback of motion on the computer, the sheer number of controls provided can add depth that might not have always been there in traditional animation. With all of the controls that CG rigs provide, it can be scary to try to decide what should move. A line drawing has a charm that CG has a hard time replicating, but the subtlety that CG can create in lighting, muscle tone, and flexion of the skin is something that is almost impossible to achieve in hand-drawn animation.

1988

OSCAR FOR *BALANCE*: *Balance* won the Academy Award for Best Short Subject: Animated Films.

1988

DISNEY AND PIXAR DEVELOP CAPS: The Computer Animation Production System (CAPS) is a proprietary collection of software programs, camera systems, and custom disks developed by the Walt Disney Company together with Pixar. Its purpose was to computerize the ink and paint and post-production processes of traditionally animated feature films. The first usage of the CAPS process was the ending rainbow scene of *The Little Mermaid*. Subsequent films were made completely with CAPS.

"I think one of the advantages of CG is the degree of subtlety in animation. It allows us to push acting in subtle levels we haven't seen before. That's one of the best parts about the computer in my personal experience. When I step frame by frame through live-action reference, I'm always amazed at all the things going on. In a simple smile, it's not just the lips...now the cheeks are involved, the nose, the nostrils, the eyelids, eyebrows, the muscles around the face, et cetera."

—*Carlos Baena*

Staying on model has always been a tough task for 2D animators. You can draw anything! You can stretch and squash to your heart's content. A sound structure while animating is so important to keeping the character believable. Traditional animators tend to have a maquette, or sculpture of the character, at their desk to help them visualize the character from all angles while they draw it.

CG didn't have an "off model" problem in the early days. The folks building rigs and working in CG didn't even dare to think that they could play with the forms of the rig without it looking broken. This is why early CG lent itself to hard-shelled characters such as bugs or toys. It wasn't until the tools advanced and more traditional animators crossed over that the ability to distort shapes in a controllable manner began to appear in CG. The computer artists had to learn how to push the model to create a pleasing shape and play up to the camera but still stay true to the character's volume and silhouette. The early rigs were more like puppets. Nowadays, rigs must be more fluid and elastic, giving more control to the animator and enabling the animator to squash and stretch the model into the most appealing shape.

This is why many traditional animators see computer-generated animation as an extension of stop-motion animation or virtual puppets. Pushing the rigs to go off model is technically quite a task today and is one of the most important features that riggers continue to work on. It is very hard to take a character off model in CG. Riggers are working harder every day to push the limits of character rigs, in order to give animators more control over the one aspect that has been lacking in a lot of CG animation: exaggeration. Eric Goldberg knows this firsthand:

1988

WHO FRAMED ROGER RABBIT IS RELEASED: This film is a landmark motion picture that combines animation and live action. The animated characters were hand-drawn without computer animation; analog optical effects were used for adding shadows and lighting to give the 'toons a more realistic, 3D appearance. The movie won four Oscars and a Special Award for Richard Williams and reinvigorated the animation field, which had become lackluster.

1988

WILLOW POPULARIZES THE EFFECT OF MORPHING: Lucasfilm used the morphing technique in *Willow*, in which a sorceress transforms into a series of animals before morphing into her final shape as a human. Over the years *Willow* has developed a cult following and is now considered one of the best films of its genre.

It's far easier and quicker to draw animation than to model, rig, and animate it in CG. I'll say something encouraging about the evolution of the CG animation technology itself. When we created *The Magic Lamp 3D* (2001) at Disney in CG, it took us a year to complete. It took a year to produce five minutes of CG animation! Today, in 2005, we just cranked out these Disneyland commercials with the same caliber of animation in CG and the same type of squash and stretch and distortion as *Magic Lamp* in record time. Yes, I know some of the 50th Anniversary commercials were put together with bubble gum and bailing wire in order to do it on such a short schedule. But, it got done in a fraction of the time! This means that: A) the technology has caught up and is able to adapt to the demands of the animator, and B) the people working in CG have a much greater awareness of why things have to distort, stretch, and go off model to create a dynamic pose. They can accommodate these needs now in CG. It's silly to say you can't do something in CG, because you can. What seems difficult and complicated now, in two years' time will seem like standard issue.

CG is still its own beast, though it has come full circle with many of the same issues traditional animators fought with pen and paper. One thing about CG that computer animators will always fight is the underwater floaty motion the computer generates, although there is one instance in which that look can work to your advantage. The floaty nature that is so easy to achieve in CG can be advantageous when working on underwater characters, such as fish. If you were to try to create a sinuous underwater motion drawing by hand, it would be quite an arduous task, but on a computer you can set a couple key frames and cycle it, and you are done.

Finally, camera angles and scale are very easy to change in CG. This can be a handicap because it makes it all too easy for people to create camera moves just for the sake of creating camera moves. The camera should always be invisible; you shouldn't be able notice it. In CG, you can create moves that are impossible to create in live action. Changing a camera move in traditional animation is a big task. In fact, changing an animated camera move is virtually impossible without completely redrawing every

"Working on *Shark Tale*, every scene is under water. Trying to animate that in 2D can be hell. Re-pegging the character can take up a lot of valuable time from animating. In CG, I hit a couple of keys in the graph editor, and in less than a minute I have my character floating."

—*Mike Surrey*

1988

OLIVER AND COMPANY DISNEY'S 27TH FEATURE AND USES CGI EFFECTS: *Oliver and Company* was the first Disney movie to make heavy use of computer layout and props; previous films *The Black Cauldron* and *The Great Mouse Detective* used it only for special sequences.

1989

OSCAR FOR *TIN TOY* (PIXAR): *Tin Toy* won the Academy Award for Best Short Subject: Animated Films. Directed by John Lasseter, it was the first 100% computer-generated film to win an Oscar. It also marks the first time a realistic human character was attempted in a computer-animated film.

1989

THE LAND BEFORE TIME RELEASED: *The Land Before Time* was originally released in movie theatres in 1988 by Universal Pictures.

aspect. Changing a camera move in CG is less of a problem, but the poses still have to be reworked to play up to the camera. However, perspective is not an issue because the camera already figures that out for you.

In summary, 2D has many advantages that CG can't touch. 2D has a charm and warmth that the computer has a difficult time getting without a lot of massaging from the rigger and animator. 2D can illustrate a style through the use of lines and drastic changes in shape. But CG can also help the animator with quick feedback. CG has an Undo button that many of us would like to have for life in general. Making changes to an action can be done fairly quickly and easily in the computer, as opposed to the endless hours you may have to spend redrawing an action that does not work in the traditional medium. The ability to change a camera quickly is another advantage of CG, but not without a caveat. When the camera is changed in CG, the animator still has to play the poses up to the new camera framing. This is more work, of course, but changing the poses to play up to the newly staged camera is still easier than having to completely redraw the entire scene over again from a different angle. With its sheer number of controls, CG has the ability to push animation to areas that have not yet been dreamed of.

Pushing Your CG Animation to a Higher Level

The Nine Old Men at Disney helped develop the principles of animation that all animators have used to learn the craft of animation. We provide a list of the actual 12 principles and a brief description of each in Appendix E of this book. This section will present some of these ideas more broadly and apply them to the actual production process within a CG pipeline. These concepts applied successfully to your work will be the glue that holds it all together. To push your animation to a higher level, you must address each of these steps with critical attention to detail. The last three sections specifically address the production process and how to handle getting your animation from storyboard to final. Here we will explain the importance of weight, contrasts in timing, reality versus exaggeration, lip-synch styles, moving holds, attention to detail, motion blur, drawing skills, and the approval, revision, and cleanup processes. Let's get started!

Weight

Weight is a tricky thing. An elephant and a mouse could both jump in the air at the same time, and in a realistic, non-cartoony world, the mouse would jump higher than the elephant (in relative terms, of course). Why? Well, even though the elephant is bigger than the mouse and you would think it would be stronger with more dense muscle than the mouse, the elephant has much more mass to move structurally. This is an

1989

MENTAL RAY RENDERER RELEASED: The Mental Ray renderer is a production-quality rendering application developed by Mental Images. As the name implies, it supports ray tracing to generate images. It awarded an AMPAS Technical Achievement Award in 2002.

1989

***THE ABYSS* RELEASED:** James Cameron's *The Abyss* won the 1990 Oscar for Best Visual Effects, including a computer-generated "water tentacle" (called the "pseudopod"). *The Abyss* won a total of three awards from the Academy of Science Fiction, Fantasy & Horror Films and the American Society of Cinematographers.

ORIGINAL CREATIVE VISIONARY TALENT

Doing it all, from design, to delivery.

The Animators

They're hip, they're driven, they're talented, but most of all, they care.

They're hip, they're driven, they're talented, but most of all, they care. Unknown artist.

 1989

PIXAR STARTS MARKETING RENDERMAN: Pixar's first tool was RenderMan, a rendering software system for photorealistic image synthesis that enabled computer graphics artists to apply textures and colors to surfaces of 3D images onscreen. Pixar licensed the tool to third parties and eventually sold upwards of 100,000 copies. For several years, while other projects were being developed, RenderMan provided Pixar with its primary source of revenues.

 1989

THE LITTLE MERMAID RELEASED:
Disney's *The Little Mermaid* grossed more than $80 million domestically and is given credit for breathing life back into Disney's feature animation division after a string of critical and commercial failures, signaling the start of a decade-long period of successful Disney animated movies.

illustration of weight. If the elephant jumped higher than a mouse, you would not believe that he was a real elephant. You educated eye knows that it would take so much power to move all of that mass, and that the elephant would barely move an inch or two in the air, while a mouse could not only jump half a foot in the air, but do so easily and quickly. Similarly, the motion of a mosquito flitting across the water would have a much lighter feel than a dinosaur charging across a field. This is what we call *weight*. You must portray weight convincingly in your animation, or it will lack believability.

On a computer, you are again dealing with the many parts that comprise a whole. You are moving a character's arms, legs, and torso to describe its weight. You need to find the center of gravity and work out from that center to show where the weight is being distributed throughout the body. The center of gravity is almost always at the center of the chest and hip areas, unless the character is being hit by something. Then, the center of gravity starts from wherever the character is being hit. Understand that you cannot just raise a leg without showing that weight shift happening throughout the rest of the body. All parts of the body react to weight shifts.

"Some people have a sort of 'cyberpuppet' attitude: When they want a character to turn its head, they turn just the head and the body remains frozen. I keep saying you can't do that. You have to slightly adjust all parts of the body to show weight shifts that compensate for the body moving around. It's like an echo effect. Everything moves. Every movement echoes down to the center of gravity, down to the source, which is the middle of the chest. Everything. No matter what you do. You move an arm, and the chest is going to rotate slightly, and the shoulder's going to adjust to that movement and so on down the tree. You turn the head to the left, and the chest is going to rotate slightly toward the left."

—*Nik Ranieri*

How do we describe weight in animation? How do the same tricks and principles of traditional animation translate to describing weight when animating on a computer? Why is weight such an issue with people who first try to animate on a computer? It all comes back to your key frames. The computer is a machine and therefore will create mechanical motion. You have to take into consideration how weight moves throughout the hierarchy of the joints as it is absorbed. A big creature needs time to build momentum. Picture an

1989

AUTODESK UNVEILS ANIMATOR: At SIG-GRAPH 1989, Autodesk unveiled a new PC-based full-featured 2D animation and painting package called Autodesk Animator. It was Autodesk's first step into the multimedia tools realm. The software-only animation playback capabilities achieved very impressive speeds and became a standard for playing animation on PCs.

1989

ALL DOGS GO TO HEAVEN RELEASED: Although *All Dogs Go to Heaven* received positive reviews from critics, it was a box-office flop. It grossed $27 million dollars, and some of this was a result of Disney's comeback with *The Little Mermaid*.

18-wheeler building up speed from a standstill or, conversely, coming to a stop from speed. Picture the forces at work bringing that massive object to a standstill from highway speed, the shrieking tires, the burning brake linings, and the shaking of the cab and trailer. What a great illustration of weight. Now picture a hummingbird coming to hover by a flower. Both objects come to a stop, but with a massive difference in weight. The momentum has to build and be dissipated. Chris Bailey explains how weight is so important to making the mechanics of motion feel natural:

> The worst thing I see is when the foot of the CGI character "slows in" to the ground on a walk. The foot should go from full speed to zero in one frame (relatively speaking). Even worse, or just as bad as the spliney feel to CG animation, is creature animation that is jerky, like bad stop-mo. Sadly, some animators just don't have the sensitivity to make CG characters run and still feel natural. Maybe it comes from a lack of understanding of weight, but I see runs on CG creatures that look like the film was sped up because their body is changing direction faster than their mass would allow in real life.

All weight shifts can be described through compression and expansion of the structure that is carrying the weight. Weight can be described through compression of the knees as you carry something heavy or the bending of a diving board as it handles the weight of a diver. Little vibrations or "staggers" in the limbs of a human can describe extreme weight. Every key frame you place will help you describe weight in your character, so do not take for granted the need for nuance in your illustration of where the weight is being shifted. Remember how the entire body plays a part in weight shifts, and make sure all of your breakdowns describe these shifts.

Contrasts in Timing

It is so easy to create even timing on the computer. If you are keying hundreds of controls on the body, it's easier to just set keys on fours for all of those controls and end up with even timing. Don't do it! Take control! Nail your poses and then finesse the timing. The finesse step is the most difficult part of animation and also the most important.

Contrast in timing is very important to natural-looking motion. Dancers spend years trying to make their movements so tight that they hit on numbered counts. If you watch your animation while counting out beats

1990

OSAMU TEZUKA DIES: Osamu Tezuka (1926–1989) is best know as the manga creator of *Astro Boy* and *Kimba the White Lion*.

1990

OSCAR FOR *CREATURE COMFORTS* (AARDMAN ANIMATION LTD): *Creature Comforts* won the Academy Award for Best Short Subject: Animated Films.

1990

MEL BLANC DIES: Mel Blanc (1908–1989), known as "the man of a thousand voices," was the first voice talent to receive screen credit. Mel Blanc joined Warner Bros. Pictures in 1936 and soon became the noted voice of a variety of cartoon characters, including Bugs Bunny, Tweety Bird, Porky Pig, Daffy Duck, and many others.

159

and you notice that all of the poses are hitting on even timing, you know you need to start shifting your spacing around to get more contrast so that the motion doesn't look rehearsed or mechanical. Unless you are animating a chorus line, even timing is not the goal. The computer will not help you create contrasts in timing; that is up to you. Scott Holmes offers his approach to timing on a computer:

> I make all of the decisions for the computer. I decide where the weight is, where the breakdowns are, and what the timing is. When I am finished with a shot, the computer hasn't done any of the thinking for me. If your shot looks like the computer did the work, it probably did, and that's why it looks floaty and wrong. I think the computer is like working with the worst assistant, like working with a guy who never understands arcs or slow ins and slow outs. You have to show him what to do every time you give him a task. So I leave as little to the machine as possible. Usually I just key the hell out of everything, and I make sure every single frame looks proper.

Again, at the risk of being obnoxious, every frame counts, and your timing has to look natural. Even jazz composers break up the rhythms they have created to make their music more interesting. You need to do the same to your animation and adjust the timing of the motion to have greater impact. The timing of your poses should have a rhythm, texture, and flow, much like great music. The beats and rests in the music between the verse and the chorus change to hold interest, and so should your animation. You decided where the keys go, so move them around until the timing feels natural. Don't let the computer animate for you, because believe me, the computer is the worst assistant you will ever work with, and it will never understand what it takes to make motion look believable.

Reality versus Entertainment Exaggeration?

Many CG animators get caught up in realism. The computer adds such an element of realism with three dimensions, lighting, fur, and so on that we lose sight of what is entertaining to watch.

Is it more entertaining to watch an animal walk toward you or to watch the animal walk toward you with intent? Is it more entertaining to watch someone propose marriage or propose marriage and fight the fear of commitment at the same time? Push your work to go past the clichéd and the trite. If the character is anxious or worried, don't have the character rub the back of his neck like everyone else has done (or rather, overdone). Find the pose that best describes the character's predicament and push it as far as you can.

1990

RICHARD WILLIAMS RECEIVES SPECIAL ACHIEVEMENT AWARD: Richard Williams was presented with a Special Achievement Oscar for directing the animation in *Who Framed Roger Rabbit.* The only time this award had been previously given for animation was to Walt Disney for *Snow White and the Seven Dwarfs.*

1990

THE RESCUERS DOWN UNDER 29TH DISNEY FEATURE: This was Disney's first sequel to an animated movie, *The Rescuers,* and the only one (besides *Toy Story 2*) that had a theatrical release.

The entertainment value of what you are animating should always be foremost in your mind. Entertainment can even defy reality if it makes sense in the scene. Suspension of disbelief is where you create something that couldn't happen in real life, but the audience believes it because it has been presented in a believable manner. Video games and high-action films know this fact. Push your poses beyond what is real to get an extreme caricature of entertainment value. Push the timing to reinforce the story and be so engaging that the audience cannot look away. Hanging onto a great pose for one more frame may just sell the idea. Forget what the rig can do and reach far back into your mind for what will reinforce the directive of the scene. If you want to hang that character in the air for just one extra frame before he falls on his butt, do it! By constantly pushing yourself to find the most entertaining and imaginative way of animating a scene, you will ensure that you are always growing as an artist. To simply satisfy what the director has asked you to provide for the scene will place you among the mediocre. Reach deep down and find out how you can make that shot stand out and reinforce its place in the story.

Dialogue and Lip-Synch Styles

Dialogue is a key component to defining a character. Dialogue is the frosting on the cake you just baked with the body movements. Cake is just not the same without good frosting.

The first approach to developing dialogue for CG is simply to apply what we call the "Henson method." This means to have the mouth open when it should be open and closed when it should be closed. Why are Jim Henson's Muppets so believable when they speak? One reason is this: The mouth is open when it should be open and closed when it should be closed. Simple and obvious, but nothing defeats believability quicker than bad lip synch. Scott Holmes offers a neat trick he uses to ensure he is hitting these beats:

> Put you finger under your chin and say the dialogue with the actor. It will give you a good indication of how many times the jaw opens and to what intensity. This is an easy way to find your accents and rhythms.

In addition to Scott's trick, most CG programs offer a great tool where you can see the waveform of the sound in the timeline. Looking at the waveform you can see where the sound is loud, usually meaning the mouth is open, and where the sound is quiet, usually meaning the mouth is closed.

1990

GRIM NATWICK DIES: Myron "Grim" Natwick (1890–1990) was an American animator and film director, regarded as one of the greatest of all time. He is best known for creating Fleischer Studios' most popular character, Betty Boop. At Disney, Natwick was a lead animator on *Snow White and the Seven Dwarfs* and was instrumental in bringing the heroine to life.

1990

3D STUDIO IS RELEASED: Autodesk formed a Multimedia division and introduced the first animation tool, 3D Studio software. 3D Studio has risen to the lead position in PC-based 3D computer animation software.

In computer-generated animation, the facial is usually established with preconceived blend shapes that describe emotions and verbal communication. Layering these shapes creates more attitude and broadens the range of what the facial can do. A good facial rig can handle this layering to create additional shapes. Mike Surrey adds:

> I try to spend time finding and creating mouth shapes that are different from what's given with a character. In CG, I noticed that a lot of the time, dialogue gets breezed over because the mouth shapes are already created, and a lazy animator will use them and will rarely tweak them to give them a unique look.

While we are on the subject of facial and mouth shapes, it is also important to think of the eyebrows as one united line. The controls in CG will enable you to break up this line because they are separated into left and right to give you more flexibility, but there should be a line of action you can follow through the brows. Think of Jack Nicholson with one brow arched in that priceless expression. That line of action flows right into the other brow, which will be down.

Finally, remember delivery and changes in attitude when listening to dialogue, and make sure you emphasize those moments. This is where entertainment values can really be "amped" to show emotion. Eyes are crucial to expressing an attitude change, so do not forget them either. Eyes and eye darts were explained in depth in Chapter 4.

Moving Holds

The moving hold is one of those juicy moments most animators hope to get in their assigned shots. The moving hold is often used when a character is thinking, and the audience gets to pause and savor that beat, that moment. The character stops moving from pose to pose and rests to make a point. But the character cannot completely stop moving, or else the suspension of disbelief is lost and the characters are dead.

The moving hold is one of those things that is so fleeting in CG. In some traditional animation, the moving hold can be created with simply a series of very tight tracings of a single drawing. The natural imperfections inherent in the drawn line lend a certain life to an image even though it is barely moving, so it doesn't seem to die quite as quickly as CG does. In CG there needs to be a bit more texture; otherwise, the depth of the medium gives it away and makes everything seem dead and lifeless. CG animators have to add a few subtle changes to make that hold real and let the viewer savor the pose.

 1990

THE JOURNAL OF VISUALIZATION AND COMPUTER ANIMATION: John Wiley & Sons begins publishing *The Journal of Visualization and Computer Animation.* This journal aimed to publish research papers on the technological developments that would make animation tools more accessible to end users.

 1991

OSCAR FOR MANIPULATION (DANIEL GREAVES): *Manipulation* won an Academy Award for Best Short Subject: Animated Films. Daniel Greaves' film used a technique called pixilation, shooting the live action of hands frame by frame alongside the character animation, making them to appear to be interacting with one another.

Moving holds also offer a place for more acting in the eyes and facial because once the body stops moving, the viewer looks right at the face to figure out what the character is thinking. Eric Goldberg explains more about how to create a successful moving hold:

> In CG, what you would have is a moving hold when the character is drifting from one position to the next over the period of the hold. Then you would have the same thing as in hand-drawn, where subtle movement would overlap that moving hold, whether it's overlap of a hat or ears catching up, or hair, or clothing, or a slight facial change, such as an eye dart or blink.

Eyes become very important during a moving hold. They transmit the character's thoughts. When the rest of the body stops moving, the audience looks at the face to find out why. This is your chance to make the eyes tell the story. You can make the character blink a few times, as if he is astonished, startled, or thinking about the situation. You can have the character look around as if he is guilty, lost, or confused. Or you can have the character simply look at another character in the scene. Holding that look for a beat can create a wonderful moment that is both powerful and subtle.

Weight also plays a big role in making a moving hold successful. You cannot just stop the body from moving, from translating. That is unnatural. As we said earlier, when people settle into a pose, different parts of the body will come to rest at different times. The computer will just stop moving everything abruptly, so you have to add that texture. The arms may dangle, the body may shift around; the hair, being lightest, will come to rest last. Let's say you ran into a room, excited because your best friend is in town for the day and is coming to visit. You find your dog has eaten all of your shoes (God forbid!), relieved himself on the bed, and chewed up the cords to the PlayStation. You would stop and assess what you see for a beat, gauging how to react. This would be a great spot for a moving hold. Your weight would shift all over your body, recovering from running down the hall. Arms, head, and torso would all regain balance as you slide into the room. Finally, all the various elements would come to a rest, and the audience would look to your face to see your reaction.

The moment the audience looks at the face is the moment you have been waiting for, so make it good. You can even use the tool presented earlier, in the "Contrasts in Timing" section, to make the hold really stand out. If the aforementioned premise is an animated scene, make the next moment drastically different in energy than the moving hold. After you see what your dog has done and you are still in the moving hold, you can contrast that motion by going nuts, running wildly with your hands flailing to get the place ready for

1991

BEAUTY AND THE BEAST NOMINATED FOR BEST PICTURE: Disney's *Beauty and the Beast* was the first animated feature to be nominated for the Academy Award for Best Picture. Up against four other contenders it didn't scoop the award, but went on to win a Golden Globe and Oscars for Best Original Score and Best Song, and it ushered in the latest Golden Age of Disney feature animation.

1991

REN & STIMPY PREMIERES: The *Ren & Stimpy Show* debuted on Nickelodeon, instantly catching the attention of both children and adults. Within a couple of months, it was the most popular show, animated or not, on cable TV.

your friend's visit. The timing of the moving hold will give a comical release to the tension of the scene. The moving-hold moment is where you can also introduce the psychological gesture and subtext that we spoke of in Chapter 4.

As we discussed in Chapter 4, psychological gesture is an acting mechanism that reveals what the character is thinking without speaking. Because in a moving hold most of the body is at rest and the character is not speaking, this is the one of the best places to use psychological gestures effectively. Psychological gestures come into play for longer moving holds with a scratch or an eye dart. These can be some of the hardest moments, but rich in acting and performance. Scott Holmes talks about moving holds:

> A moving hold seems like the simplest thing, but if a hold looks floaty or wrong or stiff, it blows your whole animation. A bad hold breaks believability in an instant and ruins the whole illusion of life. I try to add overlapping action to help break up a hold, but if every part has fallen into place and it still has to hold, I think about where the weight is and I try to animate the hips, taking the weight a bit more or settling into a pose. If I simply take a key and make it hold, it rarely works for me. Somewhere I have to break up the arc and pick a key to favor. There is a great moving hold in *Monsters, Inc.* in which Sully opens the door, stands there a second not moving as he looks around, and has that look in his eyes. Nothing else moves, and then he says, "Boo."

When you are working on moving holds, ask yourself whether it feels right. Sometimes it's hard to decipher because you're doing it in a sub-beat of the main motions. Just remember that the moving hold is one of the greatest opportunities for acting and humor.

Attention to Detail

One of the writers we interviewed for this book hit the nail on the head with her perspective on animation and details. Laura McCreary says:

> From a writer's perspective, the visual acting in animation can sometimes sell the story better than the voice acting. There's nothing worse than getting a show back from Korea and seeing a character stare into space, unblinking during an entire scene. Comic timing and emotion are all in the details. And from what I've heard, so is God, so there you have it.

1991

HANNA-BARBERA BOUGHT BY TURNER: Struggling to regain its once enviable position in the industry, Hanna-Barbera was purchased by Turner Broadcasting for $320 million.

1991

DISNEY AND PIXAR MAKE A DEAL: In 1991, after substantial layoffs in the company's computer department, Pixar made a $26 million deal with Disney to produce computer-animated feature films, the first of which was *Toy Story*.

1991

ROCK-A-DOODLE **RELEASED:** *Rock-a-Doodle* is an animated retelling of Edmund Rostand's *Chanticleer.* The film wasn't well received by critics, judging by its low box-office returns and audiences.

As Laura observes, a simple blink can make a scene funny and show what the character is thinking. Walt Disney always said, "The mind is the pilot," meaning that whatever the character is thinking drives the action. So the details will reveal to us what the character is thinking. Details include hands, eyes, and facial. As animators, we have to pay close attention to the subtle motion we add to these small but very important parts. To push these details, we need nuance, subtlety, and expression that computer-generated animation has lacked in the past. We cannot treat the characters like digital lepers who cannot touch each other or themselves because of technical issues such as penetration and collision spheres. We must embrace the fact that computer-generated animation has depth and push that further. Conrad Vernon explains how James Baxter pushed the medium on *Shrek 2*:

> James Baxter did some amazing animation tests on *Shrek 2* where Fiona put her hands on her face and drew them over her face. As she did, her eyes went down and her cheeks went down and her lips went down, and they all popped back up when she left off with her fingertips. When you draw, you can put a finger into skin, and the skin wrinkles up because you draw it. There is no reaction with the computer. You can't literally have something touch something else because then it crashes the technology. James animated the hands over the face and then animated the eyes drooping down and the skin coming down, and it was just beautiful. Unfortunately, that took so long...people don't normally go that extra mile. Computer programmers look at it and say, "Don't do that!" We are always pushing forward. It's so new. It's kind of like *Toy Story* was the *Snow White* of CG animation.

Remember that attention to detail in all of your animation will push it further than ever before. It's easy to get lost in all of the controls in CG. Just like driving a fancy sports car, you will be nervous at first. But you will find your rhythm and workflow eventually. Within that workflow, remember to pay close attention to adding the details necessary to express the state of mind your character is in and how you can express that in the clearest way. Don't view the computer as a hindrance, but as a tool with almost unlimited possibilities, as James Baxter did with Fiona.

Motion Blur and Squash and Stretch

Motion blur is being used more extensively these days because it is a valuable tool in creating realistic or believable motion and in eliminating strobing effects on fast moves. When you film any action that has a high rate of speed—for example, a pitcher throwing a ball or a tennis player serving—you will see a blurring of certain parts of the body when stop-framing the film of the action. Traditional animators usually describe

1991

ILM PRODUCES *TERMINATOR* 2: The first *Terminator* film was relatively low-budget, but *Terminator 2* was the most expensive film ever made at the time. As computer technology advanced, director James Cameron used it to create impressive special effects in his film, *The Abyss*. In *Terminator 2*, he pushed all the buttons. *Terminator 2* won four Academy Awards.

1991

SGI INDIGO WORKSTATION INTRODUCED: The Indigo, fondly called the purple box by computer artists, was considered one of the most capable graphics workstations of its era and was among the elite in the realm of hardware-accelerated 3D graphics rendering.

motion blur with drawings stretched in extreme shapes or with a dry brush effect. The more blurred the drawing is, the faster the motion of the character will appear. In CG, motion blur is an effect that can be digitally applied to the images to smooth out fast motion. Either way, this blurring should never been seen, but merely suggested to the eye (unless you are going through the animation frame by frame).

A new approach to motion blur in CG has occurred as more traditional animators have entered the field of computer-generated animation. The drawn blur frames are now being achieved in CG as extreme poses, like in hand-drawn animation. This look gives more fluid motion and squash and stretch properties to the character and is really fun to watch. Just like motion blur applied as a post-production effect, these blurred frames should not be seen for too long, or the character will look too gooey and the effect will be given away. In the world of 2D, these drawings are always exposed on single frames. Some of the best examples of hand-drawn motion blur can be found in the Warner Bros. cartoons of the '40s and '50s. Chuck Jones' *The Dover Boys* has some particularly hilarious effects. Be careful, though. Unless it's for obvious comedic effect, motion blur should be felt rather than seen.

The blur frame should just be suggested with a stretched finger or an elongated arm that overshoots a natural length. These poses should only last a frame or two to suggest an extreme motion. Think of a boxer's face when he is punched. We only see the distorted image if a camera with a super-fast shutter speed is used. Otherwise, the persistence of vision simply suggests the hit in our minds. The same thing happens in

Example of a blur frame pose and a non-blur frame in CG.

1991

AN AMERICAN TALE: FIEVEL GOES WEST: This is the sole theatrical sequel to 1986's *An American Tail* (although there were later two direct-to-video sequels) and was followed by the television series *Fievel's American Tails*.

1992

OSCAR FOR MONA LISA DESCENDING A STAIRCASE (JOAN GRANTZ): *Mona Lisa Descending a Staircase* won the Academy Award for Best Short Subject: Animated Films.

1992

CARTOON NETWORK PREMIERES: Cartoon Network started in 1992 in 2 million homes; by 1995 it was in 22 million. Since its launch in 1992, Cartoon Network has remained one of ad-supported cable's highest-rated networks.

animation, but in animation we can exaggerate that pose for even higher entertainment value. The more CG embraces going off model and creating these blur frames, the more styles will evolve out of computer-generated animation, and the less the characters will look like puppets.

Drawing Skills

This is a heavily debated topic among stop-motion, 2D, and CG animators alike. The consensus is that every-one needs to be able to draw well. Even if it's a stick figure, drawing what you envision for the scene helps you understand things about the poses that you cannot realize while acting them out or just animating right off the bat. Drawing helps you to think more logically and clearly about where the scene should go. Drawing helps you to see the whole picture. As visual artists, we must not take the opinion that any other art form is useless to us. The artist who is well-versed in a variety of media and keeps an open mind will always be ahead of those who stick to only one aspect of art. Think of Leonardo Da Vinci, who sculpted, painted, sketched, and studied music, theatre, and the natural world. Each additional skill you study will increase your value immeasurably. Drawing is a form of communication that rises above what words can accomplish, and the old adage that a picture is worth a thousand words has never been truer. Nik Ranieri tells of an experience with an animator who couldn't draw:

> I asked one of the guys working on Wilbur Robinson to draw because he was having trouble posing a figure. I asked him to draw the character and look at it as a 2D image. I wanted him to say, "Is that the way I would want it to look if I were drawing it?" Don't just settle and say, "Oh, it's a rig, so that's the best I can do." Beat it into submission if you can. Some of these rigs at the studios are pretty elaborate, and you can get the poses you want if you work at it. I thought I'd better ask him what his history was first, so I asked him if he draws. He said, "No, not really. I'm from a 3D background." I didn't say anything else to him, because what's the point of giving him that input if he doesn't draw? I think drawing really helps in the ability to pose a character out and get a good silhouette.

So, we know it's important to draw, but do you need to be a master draftsman to achieve success in the world of computer animation? Not necessarily. A simple stick figure can achieve the shorthand we are look-ing for in a drawing for animation. Thumbnails tend to be so sketchy that they are pretty close to a stick fig-ure in theory. As long as a line of action is being described in the sketch, the basic understanding of the pose and how you will get from that pose to the next is there. Taking classes to learn more about anatomy

1992

ART BABBITT DIES: Art Babbitt (1908–2004) was instrumental in developing the Goofy character for Disney. Though the character had existed previously, mostly as a background character initially known as Dippy Dawg, Babbitt's animation of the character shaped Goofy's person-ality. Art Babbitt became active in union activities and was ultimately fired by Walt Disney. His last screen credit occurred in 1948, by which time he had wandered over to UPA.

1992

FERNGULLY RELEASED: *FernGully: The Last Rainforest* is a film with an envi-ronmentalist theme about fairies living in FernGully, an area of Australian rainforest that is threatened by loggers.

and form is a tremendous help in making those sketches as simple as they can be. These classes will make your poses stronger with clarity. Ethan Hurd offers the idea that everyone can draw something and shouldn't be afraid to try:

> If you're a traditional animator, then it's very necessary to be able to draw. But in this day and age of computers, it's not completely necessary. It certainly won't hurt you to learn to draw better. Drawing will help with your illustration skills, your visual storytelling, and your silhouette. I believe that if you have the motor skills to sign your name, you have all the skills necessary to draw. Just carry a sketchbook around with you and do it all the time.

2D animators have to educate CG artists on their planning methods, including gestures and thumbnail sketches for planning out a shot. Drawing by Brian Dowrick.

1992

FROG BASEBALL ON MTV: Mike Judge's cartoon short *Frog Baseball* was the first cartoon to feature Beavis and Butt-Head. It was originally made for Spike and Mike's *Sick and Twisted Festival of Animation*. MTV picked up the short for their show *Liquid Television*.

1992

THE TUNE BY BILL PLYMPTON RELEASED: *The Tune* was animator Bill Plympton's first full-length feature.

1992

SAMMY TIMBERG DIES: Sammy Timberg (1903–1992) composed for Fleischer Studios' (later Famous Studios) Betty Boop, Superman, Little Lulu, and Casper, as well as for features such as *Mr. Bugs Goes to Town* and *Gulliver's Travels*. He is best known for "It's a Hap-Hap-Happy Day."

Drawing is not the be-all and end-all, but it sure makes things easier. It helps with the overall experience of getting inside that character's head. Stop-motion animators, like CG animators, do not need excellent drawing skills to do their job because they are dealing with puppets, not pencil and paper. However, the ability to put your ideas down on paper will make your thought process much easier.

Ethan Hurd said it best: Carry a sketchbook around and draw all the time. No one has to see inside your sketchbook. Most artists are very private about their sketchbooks, so no one will be offended if you don't let them look in there. Just draw. You think on a whole new level when you articulate what is in your head with pen and paper.

"It's not that you have to be a good draftsman to be a good animator. A poor draftsman who draws every day will yield stronger animation aesthetically than one who is a poor draftsman and, because of that, refuses to draw. My drawing skills are laughable, actually. Even after years of trying to get better at it, I just don't have the line control I need. But I can at least notate in some iconic form what I want, even if I can't faithfully reproduce that in pencil. That's okay. For me, the benefit is in drawing it out, not in drawing it out well. In years past I refused to draw because I suck at it and, by nature, I don't like to do things I'm not good at. I look at my animation from back then, and it just lacks a sense of clear line, form, force, and balance. It feels like a marionette film. My CG animation has gotten better for the effort of me drawing, even if my drawing skills themselves haven't improved nearly as much. Drawing skills aren't necessarily as key as the practice of drawing itself."

—Keith Lango

In summary, draw stick figures if you have to; you will see the benefits. In the end, the image is a two-dimensional graphic one, so thinking in that way can only help your ideas come across more clearly. Just draw!

The Approval Process

When do you show your work to a supervisor? When your ideas are most clear, but you haven't committed to them so wholeheartedly that it will feel like amputation if the ideas are cut or changed. You also have to take into account your supervisor and how he likes to work. This might take a few weeks of observation in dailies if you have never worked with the animation director, supervisors, and leads before, but pay close

1992

COOL WORLD RELEASED: *Cool World* marked Ralph Bakshi's return to feature films after nine years and his last feature film to date. The film was dismissed by critics and died at the box office, but later became a cult favorite with some of Bakshi's fans. In interviews, Bakshi praised the animation, while denouncing the story and screenplay, which he had been ordered to rewrite by Frank Mancuso Jr.

1992

END OF GOLDEN AGE OF COMMERCIALS IN LONDON: The Maastricht Treaty of European Unity combined continental advertising markets and in so doing severely limited the demand for animation commercials. This ended the Golden Age of Animation Commercials in London.

attention to their critiques, and you will figure out what they are looking for. Dave Zaboski clearly states how to size up the directive of your supervisor:

> It depends on the supervisor. If he's cool, I wait until I have roughed it out. Maybe two or three passes at it. If he is a controlling freak whose insecurities override his skill and knowledge as an animator, I will show thumbnails so we're all clear and I don't have to do extra work.

Nothing is more frustrating than having to handhold an animator through a shot. Have the confidence to see to the finish the ideas presented to you on the handoff of the shot and the ideas you are introducing. Remember, your supervisor has many responsibilities, juggling meetings with production and overseeing multiple animators through their shots. They do not have to see every single change you made and give you permission to move on. Bernd Angerer offers more on this:

> As a supervisor, I like to see many steps of an animation, but not every mouse click. Besides the poses themselves, it is important for me to have a good beat in an animation.

The only thing worse than an animator who wants to get approval for every change he makes to the scene is an animator who will not show his work until it's so far along that he feels defeated if asked to change it. If the performance is not following the directive given, the animation must change. This is why it's important to communicate where you want to take the scene with your supervisors as clearly as you can. Mike Surrey has this experience:

> You don't want to take too long working out your first pass on a scene. The faster you can get it in front of your supervisor, the better. They will most likely have changes, and because you worked quickly and invested minimal time, you should be able to turn the changes over quickly and get the scene in front of your supervisor for a second look.

Revisions are key to the process of animation. As animators, we revisit a scene over and over again for weeks to get all the bits in place. Handling approvals carefully with the supervisor will ensure your success. Communicate your intent, show your first blocking, and if the supervisor is happy with the direction, then take that ball and run with it to the finish line, and don't waste his or her time getting an approval for every change you make to the shot. Be confident. You were hired for a reason; show them why.

1992
ALADDIN 31ST DISNEY FEATURE: *Aladdin* was the most successful film of 1992, with more than $217 million in domestic revenues and more than $504 million worldwide.

1992
THE LAWNMOWER MAN (ANGEL STUDIOS AND XAOS): The climactic computer-generated animation by Angel Studios and Xaos for *The Lawnmower Man*, based on a story by Steven King, helped it become a cult favorite.

1993
OSCAR FOR *THE WRONG TROUSERS* (NICK PARK): *The Wrong Trousers* won the Academy Award for Best Short Subject: Animated Films.

The Revision Process

The revision process in animation is probably one of the most difficult and most significant. This is where all ideas about the movie, character, and shot converge. Listen closely at the handout stage because the input you are being given at that moment has come straight from the director and is what he wants to see. As we stated a moment ago, show your work when your ideas are clear. You can't sell the animation if it's mushy and vague. You shouldn't even have to explain what is going on or why, so take the time to make everything there very clear. Show other animators your rough poses so you can gauge whether the communication is there.

Keep the ideas simple. Keep your workflow simple. Many animators can block out their animation quickly, but then drown when it comes to the revision process. It's like being a swimmer in an event in which you have to swim all strokes. You shouldn't dive in doing the butterfly stroke, and then drown when you hit the backstroke. Develop a workflow that raises your performance level in all aspects of animation. We talked about this a bit in the beginning of this chapter, when we discussed using the graph editor and knowing when to change from stepped to linear to spline mode.

The revision process. Sketch by Brian Dowrick.

 1993

BEAVIS AND BUTT-HEAD ON MTV: *Beavis and Butt-Head* was first aired on MTV. Mike Judge created the aimless duo for a festival of animation when Abby Turkuhle, MTV's senior vice president, picked up an episode for the network's animated compendium, *Liquid Television.* MTV immediately contracted for 65 episodes from Judge, with Turkuhle as producer.

1993

ANIMANIACS DEBUTS: *Steven Spielberg Presents Animaniacs* (usually referred to by the shorter title *Animaniacs*) first aired on FOX from 1993 until 1995 and appeared on the WB as part of its Kids' WB afternoon programming block from 1995 to 1998.

Use Chapter 4 to help you stay lucid and efficient during the revision process. Also, don't hold onto your ideas for dear life. Your ideas are not that precious. You should be open to massaging them into something better. Most animators went to art school and were introduced to the critique process early on. If you didn't go to art school and are not familiar with this process, understand that your work will be on the big screen for all to see, and your supervisors are there to make the scene as good as possible. Take critiques in stride. Everyone is there to make the animation better and to follow the directive of the storytelling and the director's intention. Keith Roberts explains his frustration with animators who will not let go:

> It's frustrating when an animator holds onto something that is not working. Animators must not be too "precious" about their work. Be bold.

So what do you do when you're asked to take half your shot in a completely different direction? It depends on the new direction being given. If it's a subtle change, do not throw out the baby with the bathwater. If it's a new idea entirely, many times it's faster to rebuild the animation from scratch. You have already been through the shot and know the pitfalls of the rig and what will work for the shot. You can block out something new more quickly than trying to work with something that is broken. If you build a house, you want the foundation to be solid. Keith Lango offers his approach:

> The section that is being redirected will probably be torched to the ground. And if the new direction doesn't work properly with the other half that they liked, I'll likely nuke that as well and just start over from scratch. I've had to rescue enough scenes in my day, and I've always found it easier to just start over than to try and muggle something into shape. It just ends up looking muddy to me.

Remember, you will see these shots over and over again for years. You will see them in the theater, in trailers on television, again and again on cable, and when you go on an interview with these very shots on your reel. You want to be proud of them. Dave Zaboski offers what his mentor told him one day:

> My mentor, John Pomeroy, said to me once, "Don't worry about your drawings, Dave. Just imagine them blown up a hundred times their original size and shown in front of millions of people all over the world, forever."

1993

***THE NIGHTMARE BEFORE CHRISTMAS* PREMIERES:** *Tim Burton's The Nightmare Before Christmas* is a stop-motion animated musical film loosely based on drawings and a poem by Tim Burton, who served as co-producer.

1993

***JURASSIC PARK* RELEASED:** Special effects were largely credited for *Jurassic Park's* success. Through the use of CGI and conventional mechanical effects, the dinosaurs in the film appeared incredibly lifelike. The movie won Academy Awards for Visual Effects, Sound Effects Editing, and Sound, and spawned two sequels.

1993

WINDOWS NT RELEASED: Windows NT is a family of operating systems produced by Microsoft. This is important because it made the PC a player in high-end graphics, along with SGI.

It may be disheartening and frustrating at times, but stay positive and have faith in the process. Push hard in the beginning to get your ideas in there and get as much of yourself in the animation as possible. And make it all clear! The clearer and more entertaining the ideas are, the more likely they will end up on the big screen.

The Cleanup Process

Cleanup in CG is the same as in 2D. Pay attention to detail and do not start to clean up until the ideas are followed through and approved. Earlier in this chapter, we talked about awareness of supervisors and how they approach the approval process—whether they need to see everything animated down to the digits, such as fingers and facial, or whether they can visualize and/or trust you to see through those overlapping and secondary motions. You shouldn't have to think about cleanup too much because all of the important bits should already be there. It is time-consuming work, but the thought process should already be there as far as performance is concerned. Mike Murphy offers his approach to cleanup on a shot:

> When I go in and do the nitty-gritty cleanup work, typically it takes 20 percent of my time to get to the point when it's cleanup time. Then the other 80 percent of my time is cleaning up. That includes going frame by frame and fine-tuning every arc and eye blink and eye dart. This is when I layer in subtle weight shifts and adjustments and pay attention to follow-through, tongues, fingers, and breaths.

Go with the first reaction you have when you first view your rough test. Write down your thoughts. Note the frame count where you think a curve needs to be tightened or smoothed. Ask those around you what their first impressions are. A fresh eye can be very helpful. This is the step to work out any technical hiccups and make everything flow. Mark Behm has more:

> I end up spending less time in the function curve editor and more time on the 2D image itself. I always have to go in and add subtleties to curves that give things extra life. I don't want this kind of left-brain activity to interfere with my creative decisions as I'm animating and deciding on spacing and timing. It's a last step to get the kinks out, and it adds that critical level of detail that seems to be the difference between alive and dead in CG.

1993

DIGITAL DOMAIN FORMS: Digital Domain, founded by James Cameron, Stan Winston, and Scott Ross, provides visual effects for film, commercials, and music videos. The company began producing visual effects in 1993, with its first three films being *True Lies*, *Interview with the Vampire*, and *Color of Night*. It has since produced effects for more than 40 films. As of spring 2006, investment group Wyndcrest Holdings acquired the 13-year-old visual effects studio.

1994

OSCAR FOR *BOB'S BIRTHDAY* (ALISON SNOWDEN AND DAVID FINE): *Bob's Birthday* won the Academy Award for Best Short Subject: Animated Films.

Cleanup is critical to making everything flow and make sense. It's your last chance to work out the kinks and make it all look great. Bert Klein offers his concise assessment of what cleanup is:

> Broad strokes first, then I keep whittling away like it's a wood block until it resembles something.

Whittle away, animators!

[21] Johnston, Ollie and Frank Thomas. *The Illusion of Life: Disney Animation*. Disney Editions: 1995.

[22] Keyframes. http://www.siggraph.org/education/materials/HyperGraph/animation/character_animation/principles/lasseter_s94.htm#keyframes.

1994

THE LION KING 32ND DISNEY FEATURE: *The Lion King* is the highest-grossing traditionally animated feature film ever released in the US. Computer animation was used extensively in the creation of the movie. Upon general release, the film became the most successful film of the year and the most successful animated feature film ever at the time. In hindsight, the film can be seen as marking the peak of the popular success of the late-'80s-to-mid-'90s renaissance of Disney animation.

1994

FIRST TOTAL CG TV SERIES (REBOOT): *ReBoot* is a Canadian animated series credited with being the first completely computer-animated TV series.

1994

WALTER LANTZ DIES: Walter Lantz (1900–1994), head of the Walter Lantz Studio and creator of Woody Woodpecker, was a pioneer in animation. In his retirement, Lantz continued to manage his studio's properties by offering re-releases of cartoons and sales to new venues. He also continued to draw and paint, selling his paintings of Woody Woodpecker rapidly.

1994

THUMBELINA OPENS: *Thumbelina* is based on the original *Thumbelina* fairytale written by Hans Christian Andersen. This film was not as well received as most of Don Bluth's past films or any of the Disney releases.

1995

OSCAR FOR *A CLOSE SHAVE* (NICK PARK): *A Close Shave* won the Academy Award for Best Short Subject: Animated Films.

Chapter 6
Acting the Moment Again and Again and Again

Acting is the heart of your animation perform-ance. Each shot of every scene builds upon the performance and supports the intent of the story. The job of an animator involves re-motivating an acting moment in the movie again and again for weeks on end. Animators do not necessarily want to be actors (although some are real characters). To animate well, animators have to understand what an actor knows and how the actor prepares for a scene. The way an anima-tor "acts" is very different from the way an actor "acts." An animator has to be more analytical than an actor in his or her approach to a scene because the actor *acts* in the moment, and an animator has to *be* in the moment.

> "If you and I are acting on stage, and I touch your cheek, you will have an emotional reaction of some kind. You and I will both deal with that reaction, which will lead us to the next moment. An animator must create the illusion of a present moment."
>
> —*Ed Hooks*

An actor deals with internals to create the external movement you see on the stage or on the screen. An actor has to feel the emotion to have his movements, gestures, and words ring true. An animator, on the other hand, has to re-motivate an emotion for days and weeks on end. He or she has to get inside the head of the character like an actor does, but he has to deal with the externals as well. Animators are always wor-ried about a gesture or a pose reading well; actors are taught *not* to focus on these things because they are results of what is going on internally. Actors are taught that you cannot act results. There is a new technology in the world of CG that provides the director with a way to approach animation more like a live-action direc-tor would using actors. It is called *motion capture*.

1995

JOHN WHITNEY DIES: John Whitney (1917–1995) was an exper-imental animator and pioneer com-puter animator. John Whitney's active filmmaking career endured for more than 55 years, and 40 of those years were devoted to computer work.

1995

TOY STORY, FIRST CG-ANIMATED FEATURE, RELEASED: *Toy Story*, pro-duced by Pixar Animation Studios, was the first feature-length completely com-puter-animated movie released by Disney, and it took in more money at the box office than any other film in 1995.

1995

A TROLL IN CENTRAL PARK: *A Troll in Central Park* is an animated movie directed by Don Bluth and Gary Goldman. Its total domestic gross barely cleared $71 million.

"Looking at a live-action movie regarding acting alone, you can see quite a number of different styles that seem completely unrelated to one another. In 1956, you had Brando using Strasberg's Method acting on one soundstage, and across the lot you had DeMille shooting *The Ten Commandments* and directing all his actors to strike theatrical tableau poses that he carried over from his days in silent-film melodrama. I think ideally, animation can be made to mimic any style of acting appropriate to the movie and the character design. Of course, it all has to start with the voice talent. In its totality, animation will always be a much more obviously collaborative and analytical craft than live-action acting."

—*Bill Wright*

Motion Capture and Acting in CG Animation

A new technology called *motion capture* has been introduced to the world of computer-generated animation. This technology bridges the differences between the live-action actor and the key frame animator. When mo-cap is used to generate animation, the computer records the performance by an actor "in the moment." Later, an animator will clean up that data and embellish it to make it work for the movie. Successful uses of this technology involved heavy key framing by animators, such as with Gollum in *The Lord of the Rings*. That movie started a frenzy among live-action directors who have crossed into animated and visual-effects films. Movies such as *Final Fantasy*; *I, Robot*; *The Polar Express*; *Happy Feet*; *King Kong*; *Monster House*; and even crowd scenes in *Barnyard* are using motion-capture tools to generate motion and performance. Live-action directors love the idea of motion capture because it's closer to what they experience on a real set with live performers. Mark Koetsier explains how realism is the driving force behind a director's desire to pursue motion capture:

> Motion capture is the thing Steven [Spielberg] wanted to do even more of, which is kind of disheartening. They asked him if he would direct an animated picture. Spielberg's interest would lie in what Robert Zemeckis did with *The Polar Express*. I, myself, think mo-cap is dead. It looks so dead, lifeless. *Final Fantasy* was really creepy and didn't do well at all. What animation should be is a caricature of real life—not actually real life, but an exaggeration of it. I see mo-cap might be driven into a way where they don't have to have real actors. Technology is always driving to be faster and more realistic in animation because that is the ultimate drive of live action. To make things feel more real.

1995

BABE WINS VISUAL EFFECTS AWARD: *Babe* used a combination of live and computer-animated effects. Rhythm & Hues Studios was nominated for seven Academy Awards for *Babe*, which won in the Visual Effects category.

1995

FRIZ FRELENG DIES: Friz Freleng (1906–1995) was one of the giants of animation. Freleng had connections with the WB studio for more than 60 years and directed nearly 300 cartoons, four of which won Academy Awards, more than any other WB director. Even other giants of WB animation, such as Chuck Jones, have acknowledged his influence and reputation.

1995

ACADEMY AWARD FOR JOHN LASSETER: John Lasseter of Pixar won an Academy Award for development and application of techniques used in *Toy Story*.

The problem with motion capture, as Mark said, is that it strives to look too real, and the computer is too perfect in how it records the data. Think about a still frame of a boxer being hit in the face. The facial pose is a distorted mess of goo that you would never think the human face could achieve. But the sheer impact of the fist hitting the face creates this reactionary pose. We would never see this facial pose unless we had the camera to capture it. But we would feel that impact down to our bones while watching the hit. This is the exaggeration and caricature that Mark speaks of in animation. Even motion capture trying to look like real life must have these notes of exaggeration and entertainment to feel real. This is because they exist in real life, if only for a tenth of a second!

Cartoony animation is all based on real-life motion. Some of the more exaggerated poses are just held for a longer time to add comedic effect. Mo-cap can be successful in creating realistic animation, but it still requires the character animator's touch to heighten what the computer records. The animator's key frames turn the sterile data into something with entertainment value, incorporating the subtleties that mo-cap doesn't catch. The process of recording the mo-cap data is one that the live-action director can relate to better than a traditional animation pipeline.

By using mo-cap, the director has interaction with the performer and can make several takes within "the moment." With the mo-cap system, the director can decide on the fly where the staging and camera will be, instead of committing early in production during the storyboard phase, as in any regular animated film. The director can be more creative, but it also opens up a whole new set of issues for the pipeline. By changing one camera choice, you can affect the rest of the sequence.

Most live-action directors have storyboards that they use loosely, but once on set they might change camera angles and use actors' input on performance to satisfy their own creative inspirations in the moment. A great example of this would be Stanley Kubrick's *The Shining*. When on set in the large mansion, Jack Nicholson offered Kubrick the idea that if he were living inside such a spacious house, he would have the inclination to do things he would normally do outside. So, he brought out a tennis ball and threw it all over the house and down the halls, showing his character's boredom and that he is not writing like he should be. Kubrick took this idea and pushed it further by designing camera moves that followed the ball and introducing scenes with the ball rolling into the camera. In a 2D or CG animated film, this kind of creativity of changing a camera angle or recreating the whole directive of a scene rarely happens. The pipeline doesn't really allow for it because these things can be very costly within the structure and pipeline.

By using mo-cap, the director of an animated film can have a similar experience to the live-action director once the animation data is processed and inside the computer and the sets are built. As long as the creativity was worked out on the mo-cap set regarding performance and the director's vision for camera angles is

1995

PRESTON BLAIR DIES: Preston Blair (1908–1995) was an animator who wrote the book *Cartoon Animation*, which is the classic book on how to animate. Blair worked with Al Eugster on *Krazy Kat* cartoons for the Mintz studio. He later went to Disney, where he was an animator on "The Sorcerer's Apprentice" and "Dance of the Hours" sequences in *Fantasia*.

1995

POCAHONTAS DISNEY'S 33RD FEATURE: *Pocahontas* was designed as Disney's first real dramatic animated picture. However, the movie was less successful commercially than hoped. Because it dealt with more adult themes and tones, the film did not appeal as well to younger children, and the hoped-for box office performance like that of *The Lion King* never materialized for *Pocahontas*.

Sometimes advances in technology make you feel like you will never keep up. Hang in there!
Sketch by Floyd Norman.

clear, this approach can work. But these are a lot of variables that play into the equation. This approach to making an animated film can cause a lot of fear in producers and the production because it flies in the face of a traditionally animated pipeline in which everything is storyboarded out and pre-planned, and poses are played up to existing cameras. Mo-cap can provide more creativity for the director, but can be a double-edged sword because the pre-planning stage is usually eliminated, and this approach can make for a movie that goes over budget and takes a long time to nail down.

One drawback for mo-cap versus key-frame animation is that the takes made during the mo-cap session have to work. It's very expensive to go back to a mo-cap session to record info and process that data for the animators to manipulate. In the animation world, if the performance isn't working within the film, the animator can delete keys and just start over with a new idea. The key-frame animator can revisit the same

1995

WAVEFRONT AND ALIAS MERGE:
The beginnings of what is now Maya software happened when Alias/Wavefront formed in 1995. Silicon Graphics bought Alias Research and Wavefront Technologies, then merged the two. It is now owned by Autodesk, the producers of 3D Studio Max.

1995

BALTO OPENS: *Balto* was the last animated feature produced by Steven Spielberg's Amblination animation studio, which closed after Spielberg co-founded DreamWorks with David Geffen and Jeffrey Katzenberg.

1995

THE PEBBLE AND THE PENGUIN RELEASED: *The Pebble and the Penguin* grossed $3 million dollars and got low reviews But as years passed, the animated film became a cult favorite.

performance over and over again, and the director has the ability to make deliberate and subtle changes to that performance. Demanding this from a live-action actor on set can create resentment and even break down an actor's confidence. Animators are used to this process. The process of watching, adjusting, and endlessly revising a performance over and over again—or "frame f**king," as animators term it so fondly—is just another part of their job. The key to using mo-cap with a director who doesn't want to use the animation pipeline is for that director to positively know what he wants for every shot, which is rare. If the director *does* have a clear vision, the lack of pre-planning stage might not be as big a problem as Roger Vizard explains from his experience working with mo-cap on the movie *The Polar Express*:

> I just finished a film called *The Polar Express*. The director had free range as to where that camera was going to be at any given shot during a performance. This scared many of us for the first couple of days of production, but he knew where he wanted that camera generally. Not enough can be said about pre-planning; it's the most beautiful thing about animation that some forget. You are putting the audience's eyes when and where you choose! Live action, no matter how great the director is, cannot execute and duplicate a performance two or three times in order to place the camera in just the right place. Animation is a very powerful tool in the sense that your intentions and skill to compose a shot are unparalleled in almost any media in moviemaking.

Animation is truly moviemaking frame by frame. Those frames also must hold a strong silhouette and must present the idea or intent quickly and clearly. Very early in their careers, animators learn that the use of strong silhouette is the best way to achieve this.

Live-action directors rarely think about silhouette when they shoot actors. The silhouette should be there if the actor is doing his job. In contrast, the animator is *always* concerned with silhouette. Without a strong silhouette, the performance will be hard to read. A strong silhouette can read from far away or up close. A live-action actor is rarely thinking about his silhouette or whether his pose is reading well. He has to believe the movement will be honest if he is honestly acting as the character, and he never looks back to see whether it is. Ed Hooks teaches Acting for Animators classes and explains more about the differences between actors and animators:

> Live actors work in the present moment; animators do not have a present moment. (Or if they do, it's one hell of a long moment.) In the world of animation, it takes 24 drawings to create the illusion of a second of real time.

1996

OSCAR FOR *QUEST* (TYRON MONTGOMERY AND THOMAS STELLMACH): *Quest* won the Academy Award for Best Short Subject: Animated Films.

1996

BEAVIS AND BUTT-HEAD MOVIE RELEASED: Yes, *Beavis and Butt-Head*, now a feature, was released and made more than $60 million.

1996

SPACE JAM: *Space Jam* is an animated/live-action film starring Michael Jordan opposite Bugs Bunny and the rest of the *Looney Tunes* characters. Those who liked the film praised the visual effects, which were groundbreaking at the time.

We highly recommend Ed's book, *Acting for Animators, Revised Edition: A Complete Guide to Performance Animation* (Heinemann Drama, 2003),[23] as additional reading to this chapter. An actor doesn't spend weeks re-motivating a character and scene unless he is working a show on Broadway that will play every week. An actor uses internal motivation to reach his goal. An animator uses the external silhouette and poses to reach his goal. Actors are always in real time and animators are never in real time. The external visual impact is what an animator is concerned with, but this is a result of an extremely time-consuming process of manipulating every single frame of the performance. The one thing they both have in common is a vested interest in the moment.

Ed Hooks teaches Acting for Animators and has made a bridge between the tools actors use and how they can be applied to an animator practicing acting.

Improv

Animators usually learn about acting through books, observation, other animators, and trial and error. Improvisational classes are another great way to learn even more about acting. These classes are also helpful because the role in improv is to quickly assess a character for performance, and this is exactly what an animator does. Improv actors are presented with a character and a scene and have to act it out immediately. Animators are handed a folder with the scene notes, storyboards, and a few words from the director and supervisors. They are then expected to quickly create a convincing and believable performance with a small amount of information.

1996

MARS ATTACKS PREMIERES: *Mars Attacks!* is a Tim Burton film based on the popular sci-fi trading cards of the same name. During its production, the Manchester stop-motion studio Bare Bones spent nine months animating stop-motion aliens for the film, only to be told that CG images by ILM would be used instead.

1996

THE HUNCHBACK OF NOTRE DAME DISNEY'S 34TH FEATURE: *The Hunchback of Notre Dame* was loosely based on Victor Hugo's *The Hunchback of Notre Dame*. It has been acclaimed for its visual and artistic merits and its technical advances in the combination of hand-drawn and computerized animation. A notable detail includes the use of computer-generated imagery to create otherwise unfeasibly large crowds.

All action is the result of thinking. Improv helps you think quickly on your feet. It also helps you get rid of the most common ideas that pop into your head and get to the really juicy ones that an audience will react to. Improv rules tell you to not ask questions, but to always know what is going on in the scene. If you stay honest to your characters in improv, the random moments while performing will ring true with the audience and will reinforce the character and ultimately be funny.

By knowing what is going on, you act more honestly. Improv teaches character style, inner rhythm, physical limitations, age, and gender, and how you can make those distinctions through gesture, movement, and good acting. A great example of how you can get into character is to imagine the morning ritual of the character you're portraying. A truck driver might get up wearing his clothes from the previous night, pop open a beer because he is off that day, and sit back in his recliner to watch some TV. A princess might wake to her lady-in-waiting placing her fancy dress on the bed and helping her to groom for the day. How do these characters feel while they go through their rituals? How do they view their place in the world? Do they take pride in their everyday actions? How do they occupy their space physically?

Improv also teaches how to give and take in a scene and make each other look good. This applies directly to scenes with multiple characters that are split up among animators. If you understand that your character's performance will only reinforce the other character's performance, then the scene will be successful. Many times reinforcing one character with a contrasting character will make the scene even stronger. If one performer was to come out on stage with a frantic, agitated persona, it would be much more interesting if the other performer took on a contrasting personality, such as one who is calm, reserved, and controlled. Actors working in improv are taught that a scene is a negotiation. When you animate, ask yourself what is being negotiated. In every improv performance, there is a constant give and take situation among the performers. If someone was to negate or simply say "no" to a statement, the scene would be over. One person leads and the other follows, then a negotiation takes place and the power changes hands. You can illustrate this power transfer through power centers.

Helpful Improv Tools for Animators

One tool that improvisational actors use is called the *power center*, or *lead*. This helps describe how a character views himself in the world around him. Using power centers, you take a certain posture to create a character. The power center is where all of the attitude is coming from, and it leads the movement. Imagine yourself walking down the street. Where is your power center? The hips? The chest? The booty? Table 6.1 describes some power centers and the characters that would embody these leading parts.

Table 6.1 Power Centers

Hips	Moves like a supermodel on the catwalk or like a sexy Mick Jagger strut.
Chin	Moves like a queen, a statesman, or someone regal.
Chest	Moves like a boxer or a superhero.
Forehead	Moves like an intellectual; think Woody Allen.
Belly	Moves like a tubby person; think John Goodman or a pregnant woman.
Knees	Moves like a thug with a strut; think Rudy from *Fat Albert* or the rap star/actor Ice Cube.

The list goes on and on. The power center can totally change where the character is emotionally by how he moves. Power centers are intertwined with the concept of status.

Status doesn't necessarily connect with money. It can also involve rank and file in a family structure, at work, or even in a group of friends. In general, a person of high status would be very still and would make direct eye contact. A high-status person is comfortable with his place in the world, and unless you are trying to add subtext to the scene, a high-status person would conduct himself in a calm, reserved, controlled manner, much like, for example, Don Corleone in *The Godfather.* He would be direct and still as he delivers his lines, showing that he has the power in the scene. If a person of power becomes frantic and starts yelling, he illustrates that he has lost control.

In contrast, low-status folks tend to look down a lot and might touch their face often, showing insecurity or nervousness. They are uncomfortable in their world. Anthony Hopkins described how he played the butler in *The Remains of the Day* through establishing status in the space he occupied. He said the trick to playing the butler was that all of the space in the room belonged to the master. The butler only had permission to be there. It was a negotiation of space.

Anthony Hopkins hit upon a very important part of acting in his approach to the butler character. How does your character interact within his space? Space is extremely important to animation and acting and defining how the character sees his place in the world. Movement in space further describes the mindset. The big boss walking into the boardroom might move directly with a heavy and slow motion. But, say the boss's son enters. This kid doesn't really want to be there. Say his head isn't business and he just wants to just dance

1996

JAMES AND THE GIANT PEACH RELEASED:
James and the Giant Peach is a film based on the Roald Dahl book of the same name. The movie is a combination of live action and stop-motion and was nominated for an Academy Award for Best Music, Original Musical or Comedy Score (by Randy Newman), but did not win.

1996

QUAKE HITS GAME MARKET: *Quake* is a first-person shooter game by id Software. It can be said that the original *Quake* game pushed most PC hardware to its limits, due to never-before-seen features it offered: complex textured 3D environments, polygon-modeled enemies with certain intelligence, and the like.

on Broadway. He might enter the room quite differently. He might be timid and move quickly and indirectly in order to avoid interacting with anyone. There are many acting methods that can help you distinguish how your character might move and occupy the space he is in.

Take the improv method called the Laban technique. (We will touch upon only a few key methods of the technique in this chapter to illustrate how it can help an animator describe acting within a space.) Within Laban, there are four elements of dimension: space, time, weight, and flow. Space, time, weight, and flow create the action.

The space in which you move can be expressed as a big bubble around you. If the bubble is very small, your character will move in a very confined way, maybe like a disabled person. Time further explains the speed at which the character will move over the time allocated for the scene. Weight, of course, can affect time, but it also pertains more closely to acting and showing how weight might change the speed at which something moves and how direct the action can be. Finally, the term "flow" is a combination of how the character uses space, time, and weight to create an actual action.

Within these four elements of space, time, weight, and flow, there are six improv terms that can help an animator quickly assess how the character should occupy space. These labels are direct, indirect, fast, slow, heavy, and light. Space handles whether the motion is direct or indirect. Time describes fast or slow movement. Weight, of course, determines whether the motion has a heavy or light feel to it.

The following combinations of these terms can label how your character should move:

◆ Use the terms direct and indirect for space.

◆ Use the terms fast and slow for time.

◆ Use the terms heavy and light for weight.

Using each of these labels in different combinations, you can define any kind of motion. What if your character was direct, slow, and heavy? In contrast, what if the same character changed to indirect, fast, and light?

If you break down these terms further, you will get eight basic combinations of weight, space, time, and flow. These eight terms are press, wring, glide, float, thrust, slash, dab, and flick. Following are some examples of how they would break down:

◆ Direct, slow, heavy (press/wring): An elephant, a Mafioso, or a football player

◆ Indirect, fast, light (glide/float): A child, a fairy, or a hummingbird

1996

COLOSSAL PICTURES FILES CHAPTER 11: The troubled San Francisco–based studio, known for such TV shows as *Aeon Flux* and *Liquid Television*, sought protection from its creditors while seeking to overhaul its operations. Previously, it had stopped producing TV commercials and announced that it was concentrating on development projects to allow it "to reorganize its business in a profitable direction."

1996

DISNEY BUYS DREAMQUEST IMAGES: Disney bought out Dream Quest Images, the house responsible for effects in such films as *Crimson Tide* and *Total Recall*. Because of this big purchase, Disney decided to dissolve Buena Vista Visual Effects, the short-lived effects company that worked on *The Santa Clause*, among other films.

◆ Direct, fast, light (thrust, slash): A swordsman, a dancer, or a cheetah after his meal

◆ Indirect, slow, heavy (dab, flick): A drunk, a physically handicapped person, or an animator going back to work after a three-martini lunch

Again, the combinations are endless, but placing these words on your monitor as you animate will keep you on track as to how your character occupies the space he moves within. For more about improv, we encourage you to get the book *Laban for Actors and Dancers: Putting Laban's Movement Theory into Practice: A Step-by-Step Guide* by Jean Newlove (Nick Hern Books, 1998).[24]

Charlie Chaplin, Empathy, and Acting

Charlie Chaplin was a genius at creating empathy with the audience. If you do not know who Charlie Chaplin is, go back to film school—do not pass Go and do not collect $200. His Little Tramp character touched the hearts of all viewers. Why is that? The simple reason is that people could relate to the situations in which the character found himself. In a memorable scene, the Little Tramp got his foot stuck in a bucket and tried to hide the fact. Staying true to his character is what made the acting both appealing and real. The Little Tramp wanted to maintain his dignity with a bucket stuck on his foot. Instead of wildly trying to shake it off, he hid the bucket behind his other leg and limped around. The Tramp's embarrassment created empathy. The audience felt for the character and desired what he desired, which was to enter the room with grace and self-respect.

By getting inside the heads of his characters, Charlie Chaplin was able to act honestly and portray emotions that are familiar to everyone. As Leigh Rens points out, you can see the thought process going on in Chaplin's characters:

You've got to reveal the character's inner thoughts, emotions, and flaws to the audience. Charlie Chaplin would make his character hesitate, ponder his action, look for who was watching, and then do the gag. This seems insignificant, but by doing this, Chaplin spends time with his audience, shows his fear of being found out, fights with his conscience, and hides his deed from others to protect his image—all things that we as the audience would do, hence we are drawn into caring about what happens to this guy.

1997

CATS DON'T DANCE: *Cats Don't Dance* is the only animated feature produced by the short-lived Turner Entertainment animation unit. Although the film was critically acclaimed, it was a casualty of the Turner/Time Warner merger. It did substantially better when made available the following year on home video.

1997

APPLE ACQUIRES NeXT: NeXT was a computer company known to the public for its futuristic black hardware and to programmers for its outstanding object-oriented development platform. NeXT merged with Apple Computer on December 20, 1996, and its software was the foundation for Mac OS X. NeXT was headquartered in Redwood City, California.

Create empathy for your characters by crafting a persona the audience can identify with.
Sketch by Floyd Norman.

OSCAR FOR *GERI'S GAME* (JAN PINKAVA): *Geri's Game* won the Academy Award for Best Short Subject: Animated Films. *Geri's Game* was the first short film produced by Pixar since the studio shifted focus to commercials in 1989, and ultimately to feature films with *Toy Story* in 1995.

***KING OF THE HILL* BEGINS ON FOX:** As of 2006, *King of the Hill* hit their 200th episode. The series is another animation hit from *Beavis and Butt-Head* creator Mike Judge, who also voices the starring character, Hank Hill.

***PRINCESS MONONOKE* RELEASED IN JAPAN:** Hayao Miyazaki's *Princess Mononoke* became Japan's biggest motion picture hit of all time, animated or live action. It was released in the US in 1999.

Chaplin can teach an animator much about acting because he told stories without speaking. Just the look on his face or a body gesture told the whole story. Most importantly, Charlie Chaplin created a character that acted only out of his own desire to survive, as Ed Hooks reveals:

> You should watch Charlie Chaplin movies for inspiration. No matter how messed up life became for the Little Tramp, he was determined that tomorrow would be a better day. Always have your character act to survive.

Chaplin had many techniques he would use to heighten the comedy of scenes. One of his cardinal rules was, don't cut to a close-up for jokes. Charlie Chaplin's use of the long shot (or camera that includes the entire action) more clearly portrays his very physical sense of humor. In Chaplin's world, if you get too close to a character and his emotions, it might be moving, but it usually isn't funny. You achieve empathy by watching the character struggle to get what he wants. Watching Chaplin struggle with the bucket and still keep his self-respect creates empathy in the audience and therefore gets the laugh.

Buster Keaton and Harold Lloyd were also masters at comedy through empathy. Harold Lloyd said, "The more trouble you get a man into, the more comedy you get out of him." Chaplin was a king of empathy and sentiment. Keaton had the poetry of gag placement and timing down. Lloyd was a master of crowd-pleasing slapstick. Watch movies from all three of these men, and you will see some of the greatest physical acting and pantomime out there.

Another great master of acting was Peter Brook, who taught at the Royal Shakespeare Company. He taught his students three things to ensure believability in acting. These three things are:

◆ A tension line between themselves

◆ A tension line between other actors

◆ A tension line between themselves and the audience

Honest, effective acting incorporates these three lines of tension. When these connections are made, the audience can't help but root for your characters. Incorporating these lines into animation means portraying conflict within your character, within the situation, and with other characters, as well as creating conflict with your audience and empathy with the emotions being played out.

1997

HERCULES 35TH DISNEY FEATURE: *Hercules* depicts the adventures of Heracles (known in the movie by his Roman name, Hercules) in Greek mythology. There is a brief cameo appearance by Scar, the villain of *The Lion King*, as the Nemean Lion, whose skin is worn by Hercules in one scene. Andreas Deja, the animator who animated adult Hercules, also animated Scar for *The Lion King*.

1997

VIFX/BLUE SKY MERGER: In August of 1997, 20th Century Fox announced that its effects company, VIFX, had acquired Blue Sky Studios to create the newly formed Blue Sky|VIFX, a new powerhouse effects company. The talents of Blue Sky's CG animation team combined with VIFX's miniature, compositing, 2D, and 3D.

Get Inside the Character

The best acting provides a window into the character's thoughts through his actions. Like the saying goes, actions speak louder than words. By providing these windows into the character, the acting slowly reveals who the character is and why he does the things he does. Where is the character coming from? Fix the moment in your mind and make it clear. There is an old adage in acting that if you look into another actor's eyes for more than 10 seconds, you better be ready to fight or make love. If you are about to hit someone, you do not look away. Neither do you lose eye contact if you are focusing on the love of your life. Get inside the character's head and show the character's emotions through his eyes. See the thought process going on behind the eyes.

So, how do you get inside the head of your character and find out what's going on in there? A great exercise for doing this is to imagine your character waiting for a bus. What is the character's position in the world? How does the character react to waiting for the bus and to others waiting around him? What kind of person is your character? Observe people in everyday life. Animation is not about moving characters around; it is

Major Damage has great eye contact in this still from Chris Bailey's short film.

1997

ANASTASIA RELEASED: *Anastasia*, a musical in the vein of Disney animated features, is notable for being one of Don Bluth's most critically acclaimed works and for being one of the few animated features produced in the widescreen anamorphic process.

1998

OSCAR FOR *BUNNY* (CHRIS WEDGE): *Bunny* won an Academy Award for Best Short Subject: Animated Films.

1998

THE PRINCE OF EGYPT PREMIERES: *The Prince of Egypt* is the first animated film produced and released by DreamWorks SKG. It won an Oscar for Best Original Song in 1999, with the pop version of the theme song "When You Believe" interpreted by Whitney Houston and Mariah Carey.

about creating characters who move people. Mark Koetsier has another technique for getting inside the mind of a character:

> We used the McDonald's scenario. We took our main character and thought, what would he do at McDonald's? What would he buy? How would he act? We did the same with the villain. This is just one scenario. You put them into different scenarios other than the movie so that everybody gets an idea. If he is in one situation, then he will react a certain way because this is his character and everybody knows his personality.

Use everyday scenarios like a trip to McDonald's to figure out who your character is and how he would interact with others. Sketch by Floyd Norman.

1998

QUEST FOR CAMELOT RELEASED: *Quest for Camelot* is an animated feature from Warner Bros. It was retitled *The Magic Sword* in Asia. And, well, it's just bad.

1998

TITANIC LARGEST-GROSSING PICTURE IN HISTORY: *Titanic* won 11 Academy Awards, including Best Picture. As of 2006, it has the highest box-office take in movie history. It holds the record (with *Ben-Hur* and *The Lord of the Rings: The Return of the King*) for the most Academy Award wins.

1998

ALIAS/MAYA RELEASED: Upon Maya's release in 1998, Alias|Wavefront discontinued all previous animation-based software lines, including Alias Power Animator, encouraging consumers to upgrade to Maya.

When working on a short scene, turn the emotion from want to *need* to heighten the scene and make the desires of your character plain. The audience is looking for the extraordinary moment, not the ordinary moment.

The basic definition of emotion is a mental state that arises spontaneously rather than through conscious effort. How many emotions can go off at once? All of them—it's called shock. This is not to say that an over-exaggerated emotion would be better than a subtle one. Stifled emotions can work much better than full-blown emotions. It's all about staying true to your character and how he would react in the situation. Get to the core of the scene, the heart of what the character is feeling, and amplify that emotion. The improv term for this is called getting to the "seed of the scene." If the character is sad but doesn't want anyone to know it, you have to push those two conflicting emotions as far as you can, and the audience will empathize. Larry Weinberg offers more on isolating emotions:

> Isolate the emotion in action. Don't do too many things at once with the character if you want to feel his thoughts. The thinking process plays out mostly with the head, face, and hands, with the eyes being the most critical, of course. Find the pauses in the dialogue to bring out the thoughts of the character through movements. Direct the eye carefully to one thing at a time.

The seed of the scene requires you get the audience involved and develop empathy between the character and the audience. Empathy is different from sympathy. Empathy means you have felt like that character feels and you want the same thing for the character that he wants. Sympathy is just feeling for the character, but not necessarily empathizing with his plight. Sometimes sympathy can even introduce pity. You don't want pity! You want the audience to root for your character!

Remember that atmosphere plays a lot into your character's emotions as well. The place in which your character speaks has an effect on his actions. A bad car accident has a different atmosphere than a wedding. (Although that isn't to say that many marriages don't bear a striking resemblance to a car wreck!) Because an animator is expected to revisit the scene again and again for weeks on end, the acting tools described in this chapter should help you to keep the scene fresh and the intent crystal clear.

One final thought: Punctuating every verbal note with a pose is messy and confusing. Stay away from clichés. Convey the acting through the body postures first. Maintain consistency in your choices. And break from formulas that you have learned. Formulas equal hollow acting.

1998

MULAN DISNEY'S 36TH FEATURE: *Mulan* was the first of three films produced primarily at the animation studio at Disney-MGM Studios in Orlando, Florida. The character of Mulan is a departure from previous Disney female leads; she is neither a princess nor considered exceptionally beautiful, but instead is a strong and capable warrior.

1998

BOSS FILMS CLOSES ITS DOORS: Boss Films, before its announced closure in 1997, was one of the few houses in existence that could boast a pre-digital era. In fact, Boss will most likely be remembered for their wonderful work on some of the biggest effects films of the 1980s, all of which were created optically, long before the days of digital.

Body Structure

The design and body structure created for your character are crucial to how that character will act. The power center or leads described earlier will help you put together a body structure, but you must go deeper into who the character is to really come up with an effective design. A good example of body structure defined through a character's acting is Francis from *A Bug's Life*.

Francis is a ladybug. Therefore, everyone assumes he is a female. This makes for one very irritated bug. The interesting contrast comes from the scene when he becomes maternal with the child ants. It contrasts with his defiant attitude that he is, in fact, a male because he assumes the role of den mother to the Blueberry Scouts. The Blueberries are like ant Girl Scouts. This makes the indignant male role funny, and the audience likes him more because of his own inner conflict with his body structure.

Many great animated characters utilize body type, such as Marty, the zebra in *Madagascar* who doesn't know whether he is white with black stripes or black with white stripes. His very body structure and character design reinforce who he is and what his plight in the world is. It defines how he sees his status and place within the world. All of the labels, such as power centers, status, and getting inside the mind of your character, will help you reinforce how the character sees himself. This makes for a deeper understanding of how that character would react to the world around him.

Psychological Gesture and Subtext

In Chapters 4 and 5, we discussed psychological gesture and subtext briefly. These two aspects of acting will enrich your scenes. The psychological gesture is an amazing acting tool developed by the great Russian actor, director, and teacher, Michael Chekhov. These are little things we do as humans to explain what we are thinking. You can use props to convey a psychological gesture. In the movie *Missing* (1982), Jack Lemmon's character is frustrated as he tries to find his son. He uses his hat as a lid holding his emotions together. When he finally loses control, the hat comes off and he falls apart.

Some examples of psychological gestures include:

◆ Yawning

◆ Drooping or rolling eyes

◆ Scratching the head

◆ Covering one's mouth

1998

CG CARTOON *VOLTRON* PRODUCED: Voltron is a shape-changing giant mecha robot first featured in the 1980s animated television series *Voltron, Defender of the Universe*. After some initial interest, a CG series was released in 1998 (set five years after the end of the original *Lion Voltron* series) to a mixed response because of its departure from the original Lion Voltron's anime look, as well as some character changes, such as the physical appearance of Prince Lotor.

1998

AVID PURCHASES SOFTIMAGE FROM MICROSOFT: This was a good thing for Softimage because Avid would actually spend time on R&D for the software, not just port it from SGI to NT like Gates did.

◆ Tugging at one's clothes

◆ Putting one's hands behind the head, relaxed

◆ Steepling

◆ Putting hand to face in a thinking pose

If your character is tired while speaking, he might yawn, his eyes might droop, or he might sigh. If you character is indifferent to the situation, he might roll his eyes or look around aimlessly. If a character is confused, he might scratch his head or look back and forth for an answer to his plight. Another example of psychological gesture is the act of covering your mouth with your hand. This pose can be meant to hide a conversation or to illustrate nervousness. If you are playing a kind of cat-and-mouse game, your hands might come down to the table as the power play is made. Tugging at one's pants or clothes can also illustrate nervousness or trying to maintain self-control.

To impart a feeling of superiority to your character, you could pose him with his hands behind his head and an open body language that is relaxed. (Think of your producer.) By positioning your character's hands to mimic a church steeple, you can make your character look judgmental. (Think of your director.) This proud, erect stance communicates a clear sense of confidence. Steepling of the hands can also communicate smug or egotistical natures. Messing with the hair can be a defense mechanism. Evaluation gestures, such as placing a finger near the head or eyes or from hand to cheek, resemble the Thinker pose that Rodin sculpted with such accuracy. Interest, attentiveness, and critical evaluation come to mind when someone uses this gesture. Body-shifting toward the door or away from the conversation signals an intention to escape an uncomfortable situation. These are all examples of psychological gestures. It is up to you, as the animator, to find the opportunities to include psychological gesture in your scenes. They will enrich your performance immeasurably. A great book for learning about psychological gestures is *How to Read a Person Like a Book* (Pocket, 1990)[25] by Gerard Nierenberg—and it's only seven bucks on Amazon.com!

The most fun is when you mix psychological gesture with subtext. If your character is lying, he might say something with confidence and end on a note of insincerity, like looking around as he says something. A character who is angry but also thinks the scene is funny might stifle a smile or turn his head to gain his composure. Subtext is so important to getting to the heart of a scene, and psychological gesture is the tool to get you there. Try this next time you go out for lunch. When you are out with other animators, observe people and then supply your own dialogue to the observed conversation. See how the psychological gestures either complement or contradict your own interpreted dialogue. Now, that's a fun time at lunch!

1998

ANTZ OPENS: DreamWorks' *Antz* had its cinematic release somewhat overshadowed by Pixar's *A Bug's Life*, another computer-animated film based on insects. *Antz* is not as child-centric as *A Bug's Life*. It deals with slightly more complex themes, including conformity and war.

1998

A BUGS LIFE RELEASED: The story of *A Bug's Life* is a retelling of Aesop's fable of *The Ant and the Grasshopper*. The film made approximately $162 million dollars in its U.S. theatrical run, easily covering its estimated production costs of $45 million.

1999

OSCAR FOR *THE OLD MAND AND THE SEA* (ALEXANDER PETROV): *The Old Man and the Sea* won an Academy Award for Best Short Subject: Animated Films.

Stay in the Moment

As an animator, it is your responsibility to know the story that is to be played out. You must know what happened in the previous scene and you must know what is to come. As you add the nuances of psychological gesture and subtext, be sure that you stay in the moment. The next moment will play out more convincingly when it is contrasted with the previous one. Comedy depends highly on this point. This is why a straight man is so effective when contrasted with the funny guy. As an animator, you have to know when to hold back, knowing that down the line, the character will have to take it up a notch. Overacting is a big mistake. Watch any scene from television or movies with the sound off, and good acting and bad acting will become obvious. Be selective with your acting patterns and strive to nail the emotion. Ed Hooks explains why emotion is so important to creating empathy:

> Humans act to survive. Emotions—automatic value responses—are the light beacons we send to one another. We empathize only with emotion, not with thinking. An audience puts up with thinking in order to get to the emotion.

Using the acting tools and book references in this chapter will help you create richer scenes and enable you to really walk in your characters' shoes. Once you have fully absorbed the various aspects we have discussed in the previous chapters, you will be ready to move into the scary world of studio politics and where you fit into the structure. The next chapter will teach you everything you wanted to know about how animation studios work.

---

[23]Hooks, Ed. *Acting for Animators*. Heinemann Drama, 2003.

[24]Newlove, Jean. *Laban for Actors and Dancers: Putting Laban's Movement Theory into Practice: A Step-by-Step Guide*. Nick Hern Books, 1998.

[25]Nierenberg, Gerard I and Henry H Calero. *How to Read a Person Like a Book*. New York: MetroBooks, 1990.

1999

THE IRON GIANT IS RELEASED: The *Iron Giant* is a 1999 animated science-fiction film directed by Brad Bird and released by Warner Bros. Pictures. It is loosely based on a 1968 children's book by Ted Hughes, *The Iron Man*. This film won nine major awards at the 1999 Annies, which honor excellence in animation. The categories the film won include Best Picture, Director, Writing, Voice Acting (Marienthal), Music, Character Animation, Effects Animation, Production Design, and Storyboarding. Botched marketing by Warner Bros. led to poor box-office profits for this film.

Index 6: Acting Tools for Animators

Remotivating the Moment

Animators do not necessarily want to be actors, but they have to understand what an actor knows and how the actor prepares for a scene. Animators have to be more analytical than actors because the actor is in the moment and an animator has to be in the moment for weeks at a time. The externals are what an animator is concerned with, but they are a result of the internal.

Improv

Animators are expected to create a performance with a bit of information and do it quickly. All action is the result of thinking. Improv helps you think quickly on your feet. It also helps you get rid of the most common ideas that pop into your head and get to the really juicy ones that an audience will empathize with. Improv rules tell you to not ask questions, but to always know what is going on in the scene.

Power Centers

A tool that improvisational actors use is called the "power center" or "lead." This helps a lot with describing how a character sees himself in the world around him. Using power centers, you can describe any posture to create a character. The power center is where all of the attitude is coming from, and it leads the movement.

Status

A person of high status will be very still and will make direct eye contact. A high-status person is comfortable in his world and his place in that world. Low-status folks tend to look down a lot and might touch their face often. Low-status individuals are uncomfortable in their worlds.

Space, Time, and Weight

Space is so important to animation and acting. How your character occupies its space is a generous explanation of its mindset. The four elements of dimension are space, time, weight, and flow. Space, time, and weight create the flow or action. Within these four elements are six improv terms that can help an animator quickly assess how her character should occupy space. These terms are direct, indirect, fast, slow, heavy, and light.

1999

SOUTH PARK: BIGGER, LONGER & UNCUT RELEASED: *South Park: Bigger, Longer & Uncut*, based on the animated series *South Park*, is one of the most profanity-filled movies ever produced. The movie's excessive use of profanity gained it a spot in the *Guinness Book of Records* for "Most Swearing in an Animated Film" (399 profane words, 128 offensive gestures, and 221 acts of violence). The "cut-out" style of animation was entirely produced on the computer using Maya.

1999

TOY STORY 2 PREMIERES: *Toy Story 2* made more than $245,000,000 in its initial US theatrical run, far surpassing the original *Toy Story* and, in fact, every other animated movie to that date except for *The Lion King*, though both were later eclipsed by another Pixar movie, *Finding Nemo*.

Chaplin

Charlie Chaplin was a genius at creating empathy with the audience. His Little Tramp character was one that touched the hearts of all viewers. Why is that? People could relate to the character. If the Little Tramp got his foot stuck in a bucket, he would try to hide that fact. Staying true to his character is what made the acting real. The Little Tramp wanted to keep his dignity with a bucket stuck on his foot. Instead of wildly trying to shake it off, he would hide the bucket behind his other leg and limp around. The tramp's embarrassment created empathy. The audience felt for the character and desired what he desired, which was to enter the room with grace and dignity.

Emotion

Where is the character coming from? Fix the moment before the scene and lead into it in your mind. There is an old saying in acting that the only time your characters have eye contact that is lengthy is during scenes involving emotions of love, hate, or intimacy. If you are about to hit someone, you do not look away. Neither do you lose eye contact if you are focusing on the love of your life or are about to kiss that person. The eyes are the windows into the mind. Get inside the character's head and show it through the eyes. See a thought process going on behind the eyes.

Empathy

Empathy is different from sympathy. Empathy means you have felt like that character feels and you want for the character the same thing he wishes for. Animate with sincerity.

Observation

What kind of person is your character? Observe people all the time in your everyday life. Find expression in the world around you. Observation provides you with conviction. Animation is not about moving characters around. It is about creating characters that move people.

Body Structure

The design and body structure created for your character are crucial to how that character will act. The power center or leads will help you describe the body structure, but you must go deeper to reinforce the design of the character. This makes for a deeper understanding of how that character would react to the world around him.

1999

STUART LITTLE RELEASED: *Stuart Little*, based on the novel of the same name, combines live-action and computer animation. The screenplay was written by M. Night Shyamalan, acclaimed writer/director of *The Sixth Sense*.

1999

PREMIERE OF *STAR WARS* EPISODE I: *Star Wars Episode I: The Phantom Menace* was the fourth film to be released in the *Star Wars* saga, but it is the first film by chronology of events. *The Phantom Menace* used 66 digital characters composited with live action.

1999

FANTASIA 2000 38TH DISNEY FEATURE: *Fantasia 2000* used a similar format to Walt Disney's 1940 film *Fantasia*, visualizing classical music compositions with various forms of animation, with live-action introductions.

Psychological Gesture

These two aspects of acting will enrich your scenes. Psychological gesture refers to the little things we do as humans to explain what we are thinking. If your character is tired while speaking, he may yawn, his eyes may droop, or he might sigh. If your character is indifferent to the situation, he might roll his eyes or look around aimlessly. If a character is confused, he might scratch his head or look back and forth for an answer to his plight. These are all psychological gestures, and it is up to you as the animator to add these gestures to the scene to enrich the acting.

Stay in the Moment

As the animator, you know the story that is to be played out. You know what happened in the preceding scene and you know what is to come. The next moment will play out more convincingly when it is contrasted with the first beat. Comedy depends highly on this fact. This is why a straight man is so effective when placed against the funny guy. As an animator, you have to know whether to hold back a bit because down the line the character will have to take it up a notch. Stay in the moment, because your audience is!

1999

VIFX AND RHYTHM & HUES MERGE: VIFX visual effects and animation studio Rhythm & Hues purchased the VIFX portion of Marina del Rey–based effects house Blue Sky/VIFX from 20th Century Fox for approximately $5 million. Under the Rhythm & Hues banner, the combined companies are the largest privately owned visual FX house in Los Angeles.

1999

TARZAN 37TH DISNEY FEATURE: *Tarzan* is based upon the *Tarzan of the* Apes series of novels by Edgar Rice Burroughs and is the only major motion picture version of the *Tarzan* property to be animated. It is also the last bona fide hit before the Disney slump of the early 2000s, and is considered by many to be the last of the Disney renaissance era.

PART III

And Now a Word from the Producer

Chapter 7
When Push Comes to Stab

Studio politics. It's everywhere you go, and we are your studio politics "tour guides." We have experienced almost every situation in this chapter and have made many mistakes through frustration with the process of politics within the animation studio. In this chapter, we walk you through many possible sticky situations that could arise (and eventually will) and how to handle them with class and restraint.

> **"You just have to play well with others."**
> *—Cathlin Hidalgo-Polvani*

There is a different culture at every studio and on each new team of artists you work with. You must be aware of studio politics and the constants and variables, whether or not you want to work as a freelancer or a staff artist in animation. Cathlin says it well above…the key is to "play well with others." You are building a reputation with every spoken word, so choose them carefully. Take the high road when conflict arises and be the positive voice in the group.

We really tried to lighten things up here, but when we start using terms such as anal retentive, control freak, and finicky, we just come off sounding sarcastic and bitter. So, you will have to bear with us. Insert smiley face here. The three rules to working within any political arena are to play well, speak well, and avoid being dragged into negative situations.

Many creative people tend to be independent loners or perhaps are perceived this way, as the levels of concentration involved in the process of animation can be overwhelming at times. Artists know what they want and how they want to do it. The problem is, when you add the element of business to any art form, it's no longer exclusively yours. You are being paid to create something for someone else. Michelangelo had patrons he had to answer to, and it is no different in the world of animation. You offer your artistic services for the time being, subject to your employer's ideas, whims, and desires for the piece. How you handle the situation is totally up to you. This relationship will determine how long you remain in the business.

To survive in the world of animation, the artist has to see it as a team effort and learn how to modify methods and practices to work well with supervisors and coworkers. Adapt. You must be able to become everything to everyone and still have a signature style to your work that stands out above the rest. As paradoxical as this sounds, it can be done. The important thing to remember is if you continue to aspire to do great work, people will notice. The efforts you take to improve your animations skills will speak louder than any political games coworkers might play. It is your animation that will ultimately be up on the screen.

Workflow

Much of your success as an animator is dependent upon your workflow. The animator must be flexible and create a performance that reflects what the leads, supervisors, and directors require. The work must also be presented in the fashion that communicates best to those making final approvals. An artist may be seen as difficult to work with or slow if the workflow does not conform to the wishes of the supervisor as well as the pipeline.

If the supervisor does not understand stepped animation or blocking, the animator will have to be able to work in the more splined, layered fashion we talked about in Chapter 5. Flexibility in workflow is also crucial when working with the supervisor who is detail-oriented and wants to see your work every 15 minutes. In this case, just animate, be nice, do your best work, and finish your responsibilities early. Most likely that tendency to check on you will subside once he or she gains trust in your ability to produce. Granted, most people should automatically give you that trust since you were hired in the first place, but the world doesn't always work in a fair and just way.

Let's give an example of a political situation between animator and supervisor. Take a minute right now to imagine you are the supervisor. Put yourself in his shoes. You ask one of your animators to work in a stepped mode first, so the timing and poses are clear before committing to a lot of keys. The shot is not coherent as-is. How does the artist react when you request this change? Is he defensive? Does she make excuses? Or does he or she listen carefully and accept the input as a critique that will simply make the action better and more effective?

When a supervisor has different requirements for a shot in terms of your workflow, it just might force you to work in a way that you've never had to before. Why not see this as an opportunity to grow as an animator? This situation could be a blessing in disguise. It may introduce a new way of working that just might improve your speed and productivity on the next gig.

2000

DINOSAUR RELEASED: *Dinosaur* was Disney's first large scale attempt at a computer-animated feature. It combined the use of live-action backgrounds with computer animation of prehistoric creatures, notably the titular dinosaurs.

2000

BILL HURTZ DIES: Bill Hurtz (1919–2000) received an Oscar nomination for UPA's *Unicorn in the Garden* in 1953. He directed at the Jay Ward Studios from 1959 to 1984. At a Screen Cartoonists Guild meeting in 1941, Bill made the motion to launch a strike against the Disney studio; his motion was unanimously approved.

2000

HOLLOW MAN RELEASED: *Hollow Man* is a science-fiction thriller film loosely based on *The Invisible Man* by H.G. Wells.

Your goal is to be successful. To do this, you have to learn to be a chameleon and change your ways according to how others need you to work and interact. You have to adapt to the personalities of those you work with and meet their criteria. Animation is a small and extremely well-connected industry in both 2D and CG. Now that both mediums have merged, the world of animation has gotten smaller. Everyone seems to know everyone now. We will all eventually find ourselves in sticky situations in the business. Whether it is the usual ranting of the rumor mill or more personal, sometimes nasty, critiques of others' work, we must learn to step back and assess the situation as professionals. Fragile egos are easily wounded, and repercussions sometimes severe. Competition for work has never been more critical, and instances may arise in which—how should we put this?—negative tactics may used. Using unseemly political games to get ahead may seem to work for some, but in the long run it is only a matter of time before they come back to bite you. No matter how talented someone is, if he does not play well with others, word will spread, and it will become extremely difficult for that animator to find work.

Dailies

Criticism is a big part of working as an animator. Every day, your work is placed up on the big screen for all to see and there is no longer any room for excuses or political shenanigans. The proof is in the pudding at this point, and dammit, sometimes the pudding don't taste so good! Grow a thick skin and keep a pleasant attitude when dealing with criticism. Most humans have the inclination to become defensive when being criticized, and you need to push away the negative voices in your head. Slow down and really listen to what is being said. More often than not, the input you are being given is for the good of the scene rather than a personal attack on your abilities as an animator. If you recognize this one concept, you will be more receptive and open to the whole process.

Remember the rule that you are only as good as your last scene. The criticism received is vital to your shot's ultimate approval by the director regardless of what you think the shot should be communicating. Be prepared to receive and suitably respond to criticism no matter how it might tear you up inside. Everyone in that room has a common goal—to follow the directive of the film and put great entertainment on the screen. When an animator gets defensive about the creative choices made in a shot, he should remember the person giving the input probably has been in the industry a good while longer and most likely has a closer relationship to the entire directive of the project. That supervisor and/or director has the information straight from the horse's mouth as to how to get that shot approved within the context of the film. The leads, supervisors, and directors bring fresh eyes to your work and can see its place within the entire sequence because they are forced to think about the whole sequence, not just 65 frames within the movie. The ability to respond professionally to criticism will separate the winning animators from the non-hirable ones.

2000

***WALKING WITH DINOSAURS* PREMIERES (FRAMESTORE UK):** Praised by both scientists and the general public, this six-part BBC documentary series featured realistic CG dinosaur animation.

2000

***MISSION TO MARS* RELEASED:** *Mission to Mars*, with effects produced by ILM and Disney's now-defunct visual effects house, the Secret Lab, is a sci-fi thriller adventure about a rescue mission of the first manned mission to Mars, which encountered a catastrophic and mysterious disaster.

2000

PHIL MITTLEMAN DIES: Phil Mittleman created the company MAGI-Synthavision, which made the light cycle for the movie *Tron*. He also established the UCLA Lab for Technology and the Arts.

On the flip side, delivering criticism is also a delicate thing. The working relationship between animator, lead, and supervisor is one in which mutual respect will breed considerate communication instead of attitude. It's as simple as that. Remember, "once a supervisor" does not necessarily mean "always a supervisor." You may work with these people again in the future, and it will make your career much more enjoyable if you treat others in a respectful manner. As a supervisor, try to remember how you would like to be approached by the director, and draw on those same methods to speak to those working with you. Kicking a chair may not be the best way to get an animator's attention while he or she is wearing headphones! The supervisor should always strive to treat with respect those artists for whom he has been made responsible.

If nothing else, remember that the folks you work with now may go to another studio. They just might go to a studio you want to work at three years from now. Leave a good impression when you leave a show, and the good press from that will follow you to the next job. So play nicely and choose your words wisely. Like the old saying goes: It's much better to keep your mouth shut and let other people think you are a fool than to open it and remove all doubt.

Multiple Art Direction

Another aspect of playing well with others is dealing with sticky situations such as multiple art direction. In the good old days of classical animation, there were only a couple of levels of approval. You had your lead and the director. You showed the roughed-out scene to your supervisor. If he liked what he saw, it went to the director. That was it. Notice, director was singular.

It is becoming more common in CG-animated productions to have several layers of approval, somewhat like the layers of an onion or the rings of a very old tree! There is a VFX supervisor, internal and external animation supervisors, an animation director, and the actual director. Even the production studio can have input on your shots, not to mention the director's spouse (partner) and various nieces, nephews, and other dubious in-laws. Do not be alarmed when your producer trots out her precious seven-year-old to critique the scene you just spent the last 72 straight hours perfecting. Hell no, that would never happen....

Sometimes it's not quite that extreme and is simply a case of two people in charge who have differing opinions on how to make the shot successful. This is another scenario in which the artist has to watch how he handles himself. These are dangerous waters. Swim in a very careful way here. Avoid swallowing water by keeping your mouth firmly in the closed position. A smile, although forced, is always appropriate here. Oh, and a cheery nod now and then. You want to keep everyone involved happy and satisfied that their opinions

2000

HOW THE GRINCH STOLE CHRISTMAS RELEASED: A live-action remake starring Jim Carrey of one of the best-known children's books by Dr. Seuss. The movie received mixed critical reaction but became the highest-grossing film released in North America in the year 2000, earning $260 million at the box office.

2000

THE ROAD TO EL DORADO RELEASED: The creation of *The Road to El Dorado* was a challenge for the studio because DreamWorks had devoted most of its creative efforts to its first animated film, *The Prince of Egypt. El Dorado* was also plagued with a haphazard storyline, where the plot included interchanges of a children's story and adult-themed humor.

were heard. You also want to make a path for easy approvals in the future. Here is a story provided by one of our contributors that illustrates how to handle conflicting direction. David Smith had such an experience and handled it with humor:

I had the wonderful opportunity to build animatics for the original *Casper* live-action film. I worked on a shot with the ghostly trio battling Bill Pullman, simulating swordplay on a staircase. Fatso (ghost 1) was to lunge at Bill Pullman with an umbrella as a sword. Bill Pullman would duck, making Stinky (ghost 2), who was behind Pullman, the recipient of Fatso's umbrella straight into his mouth. The cause and effect gag forced the umbrella to open when jammed in Stinky's mouth—"Fwwooomp!"—expanding Stinky's head *a la* umbrella shape with all necessitated ridiculousness. When keying out the shot, director Brad Silberling stopped by and directed it quite differently than I and the animation director had thought. He says to me, "No the umbrella opens on anticipation to lunge, then it's stuffed into Stinky's mouth."

Okay, most thought differently, but I proceeded against the grain of mine and many of our animation physics and comedic sensibilities. While following that directive the next day, a voice behind me joined the chorus and said, "No the umbrella is shoved in Stinky's mouth, then it opens, expanding Stinky's comic expression."

Turning, I saw Steven Spielberg (executive producer of the film) behind me. Noting his concern and I suppose somewhat embarrassed for why it wasn't already that way, I replied, "You know, you are absolutely correct, and that's just the way I'm going to do it."

One early evening shortly thereafter, I received a call from the director's assistant's assistant, saying they'd like to know why the shot was the way it was. I replied, "Steven wanted it that way."

That was relayed and translated through murmurs and mumbles over a covered telephone receiver, and after a rather long moment the assistant returned to ask, "Steven who?"

I replied, "Steven Spielberg."

More relay, translation, and non-decipherable whispers and mumblings, and then, "Okay, see you in the morning."

However, I had an extremely difficult time getting anything through for the rest of the production.

Moral of the story... None! Just follow the directive.

2000

TITAN A.E. PREMIERES: The title of *Titan A.E.* refers to the fictional Titan spacecraft that is central to the plot, with A.E. meaning "After Earth." The film's animation technique combined traditional hand-drawn animation and extensive use of CG imagery. *Titan A.E.* was not financially successful; after it made only $9 million during its opening weekend, Fox Animation Studios was shut down.

2000

CHICKEN RUN RELEASED: *Chicken Run* proved a success with both children and adults, and showed that Peter Lord and Nick Park had the ability to handle the technical and writing challenges posed by a feature film, serving as a test bed for the 2005 movie outing for *Wallace & Gromit in The Curse of the Were-Rabbit*.

Don't say we didn't warn you. Did we mention there are a lot of levels of approval? Yeah, we think we mentioned that. Dave handled the situation well by following the directive, although he also made it hard for himself to get future shots approved.

It's best in this situation to get both parties in the same room to hash out their differences. If you can achieve this without bruising anyone's ego, you have won the battle to obtain clear animation direction for the rest of the show. If the two battling parties will not or cannot come together and discuss the multiple art direction because of geography (meaning the two are not working in the same state or country), because of big egos, or simply because of the need to strut their stuff around the room, you will merely be a pawn in their battle for power. In this case, you will have to do the best you can, as Dave did on *Casper*. Dave listened to the most reliable source for the input, the director. If you do not have access to the director, the people on the show you determine to have the closest understanding of what the director wants are your best bet.

Dealing with the bi-polar director. Sketches by Joe Scott.

THE EMPEROR'S NEW GROOVE 39TH DISNEY FEATURE: *The Emperor's New Groove* is a wacky comedy with more in common with a *Looney Tunes* or Tex Avery cartoon than a traditional Disney film. It was made and produced by Walt Disney Feature Animation over a troubled six-year timeline.

OSCAR FOR *FOR THE BIRDS* (RALPH EGGLESTON): *For the Birds* won the Academy Award for Best Short Subject: Animated Films.

2001

BOB ABEL DIES: Bob Abel (1937–2001) was a pioneer in computer animation, especially in 1970s' commercials, through his company, Robert Abel & Associates.

Sometimes we hear directors say, "I don't know what I want, but I will know when I see it." These can be the most expensive words in animation. It happens over and over again, especially when working on fantasy-based films. For the love of Pete, don't start throwing things, especially at anyone higher on the food chain than yourself. Follow the directive of what you know the scene is about and when you do, you'll hit the bull's eye. Chris Bailey talks about an experience he had working with the animators on *X-Men 2*. He just kept trying new versions to see which one would stick:

> There were these two scenes in *X-Men 2* that Bryan Singer [director] just wasn't buying. One was the reveal of Nightcrawler's tail, and the other was when Magneto was reprogramming Cerebro by rearranging a bunch of metal plates that were flying all around the room. I swear that the animators had to do at least 50 versions of each shot. "Faster, slower, more of an arc, straighter path..."; the direction changed with every version. I felt terrible for the animators as the supervisor and knew that we were presenting terrific versions of the shots. I offered the following advice: "Your job here is to make sure the shot doesn't go backward and become worse. You can't run out of ideas. Think of this as an exercise in the variety of ways to communicate this shot. Eventually one of them will be selected, and you don't want it to be one you don't believe in." To their credit, the final shots looked great in the film because the animators didn't give up. The key was in reading between the lines of what the director said and animating what he wanted.

As a supervisor and as an animator, dealing with multiple art direction can be one of the most frustrating obstacles to completing a shot. Both the supervisor and the animator have to keep moving forward on the animation. Chris did the best thing in that he kept presenting fresh ideas that still followed the directive of the story and the shot.

Mentorship Lost

The crossover from pencil to mouse has been tough for artists on both sides. Traditional animators who spent years developing a career around what they knew about motion, acting, and performance have now been thrown to the wolves, so to speak. Learning to animate on a computer can be hard for some people, especially for those to whom sending an e-mail can be a major task. Enthusiastic young CG animators sitting next to these individuals often bear the brunt of the older animators' animosity and feelings of inadequacy. Going through a major career disruption is not easy on anyone, so take pity on the grizzled old codger from the traditional world. You may have much to learn from each other.

2001

NEW CATEGORY FOR THE OSCARS: The Academy Award for Best Animated Feature was introduced because, in 2000, the Academy was disappointed that the hugely successful *Chicken Run* was not nominated for Best Picture. So, the Best Animated Feature category was introduced the following year.

2001

***SHREK* WINS BEST ANIMATED FEATURE:** *Shrek* is a computer-animated film adaptation of William Steig's 1990 fairytale picture book of the same name. It was the first film to win an Academy Award for Best Animated Feature.

In addition, CG studios do not use the same mentoring structure that 2D facilities used to create experienced, skilled artists. In a classical 2D studio, any new artist would work under an experienced leading animator for possibly many years. That new artist would not be allowed to even use the title "animator" until he had proven himself working under that mentor assigned to him. These assistant animators were middle-aged men with families to support. This was also a long time ago in 2D land, as Ken Harris affirms in an interview with Richard Williams circa 1975:

> I don't know how you get animators without them being assistants first. The average animator is an assistant for four to five years—unless he's an unusually adaptable guy. I was an assistant from June 20, 1935, to September 1, 1936. I was an assistant in-betweener and then the assistant animator, but I worked nights and animated. I probably did about 400 or 500 feet of animation in that year and a half. I got filmed tests of it; some of it they used and some they didn't. But I was no kid, you know; I was married and had to make a living. I couldn't horse around like the young guys did. They'd just go into it and say, "Well, I'm working here in this studio, and some day I'll be an animator." They didn't care about how quickly, and they didn't seem to worry much about it.

Eventually, by the '90s, this mentoring system had completely fallen away in traditional circles.

The Nine Old Men at Disney, specifically, have fond stories of what they learned involving this mentoring structure, as well as some abuse during the process. Even with the abuse, what you can learn from an experienced animator simply drawing over your poses is tremendous. We speak from experience here. When a veteran animator takes out a dry erase marker and simply draws a stronger pose on the screen on top of yours, you say to yourself, "Damn! How did I not see that?" If your lead sits down to go over thumbnails and draws out a few stronger gesture poses to illustrate a more accurate direction for the shot, the animator will learn so much more than if he was told, "Just animate it!"

If you were going to leave animation and start all over in a new career, would you do it blindly, without talking to anyone who had already been doing it for years? Does a chef go out and cook a six-course meal without ever having mentored under an executive chef? No! So why has animation let go of the mentoring organization that created some of the best animators in history?

2001

BILL HANNA DIES: William (Bill) Hanna (1911–2001) made contributions to the world of animation that cannot be overstated, from his brilliant Oscar-winning work at MGM, to the popularization of limited TV animation in the late '50s and '60s, such as *The Flintstones*.

2001

***ATLANTIS* 40TH DISNEY FEATURE:** *Atlantis: The Lost Empire* did not do well at the box office, making approximately $85 million dollars in its North American theatrical run, well below its production cost of $120 million and nowhere near the animation high-water mark of $312 million set by *The Lion King*.

Mentorship in animation is so very important. Sketch by Floyd Norman.

Quite a large number of recent animation school graduates are incredibly talented and skilled, beyond their years and working experience. Some students straight out of school have also learned to play the game at the studios and move up quickly because of their personal and political skills. Many of these young artists do not have all of the experience and understanding of motion and performance that a veteran animator would have, but they know how to sit at a computer and make something move in a reasonably convincing fashion.

2001

OSMOSIS JONES PREMIERES: *Osmosis Jones* is a part animated, part live-action film whose title character is Osmosis Jones, an anthropomorphic white blood cell. The film went through a troubled time in production. Upon its original release, the film lost a considerable amount of money and was the second-to-last production for Warner Bros.' feature traditional animation department.

2001

FAITH HUBLEY DIES: Faith Hubley made 25 personal films and won three Academy Awards with husband John Hubley. She was a great friend of the UCLA workshop.

They have grown up on computers, so it's also intuitive. Often this intuition with computers makes the younger animator faster. The younger animator might produce an acceptable result in a more rapid fashion, though the end result is not the highly finessed, more original piece of animation a more seasoned professional might offer. The younger, hungrier animator does not generally have a family at home and is willing to work very long hours in order to get the shots right or more shots animated. Recent graduates also demand a lower salary due to their lack of industry experience, increasing their marketability to a great degree. Some will work for next to nothing, just to build a reel. This is another pill that is very hard to swallow for old-timers who paid their dues on the traditional and even CG sides. You cannot assume that studios do not consider salary demands when it comes to choosing crews! No matter how long you have been in an industry, be it business, cooking, or clock cleaning, you will always be competing for shots and jobs with people who are younger, hungrier, and prettier than you.

The lack of mentoring structure has actually hindered CG over the years by placing folks with little filmmaking skill out in the trenches. Things are starting to change with the introduction of more traditional artists. However, like any big venture it will take time. Schools such as Animation Mentor (http://www.AnimationMentor.com) are trying to fill the gap that is missing at CG studios and actually mentor and teach young animators the principles they need to understand outside of running a computer. Schools such as One-On-One Animation (http://www.1on1animation.com) are working to bring back the hands-on mentoring that existed at Disney and United Film Production (UPA) so the graduating artists can be proud to call themselves animators. Mike Polvani (one of the founders of the One-on-One Animation School) tells us what it was like when he was learning about animation 22 years ago:

> Even after years of animating and having the title animator on the screen and on my paychecks, I still felt guilty calling myself an animator because I didn't have the experience to be as good as what I felt a real animator should be.

The title "animator" should mean more than it does today for all of us to take pride in what we do. More mentoring structures within the studios will raise the bar of what being an animator means. Placing value on those who have been working in animation for many years and what they have to bring to the table outside of computer skills will also encourage more of those veterans to throw a hand in teaching the fresh animators in the industry. Each veteran artist can push CG into new, unique directions and styles, making it a higher art form. This field is still in its infancy, and we have so much to learn. Studios are constantly adapting their pipelines and approaches to production because of this.

2001

JIMMY NEUTRON: BOY GENIUS NOMINATED FOR OSCAR: *Jimmy Neutron: Boy Genius* was nominated for an Academy Award for Best Animated Feature. The film was produced using off-the-shelf software by DNA Productions of Dallas, Texas. It grossed around $80 million in North America and was followed by the television series *The Adventures of Jimmy Neutron: Boy Genius* the following fall.

2001

RAY PATTERSON DIES: Ray Patterson began as an inker in Mintz's studio in 1929 and worked at Disney, MGM, and Hanna-Barbera. An animator and character designer on *Dumbo* and *Fantasia* at Disney, Ray went on to become one of Tex Avery's top animators at MGM.

> ### UPA'S CONTRIBUTIONS TO ANIMATION PRODUCTION
>
> United Film Production (UPA) was established by former Disney animators John Hubley, Zack Schwartz, Dave Hilberman, and Steve Bosustow after the animation strike against Disney in 1941. Their mission was founded in the belief that animation was an artistic form of expression that didn't necessarily have to follow the Disney model of "the illusion of life," but instead could be more graphic and experimental in the design of characters, layouts, and backgrounds. Their most critically acclaimed character arrived in 1951, the title character of *Gerald McBoing-Boing*, based on a story by children's author Theodor "Dr. Seuss" Geisel, which snagged the Academy Award®. UPA's Golden Age came to a sad and abrupt end in 1952 when Hubley fell victim to the McCarthy-era blacklisting.[26]

Some CG studios have adopted a production pipeline structure in which multiple animators work on a shot. The lead animator blocks out the shot and has a weekly footage quota. The junior and entry-level animators work on in-betweening the poses and performing cleanup. This is closer to the way classical animation production is handled. The scary part is, for 20 years now, CG animators have had control of their entire shot for the show at most other studios. This fact can be quite liberating and encourage a sense of pride in the shot. Many CG animators do not welcome a multiple-animator-per-shot pipeline because it is so different from what they are used to. CG animators want to be able to say they animated the whole shot from beginning to end. The CG industry isn't used to breaking down animation into lead and cleanup when it comes to animators. Until more studios take on this pipeline, it will be hard to enforce this tradition.

However, the multiple-animator-per-shot pipeline would reinforce the mentoring structure of the old days in 2D, as well as provide a more streamlined approval process. When we talk about mentoring structures in CG, it is not just about learning how to use the computer or fixing something technical in the shot. We are talking about actually having a veteran explain why the shot is not working and how to improve the performance.

The only way to achieve a successful CG pipeline is for the leads to take pride in teaching those working under them. This way everyone benefits from the process. The leads actually are mentoring the junior-level animators. The junior-level animators learn from taking the broad strokes set by the leads and finessing

2001

DISNEY'S SECRET LAB CLOSES:
After buying out DreamQuest Images, Disney decided that producing in-house visual effects might not be such a great idea.

2001

FINAL FANTASY FIRST CG HUMAN IN A FEATURE:
Final Fantasy: The Spirits Within was released on July 11, 2001, in the US and was the first animated feature to seriously attempt photorealistic CGI humans. Despite aggressive promotion by Sony, it also became one of the biggest box-office bombs in film history, with losses of more than $100 million.

them into something beautiful. This process provides a structure in which the assistant can learn how to "complete the sentence," so to speak. The assistant learns by observing how a lead broke down the poses and what acting choices they made to push the scene forward. Cathlin Hidalgo-Polvani explains the role of a good assistant animator:

> A good assistant understands the principles of animation and will be able to finish the thought that the animator had started.

The danger with using the animator and assistant animator structure in CG is when a junior animator is stuck working on claws and eyes for two years and never receives the mentoring that should be there to help him grow as an artist. What is he or she really learning? If this becomes the reality, then only seniority, not skill, will merit moving up within the structure, and no one grows or learns from that. There must be communication between the lead and his team and a strong bond for any animation pipeline to be successful years down the line.

Competition

In animation, the element of competition has risen to a point where camaraderie has fallen by the wayside to a large degree. 2D animators and newly graduated animation students are flooding the CG scene at enormous rates. These folks are added to the veteran CG workforce. There are more animators looking for work today than ever before. Mike Polvani explains how different the job market is today than when he started:

> One huge disadvantage for animators entering the field today is the competition. It's huge. Way bigger than when I started out 20 years ago. There is so much product out there now that everyone is saying, "I wanna do that!" It's just out of control, and a lot of people are drowning.

Animators are in such a hurry to get a quota filled, get the best shot for their demo reel, and impress a supervisor that we are all forgetting that animation is supposed to be fun. There was a time when animators shared ideas and worked together to push each other's work in a healthy and positive way. When you create this kind of sharing and similar interest in a group, the energy fuels all involved. You go to lunch and find yourself still talking about what you love about your job, instead of whining about what isn't going your way or manipulating each other to climb to the top.

2001

MONSTERS, INC. PREMIERES: *Monsters, Inc.* premiered in the US with the best opening ticket sales ever for an animated film and the sixth best of all time. It also won the Academy Award for Best Song (Randy Newman for "If I Didn't Have You") and was nominated for Best Animated Feature, Best Effects, Sound Effects Editing, and Best Music, Original Score.

2001

HARRY POTTER I RELEASED: *Harry Potter and the Sorcerer's Stone* is based on the fantasy novel of the same name by best-selling author J.K. Rowling. The film made in excess of $968 million at the worldwide box office (third all-time behind *Titanic* and *The Lord of the Rings: The Return of the King*) and received three Oscar nominations.

212

In the early years of 2D and CG, artists used to play practical jokes on each other out of genuine mutual admiration and the fun of it. We would share our shots and talk about ways to work out performance. Today, online forums and chat rooms are full of negative, bitter, and angry folks instead of people who really enjoy what they do and want to share that with others who also love animation. We are not going to start singing "Kum By Ya" here; it's just something to think about. If you put out positive stuff, you are bound to get some back.

No time to sleep; time to animate! Sketch by Floyd Norman.

Shamus Culhane observed in his book *Animation: From Script to Screen* (St. Martin's Griffin, 1990) that "90% of any group of workers are unwilling to improve their abilities by study—unless it happens during working hours and the boss supplies the means."[27] How the heck will you ever bring your skill to a higher level if you never strive to do so? Your education did not end when you graduated. Take classes in art, animation, improv, acting, sculpture, filmmaking, photography, or whatever! It's up to you to gather all the information that you now have at your fingertips, as Mike Polvani observes:

> An advantage to entering the animation market today is now, more than ever, there are more resources and references. When I started, we had nothing but the Preston Blair book and would go over it and over it and over it. But today there is so much information out there, it's crazy.

One of the most priceless technological advances for an animator today is the DVD. You can frame by frame anything to study how the problems in the shot were solved. You can even frame by frame a movie trailer online before the movie is released! The Internet provides forums and animation blogs with real-live working animators that you can correspond with. It's amazing the resources that are out there!

We are also lucky enough to be working in an industry that values versatility. There are many facets to being an animator, including understanding of kinematics, camera work, cinema, anatomy, acting...the list goes on and on. This is why animators come from so many different walks of life. Choose a class or hobby such as life drawing, sculpting, photography, or improv to improve your skills and make yourself a more well-rounded artist. Not only will it make you a more knowledgeable animator and help you understand your profession, but it will help you focus outside of work on something creative. Of course, this is assuming you have any time outside of work; many of us find ourselves working 16-hour days. Take opportunities to learn and grow on your own time. These opportunities will keep you positive and open you up to new experiences and new people. This leads to our next topic, pigeonholing, which is also dependent upon you improving your abilities outside of work hours.

2002

OSCAR FOR *SPIRITED AWAY*: *Spirited Away* won the Academy Award for Best Animated Feature one year after it was released. This incredible film was almost overlooked. It was the first movie to have earned $200 million at the worldwide box office before opening in the U.S. By 2002, a sixth of the Japanese population had seen it. The film was subsequently released in the U.S. in September 2002 and was dubbed into English by Walt Disney Pictures, under the supervision of Pixar's John Lasseter.

2002

***SPIRIT: STALLION OF THE CIMARRON* PREMIERES:** *Spirit: Stallion of the Cimarron* follows the adventures of a Kiger Mustang stallion who is nameless until the end of the movie.

Pigeonholing

Pigeonholing is a condition in which many employees find themselves because of their lack of willingness to be aggressive in an aggressive industry. This particular situation has to do with natural selection. It's just that simple. If you do not take the time outside of work to learn what you need to know to convince your employer that you have what it takes to move up or around, then you have no one else to blame than yourself.

If you want to be given better shots and higher pay, you will have to show something that merits that. Earn the respect of your supervisor and peers both technically and artistically and stretch outside of your comfort zone. Work on an animation test using an internal rig or a free rig online. The rig itself doesn't matter, it's the motion. Take classes to be competitive, as we mentioned before. Show the powers-that-be that you have what it takes to do another job within the structure if that is the path you want.

Yes. yes. You do WONDERFUL work. But, that's Exactly my POINT. Why would we Promote you, when you do such a great job, where you ARE?

Sometimes working in the structure of animation can be frustrating. Stick to your guns and show your supervisor skills outside of your comfort zone. Drawing by Brian Dowrick.

2002

OSCAR FOR *THE CHUBBCHUBBS!* (ERIC ARMSTRONG): *The ChubbChubbs!* won an Academy Award for Best Short Subject: Animated Films.

2002

LILO & STITCH 41ST DISNEY FEATURE: *Lilo & Stitch* is one of the few animated feature films to use watercolor paintings for its backgrounds. It was also the second of three Disney animated features produced primarily at its animation studio at Disney-MGM Studios in Orlando, Florida.

2002

GAMECUBE RELEASED: The Nintendo GameCube is Nintendo's fourth home video game console. The GameCube itself is the most compact and least expensive of the sixth generation–era consoles.

Core and Glitz Skills

The extracurricular classes you take to expand your artistic gifts are only one part of being a great animator. There are two sides to advancing as a computer artist. The core skills encompass everything you know outside of the technical aspects of using a computer to make art, including the classes we encourage you to take no matter what level you are at. These skills include traditional principles, drawing, and all of the right-brained talents. The glitz skills are those that help you stay ahead of software developments and continue to think outside of the box when dealing with technical issues in your shots. Glitz skills involve the software. We have a bit of advice on software: Do not be a software jockey.

Technology is something that advances so fast that you miss it quickly. The authors have learned more than 30 types of graphics software to get that paycheck over the years. HiRes QFX, Rio, Tips, TDI Wavefront, 3D Studio DOS to Max, Alias, Maya, Softimage, Photoshop, Flash, Premiere, Illustrator, Quark, Autographix— the list goes on and on and will continue until we are all old and grey. You must keep up with the creative and technical standards and advances in computer-generated images in order to stay employed. In addition, some studios have their own proprietary software they have developed in house. If you cannot or will not pick up this software quickly, you will drown and seem slow to production. For those trying to cross over to CG, this is a scary thing. For years many animators only needed to control the pencil, and now they have to master a computer and software with new releases each year.

Things can get frustrating when you are initially being taught to animate on a computer. It may seem that your slowness in the beginning is a great bother to your instructor. Take a deep breath. Avoid hitting him with any heavy, solid object. He is only doing his job, so keep an open mind. The computer can seem so remote compared to a pencil, but you will become more computer-literate with time, and more importantly, you will greatly improve your chances of employment. It takes core/traditional skills and glitzy/technology skills to make amazing CG animation.

Responsibility

Take satisfaction in touching every frame of your shot. Taking control and responsibility for the shot and any errors that happen will impress the supervisor a lot more than listening to the guy in the back of dailies who constantly makes excuses for problems in his shot. Take pride in your work, and your sense of ownership will take over. Focus and attention to detail will make the chance of embarrassing yourself in dailies much less of an issue.

2002

GLEN MCQUEEN DIES: At 41, Glen McQueen died in Berkeley in October, 2002. Glenn was a big contributor to the cinematic style that became Pixar's signature. He helped create famous characters such as Woody in *Toy Story*. He was animation supervisor on that classic film, as well as on *Toy Story 2*, *A Bug's Life*, and *Monsters, Inc.*

2002

SPIDER-MAN FIFTH HIGHEST GROSSING FILM OF ALL TIME: *Spider-Man* was a hit, grossing $403 million in its theatrical run in North America, becoming the highest-grossing film of the year and denying a *Star Wars* film (*Episode II: Attack of the Clones*) from being number one for the first time ever. Its $114 million opening weekend set a record, and the movie became the first to earn more than $100 million in a weekend.

Speaking of pride in your work, before you decide to show your supervisor anything, ask yourself, "Is this the best I can do?" Go through the shot with a fine-toothed comb and check for penetrations, technical glitches, pops, and any other carelessness that will detract from your performance.

There is a famous story about Henry Kissinger that applies here. Winston Lord was writing speeches for Kissinger, and he turned in a draft. Kissinger called Lord back a few minutes later and said, "Is this the best you can do?" And Lord said, "Henry, I thought so, but I'll try again." Lord went off and came back later with

Remember, attention to detail can make a better impression in dailies than excuses. Sketch by Floyd Norman.

2002

CHUCK JONES DIES: With the death of Charles Martin "Chuck" Jones (1912–2002), the film community lost one of its most talented artist-directors. Jones was the creator of some of the world's most beloved cartoon characters at Warner Bros. He directed many of the classic short animated cartoons starring Bugs Bunny, Daffy Duck, the Road Runner and Wile E. Coyote, Pepé Le Pew, and the other Warner Bros. characters, including the memorable *What's Opera, Doc?* (1957) and *Duck Amuck* (1952) (both later inducted into the National Film Registry), establishing himself as an important innovator and storyteller.

another draft. This process apparently went on through eight drafts, the last of which Lord supposedly stayed up all night finishing before he turned it in. Kissinger called Lord back again and said, "Is this the best you can do?" Lord said, "Henry, I've beaten my brains out—this is the ninth draft. I know it's the best I can do: I can't possibly improve one more word." Reportedly Kissinger then replied, "In that case, now I'll read it."[28] Take responsibility for presenting the best work possible. Don't just meet the needs of the scene. Dave Brewster has a great story to share that illustrates the responsibility you have to your shots and to yourself:

> I'm in Ireland working for Don Bluth. I am working on this scene of Carface from *All Dogs Go to Heaven*. It's Thursday and the scene is due Friday. I spent the week thinking how great it's going to be, how hard I worked to make the perspective perfect, the motion smooth, and making it dead on model. So I am shooting the test on the Lyon Lamb, I look up to the screen and view what I suddenly come to see as the emptiest piece of crap I have ever produced. A bead of cold sweat rolls down my face as the realization that I had missed the entire point of the scene kicks in. I had spent my time polishing an idiotic, egotistical, self-indulgent, off-topic bad idea. I trashed every drawing. Two days of terror followed as I redid the scene and tried only to keep it to what Don had asked. For some reason just by doing this I was able to hit the scene exactly. Everyone was pleased. The lead on Carface, Linda Miller, came up later and said, "Nice"—something she rarely did. I collapsed in exhaustion later that night, swearing never to let that kind of thing happen again. Never did, not like that.

Ask yourself before you decide to show anything, "Is this the best I can do?"

You are an animator! You were hired to do a job, and you should honor that responsibility. This means you own your shot and you should constantly push the limits of what you can do with it. So why not work on the facial when you know the director won't be back for dailies until tomorrow. The goal is not to get notes here. The goal is to get some crazy fantastic animation in front of the folks who are chomping at the bit to see something new! If your supervisor advises you to make a change, don't tell him you want to wait and show it as-is to the director! Give that supervisor the same respect you would like in return. The supervisor is there to guide the shot and make sure it's following the arrangement the director has in mind. In fact, most successful animators take advantage of an opportunity, like a day's worth of no input, to work on some fresh ideas and create a more original performance. Make that scene work so well that you get a standing ovation!

2002

ICE AGE IS RELEASED: *Ice Age*, created by Blue Sky Studios and released by 20th Century Fox, contains a humorous subplot in which an animal named Scrat makes many comical attempts to bury his beloved acorn.

2002

TREASURE PLANET 42ND DISNEY FEATURE: *Treasure Planet* employed a novel technique of hand-drawn 2D traditional animation set atop 3D computer animation. A similar method was used for the character of the cyborg John Silver: His natural body was hand-animated, but his mechanical arm and eye were computer-animated.

Communication between Departments

There are many departments of specialization in a CG animation production. In a 2D production there were also many different departments, such as visual development, story, layout, animation, inking, and camera, but the main tools used were pencil and paper and drawing was the craft. Many artists could move around easily without necessarily needing to learn new tools. The problem with computers is you introduce a technical side to production that is very specialized. There are additional positions, such as lighting and pipeline tools, requiring a mind that is creative but also very technical and mathematical. Right- and left-brained people are very different in how they approach problems. Your communication skills will be tested when speaking with riggers, lighters, match movers, as well as CG tool and pipeline specialists.

You interaction should always be respectful and understanding of their contributions to the picture. Make nice with your rigger because he will make or break your ability to animate well. Imagine your favorite pencil is discontinued. What are you going to do? You go to every store in town to buy the last box of those pencils, right? Imagine the rigger you have worked with for the past two years is leaving to go to another studio. In CG, a solid rig is akin to a solid drawing. What do you do? You get to know the new guy and let him know you are supportive of his role and that you want a good working relationship.

So many people in this business these days get caught up in their small role in the production and forget that it takes an army of people to make a CG film and every single person is important to that production. It seems a simple rule to treat everyone with respect, but in a heated situation when you are emotionally invested in your work, you can lose sight of things. Everyone has the same goal—to make the best film possible. So before you touch another person's shot because you think you know better, or before you speak unfavorably about another artist, think about how you would feel if you were on the receiving end of those actions.

When dealing with other departments, try to understand their plight. Try to observe how many shots they are working on and how much overtime the artists have already done that week. One day some of the animation created will break the fur or the cloth or the feathers, and a really cheesed-off guy is going to give you a call. You might also be really stressed over the six retakes you are expected to finish by the end of the day, and now he wants you to look at the last shot you submitted to be rendered. Do you:

A. Tell him he has to fix it because it's his job and hang up, slamming the phone.

B. Start to weep. There is nothing like a hysterical bout of the jaggies to make the person on the other end of the line feel bad for you.

C. Tell him that you are kind of busy but promise to check out the file on your lunch hour, so he should just e-mail the path so you can get back to him as soon as possible.

2002

STAR WARS EPISODE II RELEASED: *Star Wars Episode II: Attack of the Clones* was the first film to be shot completely on a high-definition digital 24-frame system. This is the only *Star Wars* film that was not the highest-grossing film for the year in which it was originally released. It was out-grossed by *Spider-Man* and *The Lord of the Rings: The Two Towers*.

2002

HARRY POTTER 2 PREMIERES: *Harry Potter and the Chamber of Secrets*, the second film in the popular Harry Potter series, was released in 2002.

2002

SCOOBY-DOO RELEASED - ZOINKS!: *Scooby-Doo* is a live-action movie based upon the popular Hanna-Barbera Saturday morning cartoon *Scooby-Doo*.

Respect your coworkers and their efforts. Touching someone else's scene without asking is a no-no. Articulate if you want a change. Take responsibility for being able to articulate what you think should be touched. Drawing by Brian Dowrick.

The answer is B. No, wait—it's C, of course. The best way to diffuse the situation is to communicate and share the responsibility of getting that shot completed. Or cry—that works too.

Another tricky technological advancement is e-mail. E-mail is an amazing form of communication. You can send necessary information to another artist or your supervisor without disturbing their flow and their own demands throughout the day. They can deal with the topic when they are ready to do so. E-mail is also great when applying for a job. Again, without putting someone on the spot, you can send a brief e-mail stating you are following up on a reel or an interview.

A general rule of thumb when it comes to e-mail is brevity. If you are typing more than a paragraph, then most likely you need to be having the conversation in person. Just try and tell your 13-year-old daughter that

2002

STUART LITTLE 2 RELEASED: *Stuart Little 2* is a sequel to the 1999 film *Stuart Little* and includes characters from the children's book by E. B. White, such as Margalo the bird.

2002

LORD OF THE RINGS 2 USES AI ON DIGITAL ACTORS: *The Lord of the Rings: The Two Towers* is the second part of the *Lord of the Rings* film trilogy. This film employed the first use of AI for digital actors using the Massive software developed by Weta Digital. The movie was very well received critically and was an enormous box-office success, earning more than $900 million worldwide and making it the fourth most successful film in history at the time of its release.

when she is on her fourteenth straight hour of senseless IM-ing. E-mail is a great way to collect your thoughts and express them in a clear manner, but if this takes several paragraphs, then it will most likely be more productive to go talk to the person about the situation directly. E-mail can give a false sense of intimacy because you are not directly in front of someone else, and you may say things that you might not say in person without realizing it. Also, if someone doesn't know you well, your own words can be twisted into something that comes across as short, curt, and snappy instead of the brief, succinct text you intended. Placing "smileys" all over an e-mail also doesn't always help. Never send an e-mail when you are angry or upset. Overall, it's best to speak directly to the person, but if you need to reference a specific file or pipeline situation, e-mail is very helpful in that respect. Just remember, when you send an e-mail, the person who is reading it has many other things going on in his day and life, so keep it brief and light.

Another touchy aspect of communication between departments is how to deal with difficult people. Sometimes you just run into a real bastard who, for whatever reason, seems to have it in for you. In general, it's best to use the philosophy that you get more flies with honey than you do with vinegar, and be as polite and civil as you can. But this method can be taxing on the soul in some situations, and sometimes can set you up to be taken advantage of during the production. The first thing to do when dealing with a difficult person is to try and figure out why. Don't spend a lot of time on this, of course—no analyzing for days. Just try to see this guy's point of view.

Most people are difficult because of a perceived sense of threat and their own fears and insecurities. If you view the person who is being difficult in this way, it makes it a lot easier to empathize with him and find new ways to approach him. Just like we described in Chapter 3, any villain sees himself as a hero in his world, and so does this difficult person you deal with day in and day out. If he feels threatened by you or the production, try to speak to him in ways that will put him at ease. You can fight the situation, but where is that going to get you, really? Instead, realize that it's just a job and you do not have to work with this person forever. It's always best to talk to the person you are having difficulties with directly before going to anyone else in production. Try to put yourself in his shoes when you do go to talk to him about the problem, and think how you would like to be approached in the same situation. Conversely, ignoring the situation will likely make matters worse, so be brave and confront the problem before it escalates. Working for a difficult person can be trying. When that person is much younger than you, it can be particularly grating.

The lack of mentoring structures in CG, especially at smaller studios, has made the possibility of working for someone less experienced a reality. More and more visual-effects boutiques are branching out into character animation. But studios that have made their bread and butter doing explosions, spaceships, and futuristic planes aren't necessarily well-equipped to deal with the subtle aspects of character animation. There are very few experienced character animators or supervisors at the compositing and visual-effects boutiques.

2003

OSCAR FOR *HARVIE KRUMPET* (ADAM ELLIOT): *Harvie Krumpet* won the Academy Award for Best Short Subject: Animated Films, in addition to numerous festival awards and the 2004 Australian Film Institute Best Short Animation award.

2003

FINDING NEMO WINS BEST ANIMATED FEATURE: By March of 2004, *Finding Nemo* was one of the top 10 highest grossing films ever, having earned more than $850 million. The film received an Academy Award for Best Animated Feature Film in 2004.

2003

SINBAD: *LEGEND OF THE SEVEN SEAS* PREMIERES: *Sinbad: Legend of the Seven Seas* was produced by DreamWorks SKG. Sin-*bad* is right.

Underbidding by visual effects and compositing studios to bring character animation shows in house has led to a situation in which budget is dictating the quality of artist on the show. If a studio cannot afford to hire an experienced character animation supervisor, this will be reflected in the quality of the work. In contrast, an animator is worth his weight in gold if he knows how to problem-solve and work out issues in the shot without a lot of direction.

Remember, animation should be fun. Violence is never the answer. Sketch by Floyd Norman.

2003

BROTHER BEAR 43RD DISNEY FEATURE: Originally titled *Bears*, this was the third and final Disney animated feature produced primarily by the Feature Animation studio at Disney-MGM Studios in Orlando, Florida. *Brother Bear* made $85 million during its domestic theatrical run, and Disney considered the film a failure. However, it went on to be a hit around the world, amassing $164 million more worldwide than *Lilo & Stitch*, bringing its worldwide total to $250 million.

2003

DAVID BROWN DIES: David Brown was a marketing executive with CBS/Fox Video and later cofounded Mathematics Application Group, Inc. (MAGI) Synthavision and Blue Sky Studios.

Problem-Solving

Every supervisor has a story about the one animator who just came in, did his work, and left. The person's work looked amazing, but the supervisor never saw him or heard from him. It's like little elves came in and did the work and disappeared. This is an example of good problem-solving. That animator knew how to make decisions for himself. It's guaranteed he ran into an issue in which the rig didn't work the way he hoped, or the tracking was off, or the frame rate given by the producer didn't match the file settings. You know what the "magic elf animator" did? He took care of it. He fixed the tracking himself. Or he spoke with the rigger and got him to make a quick change, or, even better, he actually communicated with the producer about a simple typo. This is called problem-solving. And it makes you look good.

Your supervisor is handling close to 30 or even 40 animators a day, as well as attending meetings with his supervisor, the client, and other departments. He doesn't need to track down why your shot is 37 frames on the list, but your file is 42 frames long. Be proactive. Be willing and able to overcome technical and artistic challenges. When faced with a problem, don't be someone whose first instinct is to run to a supervisor and ask for help when faced with performance or non-technical issues. Think creatively. Approach the problem from a different angle. If the supervisor said pick up the left foot, but you realize that the left foot will have to penetrate the leg of a chair in the shot, work it out. Lift the leg in a different way, or lift the right foot and explain why later. He will get it. Be a self-starter and proactive. Your supervisor will love you for it.

Freelancing

Freelancers are a big part of the animation workforce. There are both benefits and hazards to working as a freelance animator. If you are the type of person who needs security and doesn't like change, you might want to make a staff position your goal. If you like to work on different types of projects that *you* choose, if you don't mind being called in the last three months of a project during the most hectic time, and if you like moving around and meeting new people, then freelancing might be your bag. A successful freelancer can stay employed, only work nine months out of the year, and still make more than a staff artist.

However, the freelancer has to be really good with his or her money, good with people, and a good animator to be successful. Understanding that you may work only nine months out of the year is crucial to figuring out how to set your rate and manage your money as a freelancer. If you are only working 75 percent of the year and not receiving benefits and sick days, your rate must offset these losses.

The only factors a freelancer really needs to know when signing a contract are when it starts, when it ends, the rate, and whether the contract is "at will." The "at will" part lets you know whether they can dump you with no notice or whether you can leave with two weeks' notice. Really, you should be able to give no notice

2003

LOONEY TUNES: BACK IN ACTION RELEASED:
Looney Tunes: Back in Action combines live-action and animation. Grossing around $21 million ($68 million worldwide), it was a considerably large bomb, partially due to stiff competition from *Elf* and *The Cat in the Hat*, but earned relatively positive reviews from critics, including those who gave *Space Jam* bad reviews.

2003

TRIPLETS OF BELLEVILLE PREMIERES: *Les Triplettes de Belleville* is a 2003 Belgian-French-Canadian animated feature film highly praised by audiences and critics for its unique style of animation. It was nominated for Academy Awards for Best Original Song and Best Animated Feature.

as well, but then you may never be able to go back, so it's best to communicate with those who are employing you. Your rate will also depend on whether you set your status as an independent contractor being paid by invoice without taxes taken out, or whether you will be a "true freelancer," employed by the studio and paid through their payroll company, deducting taxes.

A freelance job in CG animation is defined as one that is short-term and does not involve benefits, sick days, or any of the perks that come with a staff position. You do have the opportunity to pick and choose what work you will take. You have the freedom to choose which projects ultimately end up on your reel. However, you pay for this flexibility by losing stability, benefits, sick days, and/or vacation. It's a big tradeoff. The positive of this tradeoff is, as a freelancer, your pay rate is generally higher in CG animation. Depending on skills and experience, it can be almost 1 1/2 times that of a staff animator.

What do you buy when you are working for peanuts? Drawing by Brian Dowrick.

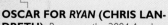

OSCAR FOR *RYAN* (CHRIS LANDRETH): *Ryan* won the 2004 Academy Award for Best Short Subject: Animated Films and the 25th Genie Award for Best Animated Short. It was also very well received at the Cannes, Venice, Sundance, and Toronto film festivals.

THE INCREDIBLES WINS BEST ANIMATED FEATURE: Pixar's *The Incredibles* won an Academy Award for Best Animated Feature. It was originally developed as a traditionally animated movie, but after Warner Bros. shut down its animation division, writer Brad Bird moved to Pixar and took the story with him. *The Incredibles* is Pixar's sixth film. The big question here is…if there wasn't a separate category for best animated film, would it have won the Oscar for Best Picture? Hmmm….

When freelancing, you are the one who sets the rate. You are an artist the studio must have on board to finish the project; therefore, you have a little more power in the negotiation. There will, of course, be some give and take. Some studios will not be able to afford your rate. It will be up to you to make the decision whether a lower rate is worth trying to get that particular project on your reel. Sometimes smaller studios will offer perks such as sick days or benefits to offset the fact that they have not met your full freelance rate.

The key to being a successful freelancer and getting your rate every time is being able to walk away. It is vital to any negotiation to be able to say no to a low rate. Nine times out of ten, you will walk out of that office and have a call on your cell before you get to the car. The only way you can do this is to manage your money well. You have to be careful and remember that you might only work nine months or less out of a year! This means if you are paid well, you have to stow it away for a rainy day. Don't act like you are rich and buy a Lotus and a house in Malibu. In the future, there will be more demand for the freelancer as studios try to lower their overhead costs and smaller boutiques branch into character animation. So, the next step to becoming a successful freelancer is to learn how to network.

Networking

For a freelancer, networking is so important that it should become your second art and passion. This industry is small, and now with 2D and CG artists merged, it's even smaller. The briefest encounter can have the most profound effect on your career. You might be at a non-animation-related party and meet a guy who works at another studio. You two hit it off with the same views about the industry. He sees you are really passionate. A year later, you have kept up a correspondence through e-mail, seen him at a few festivals and shows, and stayed in touch. One day, he tells you about a new opening at the studio where he works.

Contacts help you get in the door every time. If you had a choice between working with someone you know nothing about and working with someone your coworker has worked with or knows on a social level and can vouch for, whom would you choose? There are too many artists out there with big egos and attitude (not to mention hygiene issues) to take a chance. It's also a game that works from a karmic angle. If you help someone you know get a position, one day he might do the same for you.

The contact will not keep you at that job or pave your path with gold, however. Your skills and professionalism are what will keep you employed. Your attitude will also reflect on the person who referred you, so keep that in mind. Even when you are spending time with coworkers at lunch or socially, your behavior will continue to develop their opinion of you. This does not mean you should hang out with people you do not like. People will see through your motives. In contrast, it is also important to remember that if you make enemies, it will only work against you in the future. You do not want negative press; it will counter

HOME ON THE RANGE 44TH DISNEY FEATURE: *Home on the Range* was the last Disney movie to date to use traditional animation. Disney animated films have used some CG effects for many years, but after *Home on the Range*, Disney announced plans to move entirely to computer animation.

2004

SHREK 2 PREMIERES: This sequel to 2001's *Shrek* scored the second-largest three-day opening in US history, as well as the largest opening ever for an animated movie.

SHARK TALE RELEASED: Even though critics didn't like *Shark Tale*, the film still managed to make $363 million worldwide, making it another smash for DreamWorks.

any good things that have been said. Ido Gondelman offers a story about how you can create your own good and bad press:

> I remember working on a test for a CG feature back in 1996. The animation supervisor was a total whack job! I mean, this guy was crazy; you never knew if he would be happy or angry that day. After a week of working on a shot under his direction, we showed it in weeklies. The animation director and the VFX sup didn't agree on the shot, so my animation supervisor hung me out to dry and said, "What the f**k are you doing? This is not what I asked you to animate!" He then proceeded to make a fellow female animator cry. The animation supervisor was let go a week later. Funny thing is, after making my life hell and being a total ass, he ended up using me as a reference while I was working at another studio. He was trying to get a job there...ha, ha, ha. The lesson is, it's a small world. Be nice to people and don't take crap from anyone. We all deserve respect.

Reputation is like magic. With one stroke of a wand it doubles your strength. So take great care in your reputation and honor it with professionalism and respect when dealing with others. Your reputation will enter the room before you do; follow it with dignified grace. If you network successfully, people will come to you because of your reputation. Networking is the one thing that will keep a paycheck coming. You are networking even when you are a staff employee. People talk about your work when they are out to dinner, at a party, or just hanging with their friends and family. Remember that word of mouth can be your best asset or your worst enemy. It's up to you.

Mass Production of CG Animation

With so many CG productions being made today, the system does not promote for skill as much as sheer volume and willingness to work incredibly long hours. The mass-production approach to creating CG features has spawned a huge staff of animators expected to produce an enormous amount of footage a week. Producers are trying to find more ways to streamline production. Studios are underbidding each other to get work. In this environment, concepts such as respect seem to fly out the window, along with our salaries.

CG animation producers are hiring more kids straight out of school to meet the mind-boggling quotas the studios require. Producers try to get more footage out of animators by advising them to work late without pay, and the animators do it in order to compete in dailies the next day. It's a never-ending cycle. This new mass-production environment views veteran animators as too expensive, and unless they have someone to

2004

THE POLAR EXPRESS BRINGS AN ALL MO-CAP MOVIE TO THE SCREEN: *The Polar Express* is a feature film based on the children's book of the same title by Chris Van Allsburg. It was the first CGI movie to use performance capture for all actors.

2004

I, ROBOT PREMIERES: Criticism did not stop the $120 million *I, Robot* from being a solid box-office success, earning almost $145 million in North America and more than $200 million overseas.

2004

HARRY POTTER 3 RELEASED: *Harry Potter and the Prisoner of Azkaban* is the third book in the *Harry Potter* series by J. K. Rowling. The film based on the book made $249 million domestically.

champion them, they will find themselves up against a brick wall looking for work. Hope against hope that producers will eventually tire of that guy reanimating a shot 12 times to get what the director wants at a third of the pay rate of an experienced animator. The pay rates may look good on paper with the fuzzy math applied, but in the long run they will cost everyone the movie.

The answer to this problem is to create a balanced team that will ultimately provide for the best experience, budget, and harmony overall. Imagine delivering a show on time and without three months of overtime at the end of the schedule. As long as respect and mentoring philosophies are encouraged, a mixed bag of entry-level, junior, senior, and supervisory-level artists will provide the most productive team. Larry Weinberg tells us when the best experience is had with a team and why:

> I've worked on a number of projects, and the ones that produced the best results had the highest level of respect between director to supervisor to animator.

When the mixed bag of experience has synergy with an appreciative director and producer, everybody wins. However, the new age of mass production in animation has roused the monster called outsourcing.

Death, Taxes, and Outsourcing

Following trends in animation is imperative to staying employed and evolving with an ever-changing field. The whole need for this book came out of denial and reluctance to observe trends and changes in the animation audience by traditional animators. Traditional animators felt blindsided by the shifts that happened after *Toy Story* was released, even though most saw the shift happening. We all heard people saying, "The computer can never do my job," and "Computer-generated animation is too sterile to appeal to any audience," and "Those computer geeks will never create a performance with the charm and warmth that a hand-drawn film has."

While some of these comments still hold some truth, we cannot deny the popularity of CG animation with the audience. These same traditional animators have either already made the shift to animating on a computer or are trying to make the shift today. The remaining traditional animators stay purists and have had to find other ways to make a living or work in television animation creating storyboards that eventually go overseas for animation. History now repeats itself with forums and e-mail lists discussing, speculating on, and denying the prospect of countries such as India, China, Singapore, and the Philippines producing animation at half the price today for the CG feature market.

2004

SPIDER-MAN 2 IS THIRD-HIGHEST GROSSING MOVIE OF 2004:
Spider-Man 2 is the Academy Award-winning sequel to the popular 2002 film *Spider-Man*. In its first six days of release, *Spider-Man 2* generated a record $180 million at the North American box office. Altogether *Spider-Man 2* made $373 million in North America, making it the third-highest grossing movie of 2004 and the ninth-highest grossing US movie of all time.

2004

SCOOBY-DOO 2 RELEASED:
Scooby-Doo 2: Monsters Unleashed is a sequel to *Scooby-Doo*.

Any animator is living in a dream world if he does not recognize outsourcing as a reality when it comes to his job going overseas. We would all like to think that the art of animation will hold its integrity against streamlining production and using cheaper labor. However, when a field brings the kind of profits CG animation is currently earning, it's inevitable the suits will look to finding ways to increase that profit margin even more. A perfect example is the movie *Hoodwinked*, which grossed $16.6 million over the four-day Martin Luther King holiday weekend in 2006. According to Box Office Prophets, "The average production cost for the last three Pixar films was $100 million, while Hoodwinked was made for only $15 million, as it was produced mostly in Asia, using over-the-counter animation software. Suddenly, we have a film that isn't forced to earn $30 million in its first weekend to be any kind of success, and can be shopped to any of the studios, big or little."[29] We couldn't have said it better ourselves. If bigger profits than a live-action film can be made without having to pay Demi Moore the entire price tag of *Hoodwinked* to be in the film, then why not go overseas to produce it and laugh all the way to the bank?

So what is the answer? The artistic integrity is still very low overseas. Think back to when we all started in CG animation in the '80s—computer-generated animation was awful. Think back to the rolling spheres on checkerboard planes. This is where the overseas artists are starting, but they will learn just like we all did, and they *will* train up fast because there are more resources out there today than ever before. They need the experienced Hollywood artists to show them the way. We need to embrace this shift or it will pass us by, just like the traditional animators experienced with the introduction of the computer. These countries are filled with artists who have the technical understanding, the work ethic, and the willingness to work for less. They will catch up.

If you apply the blueprint of how traditional television animation is being created today to overseas CG feature production of the future, you can see how the U.S. story and animation artists block out broad brush strokes of what the animation will be. That pre-viz, choreography, or whatever you want to call it will be shipped overseas to have breakdowns and cleanup worked out at a much cheaper price. The final work will be shipped back to the U.S. and then re-purposed again, if necessary, to work for the final cut. This is the future for CG feature production overseas, and it's something we should all recognize as a real movement for the animation business. Your role will be to plan out the shots and have someone overseas fill in the notes of the composition, much like the old model at Disney functioned with a lead animator, assistant animator, and cleanup artist.

To help us all deal with outsourcing, we have provided a list of the top 10 things you might consider:

10. Join the military.
 9. Get a government job.
 8. Keep your passport up to date.
 7. Learn a foreign language.
 6. Become a firefighter.
 5. Marry a very rich person.
 4. Win the lottery.
 3. Become a survivalist and hunker down in a cabin with your firearms and wait for Armageddon.
 2. Embrace minimalism.
 1. Learn to eat animals you normally consider pets.

Schedules and Production

The first week will define how you are perceived on the whole project. Many animators ask themselves when they start on a new show, "What do they expect of me?" They expect you to produce quality work within a reasonable time with little drama. Some studios have turnaround times that are extreme because they underbid the project, the project was in trouble for political reasons, or the production schedules were mismanaged. Some studios have more reasonable schedules on their shows. Sometimes it's not the studio culture, but it's simply the nature of the show.

The best thing to do when you start with a new studio or on a new show with people you haven't worked with is to stay neutral. Do not attack the work, producing at 110 percent your first week. Ease your way in. Learn about the people you are working with through observation. Watch the dynamic of those who have been working there for a while and their interaction with others. When you first begin on a show, work at a steady and meaningful level. They hired you because you have the skills and you have nothing to prove. Wait for the long hours and stressful nights to show them what you've got.

2005

OSWALD THE LUCKY RABBIT SOLD: In February 2006, the rights to *Oswald the Lucky Rabbit* were acquired by the Walt Disney Company from NBC Universal as part of a trade that sent sportscaster Al Michaels from Disney's ABC and ESPN to NBC Universal. The deal included the rights to the character and the original 26 short films made by Disney. This marks the first and most likely last time in history that a live person was traded for a cartoon character.

2005

ROBOTS RELEASED:
Robots is a computer-animated film produced by Blue Sky Studios for 20th Century Fox, the same companies behind the film *Ice Age*.

If you produce way above your normal speed, you can have even more put on your plate and then get burnt out too quickly. You could make someone who is around feel you are trying to make them look bad. It's not true, of course, but perception has a lot to do with first impressions. Different artists work at different rates and it's a competitive market, so the best approach with schedules is to blend in. Later, you can show them your stuff. What your producer and supervisor want from you is work that is created exactly as the client sees it and within a reasonable schedule. They want to feel like little elves came in and completed it with no hassles. If there is drama or a squeaky wheel, you could be branded as difficult. Now, let's move on to the crunch time of a project and how you handle it.

It can get crazy. You are working 24/7 and you are dreaming about the characters you are animating. You have to finish this show because not only do you believe in it, but you can't wait to see these shots on your reel. The worst part is thinking about another 16-hour day. If you don't give it your all, that two-second shot on the big screen will haunt you for years as the movie repeats on cable. Well, while you are stressing over the hours you are putting in and the fact that you really need to get some sleep, read this bedtime story about a guy who has to hide to get away from his producer:

The most fun time I had was working on *Hunchback*. It was a great crew. I loved working with that crew. I was working with my lead on Esmerelda. The lead is one of those guys who is hard to find to begin with. He is one of those guys that if you call him, he doesn't call you back necessarily. So, my lead was getting a backlog of scenes in his room that he had to go over. The lead would make drawings over a scene before it went to cleanup. Back then, they were pushing you to do more than just draw over but complete the scene, especially the leads. They were approving it in its really, really rough stage. It was so far from being done. The production people were saying, "Oh, we can count this for this week? Yay! We can meet our deadline!" So they could put the numbers down, but in the meantime my lead had to get started on another scene. So, he was getting a backlog of scenes that were approved through the production. They were always on his case, asking, "Do you have this sequence done? Do you have that sequence done?" At a certain point, I was in his room and he started to hide. He would lock his door. I would be in his room talking about a scene, and all of a sudden you would hear a knock on the door. It would be the production supervisor saying, "Hey, you in there?" He would look over at me and say, "Shhhhhh!" So we wouldn't say anything and be really quiet. He would get up and walk behind the door in case she opened it. She had even-

2005

STEAMBOY RELEASED AND IS EXPENSIVE: *Steamboy* is director Katsuhiro Otomo's second major (anime) release, following *Akira*. With an initial production cost of $26 million, *Steamboy* is the most expensive full-length Japanese animated movie made to date, but is still cheap compared to Hollywood productions.

2005

MADAGASCAR RELEASED: DreamWorks' *Madagascar* made about $193 million overall in the theaters.

tually decided that he was hiding in his room and she would get a key for the door and open up the door. This actually happened a couple of times. One time I was in there with my lead, and he hid behind the door and she opened it up right then. I was sitting there and she said, "Where is your lead?" I said, "I am looking for him too. I was just going to sit and wait until he got here." Then she would say, "Ah, jeez!" and close the door and walk out, but he was right behind the door! It was so funny. He would just continue hiding from them because there was no way you could get the stuff done that they wanted.

Laugh at those times you feel like hiding behind the door when the producer comes to call.
Sketch by Floyd Norman.

TIM BURTON'S CORPSE BRIDE RELEASED: *Tim Burton's Corpse Bride* is a stop-motion film based loosely on a 19th-century Russian-Jewish folktale and set in a fictional Victorian-era England. It was nominated for an Academy Award for Best Animated Feature. Ironically, it lost to another stop-motion animated feature, *Wallace & Gromit: The Curse of the Were-Rabbit.*

VALIANT BOMBS: Computer-animated film *Valiant* was received rather poorly by critics, many of whom felt the film lacked originality and quality humor. *Valiant* had a worldwide total of $61 million, which is considered low by CGI animated film standards.

Laugh to yourself when you are stressing over long hours on a shot, because there is always some guy out there hiding behind a door for the same reason.

The most pleasant people to be around are those who keep their sense of humor during these intense scheduling times of production. Who wants to sit next to the guy complaining all day about having to be at work and not at home relaxing? We all have to be there, so let's make the most of it! Keep your head up and laugh about it, and the time might go by a little easier. Your ideas might flow a little cleaner. And you just might finish a little faster. As a closing note on long hours, Darin McGowan has one last tip for you:

> Helpful tip: Remember that most company first-aid cabinets have cold medication. Some cold medication contains speed! Keep that in mind for the next all-nighter you have to pull.

Don't stay too late…there is always tomorrow.

[26]UPA Studios. http://www.vegalleries.com/upa.html.

[27]Culhane, Shamus. *Animation from Script to Screen*. St. Martin's Griffin, 1990.

[28]National Security Archive. George Washington University. Contents of this website Copyright 1995–2004 National Security Archive. All rights reserved. http://www.gwu.edu/~nsarchiv/coldwar/interviews/episode-15/lord1.html. Department of Defense. The Pentagon Washington. Speech. http://www.defenselink.mil/speeches/2002/s20020529-depsecdef.html.

[29]Box Office Prophets. http://www.boxofficeprophets.com/column/index.cfm?columnID=9367.

2005

HOODWINKED OPENS THE DOOR TO OUTSOURCING:
Hoodwinked is an American computer-animated family comedy produced in a large house in the Philippines. The film exceeded expectations by nearly doubling what had been predicted for its box office debut, and it reportedly cost $15 million to make, including marketing and distribution. The quality of the film's animation has been criticized, specifically by animators who believe that the success of the movie shows a disregard for quality and will eventually hurt the industry.

2005

AUTODESK BUYS ALIAS:
Autodesk agreed to purchase Alias for $182 million. Who knows what will happen to Maya, which is a staple software program among CG animators working in film and commercials.

Sketch by Joe Scott.

HOWL'S MOVING CASTLE PREMIERES: More from the Japanese Walt Disney, *Howl's Moving Castle* is a Japanese anime film based on Diana Wynne Jones' novel of the same name and directed by Hayao Miyazaki. Mamoru Hosoda was originally selected to direct but abruptly left the project, leaving the then-retired Miyazaki to take up the director's role.

THE SIMPSONS 16TH SEASON: In its 16th season, *The Simpsons* has become the longest running television comedy series ever made, surpassing *The Adventures of Ozzie & Harriet*, which tallied 15 seasons from 1952–1966.

Chapter 8
The End of the Beginning

"Our studio has a tiny yard in the back, and it was raining one day. I had only been an employee for a few weeks, and I took a break to watch the rain fall. As I stood there and watched, the company president walks up and stands next to me, casting his gaze to the rainfall. I had only met him briefly before and not really spoken with him—and definitely not one on one. I thought to myself, 'Wow, I wonder what words of wisdom he might bestow upon me at this moment. I wonder what my reply will be, and if I'll make a good impression?' The company president then says, 'Sure is a lot of mud out there.' My reply was, 'Yeah....'"

—*Roberto Smith*

Bridging the Gap

Much like Roberto observed from the president of his studio, sometimes there "sure is a lot of mud out there." We are now armed with all the ammunition that history has provided us to march through that mud on our way to something great! We are but fleas on the shoulders of giants in this industry. We have much to learn from our animation forefathers, such as John Whitney Sr. and Jr., Walt Disney and his Nine Old Men, Chuck Jones, Tex Avery, Bob Clampett, Robert Abel, Richard Taylor, and so many others. We have much to examine as this young field we call CG animation unfolds and reveals the new pioneers, such as John Lasseter, Chris Wedge, Brad Bird, and more to come. The only way to predict trends in an industry driven by art, commerce, and technology is to look at the past and learn.

2005

STAR WARS III OPENS: *Star Wars Episode III: Revenge of the Sith* is the sixth and final film released in the *Star Wars* saga, and the third in terms of the saga's chronology. It broke several box-office records in its opening week and went on to earn more than $850 million worldwide, making it the highest grossing film of 2005 in the U.S., the second-highest grossing film of 2005 worldwide (right behind *Harry Potter and the Goblet of Fire*), and the twelfth-highest grossing worldwide film of all time.

All three mediums of traditional, CG, and visual-effects animation have influenced one another over the years. Your mission, should you choose to accept it, is to get out there and kick some serious booty as an animator. Don't let a little rain stop you! Put on your mud boots! Take no prisoners in your quest to put your best work up there on the screen. Oh, and if you decide to take any prisoners, please remember to treat them nicely. Utilizing what you have learned in this text, you should be well armed to take on the future as an animator. You can only do something well if you are willing to do it again and again and again, so keep on drawing and animating.

2005

THE CHRONICLES OF NARNIA OPENS: *The Chronicles of Narnia: The Lion, the Witch and the Wardrobe* is based on the C.S. Lewis children's fantasy novel of the same name. It won the 2005 Academy Award for Best Makeup and was nominated for Best Visual Effects and Best Sound Effects Editing. *Narnia* opened with $23 million and took in a total of $65 million on its opening weekend, the 24th-best opening weekend of all time.

2005

HARRY POTTER 4 RELEASED: *Harry Potter and the Goblet of Fire*, directed by Mike Newell, is the fourth film in the popular *Harry Potter* series. It enjoyed a successful run at the box office, earning more than $892 million worldwide, making it the highest grossing film of 2005 worldwide and the eighth-highest grossing worldwide film of all time.

2005

JOE RANFT DIES: Joe Ranft, Pixar Animation Studios' head of story for more than a decade, died in a car crash at 45. Ranft was a co-writer on 1995's *Toy Story*, for which he earned an Oscar nomination, and 1998's *A Bug's Life*. Before Pixar, he was a leading member of the story department at Walt Disney Feature Animation, where he was a writer on 1991's *Beauty and the Beast* and 1994's *The Lion King*.

2005

***KING KONG* RELEASED:** *King Kong* is the Academy Award–winning remake of the original 1933 *King Kong*. The remake won three Oscars, for Visual Effects, Sound Mixing, and Sound Editing. It had an opening weekend of $50 million—good for most movies, but short of the inflated expectations caused by the movie's enormous budget and marketing campaign.

PART IV

Appendixes

Appendix A
Author Bios

Authors

Angie Jones

Angie escaped the Deep South after graduating from Atlanta College of Art in 1994. Her first introduction to animation was at a San Diego studio of more than 150 traditional animators called Lightspan. As a female animator, she was a novelty. Even rarer at this traditional studio was her willingness to create animation with a computer. Although she was trained at a fine art school, she took to the computer, and for the past 10 years she has worked on productions including *Stuart Little 2*, *Oddworld: Abe's Exoddus*, *Garfield*, *Scooby-Doo 2*, *Dino Crisis 3*, Disney's 50th Anniversary commercials, and *X-Men 2*. To find out more about Angie, go to http://www.spicycricket.com.

Jamie Oliff

Educated at Sheridan College of Art and Design in classical animation, Jamie has worked in the animation industry for more than 20 years. An award-winning director and longtime feature film animator, Jamie's credits include the first season of *The Ren & Stimpy Show* and many feature-length animated pictures, such as *The Hunchback of Notre Dame*, *Mulan*, *Hercules*, and *The Emperor's New Groove*, as well as CGI animation on titles ranging from *Kangaroo Jack* to *Scooby-Doo 2* and *National Treasure*. He lives in Burbank, California, with his wife and two children and a biplane project that he never finds enough time to finish.

Contributing Authors: Directors

Henry Anderson

A graduate of the CalArts Character Animation program, Henry directed his first CG project at Rhythm & Hues in 1989. Since then, he has directed at PDI, Digital Domain, Pixar, Blue Sky, Sony Pictures Imageworks, and DreamWorks. He was nominated for an Academy Award for his work as animation director on the film *Stuart Little* and won a Primetime Emmy for his work on *The Last Halloween*—the first TV special to incorporate CG characters into a live-action show. Years before working on *Stuart Little*, Henry studied biology at UC San Diego, where he worked with lots and lots of real mice.

Tony Bancroft

Best known for his clock, Cogsworth, in *Beauty and the Beast*; his warthog, Pumbaa, in *The Lion King*; his parrot, Iago, in *Aladdin*; and lovable dumb-guy Kronk from *The Emperor's New Groove*, Tony Bancroft has become known as the creator of loveable freaks. Jumping from a career at Disney to cofounding Toonacious Family Entertainment was literally a "leap of faith," according to Tony. As a director and an animator, Tony's experience in both traditional animation and CG animation spans a career of more than 15 years in the movie business.

Eric Goldberg

Eric Goldberg is a veteran director and animator who has worked extensively in London and Hollywood. He directed and animated television commercials for the Richard Williams Studio in London before opening his own studio there, Pizazz Pictures. In 1990, he joined Walt Disney Feature Animation, where he was the supervising animator of the irrepressible Genie in *Aladdin* and Phil in *Hercules*. He was also co-director of *Pocahontas* and director-animator of two sequences in *Fantasia 2000*—"Carnival of the Animals" and "Rhapsody in Blue," the latter based on the work of Al Hirschfeld. In recent years, he has worked on a variety of projects, including the animation direction for the recent CGI "Disneyland's 50th" television spots.

Darin McGowan

One time, Darin moved out to LA and got this job storyboarding. And then this other time, Darin got this other job as an animation director. And then, once, he started pitching his own TV show ideas around Hollywood, and then got them all optioned, and then he started directing his own pilots. And then one time he went international when this studio in Australia started looking at his stuff. And then he started drinking and making a fool of himself in public. And then one time he woke up on a public bus without any pants. Now, Darin can be seen selling hotdogs out of his van on Cherokee and Hollywood—and you gotta tell him if you're a cop, because that's the law.

Tom Sito

Tom Sito's screen credits include the Disney classics *The Little Mermaid*, *Beauty and the Beast*, *Aladdin*, *The Lion King*, *Who Framed Roger Rabbit?*, *Pocahontas*, *Dinosaurs*, and *Fantasia 2000*. In 1995, he left a Disney directorship post to help set up the DreamWorks Animation unit. He worked on *The Prince of Egypt*, *Antz*, *Paulie*, and *Spirit: Stallion of the Cimarron*, as well as the Oscar-winning film *Shrek*.

Tom also helped animate the title sequence of *City Slickers*, the 1982 Emmy award–winning ABC special *Ziggy's Gift*, and he did 22 hours of Saturday-morning television, including *Fat Albert*, *He-Man and the Masters of the Universe*, *She-Ra*, *Super Friends*, as well as numerous commercials. Tom directed the animation for Warner Bros.' *Osmosis Jones*, was a storyboard artist/animator for Warners Bros.' *Looney Tunes: Back in Action*, and led the storyboard team for Fox's *Garfield*. Today, Tom is an owner of Gang of Seven Animation, where he did a TV series for the BBC called *Legend of the Dragon*, the film *Son of the Mask*, and a new season of *Biker Mice from Mars*.

Tom has produced short films, is an adjunct professor of animation at the University of Southern California and UCLA, and has written numerous articles for *Animation Magazine* and Animation World Network. He has lectured on animation around the world, from Denmark to Beijing. He served three terms as president of the Hollywood Animation Guild (1992–2001) and is vice president of the International Animated Film Society (ASIFA/Hollywood). He is currently working on a book on animation union history, *Drawing the Line: The Untold Story of Animation Labor from Silents to CGI*. He is a member of the Motion Picture Academy, the National Cartoonists Society, and Hollywood Heritage. In 1998, he was named in *Animation Magazine*'s list of the 100 most important people in animation.

Richard Taylor

Richard Taylor has an extensive background in live-action direction, production design, special effects, and computer-generated images for theatrical films, television commercials, and computer games. He began his career as an artist and holds a BFA in painting and drawing from the University of Utah. Richard began making short films in 1965, and in 1967 he co-created *Rainbow Jam*, a multimedia light show and graphics company. *Rainbow Jam* toured with the Grateful Dead and regularly preformed concerts at the Family Dog, the Fillmore, the Winterland, and other rock venues with bands such as Santana, Led Zeppelin, Crosby, Stills & Nash, Jethro Tull, and many more. In 1971 Richard received The Cole Porter Fellowship to USC graduate school, where he earned his Master's degree in photography and printmaking.

In the past 30 years, Richard has lent his talent to a number of companies, resulting in many award-winning commercial spots and seven Clio awards, along with two Hugo awards and two Mobius awards. Richard was a member of the team at Magi, whose commercial for Atari's *Worm War I* was the first to win a Clio for computer animation. His other commercial work includes spots for companies such as Ford, RCA, Kellogg's, Reebok, McDonald's, UPS, Honda, Toyota, Bud Light, Intel, Norwegian Cruise Lines, Census 2000, Warner Bros., Disney, Duracell, and 7-Up, for whom he launched the internationally acclaimed "Spot" campaign.

Richard's years in the industry have provided him with a wide array of opportunities in addition to commercial work. He has done everything from directing promotional films for major networks, to designing, supervising, and directing special effects and computer-generated images. Richard has worked in various capacities on features such as *Tron*, *Star Trek: The Motion Picture*, *Looker*, *Something Wicked This Way Comes*, and *Where the Wild Things Are*. Presently Richard is cinematics director at Electronic Arts Los Angeles. Over the last four years he has designed and directed cinematics for such games as *Top Spin*, *Links 2004*, *Lord of the Rings: The Battle for Middle Earth 1* and *II*, and *Command and Conquer 3*.

Conrad Vernon

Conrad Vernon, born in Lubbock, Texas, began his film career in 1991 doing a little bit of everything on Paramount Pictures' *Cool World*. His credits included animator, effects animator, gag writer, layout artist, and character designer. From there, he went on to write and storyboard on Hanna-Barbera's *2 Stupid Dogs* and Nickelodeon's *Rocko's Modern Life*. In 1994, Vernon went to Film Roman, where he was a storyboard artist on the popular animated television comedy, *The Simpsons*. Other credits include directing for Hyperion's *Itsy Bitsy Spider*, writer and storyboard artist on Nickelodeon's *The Ren & Stimpy Show*, writer and storyboard artist on Disney's television show, *Nightmare Ned*, and a storyboard artist on Sony Pictures' *Harold and the Purple Crayon*.

Vernon joined DreamWorks Animation in 1996 as a storyboard artist on PDI/DreamWorks' first animated feature, *Antz*, as well as the animated comedy, *The Road to El Dorado*. He served as a storyboard artist, additional dialogue writer, and voice of the Gingerbread Man on the original *Shrek*. Vernon made his directorial debut in 2004 with *Shrek 2*, the sequel to the Academy Award–winning blockbuster. He is currently writing a screenplay and directing his second feature for DreamWorks Animation.

Contributing Authors: Supervisors

Bernd Angerer

Bernd Angerer started his CG career back in 1987 in a small video studio in Vienna, Austria, where he worked as a graphic artist mainly for TV commercials and music videos. After his first experience with 2D cel animation and some stop-motion experiments, he created the first fully CG-animated commercial in Austria, *Jolly*, and he specialized in digital character animation. In 1994, he directed and animated *Der Winzer Und Der Wein*, a computer-generated short video about the process of making wine.

In 1996, Bernd joined Digital Domain to animate on James Cameron's *Titanic* and then continued his animation career as animation supervisor on *The Little Vampire* and numerous commercials, amongst them "Adidas Mechanical Legs" and "Disney's 50th Homecoming" spots. Over the years, Bernd has worked as lead animator and animation supervisor on features such as *What Dreams May Come*; *Lord of the Rings*; *Tightrope*; *I, Robot*; and *Aeon Flux*. In 2004, he joined the team at Sony Imageworks for *Spider-Man 3*.

Dave Brewster

Dave Brewster worked as the supervising animator on numerous films, including *Curious George, Looney Tunes: Back in Action, Osmosis Jones, The Road to El Dorado*, and *The Prince of Egypt*. He was an animator on *Eight Crazy Nights, The Hunchback of Notre Dame, Rock-a-Doodle, All Dogs Go to Heaven, Asterix et le Coup du Menhir, The Land Before Time, Asterix Chez Les Bretons*, and *Rock & Rule*.

Dave was storyboard artist as well as the leading character animator for Krysta in *Fern Gully: The Last Rainforest*. He was the animator poster and key animator for *The Nutcracker Prince*, the designer and supervising animator for *The Care Bears Movie*, and an animator, supervising animator, and storyboard artist for *Asterix in Amerika*.

Dave has also worked on numerous series, including episodes of *Strawberry Shortcake, The Flintstones*, and *Scooby-Doo*. His other work includes the title sequence for *Son of the Pink Panther, George Burns Comedy Week, The Get-Along Gang*, and *Herself the Elf*. His work on commercials includes companies such as Rice Krispies, Lucky Charms, 21st Century Insurance, 7-Up, Burger King, Alpha-Bits, and Shake and Bake.

Chris Bailey

Chris Bailey lives near Hollyweird, California, and thrives as an animator/director. Bailey's career in CG goes back to before IK, when animators only dreamt of long lines of people waiting to see a feature-length cartoon. His notable credits include the Oscar-nominated *Runaway Brain*, *Mighty Joe Young*, *Kim Possible*, *X-Men 2*, *Garfield*, and *Fat Albert*. His *Major Damage* comic digest and DVD featuring a 3D-animated superhero short can be found online at http://www.majordamage.net and in better funny book stores.

Tom Capizzi

Tom Capizzi started life as a disillusioned youth and a juvenile delinquent. Determined to waste his entire life, he decided to pursue art full time as a career. He spent several years working as an illustrator in various graphic design firms, and one year was faced with a dramatic choice. He had to learn how to use the computer to create art or become employed in the satisfying field of food service. He chose to learn more about computer graphics. Since then, he has worked as an industrial designer in Detroit, an art director for Atari Games, and a technical director at Rhythm & Hues. He is currently working in a place called Orange County, supervising the lighting staff on a film called *The Barnyard*. Tom has worked on such unforgettable films as *Spawn* and *Gigli*, and he even did a little work on *Battlefield Earth*. His other, less pungent credits include *Scooby-Doo* and *Scooby-Doo 2*, *Garfield*, *Daredevil*, and *X-Men 2*. One day, Tom dreams of returning to his roots and spending the rest of his days lying on a beach, drinking Bloody Marys, and talking about how cool things used to be.

Fred Raimondi

Recognized as one of the preeminent digital artists in the world today, visual effects supervisor Fred Raimondi has partnered on projects with Michael Bay, David Fincher, Mark Pellington, Lance Acord, and Alex Proyas. Historically, he has always been ahead of the curve. At a time when visual effects were reserved for film optical houses, his early work set the standard for electronics visual effects compositing with *The Twilight Zone*, *Max Headroom*, and the first season of *Star Trek: The Next Generation*. As a founding member of Planet Blue in 1988, his early work with digital compositing helped pave the way for today's generation of visual effects and compositing platforms, tools, and techniques that are widely recognized as industry standards today.

October 1993 saw Raimondi join the startup phase of visual effects and creative hotbed Digital Domain in Venice, California. He was among the first 15 employees at Digital Domain and played a large part in setting the stage and feel for Digital Domain's Commercial division. His need to be closer to the production process and desire to take visual effects in commercials to a much higher level saw him become one of the first visual effects supervisors in the commercial arena. As a result, he helped the art form move from a "post-production only" process to an integrated part of the whole filmmaking process. An accomplished editor, photographer, and musician, Raimondi brings a unique skill set and creative vision to the projects he chooses. His experience as a "complete filmmaker" brings a unique blend of art and technology to his projects. Raimondi's work has garnered Gold and Silver Cannes Lions, Gold and Silver Clios, an MTV Video Music Award, numerous AICP Awards, and a Grammy. Some of his clients include Adidas;

245

Budweiser; Nike; Levi's; Cingular; Sony; Visa; BBDO; Chiat/Day; Goodby, Silverstein & Partners; DDB Needham; and McCann-Erickson. He is currently the senior visual effects supervisor in the Commercial division of Digital Domain in Venice, California.

Nik Ranieri

Nik Ranieri was born August 23, 1961, in Toronto, Canada. After graduating in 1984 from the animation program at Sheridan College (also in Canada), he went on to a lengthy career in the animation industry, which included several commercial houses in the '80s and a 15+ year position at Walt Disney Feature Animation. Nik's work has been included in such animated classics as *Who Framed Roger Rabbit?*, *The Little Mermaid*, and *Aladdin*, and he has supervised and/or created such characters as Lumiere, the candlestick from *Beauty and the Beast*; Meeko, the raccoon from *Pocahontas*; Hades from *Hercules*; and Kuzco from *The Emperor's New Groove*. Nik has recently taken the leap to CGI and has just finished working on Disney Feature Animation's first all-digital 3D film, *Chicken Little*. Nik and his wife of 10 years, Jennifer, have five children: Jenna, Belle, Quinn, Emily, and Lily. They reside in Canyon Country, California.

Keith Roberts

If you have seen the film *Billy Elliot*, you've seen Keith Roberts's childhood. When growing up in the north of England, he told his dad he wanted to draw and paint for a living, and his father's reply was, "What's wrong wi' ya? Go get a proper job!" After glassblowing for five years (a proper job), he went to college to learn how to use the computer to extend his visual capability. Using this, he worked his way into The Moving Picture Company in London and finally got the opportunity to animate full time when he hopped across the pond to Rhythm & Hues. Keith has been animating and supervising animation at Rhythm & Hues for more than eight years now, and his dad is very proud—or at least he tells him he is!

Mike Surrey

Mike Surrey is a graduate of Sheridan College and, like many of his fellow Canadian animators, he has traveled a great deal to work in animation. Over the last 17 years, he has worked in London, Paris, and Los Angeles. Mike worked at Disney for 13 years on seven films, *Beauty and the Beast*, *Aladdin*, and *The Lion King* being some of the most memorable. Timon from *The Lion King* was Mike's first crack at supervising a character. Not a bad way to start. He was nominated for an Annie Award for his work on Clopin in *The Hunchback of Notre Dame*. He continues to work in animation as it moves into the CG world full time. DreamWorks was kind enough to train Mike in Maya and didn't waste any time putting him to work on *Shark Tale*. He has returned to Disney, working in story and animation. As the studio moves forward with Pixar at the helm, Mike looks forward to the challenges Disney will offer him in his animation career.

Troy Saliba

Animation supervisor Troy Saliba has worked in the animation industry for more than 15 years, with wide-ranging experience in both traditional and CG character animation. Currently, Troy is in production as animation supervisor on the animated feature film *Monster House*, which utilizes the proprietary Imagemotion™ performance-motion-capture technology developed by Imageworks. In 2003, Troy wrapped production as animation supervisor on Disney's *The Haunted Mansion*, working with visual effects supervisor Jay Redd and director Rob Minkoff (*The Lion King*, *Stuart Little*, and *Stuart Little 2*). He most recently completed work for the blockbuster sequel *Spider-Man 2*. Since joining Sony Pictures Imageworks in 2001, Troy has worked on *Stuart Little 2*, winner of the VES Award (Visual Effects Society) in 2003 for Best Character Animation in an Animated Motion Picture, as well as the company's first CG short film, *The ChubbChubbs*, which won an Academy Award for Best Animated Short Film. In 2001, Troy was supervising animator on Nickelodeon's Academy Award–nominated *Jimmy Neutron: Boy Genius*, one of the first animated features to ever be nominated for an Oscar.

Troy began his career in Dublin, Ireland, working for Don Bluth Animation on such features as *Rock-a-Doodle* and *Thumbelina*. While in Dublin, Troy also taught animation at Ballyfermot College in a program based upon the curriculum of the animation program at Sheridan College. He then took his talents to Walt Disney Television Animation in Sydney, Australia, where he worked on numerous television shows and direct-to-video features as both a character animator and animation supervisor. Moving to Fox Animation in Phoenix, Arizona, in 1995, Troy was promoted to directing animator and served in that capacity on the feature films *Anastasia* and *Titan A.E.*

Don Waller

Don Waller has been in the animation business for 28 years. He cites Ray Harryhausen as being his sole inspiration to become an animator. Don began his animation career in Pittsburgh, Pennsylvania, at a studio called The Animators, and gradually worked his way to Los Angeles, with a five-and-a-half year stop in Iowa along the way. While in Iowa, he worked at a graphic arts studio called Hellman Associates, and designed and animated many national 2D commercials, as well as doing some stop-motion work. He was also able to work directly with many of the day's top advertising agencies. That stint enabled him to put together a demo reel for the journey onward to California. After arriving in Los Angeles in the mid '80s, Don soon landed a job as the "dinosaur family" animator for the second season of *Pee-Wee's Playhouse*, a popular children's (and adults') program at the time. Since then, he has animated on many music videos, children's films, and television commercials, as well as doing stop-motion and CG animation and effects for feature films. His feature film credits include *Nightmare on Elm Street 5*, *The Addams Family* movies, *RoboCop 1* and *2*, *Jurassic Park*, *Dinosaur*, *Stuart Little 2*, *Holes*, and *The Last Samurai*. In 2001, Don was also nominated for an Emmy for his animation direction on the Discovery program, *When Dinosaurs Roamed America*.

Larry Weinberg

Larry Weinberg has been active in computer animation production since 1983, including 10 years with Rhythm & Hues Studios. His contributions to animation, software, and animation supervision have helped win four Clio awards, a special effects Emmy (for *Star Trek: Deep Space Nine*), and an Academy Award for Best Special Effects (for *Babe*). He was an FX supervisor and lead animator on the award-winning motion-base ride film "Seafari," produced for Universal Studios. Other animation supervision credits include two Coca-Cola Polar Bear spots, a series of Mr. Peanut ads, the Matchlight Charcoal ads, the

"Spider-Man" ride film for Universal Studios, and the movies *Stay Tuned*, *Scooby-Doo 2*, and *Garfield: The Movie*. Larry is the creator and lead developer of the Poser software product (published by Curious Labs). He is also the grandson of animation director Dave Fleischer who, with brother Max Fleischer, was a pioneer in the early days of cartoon animation with their Koko the Clown, Betty Boop, Popeye, and Superman cartoons produced by Fleischer Studios. Larry graduated with a B.A. in film from Yale University in 1982, where he studied with John Canemaker and Faith Hubley. He was also once a Good Humor (http://www.goodhumor.com) ice cream man.

Contributing Authors: Animators

Carlos Baena

Carlos has been animating for more than eight years. He specializes in computer animation and has had experience in the traditional and stop-motion mediums, as well as drawing and film. Carlos has been working at Pixar Animation Studios (http://www.pixar.com) for the last few years, where he has worked on films such as *Finding Nemo* and *The Incredibles*. He's currently working on *Cars* (2006). He previously worked at Industrial Light & Magic (http://www.ilm.com) as an animator on the films *Jurassic Park III*, *Star Wars: Episode II — Attack of the Clones*, and *Men in Black II*. Before jumping on to work on feature films, he worked on commercials, documentaries, and short films such as Wild Brain's *Hubert's Brain* and Will Vinton Studios' M&Ms commercials. Carlos is also cofounder and creative director of Animation Mentor (http://www.animationmentor.com), an online animation school taught by professional animators and with students from all over the world. In his free time, Carlos has been working on video projects, creating music, and animated short films (http://www.carlosbaena.com).

Mark Behm

Mark Behm got a copy of *The Illusion of Life* for Christmas when he was nine. From there on out, he worked diligently at filling the corners of all his childhood books with flipbook doodles. An old Bolex and lots of Harryhausen films soon got him into stop-motion. Alas, growing up in the northeast gave him a clear understanding that people can't actually grow up to be animators. So he went to school for and spent a couple years in the illustration world, following in his father's footsteps. Being fond of food, he soon began to work in multimedia and discovered that people were actually making a living as animators after all. He saw *Toy Story* and promptly went out and spent way too much money on a little SGI and a copy of Maya to try to make this animation thing work. A couple years later, he got his first real animation gig in the NY commercial scene. He then bounced over to Big Idea Productions to work on the *3-2-1 Penguins!* video series, then to Blue Sky Studios for *Robots*, and now DNA Productions for *The Ant Bully*.

Brian Dowrick

Brian Dowrick is an animator who works on movies and commercials doing special effects. He loves doing things with his hands. He can fix almost anything, but he is lost under the hood of a car. Movies should have explosions, music should have a beat, and spoons should be bigger. Sports: He can play, and likes to, but as for watching sports…he gets bored quickly. When he is not reading or eating chocolate,

Brian can be dragged to a 5k or 10k run for charity. He can, however, be found sleeping on occasion. With a day off and nothing to do, he can sleep until noon. The people at Home Depot, Pizza Hut, and Jamba Juice know him by name. When he is not out saving small children from hunger, he is buying gold and leaving origami twenties in restaurants. You may have seen him and not known it. A flash, and then nothing. His style changes almost daily. He can sew and make his own Halloween costumes. Brian likes all styles of music (except anything with an accordion in it). He is good with money, but he is an impulse buyer. He knows how much he can spend, and he usually spends right up to that amount. He also makes good beer bread. Somewhere along the way, Brian got beat up enough by older kids to make him go into art, thereby exacerbating the problem. He now laughs at their puny lives as his name rolls up on movie credits, and he draws their faces in childish caricatures. The end.

Cory Florimonte

Known as Cory to half the world and as Rocco to the other, Cory Rocco Florimonte suffers from an identity crisis—he doesn't know who you think he is. It also makes for embarrassing moments when he draws a blank while trying to decide which name to use when meeting someone new. Cory was lucky enough to shift from a photography education into CalArts when the Character Animation program had just a fledgling interest in 3D. That forced him to attend all of the "pencil classes" in the animation curriculum and pack in the CG where he could. Even with 10 hours of life drawing a week, Rocco's pencil skills never really improved, but the knowledge he took from the other traditional classes—when he could stay awake—has proven invaluable. Rev. Florimonte tends to make a regular rotation from feature animation to VFX post-production studios, leaving a trail of broken glass, crushed ice, and swizzle sticks in his wake.

Dan Fowler

Daniel Fowler began his journey as an artist right out of high school when he signed a recording contract and toured with a rock band. After several years on the road and with his constant pursuit of creative expression, he discovered and began studying character animation. With his drumming and musical background, he connected with the idea that music and animation are a lot alike—each are phrases in subdivided time relying on beats, timing, cues, rhythmic hits, and, for animation, poses. Since the early '90s, Daniel has been fortunate to work on award-winning feature films, commercials, and video games at some of the industry's top studios. His reputation precedes him with reliable high-quality work, and he has worked consistently with directors including James Cameron, Ron Howard, Robert Rodriguez, Rob Legato, and Joe Pytka. Currently, Daniel continues to work and study character animation; contributes to motion capture and virtual productions pipelines; and continues to write, produce, and perform music in all of its forms.

Ido Gondelman

A Canadian who started with animation early on in life, while in high school, Ido got a part-time job working for an animation house in Toronto. Ido worked as an in-betweener and occasionally inked cells. He graduated from Sheridan College of Art and Design with four years of education in illustration and CG animation. That same year, Ido moved to Los Angeles. He worked at a few places, such as VIFX, CFX, Centropolis FX, Digital Domain, and Rhythm & Hues. It has been 10 years since Ido joined the animation industry. His credits include, in no particular order, *Face/Off*, *Planet Ice*, *T-REX*, *Back to the Cretaceous*, and a short film called *Tightrope*, as well as *Willard*, *Red Planet*, *Eight Legged Freaks*, *How the Grinch Stole Christmas*, *Scooby-Doo 2*, and *Garfield*. Ido served as an animator, an animation supervisor, and a TD for some commercials and music videos. He has also worked as a lead on some award-winning features. He lives in Los Angeles, California, with his wife and their latest major project—their company.

Angie Glocka

Angie Glocka was born a long time ago in a galaxy far, far away (Milwaukee, Wisconsin). In Wisconsin at that time, art was considered a nice hobby you did when you came home from your real job. So after taking a number of classes in art, film, and anything even vaguely animation-related at the University of Wisconsin, Angie and her husband (Owen Klatte, also an animator) hightailed it out to San Francisco.

After nosing around for a while in the Bay Area feature film and commercial scene, they landed jobs as stop-motion animators for *The New Gumby* TV series. Basically, Angie learned while her stuff got on TV. After a year and a half of doing animation every day, Angie managed to learn something about it and also got very good with shop tools. Because of all the wonderful folks she met and learned from (exec producer David Bleiman, art director Ken Pontac, and director Henry Sellick among them), she managed to be invited by Henry to work as a stop-motion animator on *The Nightmare Before Christmas*.

When that wrapped, Angie's pals Dave and Ken became creators of the TV series *Bump in the Night*. She animated for six months and then became assistant animation director for another six. She was very grateful for this opportunity, but after working nonstop for about five years she had to stop in mid-season and take a break. However, before she could take a breath, Angie was invited to interview for Pixar's *Toy Story*, and John Lasseter (another one of her favorite people in the entire world) hired her to learn CG animation. Even though she was on hiatus, Angie couldn't pass up the opportunity. It was definitely a seat-of-the-pants learning situation—two days of training with no computer background and no documentation. (Pixar has its own proprietary software.) Amazingly, she managed to do about 25 shots that she'll be forever proud of.

It was unclear at Pixar what the future would hold for Angie at the time, and both she and her husband were offered jobs on Disney's *Dinosaur*. So, they moved down to Los Angeles, where they still live. It was great working for Disney, and since *Dinosaur* wrapped Angie has been studio-hopping a bit, working at places such as DreamWorks and Digital Domain (where she met the fabulous Angie Jones) and raising her seven-year-old daughter, Julia. Angie just completed work on Sony's second motion-capture feature, called *Monster House*.

Scott Holmes

Born of parents. Raised in an apartment. Went to school. Finished school. Draws, paints, and animates.

Victor Huang

Some people call Victor an alcoholic. He likes to be called a raging alcoholic! He has been partying and drinking on the job as an animator for about eight years now. You've seen his works on projects ranging from games to commercials to films; he recently completed *The Matrix Reloaded*, *The Matrix Revolutions*, *Catwoman*, and Peter Jackson's *King Kong*. After a few years at ESC Entertainment and months at Digital Domain, Victor taught some animation classes at the Academy of Art University in San Francisco, then hopped across the South Pacific to chase his dreams of making a giant gorilla terrorize Skull Island and NYC, compliments of Weta Digital. Now saying "sweet as" every 10 minutes, he's living in Wellington, New Zealand, itching to get home so he can scarf down an In-N-Out burger. He likes to think that taking pictures keeps him from going crazy. What he doesn't know is that he's already crazy. Check out his site at http://www.tincast.com.

Ethan Hurd

Ethan originally planned on drawing his animation with a pencil. He studied the art of drawing animation at CalArts. But very soon after graduating, he discovered that his skills were better suited for pushing a mouse than drawing with a pencil. He has been happily animating with a mouse ever since. He has worked on such feature films as *Toy Story 2*, *Shrek*, *Shrek 2*, and *Madagascar*. He is currently working on the feature film *Open Season* at Sony Imageworks. Besides feature films, he has also pushed a mouse on various commercials, theme park rides, and video games. Ethan likes to write about his experience pushing a mouse at http://persistenceofvision.blogspot.com.

Bert Klein

Bert Klein has been making animated films since he was 13. He has a love for old-fashioned animation and believes it still has a place in our modern age. Bert met his friend and collaborator Teddy Newton while both were working at Disney Feature Animation in the early '90s and began work together on *Boys Night Out* several years later. He recently completed work as supervising animator on the animated sequences of the *Fat Albert* movie at Warner Bros.

Keith Lango

An escapee of the wild winter devastation of Buffalo, New York, Keith has been animating characters digitally for more than 10 years. A self-taught, no-talent hack, Keith has managed to remain gainfully employed somehow. As of this writing, he is serving as an animation supervisor at ReelFX Creative Studios in Dallas, Texas. Before that he served tours of duty at Blur Studio in Venice, California, and Big Idea Productions in Chicago, Illinois. He has done stints as an animator, senior animator, animation supervisor, VFX supervisor, CG supervisor, animation director, and director on a variety of projects ranging from interactive media, to commercials, to direct-to-video and feature films. In addition to the many animation-related roles, Keith has served in other production capacities, such as writer, storyboard artist, editor, layout artist, modeler, rigger, texturer, lighter, voice talent, production manager, render monkey, and compositor. He has even written and illustrated a published children's book, which some people reportedly bought with real money. Keith likes to pretend he's a filmmaker and has been accused of making several animated short films. Some people even allegedly watched them and didn't vomit. He even washed a few dishes once. Even though this all sounds very pompous and important, it's not of any significance to his lovely wife of 17 years and his three supernaturally adorable children. They like him for his ability to dig holes in the garden and pretend that he's Darth Vader by breathing into a plastic cup when playing light saber fights with Tinkertoys.

Cameron Miyasaki

Cameron Miyasaki never intended to become an animator. It was by chance, or maybe fate, that he stumbled upon computer animation while studying architecture at U.C. Berkeley. He hasn't been the same ever since. After dedicating himself to the craft, Cameron went on to graduate from the Academy of Art College in 2002, landing internships at Sony Pictures Imageworks and Pixar Animation Studios along the way. Cameron is currently employed as an animator at Pixar, where he has worked on such films as *Finding Nemo*, *The Incredibles*, and *Cars*.

Mike Murphy

Mike studied animation at CalArts. He almost got kicked out for painting the walls green, but that's a different story. After graduating, he got a brief stint at the lovely Rhythm & Hues. After being trained on the PC at R&H, he rolled over to Warner Bros. Feature Animation and animated on *The Iron Giant*. From there he went to Sony Imageworks and worked with the talented crew on *Stuart Little*. Then it was off to Warner Bros. again for *Osmosis Jones*, then back to Sony for *Stuart Little 2* and *Harry Potter and the Sorcerer's Stone*, then back to Warner Bros. (detecting a pattern?) for *Scooby-Doo*. Then he was coerced into going to New Zealand for "three months" to animate Gollum on *Lord of the Rings*. Three months became two-and-a-half years. Mike has also freelanced on various commercials and straight-to-video features, and he has done animatics for video games (*Halo 2*). He is currently developing his directing reel and hopes to make the plunge into working really long hours.

Eddie Pittman

Eddie Pittman grew up in Atlanta, Georgia, where he taught himself how to draw in the back row of math class. He began his animation career with Walt Disney Feature Animation Florida working on *Mulan*, *Tarzan*, *Fantasia 2000*, *The Emperor's New Groove*, and *Lilo and Stitch*. After escaping from the cleanup chain gang, Eddie left Disney to make his directing debut with *Legends of the Night Sky: Orion*, the world's first full dome (360°×180°) traditionally animated movie, which gives planetarium audiences the sensation of being immersed in a cartoon environment. Eddie is currently a freelance animator and character designer with most of one foot in the digital world.

Mike Polvani

Michael Polvani is a veteran animator with more than 20 years of experience in the animation industry. His grandfather (a New York cinematographer) sparked his strong interest and love for animation at the age of three. There are many school textbooks featuring flipbook animation in *all* the borders floating around the Arizona school system as a result. He has worked on everything from feature films, television commercials, television series, television pilots, educational films, and public service announcements to interstitials, theatrical short subjects, televised Academy Award ceremonies, and music videos in the capacities of traditional as well as computer-generated animation. Over his extensive career, he has worked his way to veteran animator by way of live-action gopher, assistant editor, in-betweener, breakdown artist, assistant animator, key cleanup, storyboard artist, layout artist, character designer, sheet timer, and assistant director. Michael has studied under such artists as Disney Studios' Walt Stanchfield, Dale Baer, Tom Sito, Dan Hansen, Michael Giaimo, Bill Kroyer, and Glen Vilppu. Michael is currently the co-founder (along with fellow veteran animator Wayne Carlisi) of a new animation school called 1 on 1 Animation.

Cathlin Hidalgo-Polvani

Cathlin Hidalgo-Polvani has worked in the animation industry since 1994. Her love of animation began while watching *Winky Dink* as a child. She got in trouble for using her crayons to draw a bridge on the television screen to help Winky get across the river. A graduate of California Institute of the Arts, her instructors were veteran animation professionals Mike Giaimo, Chris Buck, Glenn Vilppu, Robert Lence, and legendary Disney and graphic design artist Bob Winquist. Cathlin has worked on various traditional animation projects, including the feature films *Cats Don't Dance*, *The Prince of Egypt*, *The Iron Giant*, *The Powerpuff Girls Movie*, and the television show *The Powerpuff Girls*. Her most recent project was the Flash-animated *Hi Hi Puffy AmiYumi* show. She started her career with a foot-in-the-door job as a production assistant, and since then has worked as an in-betweener, breakdown artist, assistant animator, character model cleanup, and character layout artist.

Leigh Rens

Born a colonial in deep, dark Africa, Leigh learnt the hard way about the difference between animation and reality when he bumped a kid on the head in kindergarten and was banished to a life of artistic pursuit. After graduating from art college in 1986, he took a few years odd-jobbing at art galleries and print shops, and working as a camera grip. In 1990, he entered into the fresh, new world of computer graphics, and by '95 he had made his way to the mother ship in L.A. Since arriving, he has worked on ride shows for Disneyland, Legoland, and Universal theme parks. He has also had some fun working on such memorable films as *Dragonheart: A New Beginning*, *Dungeons & Dragons*, *Spy Kids*, *Dr. Dolittle 2*, *Scooby-Doo 2*, *Garfield*, and *Herbie Fully Loaded*. He can often be found wiping a tear off his sketchbook as he looks at the small sack of stardust that he kept after his first Hollywood film.

David Smith

Artist, storyteller, animator, and director. A graduate of Canada's widely recognized Sheridan College animation arts program, David cut teeth with Nelvana Ltd. on the feature animation icon, *Rock & Rule*. Shortly thereafter, he became conscript to a few formative years of animated filmmaking with Gaumont Film in Paris and the commercial and music video studios in London's Soho district. That gypsy wind soon surrendered him home to his hemisphere…then Hollywood. Ten years with Disney and high-profile

253

projects with Amblin, several West coast commercial houses, Jim Henson, ILM, Paramount, and Warner Bros. brought wonderful experiences, lifelong friends, and most importantly, clear focus on his lifelong ambition of creating a studio. Now cofounder and the creative vision behind Pow Wow Worldwide, David is directly involved in creating original content while keeping his eye on the big picture, his ultimate goal…100 minutes, a darkened theater, a captive audience, and a decent budget.

Roberto Smith

Born in the Canal Zone, Panama, Roberto had an interest in visual arts at an early age. For years he drew for himself and friends, but never considered the opportunities the visual arts could bring. Finally, in order to make sure he was chosen as "Most Talented" in the high school yearbook, he signed up for art classes. Roberto was neck-deep in it, doing art work for theatrical productions, school newspapers, t-shirts, and class publications. In his senior year of high school, Roberto, knowing no one else in the tiny country of Panama who wanted to get into animation, had the silly thought that animation would be fun and relatively easy to get into. With encouragement from his high school art teacher, Roberto submitted an application and was accepted to Ringling School of Art and Design as a computer animation major in Sarasota, Florida. There, he learned just how challenging and competitive the animation industry really is. Upon graduating in June of '95, Roberto accepted a position at Rhythm & Hues Studios and started employment at their new location near the beach in Los Angeles as a technical director. Taking advantage of the opportunities at the expanding studio, Roberto progressed from lighting and compositing to animation. In his years at Rhythm & Hues Studios, Roberto has animated, supervised animation, and acted as lead on such projects as the Coca-Cola Polar Bears commercials, *Cats & Dogs*, *The 6th Day*, *Babe: Pig in the City*, and *Scooby-Doo 1* and *2*, just to name a few. He has also had the opportunity to travel to work on location as a pre-visualization artist.

Bill Wright

William R. Wright studied film production at NYU and worked on commercials, television series, and music videos as a stop-motion animator and photographer, sculptor, and writer. After producing and directing a few award-winning MTV station IDs, he moved to the West coast, where he uses computers to make characters walk around and talk in movies such as *The Fantasia Legacy: Fantasia Continued*, *Dragonheart*, *Star Wars: Episode I*, and in commercials and video games as well. He is currently animating on Sony's full-length CG feature, *Open Season*.

Paul Wood

Paul Wood graduated from USF and the Academy of Art College in 1988 with a degree in graphic design, but fell into animation after a friend mentioned a demand for Sega and Nintendo game animators for the new 16-bit video game consoles. In 1996, after five years in games, six titles, and hundreds of six-frame walk cycles, he packed the family in the truck and moved to L.A. to a new job at Disney Feature Animation. In 2002, he left Disney and has since been jumping around to studios that include Rhythm & Hues, Digital Domain, and Sony Imageworks. Some of the film credits Paul has earned in the past nine years include *Dinosaur*, *Reign of Fire*, *Kangaroo Jack*, *Scooby-Doo 2*, and *Garfield*.

Roger Vizard

Roger Vizard attended Sheridan College in Canada for two years. His traditional animation credits include *Rock-a-Doodle*, *Cats Don't Dance*, *The Iron Giant*, and *The Thief and the Cobbler*. Roger's CG credits include *Stuart Little 2*, *The ChubbChubbs*, *The Polar Express*, and *The Chronicles of Narnia: The Lion, the Witch and the Wardrobe*. Roger was born in Worchester, Massachusetts, on November 11, 1964. Just in case anyone wants to send him a birthday gift.

Dave Zaboski

Dave Zaboski has left the building. Having worked for Disney for eight years during the last Golden Age of animation, Dave bounced from Warner Bros. to Sony and back to Warner Bros. in pursuit of the next great story. He didn't find it, so he left them to fend for themselves. He went solo, and the funny thing is, he couldn't be happier. With nothing to complain about, he paints and draws for clients all over the place all the time. His pet project is the Dreamstir Project, wherein he creates allegorical paintings that reflect the highest thought of his clients. He also teaches creativity through his company, "What's the Big Idea?" He lives with his wife and daughter on a small ranch (okay, it's more of a ranchette) in Chatsworth, California, where they plan to add a dog in about a year.

Contributing Authors: Story Artists/Writers

Mark Koetsier

Born in Hamilton, Ontario, Canada, Mark Koetsier graduated from Sheridan College in animation, jumping right into the industry. He was able to start on some (ahem) memorable TV shows doing character layouts before he got a chance to work as an animator for a TV series in Canada. After this, he shuffled back to Toronto to work on a few low-budget features (*Babar* and *Astérix & Obélix*). Then, he was discovered by Don Bluth Studios and made his way to California to animate on *Rock-a-Doodle*. This project bumped him into such enterprises as *Rover Dangerfield*, *A Wish for Wings That Work*, and a few other "blah de blah" projects until he started his ultimate goal…Disney! Finally, where he had always dreamed of working! The movie was *The Lion King*. What a blast! It was everything Mark had hoped it would be. Moving from picture to picture over a nine-year period (*Pocahontas*, *The Hunchback of Notre Dame*, *Dinosaur*, *Tarzan*, *Atlantis*, *Home on the Range*, and *Brother Bear*), animating at Disney lost its luster—which brings him to his change in career and his adventures as a story artist at DreamWorks for the past three years.

Ed Hooks

Ed came to the world of animation in 1996, after working as an actor for 25 years. He is the author of *Acting for Animators* and *Acting in Animation: A Look at 12 Films*. He teaches often at leading animation schools and studios.

Evan Gore

Evan Gore can't draw a bath, but he types very, very fast. As the handsome half of TV animation writing dynamos Gore & Lombard, he has written for *Futurama*, *Jimmy Neutron: Boy Genius*, *Ozzy & Drix*, and *The Weekenders*. Evan was Annie-nominated in 2004 for *Dave the Barbarian*. Gore & Lombard were story editors on the second season of *Lilo & Stitch* and the upcoming series, *Katbot*. Currently, he is trying to make this bio entertaining and would still like to mention that he was a co-writer on the CG *Here Comes Peter Cottontail: The Movie*, for which he also served as voice director.

Floyd Norman

Floyd Norman began his cartooning career while still in high school, assisting Bill Woggon on the *Katy Keene* series for Archie Comics. He attended Art Center College of Design as an illustration major. Floyd started working as an animation artist for the Walt Disney studio on *Sleeping Beauty* and eventually graduated to the story department, where he did story sketch on *The Jungle Book*. He had the opportunity to work with Walt Disney on the last film the old maestro personally supervised. Afterwards, he and his associates launched their own production company in the late '60s. Floyd served as a writer-director in the production of educational media. Vignette Films, Inc. was one of the first companies to produce films on the subject of African-American history. Moving to public television, Floyd wrote and produced animated segments for *Sesame Street*, *Villa Alegre*, and dozens of educational films. In the '70s, Floyd supervised animation layout at Hanna-Barbera Productions and storyboarded several shows, including *The Flintstones*, *The Smurfs*, and *Scooby-Doo*. He wrote scripts for *The Kwicky Koala Show*, *The Real Ghostbusters*, and *Monster Tales*. Floyd returned to Disney in the early '80s to join Disney Publishing Group. He wrote the syndicated *Mickey Mouse* comic strip and contributed stories for Disney Comics. As projects supervisor in creative development publishing, Floyd created, wrote, and designed several children's books. After a 10-year absence from film, Floyd returned to Disney Feature Animation to storyboard on *The Hunchback of Notre Dame*, *Mulan*, *Dinosaur*, and *The Tigger Movie*. In 1997, Floyd moved north to Pixar Animation Studios, where he joined the story crew for *Toy Story 2* and *Monsters, Inc*. Intrigued by the new digital realm and interactive computer media, Floyd worked with Disney Interactive to develop computer software for painting and animation. The result was the award-winning software program, Disney's Magic Artist. Like hundreds of Disney artists, Floyd "retired" from Walt Disney Feature Animation, but continues to write and create storyboards for various studios and clients.

Laura McCreary

Laura McCreary left Houston for California at the age of 18, with dreams of fame, fortune, and year-round 70-degree weather. After graduating with a BFA in film and television from the University of Southern California, Laura went on to work on various animated and live-action "tween" television shows. She was executive story editor on Fox's *Angela Anaconda* and has worked as writer and story editor on various Disney shows, including *Pepper Ann*, *Lilo & Stitch*, *Kim Possible*, and the upcoming *American Dragon*. Currently, Laura is a writer on the live-action Nickelodeon show, *Unfabulous*. She is happy to report that, while she has yet to achieve the aforementioned fame or fortune, at the time of this writing, it's 84 degrees in January.

Joe Scott

Joseph Scott was born in Manchester, New Hampshire. He successfully fled the tropical climes of New England as a boy and landed in San Diego during the heyday of the filmation stranglehold of television animation. He never gave up on this favorite art form and vowed to avenge the banality and mediocrity of mid-'70s animation…someday!

Incessant doodling and early, unrefined impressions of TV and cartoon stars brought him to the attention of local art impresarios. This led him nowhere, until eventually he attended San Diego State University as an art major, Richard Williams Master Classes, and the Animation Academy. He is a director and story-board artist who has worked extensively in San Diego, Hollywood, and the UK. He has worked for studios such as Lightspan Partnership (where he met the dark mistress of the timing and spacing continuum, Angie Jones), Fox Studios, Renegade Studios, Warner Bros. Classics, Klasky Csupo, O-mation, Mike Young Productions, and Kickstart Productions. Over the past 10 years, he has contributed to a variety of projects, including the *Rugrats* (Emmy Award), *The Wild Thornberrys*, *As Told by Ginger*, *Rocket Power*, *Barnyard*, the *Bratz* TV series, and several Looney Tunes commercials. Joe is currently directing 38 episodes of *Finley the Fire Engine* for Hallmark Television. Animation is his raison d'être.

Contributing Author: Rigger

Javier Solsona

Javier Solsona is currently the lead creature TD at Propaganda Games, a new Disney-owned studio recently opened in Vancouver, Canada. He was born in Buenos Aires, Argentina, and his journey to Vancouver was a long one.

Javier has always been interested in computers, ever since his father bought one of the first Commodore 64s in his little town in Patagonia. Javier used to spend hours and hours playing and doing graphics on it. Through the years, his interest didn't diminish, so studying computer science made the most sense. He didn't particularly enjoy his degree, probably because he's just not a good programmer! Toward the end of his university degree, Javier came across a multimedia course offered at a small private institution in Cape Town, and he dove right in. At the time, South Africa had seen little to no graphics, and courses were hard to come by. On the course of study, he was introduced to 3D, and there was no turning back. Javier spent a lot of his time in Brazil, getting more and more acquainted with 3D. When he arrived in Vancouver after three years of doing 2D graphics in Photoshop in London, he decided to get more into the 3D world. After working for a few months at the local VFX company, Lost Boys, he was offered a job at Electronic Arts as an animator, which was the direction he wanted to go until he realized that he was probably a way better TD than animator. This is why he now finds himself rigging all types of different creatures. It's been an interesting journey, and it continues to be so.

Appendix B
Traditional and CG Productions 1994–2005

The charts in this appendix prove an obvious point. Animation for feature films has been affected by the rise of the digital image in a profound way and in a relatively short span of time. The reasons for the lack of box-office draw from the latest batch of hand-drawn films cannot be attributed to simply poor marketing or less than palatable storylines, although you would not want to rule that out in most cases! The visual taste of the audience has always ebbed and flowed with the times. However, movie-goers have always been drawn to technical advances that enhance the movie-going experience. The rise of CG and the fall of 2D are clear when you look at the productions released in the last 10 years and how they performed at the box office. These charts might help to clarify some misconceptions regarding 2D versus 3D animation box-office results and illustrate the impact the visual-effects industry has had on our art form. So read at your own risk and draw your own conclusions, no pun intended.

Specs decided by authors for this chart: All monies reported in these charts are rounded to the nearest even number for simplicity in reporting, and all sales are domestic. Visual-effects movies reported had to make more than $100 million and contain a heavy amount of computer-generated effects to be included. CG productions were defined by either a 100-percent CG production or having a titled character animated in CG who was on the screen more than the live-action actors. All 2D productions were reported regardless of sales.

All information in the following table was gathered from http://www.boxofficemojo.com, including box-office sales.

1994

Traditional	$	Stop-Mo	$	CG	$	EFX	$
The Lion King	312m					The Flintstones	130m
						The Mask	119m
1 prod	312m	0 prod	0	0 prod	0	2 prod	249m

1995

Traditional	$	Stop-Mo	$	CG	$	EFX	$
Pocahontas	141m			Toy Story	191m	Batman Forever	184m
A Goofy Movie	35m			Casper	100m	Jumanji	100m
Balto	11m						
3 prod	187m	0 prod	0	2 prod	291m	2 prod	284m

1996

Traditional	$	Stop-Mo	$	CG	$	EFX	$
The Hunchback of Notre Dame	100m	James and the Giant Peach	28m			Independence Day	306m
Space Jam	90m					Twister	241m
All Dogs Go to Heaven	27m					101 Dalmatians	136m
3 prod	217m	1 prod	28m	0 prod	0	3 prod	683m

1997

Traditional	$	Stop-Mo	$	CG	$	EFX	$
Anastasia	58m					Titanic	600m
Cats Don't Dance	4m					Men in Black	250m
						The Lost World: Jurassic Park	229m
2 prod	62m	0 prod	0	0 prod	0	3 prod	1.08b

1998

Traditional	$	Stop-Mo	$	CG	$	EFX	$
Mulan	120m			A Bug's Life	162m	Armageddon	201m
The Prince of Egypt	101m			Antz	90m	Dr. Dolittle	144m
The Rugrats Movie	100m					Godzilla	136m
Quest for Camelot	22m						
4 prod	343m	0 prod	0	2 prod	252m	3 prod	481m

1999

Traditional	$	Stop-Mo	$	CG	$	EFX	$
Tarzan	171m			Toy Story 2	245m	Star Wars: Episode I – The Phantom Menace	431m
The Iron Giant	23m			Stuart Little	140m	The Matrix	171m
Princess Mononoke	2m					Wild Wild West	113m
3 prod	196m	0 prod	0	2 prod	385m	3 prod	715m

2000

Traditional	$	Stop-Mo	$	CG	$	EFX	$
Chicken Run	106m			Dinosaur	137m	How the Grinch Stole Christmas	260m
The Emperor's New Groove	89m					Cast Away	233m
Rugrats in Paris: The Movie	76m					Mission Impossible II	215m
Fantasia 2000 (35mm and IMAX)	61m					The Perfect Storm	182m
The Road to El Dorado	50m					X-Men	157m
The Tiger Movie	45m					Crouching Tiger, Hidden Dragon	128m
Titan AE	22m					The Nutty Professor	123m
6 prod	449m	0 prod	0	1 prod	137m	7 prod	1.3b

2001

Traditional	$	Stop-Mo	$	CG	$	EFX	$
Atlantis: The Last Empire	84m			Shrek	267m	Harry Potter and the Sorcerer's Stone	317m
Osmosis Jones	13m			Monsters, Inc.	255m	LOTR: The Fellowship of the Ring	313m
						Jurassic Park III	181m
						Planet of the Apes	180m
						Lara Croft: Tomb Raider	131m
						Dr. Dolittle 2	112m
2 prod	97m	0 prod	0	2 prod	522m	6 prod	1.2b

2002

Traditional	$	Stop-Mo	$	CG	$	EFX	$
Lilo and Stitch	145m			Ice Age	176m	Spiderman	403m
Spirit: Stallion of the Cimarron	73m			Scooby Doo	153m	LOTR: The Two Towers	339m
Treasure Planet	38m			Stuart Little 2	64m	Star Wars: Episode 2 – Attack of the Clones	302m
Hey Arnold! The Movie	13m					Harry Potter and the Chamber of Secrets	261m
The Powerpuff Girls Movie	11m					Men in Black II	190m
Spirited Away	10m						
6 prod	290m	0 prod	0	3 prod	393m	5 prod	1.5b

2003

Traditional	$	Stop-Mo	$	CG	$	EFX	$
Brother Bear	85m			Finding Nemo	339m	LOTR: The Return of the King	377m
Sinbad: Legend of the Seven Seas	26m					Pirates of the Caribbean	305m
Piglet's Big Movie	23m					The Matrix Reloaded	281m
Looney Toons: Back in Action	20m					X2: X-Men United	214m
The Triplets of Belleville	7m					Elf	173m
						Terminator 3: Rise of the Machines	150m

2003 (continued)

Traditional	$	Stop-Mo	$	CG	$	EFX	$
						The Matrix Revolutions	139m
						Hulk	132m
						Daredevil	102m
						The Cat in the Hat	101m
5 prod	161m	0 prod	0	1 prod	339m	10 prod	2b

2004

Traditional	$	Stop-Mo	$	CG	$	EFX	$
Home on the Range	50m			Shrek 2	441m	Spider-Man 2	373m
				The Incredibles	261m	Harry Potter and the Prisoner of Azkaban	249m
				The Polar Express	162m	The Day After Tomorrow	186m
				Garfield the Movie	75m	Scooby-Doo 2: Monsters Unleashed	84m
						Lemony Snicket's A Series of Unfortunate Events	118m
						I, Robot	144m
1 prod	50m	0 prod	0	4 prod	939m	6 prod	1.15b

2005

Traditional	$	Stop-Mo	$	CG	$	EFX	$
Pooh's Heffalump Movie	19m	Wallace and Gromit in the Curse of the Were-Rabbit	56m	Madagascar	194m	Star Wars: Episode III – Revenge of the Sith	380m
Steamboy	10m	Tim Burton's The Corpse Bride	53m	Chicken Little	135m	The Chronicles of Narnia: The Lion, the Witch and the Wardrobe	290m
Howl's Moving Castle	5m			Robots	128m	Harry Potter and the Goblet of Fire	290m
				Valiant	19m	War of the Worlds	234m
				Hoodwinked	51m	King Kong	217m
						Charlie and the Chocolate Factory	206m
						Batman Begins	205m
						Fantastic Four	154m
3 prod	34m	2 prod	109m	5 prod	527m	8 prod	2b

Appendix C
The Digital Age of Animation Begins

Animation trends are defined by history. History repeats itself and demonstrates how shifts in culture can create appeal in popular media. This is not intended to be a complete list of movies for each era, but highlights of films for study and appreciation. We encourage you to look at these particular films for their value in history and/or their quality as animated movies. These pictures can usually be found on DVD, or you can find them online for download at sites such as http://www.animationarchive.org. Frame by frame you can watch and study these movies to see what our animation forefathers discovered over the years.

Also, if a film had an important character premiere, we placed the character's name next to the movie for its significance. All the data in this appendix was compiled from http://www.cartoonresearch.com/feature.html (The Animated Movie Guide 1937 to 2005). Thanks to Jerry Beck for personally helping to verify this information.

The Golden Age of Animation (1928–1941): The Beginning of the Art Form

The Golden Age of animation was a time in American animation history that began in 1928 and lasted into late 1942. Some of the most memorable characters that came from this period included Mickey Mouse, Donald Duck, Goofy, Bugs Bunny, Daffy Duck, and Porky Pig.

Walt Disney Productions

◆ *Trolly Troubles* (1927): First appearance of Oswald the rabbit.

◆ *Plane Crazy* (1928): First Mickey Mouse cartoon ever made.

◆ *Steamboat Willie* (1928): First Mickey Mouse cartoon released and first Disney cartoon with a synchronized sound recording.

◆ *The Skeleton Dance* (1929)

◆ *Flowers and Trees* (1932): First Disney short produced in color. First Academy Award (Short Subjects - Cartoons).

◆ *Three Little Pigs* (1933): Academy Award (Short Subjects - Cartoons).

◆ *The Wise Little Hen* (1934): First appearance of Donald Duck.

◆ *The Tortoise and the Hare* (1934): Academy Award (Short Subjects - Cartoons).

◆ *The Band Concert* (1935): First complete Mickey Mouse cartoon made in color.

◆ *Three Orphan Kittens* (1935): Academy Award (Short Subjects - Cartoons).

◆ *The Country Cousin* (1936): Academy Award (Short Subjects - Cartoons).

◆ *The Old Mill* (1937): First use of Disney's multiplane camera and wins Academy Award (Short Subjects - Cartoons).

◆ *Clock Cleaners* (1937)

◆ *Snow White and the Seven Dwarfs* (1937): First animated feature for Disney.

◆ *Brave Little Tailor* (1938)

◆ *Ferdinand the Bull* (1938): Academy Award (Short Subjects - Cartoons).

◆ *Donald's Better Self* (1938)

◆ *Mickey's Trailer* (1938)

◆ *The Ugly Duckling* (1939): Academy Award (Short Subjects - Cartoons).

◆ *Pinocchio* (1940)

◆ *Fantasia* (1940)

◆ *Dumbo* (1941)

◆ *Lend a Paw* (1941): Academy Award (Short Subjects - Cartoons).

Warner Bros.

◆ *Sinkin' in the Bathtub* (1930): First Warner Bros. theatrical cartoon short and first appearance of Bosko.

◆ *I Haven't Got a Hat* (1935): First appearance of Porky Pig.

◆ *Gold Diggers of '49* (1935)

◆ *Porky's Duck Hunt* (1937): First appearance of Daffy Duck.

◆ *Porky in Wackyland* (1938)

◆ *You Ought to Be in Pictures* (1940)

◆ *A Wild Hare* (1940): First "true" Bugs Bunny cartoon.

MGM

- *Fiddlesticks* (1930): First appearance of Flip the Frog and first full-length color sound cartoon ever produced.
- *Room Runners* (1932)
- *Peace on Earth* (1939): Only cartoon ever nominated for the peace prize.
- *Puss Gets the Boot* (1940): Tom and Jerry get their first Oscar nomination.
- *The Milky Way* (1940): Academy Award (Short Subjects - Cartoons).

Fleischer Studios

- *I'm Afraid to Come Home in the Dark* (1930)
- *Dizzy Dishes* (1930): Betty Boop's first appearance.
- *Swing You Sinners!* (1931)
- *Bimbo's Initiation* (1931)
- *Minnie the Moocher* (1932): Younger Betty Boop appears.
- *Snow White* (1933): Betty Boop is fairest in the land in this rendition.
- *Popeye the Sailor* (1933): First appearance of Popeye.
- *Popeye the Sailor Meets Sinbad the Sailor* (1936)
- *Goonland* (1938): Popeye meets his father for the first time in a cartoon.
- *Gulliver's Travels* (1939)
- *Superman* (1941)
- *Mr Bug Goes to Town* (1941): First full-length comedy, musical cartoon.

Walter Lantz

- *Race Riot* (1929): New series of Oswald the Rabbit shorts begins with *Race Riot*.
- *Confidence* (1933)
- *Life Begins for Andy Panda*: First appearance of Andy Panda.
- *Knock Knock* (1940): First appearance of Woody Woodpecker.

Others

- *Dinner Time* (1928): The first publicly released sound cartoon with Farmer Alfalfa, Paul Terry.
- *Pink Elephants* (1937)
- *The Mouse of Tomorrow* (1942): Super Mouse in this cartoon, soon to become Mighty Mouse.

Wartime Era (1942–1945): Propaganda

The wartime era in the 1940s created a slump for theatrical animation. Many animators went overseas to fight in the war, and those left behind were producing animated films that promoted the war effort with very different content than before.

Disney

- *Bambi* (1942)
- *Der Fuehrer's Face* (1942)
- *Yankee Doodle Mouse* (1943): Academy Award (Short Subjects - Cartoons).
- *Saludos Amigos* (1943): First appearance of Jose Carioca.
- *The Three Caballeros* (1944)
- *Hockey Homicide* (1945): All the players were various members of the Disney staff.

Warner Bros.

- *The Dover Boys* (1942): Earliest example of stylized animation.
- *The Ducktators* (1942)
- *Private Snafu* (1943–1946)

UPA

- *Hell-Bent for Election* (1944): UPA's first major success. Made in an apartment with the help of moonlighters from various local Hollywood animation studios.
- *Brotherhood of Man* (1945)

Paramount/Famous Studios

- *Spinach Fer Britain* (1943): Popeye fights a Nazi submarine; guess who wins?
- *Cartoons Ain't Human* (1943)
- *The Friendly Ghost* (1945): First appearance of Casper in a film.
- *Tulips Shall Grow* (1942): George Pal Puppetoon.

Walter Lantz

- *The Barber of Seville* (1944): Woody Woodpecker's appearance is streamlined.
- *Apple Andy* (1946)

MGM

- *The Yankee Doodle Mouse* (1943): Academy Award (Short Subjects - Cartoons).
- *Dumb-Hounded* (1943): First appearance of Droopy.

◆ *Red Hot Riding Hood* (1943): The wolf in this film reacts so lustfully that censors demanded cuts.

◆ *Mouse Trouble* (1944): Academy Award (Short Subjects - Cartoons).

◆ *Quiet Please!* (1945): Academy Award (Short Subjects - Cartoons).

Post War (1946–1980): Animated Television Influences

Some animators who remained in the States during the war participated in strikes that severed many ties between artists and the studios. Some of these folks started new studios such as UPA, Shamus Culhane Productions, and Famous Studios, which introduced new styles and genres in the 1950s. This is apparent by the number of Oscars presented to independent studios during this time. Unfortunately, many of these smaller studios that created new styles collapsed during the recession of 1959–1960. Television began to influence animated features at this time. The new studios brought us new characters, such as Droopy Dog, Tweety, Sylvester, Heckle and Jeckle, Casper the Friendly Ghost, and Mr. Magoo.

Disney

◆ *Song of the South* (1946)

◆ *Fun and Fancy Free* (1947): "Mickey and the Beanstalk" segment in this film marks the last time Walt Disney would perform the voice of Mickey Mouse.

◆ *The Adventures of Ichabod and Mr. Toad* (1949): The last of the wartime films.

◆ *Cinderella* (1950): First full-length feature produced by the studio since *Bambi* in 1942.

◆ *Alice in Wonderland* (1951)

◆ *Toot, Whistle, Plunk, and Boom* (1953): Academy Award (Short Subjects - Cartoons).

◆ *Peter Pan* (1953): Final Disney film where all of the Nine Old Men worked together as directing animators.

◆ *Lady and the Tramp* (1955)

◆ *Sleeping Beauty* (1959): Last cel animated feature from Disney to be inked by hand.

◆ *101 Dalmatians* (1961): Introduction of Xerography, recognizable by its thick black lines.

◆ *The Jungle Book* (1967): Last animated feature produced by Walt Disney; he died during production.

◆ *Winnie the Pooh and the Blustery Day* (1968): Academy Award (Short Subjects - Cartoons).

◆ *It's Tough to Be a Bird* (1969): Academy Award (Short Subjects - Cartoons).

◆ *The Aristocats* (1970)

◆ *Robin Hood* (1973)

◆ *The Many Adventures of Winnie the Pooh* (1977)

◆ *The Rescuers* (1977): This film was the last project for John Lounsberry, one of Disney's Nine Old Men.

Warner Bros.

- *Book Revue* (1946): A favorite among animators.
- *Tweetie Pie* (1947): Academy Award (Short Subjects - Cartoons).
- *Haredevil Hare* (1948): First appearance of Marvin the Martian.
- *For Scent-imental Reasons* (1949): Academy Award (Short Subjects - Cartoons).
- *Rabbit of Seville* (1950): Another big favorite among animators.
- *Rabbit Fire* (1951): Is it duck season or rabbit season?
- *Duck Dodgers in the 24 1/2th Century* (1953)
- *Duck Amuck* (1953)
- *Speedy Gonzales* (1955): Academy Award (Short Subjects - Cartoons).
- *One Froggy Evening* (1955): Frog had no name, but Chuck Jones later named him Michigan J. Frog after the song.
- *What's Opera, Doc?* (1957): If you see anything on this list, see this.
- *Birds Anonymous* (1958): Academy Award (Short Subjects - Cartoons).
- *Knighty Knight Bugs* (1959): Academy Award (Short Subjects - Cartoons).
- *The Incredible Mr. Limpet* (1964)
- *Gay Purr-ee* (1962)
- *The Great American Chase* (1979)

Terrytoons

- *Flebus* (1957)
- *Juggler of our Lady* (1957)
- *Topsy TV* (1957)

UPA

- *Ragtime Bear* (1949): First appearance for Mr. Magoo.
- *Gerald McBoing-Boing* (1950): Academy Award (Short Subjects - Cartoons).
- *Rooty Toot Toot* (1952)
- *The Tell-Tale Heart* (1953)
- *When Magoo Flew* (1955): Academy Award (Short Subjects - Cartoons).
- *Mr. Magoo's Puddle Jumper* (1956): Academy Award (Short Subjects - Cartoons).
- *1001 Arabian Nights* (1959)

MGM

- *The Cat Concerto* (1946): Academy Award (Short Subjects - Cartoons).
- *King-Size Canary* (1947)
- *The Little Orphan* (1948): Academy Award (Short Subjects - Cartoons).
- *The Two Mouseketeers* (1951): Academy Award (Short Subjects - Cartoons).
- *Johann Mouse* (1953): Academy Award (Short Subjects - Cartoons).
- *The Phantom Tollbooth* (1970)

Walter Lantz

- *Crazy Mixed-Up Pup* (1954)
- *The Legend of Rockabye Point* (1955)

Columbia

- *The Huckleberry Hound Show* (1958): Yogi debuted in 1958 as a supporting character on *The Huckleberry Hound Show*.
- *Hey There! It's Yogi Bear* (1964)
- *The Man Called Flintstone* (1965)

United Artists

- *The Yellow Submarine* (1968): The style contrasts to Disney, and the Blue Meanies wear Mickey Mouse–shaped ears.
- *The Pink Phink* (1964): Academy Award (Short Subjects - Cartoons).

Anime

- *Alakazam the Great* (1960)
- *Magic Boy* (1961)
- *Adventures of Sinbad* (1962)
- *Little Prince and Eight Headed Dragon* (1964)
- *Gulliver's Travels Beyond the Moon* (1966)
- *Nutcracker Fantasy* (1979)

Rankin-Bass

- *Wacky World of Mother Goose* (1967)
- *Mad Monster Party?* (1969)

Ralph Bakshi

- *Fritz the Cat* (1972): First X-rated cartoon.
- *Heavy Traffic* (1973)
- *Nine Lives of Fritz the Cat* (1974)
- *Coonskin* (1975)
- *American Pop* (1981)

Fox

- *Raggedy Ann and Andy: A Musical Adventure* (1977)
- *Wizards* (1977)

Paramount

- *Herb Alpert and the Tijuana Brass Double Feature* (1966): Academy Award (Short Subjects - Cartoons).
- *Charlotte's Web* (1973)
- *Race for Your Life, Charlie Brown* (1977)
- *Bon Voyage, Charlie Brown (And Don't Come Back!)* (1980)

Other

- *Professor Small and Mr. Tall* (1943)
- *Moonbird* (1959): Academy Award (Short Subjects - Cartoons).
- *Munro* (1960): Academy Award (Short Subjects - Cartoons).
- *Ersatz* (1961): Academy Award (Short Subjects - Cartoons).
- *The Hole* (1962): Academy Award (Short Subjects - Cartoons).
- *The Box* (1967): Academy Award (Short Subjects - Cartoons).
- *The Plumber* (1966): Shamus Culhane Productions.
- *My Daddy the Astronaut* (1967): Shamus Culhane Productions.
- *A Boy Named Charlie Brown* (1969)
- *Is it Always Right to Be Right?* (1970): Academy Award (Short Subjects - Cartoons).
- *The Crunch Bird* (1971): Academy Award (Short Subjects - Cartoons).
- *Snoopy Come Home* (1972)
- *A Christmas Carol* (1972): Academy Award (Short Subjects - Cartoons).
- *Closed Mondays* (1974): Academy Award (Short Subjects - Cartoons).
- *Great* (1975): Academy Award (Short Subjects - Cartoons).

◆ *Sand Castle* (1977): Academy Award (Short Subjects - Cartoons).

◆ *The Lord of the Rings* (1978)

◆ *Every Child* (1979): Academy Award (Short Subjects - Cartoons).

The Second Golden Age of Animation (1981–1995): A Rabbit, Mermaid, and a Tail to Bring the Audience Back!

It wasn't until *Who Framed Roger Rabbit?* was released in 1988 that American animation experienced a resurgence. *Who Framed Roger Rabbit?* won four Academy Awards: Best Effects, Sound Effects Editing; Best Effects, Visual Effects; Best Film Editing; and a Special Award for Richard Williams for "animation direction and creation of the cartoon characters." The audience was back for animated films, and so began the second Golden Age of animation. Hot on the heels of *Roger Rabbit* came *The Little Mermaid* and *An American Tail*. The boom had begun. In addition, Japanese anime was flourishing as well, and entering the American market by 1987. New animation studios opened during the 1990s, attempting to gain a foothold in this lucrative market, and by 1994 *The Lion King* from Disney marked the height of the second boom for animated films, grossing more than any other animated film before.

Walt Disney/Touchstone Productions

◆ *The Fox and the Hound* (1981): The remaining three of the Nine Old Men worked on this, and a new crop of animators began to emerge.

◆ *Sundae in New York* (1983): Academy Award (Short Subjects - Cartoons).

◆ *The Black Cauldron* (1985): A train wreck. If you must see this, look for the cool CG smoke.

◆ *The Great Mouse Detective* (1986): Ratigan and the clock gears scene are amazing.

◆ *The Brave Little Toaster* (1987): Joe Ranft worked on story; a must see.

◆ *Oliver and Company* (1988): If you like Billy Joel, see this one.

◆ *Who Framed Roger Rabbit?* (1988): Every character you can think of together on one screen.

◆ *The Little Mermaid* (1989): Rebirth of the classic fairytale at Disney.

◆ *The Rescuers Down Under* (1990)

◆ *DuckTales the Movie: Treasure of the Lost Lamp* (1990)

◆ *Beauty and the Beast* (1991): Just see this one, if you haven't already.

◆ *Aladdin* (1992): Machine-gun pacing and the genie.

◆ *The Nightmare Before Christmas* (1993)

◆ *The Lion King* (1994): Highest-grossing film for Disney, but marked the end of the second Golden Age, traditionally speaking.

◆ *Pocahontas* (1995)

◆ *A Goofy Movie* (1995)

Anime

- *Galaxy Express* (1981)
- *Laputa: Castle in the Sky* (1989)
- *Akira* (1989): A monumental piece of filmmaking. Set the bar for anime movies in this country.
- *Robot Carnival* (1991): Ensemble movie that is really nine small stories animated/directed by different teams.
- *Little Nemo: Adventures in Slumberland* (1992)
- *My Neighbor Totoro* (1993): Fantastic on so many levels. One of the most charming movies ever made.
- *Space Adventure Cobra* (1995)

Pixar

- *Luxo Jr.* (1986): First film produced by Pixar following its establishment as an independent film studio.
- *Tin Toy* (1988): First time a realistic human character is attempted in a computer-animated film. Academy Award (Short Subjects - Cartoons).
- *Toy Story* (1995): This film arguably began the demise of traditionally animated pictures. It only took a few years.

Warner Bros.

- *The Looney Looney Looney Bugs Bunny Movie* (1981)
- *1001 Rabbit Tales* (1981)
- *Twice Upon a Time* (1983): First animated film George Lucas produced.
- *Daffy Duck's Fantastic Island* (1983)
- *Rainbow Brite and the Star Stealer* (1985)
- *Daffy Duck's Quackbusters* (1989)
- *Batman: Mask of the Phantasm* (1993): Dark nature of the film is respected by animation fans.
- *The Nutcracker Prince* (1990): Uhh…yeah.

Fox/Bluth Studios

- *The Secret of NIMH* (1982): Bluth's answer to his perception of the growing lack of quality in feature animation at Disney.
- *Rock-a-Doodle* (1991)
- *A Troll in Central Park* (1994)

Universal

- ◆ *Casper* (1995): First computer-generated title character in a live-action movie.
- ◆ *Balto* (1995): Universal Pictures did not release another animated film until *Curious George* in 2006.

United Artists

- ◆ *All Dogs Go to Heaven* (1989): Even though *The Little Mermaid* kicked its butt at the box office, you should still see this film.
- ◆ *An American Tail* (1986): At the time, the highest-grossing non-Disney animated feature in first release.
- ◆ *An American Tail: Fievel Goes West* (1991)

Others

- ◆ *Heavy Metal* (1981): Bloody violence, nudity, and sexuality. What more could any child want?
- ◆ *The Last Unicorn* (1982): American film, but work was subcontracted to the Japanese company Topcraft, which eventually became Studio Ghibli.
- ◆ *Mighty Mouse in the Great Space Chase* (1982)
- ◆ *Hey Good Lookin'* (1982): Knife fight is worth the rental.
- ◆ *Amazing Stories: Book Two (Family Dog)* (1992): Combination of Tim Burton designs, Brad Bird writing, and Spielberg producing makes this one a winner, and we like the dog too.
- ◆ *Tom and Jerry: The Movie* (1993): First feature to star Tom and Jerry. Not to be confused with the classic MGM cartoons of the '40s and '50s.
- ◆ *Arabian Night (The Thief and the Cobbler)* (1995)
- ◆ *Crac* (1981): Academy Award (Short Subjects - Cartoons).
- ◆ *Anna & Bella* (1985): Academy Award (Short Subjects - Cartoons).
- ◆ *The Man Who Planted Trees* (1987): Academy Award (Short Subjects - Cartoons).
- ◆ *Balance* (1989): Academy Award (Short Subjects - Cartoons).
- ◆ *Rock & Rule* (1985): Nelvana's first animated feature film. Nelvana's last animated feature.
- ◆ *When the Wind Blows* (1988)
- ◆ *Fire and Ice* (1983): Frank Frazetta designs make this film.
- ◆ *The Thief and the Cobbler* (1995): Richard Williams' 23-year pet project; everyone is awaiting the original restoration of this project. The war machine scene is worth it.

The Digital Age of Animation (1996–?)

1995 brought the first computer-animated feature-length film, *Toy Story*, and the rise of the Digital Age of animation was obvious. The only traditionally animated film in 2004 was *Home on the Range*, grossing $50 million domestically, while the three computer-animated productions out that same year—*Shrek 2*, *The Incredibles*, and *The Polar Express*—grossed more than $800 million domestically. This boom in CG animation will continue to rise with the mainstream popularization of anime, the decline of Saturday morning cartoons (especially traditionally animated ones), and the rise of Nickelodeon and Cartoon Network shows that are also computer-animated, whether in CG or with Flash. In 2005, Disney closed all facilities for hand-drawn traditional animation, concentrating on computer animation for their feature films. It would appear that the traditional hand-drawn feature is truly a thing of the past, at least in Hollywood. But in light of the acquisition of Pixar by Disney, who knows what the future holds.

Walt Disney Productions

◆ *The Hunchback of Notre Dame* (1996): James Baxter's work is amazing.

◆ *James and the Giant Peach* (1996)

◆ *Hercules* (1997): Phil and Hades, study them! Kudos to the animation crews on these characters!

◆ *Mulan* (1998): *Mulan* is a wonderfully realized female lead. And Mushu rocked.

◆ *Tarzan* (1999): Watch Tarzan surf the vines! Watch Rosie O'Donnell act like an ape.

◆ *Fantasia 2000* (1999)

◆ *The Emperor's New Groove* (2000)

◆ *Lilo & Stitch* (2002): Kata Bakka Dooka?

◆ *Spirit: Stallion of the Cimarron* (2002): Baxter does it again, beautiful animation.

◆ *Brother Bear* (2003)

◆ *Chicken Little* (2005): Disney's first CG feature attempt since *Dinosaur*.

Pixar

◆ *Geri's Game* (1997)

◆ *A Bug's Life* (1998)

◆ *Toy Story 2* (1999): Two Buzz Lightyears interacting differently in the same scene; nice stuff.

◆ *Monsters, Inc.* (2001): Blue fur. A lot of blue fur.

◆ *For the Birds* (2001)

◆ *Finding Nemo* (2003): Academy Award (Best Animated Feature). Great fish animation. Better than the other fish movie.

◆ *The Incredibles* (2004): Academy Award (Best Animated Feature). Pixar and Brad Bird raise the bar. Way up.

Fox/Bluth/BlueSky

◆ *Anastasia* (1997)

◆ *Bunny* (1998)

◆ *Ice Age* (2002): Great entertainment. Scrat is a standout.

◆ *Robots* (2005)

Sony Pictures

◆ *Stuart Little* (1999): Second to Casper, a titled CG character to be mixed with live action.

◆ *Final Fantasy* (2001): Nice hair and lighting in CG.

◆ *Stuart Little 2* (2002)

◆ *The ChubbChubbs!* (2002)

DreamWorks/PDI Animation

◆ *Antz* (1998)

◆ *Chicken Run* (2000): Funny, funny stuff. From the Wallace and Gromit gang.

◆ *Shrek* (2001): Academy Award (Best Animated Feature). Huge success for DreamWorks. Rumors of painting the entire studio green are not without foundation.

◆ *Shrek 2* (2004): Studio now to be painted green.

◆ *Madagascar* (2005): Insane breaking of joints and drastic animation stylings. Made Aladdin look slow.

◆ *Wallace & Gromit in the Curse of the Were-Rabbit* (2005): Academy Award (Best Animated Feature).

Anime

◆ *Ghost in the Shell* (1996): Great movie on what it is to be human and raises the question of how much of your humanity can be removed/replaced and still leave you human. Plus it has cool fight scenes.

◆ *Tenchi Muyo in Love* (1996)

◆ *Princess Mononoke* (1997): More top-notch cinema from Miyazake the Master.

◆ *Pokemon: The Movie* (2000)

◆ *Spirited Away* (2001): Academy Award (Best Animated Feature). Interesting that a traditional hand-drawn film can still win an Academy Award in the era of CG.

◆ *Pokemon Heroes* (2003)

◆ *Cowboy Bebop: The Movie* (2003)

◆ *Ghost in the Shell 2: Innocence* (2004): Great, though under-appreciated, sequel. More about the human condition.

◆ *Steamboy* (2005)

◆ *Howl's Moving Castle* (2005): Academy Award (Best Animated Feature).

Aardman

◆ *Creature Comforts* (1990): Brilliant.

◆ *The Wrong Trousers* (1993): Brilliant.

◆ *A Close Shave* (1995): Brilliant.

Warner Bros./Paramount

◆ *Space Jam* (1996)

◆ *Cats Don't Dance* (1997)

◆ *Quest for Camelot* (1998)

◆ *The Rugrats Movie* (1998)

◆ *The Iron Giant* (1999): Recommended viewing for everyone.

◆ *South Park: Bigger, Longer & Uncut* (1999): If you really like cussing and vulgarity, this is for you.

◆ *Jimmy Neutron* (2001): No cussing or vulgarity here.

◆ *Osmosis Jones* (2001)

◆ *Looney Tunes: Back in Action* (2003): Don't quite know what to say here.

◆ *The Polar Express* (2004)

◆ *The SpongeBob SquarePants Movie* (2004)

◆ *Corpse Bride* (2005)

Others

◆ *Beavis and Butt-Head Do America* (1996): Cussing and vulgarity...pattern emerging?

◆ *Swan Princess II: Escape from Castle Mountain* (1997)

◆ *I Married a Strange Person* (1998)

◆ *Jonah: A Veggie Tales Movie* (2002)

◆ *The Triplets of Belleville* (2003): No dialogue in the whole film. Proving Hitchcock's adage about using dialogue as a last resort in a big way. The first traditionally animated independent film in years.

◆ *Kaena: The Prophecy* (2004)

◆ *The Sandman* (1992)

◆ *The Old Man and the Sea* (1999)

◆ *Father and Daughter* (2000)

◆ *Harvie Krumpet* (2002)

◆ *The Moon and the Son: An Imagined Conversation* (2005)

The Future

What is next for animation? As movie executives desire even greater profit margins, the medium will lose its craft and embrace mass production. Animation production moving overseas is part of the future. There will always be a few studios in America that set the bar highest for themselves and still welcome the artistry of the art form over a box-office profit, but those will become fewer and more elitist with time. We can only hope the audience will reject productions made at half the price overseas because of lack of solid storytelling and level of artistry, but if television is any indication, then pack your bags.

We believe that if you continue to master your craft, you will only become even more valuable a commodity to those overseas who do not have your amazing skills. The jobs that most likely will not be outsourced are those involving look development, story, and pre- and post-production roles of all sorts, such as storyboarding, character design, editing, and creative content. We encourage you to learn everything you can about animation and filmmaking. In the end, the only real security you have is your artistic ability. Strive to learn every day and embrace the new tools that are coming. That is the future. Your future.

Appendix D
Animation Hall of Funny

The director/supervisor takes you aside because he has some very important art direction for your scene, and he says (and yes, these are real comments;, we could not make this stuff up)....

◆ "Make the shot less salamandar-y."

◆ "I need you to sharpen it, then smooth it."

◆ "Can you make it 10 percent cooler?"

◆ "It needs to be 10 percent less funny."

Comic made with Strip Generator. http://www.stripgenerator.com.

◆ "We need no descriptive sense of foreboding."

◆ "I need it to be less animation-y."

◆ "Are we worried about production or are we worried about making a movie?"

Comic made with Strip Generator. http://www.stripgenerator.com.

◆ "You have to take about 85 percent of the energy out of the scene."

Response: "Um…yes, but that energy is in the dialogue."

"Well, if it's in the dialogue, then you don't need it in the character."

◆ "Make it more blue, because blue is more mysterious."

◆ "You're going to add lip sync to that, aren't you?"

◆ "Okay…well, that doesn't totally suck."

◆ "Make it more *Star Wars*-y!"

Comic made with Strip Generator. http://www.stripgenerator.com.

- ◆ "I'm not sure what I want, but that's not it."
- ◆ "I can't judge the animation on that; it's the wrong color."
- ◆ "It should be more poom, poom, poom, *not* vroom, vroom, vroom."
- ◆ "Fix it so that NASA won't laugh at us when they see it."
- ◆ "Could you make it all…less animated?"

just do it

Comic made with Strip Generator. http://www.stripgenerator.com.

- ◆ "If you fix something long enough, you'll break it."
- ◆ "I love the dynamics on the ears."

   Response: "The dynamics have not been added yet."

   "Oh…then I guess we have to change it."

its version 16

Comic made with Strip Generator. http://www.stripgenerator.com.

◆ "There are too many keys on your curve. Delete some and get rid of the clutter."

◆ "Can you shift that half a frame south?"

◆ "Why do you keep moving the body? I just want him to raise his leg."

◆ "Don't think; just do what I say."

Comic made with Strip Generator. http://www.stripgenerator.com.

◆ "I want it to sound like nothing going through nothing."

◆ "More lens flares. Lens flares make it look real."

◆ "I know [the director] said this, but I was thinking…."

◆ "Show me the funny!"

◆ "I know you want it to look good, but I want it to look good *and* be approved."

Comic made with Strip Generator. http://www.stripgenerator.com.

◆ "Make the animation a bit more 'eeeeek.' You know, 'eeeeek?'"

◆ "Make it more flowery."

◆ "More of frame 35, less of frame 36; that will sell it!"

◆ "Trust me; I know funny, and that frame is not making me laugh."

◆ "Can you give me more ERRRRRR!?"

◆ "Could you rotate that hoof just three degrees?"

◆ "Take out one frame and it will work…."

Appendix E
Principles of Animation

These are the 12 principles of animation, as defined by Frank Thomas and Ollie Johnston in their book *The Illusion of Life: Disney Animation* (paraphrased by Nataha Lightfoot). This information was provided by Frank Thomas and Ollie Johnston's Web site: http://www.frankanollie.com/PhysicalAnimation.html.

Squash and Stretch

This action gives the illusion of weight and volume to a character as it moves. Also, squash and stretch is useful in animating dialogue and doing facial expressions. How extreme the use of squash and stretch is depends on what is required in animating the scene. Usually it's broader in a short style of picture and subtler in a feature. It is used in all forms of character animation, from a bouncing ball to the body weight of a person walking. This is the most important element you will be required to master and will be used often.

Anticipation

This movement prepares the audience for a major action the character is about to perform, such as starting to run, jump, or change expression. A dancer does not just leap off the floor. A backward motion occurs before the forward action is executed. The backward motion is the anticipation. A comic effect can be done by not using anticipation after a series of gags that used anticipation. Almost all real action has major or minor anticipation, such as a pitcher's wind-up or a golfer's backswing.

Staging

A pose or action should clearly communicate to the audience the attitude, mood, reaction, or idea of the character as it relates to the story and continuity of the storyline. The effective use of long, medium, or close-up shots, as well as camera angles, also helps in telling the story. There is a limited amount of time in a film, so each sequence, scene, and frame of film must relate to the overall story. Do not confuse the audience with too many actions at once. Use one action clearly stated to get the idea across, unless you are animating a scene that is to depict clutter and confusion. Staging directs the audience's attention to the story or idea being told. Care must be taken in background design so it isn't obscuring the animation or competing with it due to excess detail behind the animation. Background and animation should work together as a pictorial unit in a scene.

Straight-Ahead and Pose-to-Pose Animation

Straight-ahead animation starts at the first drawing and works drawing to drawing to the end of a scene. You can lose size, volume, and proportions with this method, but it does have spontaneity and freshness. Fast, wild action scenes are done this way. Pose-to-pose is more planned out and charted with key drawings done at intervals throughout the scene. Size, volume, and proportion are controlled better this way, as is the action. The lead animator will turn charting and keys over to his assistant. An assistant can be better used with this method so that the animator doesn't have to draw every drawing in a scene. An animator can do more scenes this way and concentrate on the planning of the animation. Many scenes use a bit of each method of animation.

Follow-Through and Overlapping Action

When the main body of the character stops, all other parts continue to catch up to the main mass of the character, such as arms, long hair, clothing, coattails or a dress, floppy ears, or a long tail. (These follow the path of action.) Nothing stops all at once. This is follow-through. Overlapping action is when the character changes direction while his clothes or hair continues forward. The character is going in a new direction, to be followed, a number of frames later, by his clothes in the new direction. "Drag" in animation, for example, would be when Goofy starts to run, but his head, ears, upper body, and clothes do not keep up with his legs. In features, this type of action is done more subtly. Example: When Snow White starts to dance, her dress does not begin to move with her immediately, but catches up a few frames later. Long hair and animal tails will also be handled in the same manner. Timing becomes critical to the effectiveness of drag and the overlapping action.

Slow-In and Slow-Out

As action starts, you have more drawings near the starting pose, one or two in the middle, and more drawings near the next pose. Fewer drawings make the action faster, and more drawings make the action slower. Slow-ins and slow-outs soften the action, making it more lifelike. For a gag action, we may omit some slow-out or slow-in for shock appeal or the surprise element. This will give more snap to the scene.

Arcs

All actions, with few exceptions (such as the animation of a mechanical device), follow an arc or slightly circular path. This is especially true of the human figure and the action of animals. Arcs give animation a more natural action and better flow. Think of natural movements in terms of a pendulum swinging. All arm movement, head turns, and even eye movements are executed on arcs.

Secondary Action

This action adds to and enriches the main action and adds more dimension to the character animation, supplementing and/or reinforcing the main action. Example: A character is angrily walking toward another character. The walk is forceful, aggressive, and forward-leaning. The leg action is just short of a stomping walk. The secondary action is a few strong gestures of the arms working with the walk. Also, there is the possibility of dialogue being delivered at the same time with tilts and turns of the head to accentuate the walk and dialogue, but not so much as to distract from the walk action. All of these actions should work together in support of one another. Think of the walk as the primary action, and arm swings, head bounce, and all other actions of the body as secondary or supporting action.

Timing

Expertise in timing comes best with experience and personal experimentation, using the trial-and-error method in refining technique. The basics are as follows. More drawings between poses slow and smooth the action. Fewer drawings make the action faster and crisper. A variety of slow and fast timing within a scene adds texture and interest to the movement. Most animation is done on twos (one drawing photographed on two frames of film) or on ones (one drawing photographed on each frame of film). Twos are used most of the time, and ones are used during camera moves such as trucks, pans, and occasionally for subtle and quick dialogue animation. Also, there is timing in the acting of a character to establish mood, emotion, and reaction to another character or to a situation. Studying movement of actors and performers on stage and in films is useful when animating human or animal characters. This frame-by-frame examination of film footage will aid you in understanding timing for animation. This is a great way to learn from the others.

Exaggeration

Exaggeration is not extreme distortion of a drawing or extremely broad, violent action all the time. It's like a caricature of facial features, expressions, poses, attitudes, and actions. Action traced from live-action film can be accurate, but stiff and mechanical. In feature animation, a character must move more broadly to look natural. The same is true of facial expressions, but the action should not be as broad as in a short cartoon style. Exaggeration in a walk, an eye movement, or even a head turn will give your film more appeal. Use good taste and common sense to keep from becoming too theatrical and excessively animated.

Solid Drawing

The basic principles of drawing—form, weight, volume solidity, and the illusion of three dimensions—apply to animation as they do to academic drawing. You draw cartoons in the classical sense, using pencil sketches and drawings for reproduction of life. You transform these into color and movement, giving the characters the illusion of three- and four-dimensional life. Three-dimensional is movement in space. The fourth dimension is movement in time.

Appeal

A live performer has charisma. An animated character has appeal. Appealing animation does not mean just being cute and cuddly. All characters have to have appeal whether they are heroic, villainous, comic, or cute. Appeal, as you will use it, includes an easy-to-read design, clear drawing, and personality development that will capture and involve the audience's interest. Early cartoons were basically a series of gags strung together on a main theme. Over the years, the artists have learned that to produce a feature, there is a need for story continuity, character development, and a higher quality of artwork throughout the entire production. Like all forms of storytelling, the feature has to appeal to the mind as well as to the eye.

Appendix F
Character Animation Terms

180 degree rule. The 180 degree rule is a rule relating to the staging or blocking of characters or actors, relative to the camera. In the simplest case, imagine two characters facing each other in a shot, with a line connecting character A to character B. The camera can be on either side of this line, but to maintain continuity, it should not cross the line. This is called the 180 rule because this line creates 180 degrees of freedom for the camera, but the camera cannot go a full 360 degrees around the character. From the camera's point of view, if character A is on the left and character B is on the right of the screen, and the camera were to cross the line, the characters would appear to switch sides, and thus confuse the viewer. Typically, all cameras for a shot or group of shots should stay on the same side of the line. If a new character enters or leaves, then a new 180 degree line can be created and used.

acting. Animation is acting. Always keep this in mind. What are your character's motivation and emotional state? Such information should be revealed in your performances. A shot's story can't be told if the characters are simply moving through the scene without any indication of intention or personality. Always ask why. Every movement should have a purpose. Arbitrary motions rarely contribute anything to a character's performance. Contrasts are an important element in acting as well. Animating the same character with significant contrasts in timing can imply completely different personalities and motivations.

animatic. *See also* storyboard. Sometimes images in a storyboard are filmed with audio and are timed so each image is recorded for the appropriate amount of time. This produces a sort of pseudo-animation with hard cuts at key points. This is known as an animatic. It is also known as a Leica reel (original term), pose reel, or, more commonly, a story reel.

animating on 1s/2s. *See also* frames per second, FPS. Basically, 1s and 2s refers to how long a drawing is held when it is shot. (This is a traditional animation term.) For example, film is 24 frames every second. If there is a new drawing every frame (i.e., 24 per second), then it is shot/animated on 1s. However, one could draw 12 frames of animation and shoot each image for two frames. This is animating on 2s. The result is, in most cases, indistinguishable. However, some fast-paced actions or those actions in which a panning background is involved usually require animating on single frames.

animation. The illusion of life and motion typically created by displaying sequential images in rapid succession.

animation cels. The individual character (or prop requiring animation) painting on clear celluloid, which is photographed along with other cels and a background in a setup, creating the complete image for a single frame of film.

arcs. In nature, almost all actions move in an arc due to the physical makeup of humans and other creatures. When creating animation, one should try to have motion follow curved paths rather than linear ones. This will help to eliminate the robotic look often associated with early CG animation.

anticipation. *See also* follow-through. Action in animation usually occurs in three sections: the setup for the motion, the actual action, and then the follow-through of the action. The first part is known as anticipation. In some cases anticipation is needed physically. For example, before you can throw a ball you must first swing your arm backward. The backward motion is the anticipation; the throw itself is the motion. In addition, anticipation is used to lead the viewers' eyes to prepare them for the action that follows. Generally a greater amount of anticipation is needed for faster actions.

appeal. Appeal means anything that a person likes to see. This can be quality of charm, design, simplicity, communication, or magnetism. Appeal can be gained by correctly utilizing other principles, such as exaggeration in design, avoiding twins, using overlapping action, and others. One should strive to avoid weak or awkward design, shapes, and motion.

background paintings. A painting or other artwork depicting the environment in which the character operates is the background painting. First, the background stylist made small color sketches called key backgrounds, which were created to establish the color scheme and mood. These keys acted as a model for the other background artists to follow. Key backgrounds were also referred to as preliminary backgrounds. Backgrounds which were rejected or cut from the film were called N.G. backgrounds. Although hundreds of animation drawings and cels would be required for a scene, typically there was only one background. A setup featuring a cel and background from the same scene is often incorrectly referred to as a key background setup, but a more accurate description would be a matching background setup.

blocking. This term comes from traditional theater, where it means figuring out where the actors will be on the set at specified points in the script. For computer animation, the definition is basically the same. Usually blocking means a very rough animation pass that shows the characters in the scene with a basic set of poses and timing to get a feel for how the shot will look. It can be very, very rough, as in simple block shapes moving around, or it can be more detailed, with actual poses off of which a more finished animation could be based. Blocking can also be defined as the act of protecting oneself from another animator after giving a scathing critique of his or her work.

A third method of animating, as opposed to straight-ahead or pose-to-pose. This method (very often utilized in CG) involves initially establishing the overall posing, timing, and trajectories of your character as a "blocking" phase. Details are added after these global issues are refined and approved. Similar to the (sometimes) preferred method of painting, in which the overall composition and colors are established rather abstractly and the image slowly comes together as a whole as the details are refined with smaller and smaller brushes, as opposed to finishing one corner of the painting before moving on to another. This blocking/refining method is especially desirable in CG so that global timing can be refined before there is a huge number of keyframes to tweak.

cels. Sheets of clear plastic, containing the images of the characters, which are placed over a background, and then photographed in succession to give the illusion of movement in the completed film. The outline of the image, whether hand-inked or Xeroxed, is applied to the front of the cel. The colors are painted by hand onto the back of the cel to eliminate brushstrokes.

character model sheets. Standardized renderings of characters, expressions, props, and costumes. Character designs would be created by concept artists or lead animators, and once they were approved, photographic stats called model sheets would be produced and distributed to the various departments to ensure absolute consistency between the sketches of all of the artists working on a project. Hundreds of photostats would be produced from a single paste-up, consisting of various drawings trimmed and applied to a board. Sometimes animators would create their own model sheets, traced from their own or other artists' drawings.

cleanup. Tracings of the original animation roughs, which are often more detailed and refined than the drawings that preceded them. Created by the assisting department, these clean drawings represent the final stage of animation before the image is transferred to the cel via hand-inking or xerography. These sketches often include colored lines to indicated different ink colors, color markups to tell the painters which areas to paint which colors, and notes to the ink and paint department about parts of the character that needed to be registered to other characters or background elements.

color model cels. A cel created by the ink and paint department to act as an example for inkers and painters to follow. Color models may be exact duplicates of the cels appearing in the film, or they may be test models, exploring various inking techniques or color palettes. Although many collectors assume that color models are less valuable than cels used under the camera, this is not always the case. Since color model cels acted as an example for the inkers and painters to follow, great care was taken to make them absolutely flawless. Cels under the camera occasionally had flaws due to repairs or corrections quickly done in the heat of production.

composition. *See also* staging and silhouette. Composition of an animation, like composition of a painting, requires an interesting mix of positive space (your subject) and negative space (your background) while providing a clear focus point for your audience to "find" the action within the frame. As a general rule, symmetry in composition is a no-no. It's more interesting to see things out of balance.

concept art. Inspirational sketches or paintings used to establish the situations, color choices, or mood of a particular sequence. These are rendered in a wide range of media, from pastels and graphite to watercolor and computer-generated images.

cut. A clean, abrupt change from one scene to another.

dailies. Animation or footage that has been developed and printed overnight. Many CG houses will render out sequences overnight and then discuss changes needed the next morning in "dailies" sessions.

details. Sometimes the difference between a good animation and a great animation comes from effective attention to detail. You never know where a viewer's eyes may be wandering. Just because the main focus of a shot is on your character's face, don't forget to animate the toes. Details such as thigh muscles jiggling when a foot hits the ground add to the naturalism of a performance and can help tell the story. Introducing naturalistic imperfections will also add to the believability of your shot. Keep in mind, however, that it is usually not desirable to confuse the action with too many details. Watch out for technical glitches such as geometry intersections and IK "pops." Material integrity is also an important detail to consider. Is it appropriate to squash and stretch a rigid object, such as a stone? Some animators will do this as an aesthetic choice. Others prefer to follow realistic rules of physics. And don't try to hide animation errors behind overly detailed modeling, lighting, texture maps, and particle effects. This is an undesirable variation of the "attention to detail" concept.

ease-in/ease-out. This term deals with the positioning of an object between key frames. In most computer software you can adjust the speed at which an object enters or leaves a key frame. By making an object slow down as it approaches (ease-in) or slowly speed up as it leaves (ease-out), you can smooth out action. For example, when a ball is bouncing it will slowly come to a stop at the top of its climb (ease-in), and then slowly accelerate as it rushes toward the ground (ease-out). Obviously the amount of drawings will be greater the slower the action. The action of the ball slowing down as it runs out of vertical energy will require a slow-in to the key at that point. Conversely, as the ball starts to drop from that key frame, it will slow-out.

exaggeration. The idea behind exaggeration is to accent the action. This is often used in situations in which comedic effect is desired. It is akin to caricature in the cartoon world, where you accent certain facial or body attributes. However, it should be balanced and not used arbitrarily. One should figure out the reason for an action (or even sound effects, character design, and so on) and how to exaggerate the needed sections.

exposure sheet. A form an animator fills out that has detailed camera instructions for each frame. It may also have some of the same information as a bar sheet. Also known as an X-sheet. Some 3D software, especially dialogue/lip sync software, contains virtual exposure sheets.

Field, 12. An industry-standard size for cels, backgrounds, and drawings, measuring roughly 10 1/2" by 12 1/2".

Field, 16. An industry-standard size for cels, backgrounds, and drawings, measuring roughly 12 1/2" by 16 1/2".

fielding. Refers to the size of the area on the artwork that falls within the sight of the camera. Thus, a 12 field is roughly 12 inches across, and a 9 field is 9 inches across. Even though a drawing or cel may be of a standard 12 or 16 field size, the camera may have been zoomed in to an 8 or 9 field, focusing on a tighter area of the artwork, eliminating the outer margins of the sheet. Most early pictures conformed to a field referred to as the academy format. Later films, which were shot in widescreen or Cinemascope, had a more rectangular active area.

fielding: panning shots. Wider cels, backgrounds, and drawings were used in moving camera shots. A good example of a pan background would be in *The Flintstones*, where a character is running in place and the background element is rolling by. This is actually a repeat background because the panning element would be rolled back and reshot (hence the repetition of objects in the background). In films shot in Cinemascope or Technirama (such as *Lady and the Tramp* or *Sleeping Beauty*), panning cels were used in many scenes to accommodate the wider fields needed for the widescreen process.

follow-through. *See also* anticipation. Follow-through is the movement at the end of a motion. In most cases objects don't stop suddenly, but tend to travel a little farther past their end point. Objects of varying weights will come to rest at differing times. For example, when throwing a ball, after releasing the ball your arm will continue to move a bit. This is known as follow-through. Drapery and hair are obvious examples; their light weight means that they will tend to remain in motion after most other body parts have come to rest.

forces. An object moves when forces are applied to it. Consider where these forces are coming from. Are they being generated from within (desire, intention, muscle movement) or from without (gravity, the wind, a push from another character)? The origin, magnitude, direction, and duration of these forces will dictate how your characters move. How is your character affected by these forces? Does your character resist them or does he "go with the flow?" Do multiple forces cancel out one another? Understand a force's "attack and decay." How powerful is the initial hit of the force? How long does an object continue reacting to the force? Consider the material of the object. Rubber decays slower than cloth.

frame. A frame is the unit of time used in creating animation. Essentially there is one image per frame. Each drawing or frame is shown sequentially, and the images appear to move. A frame is also a single, complete picture in video or film recording.

frames per second (FPS). This is the rate at which animation frames are displayed. NTSC Television in the U.S. and Canada shows 30 images every second, so animation on TV is played at 30 FPS. PAL format used in Europe and SECAM in France use 25 FPS. Film uses 24 FPS.

hold. *See also* moving hold. A hold is a period of time in which a character remains in one pose. In general, having a character remain completely stationary kills the illusion of life. Therefore, holds are usually implemented as moving holds—unless of course you are dealing with cheaper limited television animation, where one drawing may hold for a long period due to budget constraints.

hookups and continuity. To maintain flow and readability, each scene needs to "cut" properly to the next. Are the spatial relationships between your characters consistent from one scene to the next? Does an object's trajectory look like it continues sensibly after a camera cut? Does the new camera position confuse the clarity of the action? If you cut away from a particular action and then return later, do the changes in the scene make sense with the length of the time lapse? Do your actions overlap? Should they? Sometimes it is desirable to intentionally break the rules of continuity, but care should be taken when doing so.

in-betweens, in-betweener. Typically, animation is created by posing an object at a specific position at a given time. The position of an object between any two "key" poses is the in-between pose. Most computer software allows the animator to create these key poses while the software "in-betweens" the additional frames.

In traditional animation, animators typically drew "key" poses/drawings, and the in-between drawings were taken care of by another animator, also called an "in-betweener."

key frame. 3D animation is usually created by posing a character in a specific way at a given frame. This frame is called a key frame. Usually you position an object at two different frames and let the computer in-between the motion between these key poses. In traditional animation, the animator usually draws key cels, and the in-betweener creates the motion between the poses.

Note that these poses do not need to be the extremes (though typically they are). For example, in releasing a thrown ball the two extremes might be the arm coiled back and then out very straight and stretched (for follow-through). Then there would be an additional key frame of the arm coming back to a more natural position but still out (end of the follow-through). So those are three key drawings. But the most extreme is in the middle.

layout drawing. A detailed pencil drawing that indicates the fielding, the character's action, or the design of the background, which acts as the scenery behind the character. There are two types of layouts: character layouts, which outline the character's path of movement, expressions, and action within the scene; and the background layout, which generally consists of a line drawing of the environment in which the character exists. These layouts are used as reference by the animator and the background painter, respectively.

Leica reel. *See* animatic.

moving hold. A moving hold is one in which a character stays in one basic pose for a period of time but still has some part or all of him subtly moving. This movement can help keep the illusion that the character is alive. Anything from animating a breathing ribcage to animating eye blinks can be used to create a moving hold. In general, two very close poses are in-betweened. The result is a slight motion that keeps the character from looking frozen.

overlapping action. When objects with loose parts or appendages move, these parts tend to move with a different timing than the main section. The difference in timing of these loose parts is known as overlapping action. For example, if a dog is running and comes to a stop, its ears will tend to continue to swing forward and then back, and will stop moving after the dog itself has stopped. This overlap tends to create more interesting and realistic animation.

Another important note is that no action should come to a complete stop before another action is started. Even though ideas should be presented clearly (*see* staging) there should be some overlap in activity and action to maintain continuity.

pencil test. *See also* rough. With drawn animation, each sequence is usually first checked by filming the original drawings. This allows the animators to see any potential problems and fix the animation before the cels are actually inked and painted. This is the same concept as a preview test (Playblast) in 3D computer graphics.

planning ahead. It's always a good idea to plan out a performance before starting. Act out the motion with a stopwatch and take down some numbers. This is very important in stop-motion, where it's impossible to go back and fix an individual part of a performance after it has been filmed. It's especially important to plan ahead when you have a deadline. Most of us rarely have the opportunity to animate by trial and error. As the carpenters say: Measure twice, cut once.

personality. This word isn't actually a principle of animation, but refers to the correct application of the other principles. Personality determines the success of an animation. The idea is that the animated creature really becomes alive and enters the true character of the role. One character would not perform an action the same way in two different emotional states. No two characters would act the same. It is also important to make the personality of a character distinct, but at the same time familiar to the audience.

posing. A subset of staging. Interesting poses are extremely important for effective and natural-looking animation. Pay attention to center of gravity issues. (Does your character look as if he's going to fall down?) It's usually a good idea to avoid too much symmetry in your poses. One hip is often a little higher than the other. Weight is rarely distributed evenly over both feet. How does the silhouette read? This is more or less a subcategory of "staging" and "appeal," but, again, it is so important that I think it should be listed separately. Pay close attention to anatomy (understand the underlying structure) and "appealing" poses. Watch out for center-of-gravity placement and off-balance problems, as well as twinning or symmetrical poses.

pose-to-pose animation. *See also* straight-ahead animation. One of two basic approaches to animation. Pose-to-pose animation is created by drawing or setting up key poses and then drawing or creating in-between images. This is the basic computer "key frame" approach to animation. It is excellent for tweaking timing and planning out the animation ahead of time.

rotoscope. This is a machine that projects a live actor on film to an animation disc. The device was patented in the 1920s by the Fleischer brothers and was designed to allow animation to be matched to live action. Max Fleischer was among Bray's most illustrious graduates, contributing an innovative little series called *Out of the Inkwell*. Koko (sometimes spelled "Ko-Ko") was its star, debuting in a one-minute 1916 outing called, simply enough, *Out of the Inkwell*. Koko was the first 'toon to be rotoscoped, with Max's brother, Dave, acting out the clown's part for animators to trace. The character wasn't rotoscoped all the time, however, because the process proved not quite the labor-saver Max, who invented it, had hoped it would be.

rough. *See also* pencil test. Traditionally, a rough is a drawing or sequence that shows the general motion but lacks details. With computers, a rough is usually a quick first-pass animation typically lacking things such as finger or facial movement, or subtle secondary and overlapping action.

A rough is also the original, first-generation sketch by the animators in creating the movement in a scene. Roughs can be divided into three basic types: key drawings, which were drawn by the principle animators themselves; breakdowns, which were drawn by both animator and his assistant; and in-betweens, which were the work of the assistant animators alone. Generally, the animator would sketch out a key drawing for every five or six frames and leave the drawings between his keys for the assistants to fill in. Once the rough animation was approved, the drawings would be delivered to the assisting department for cleanup. Many animation art collectors prefer roughs to cleanups because they are often more spontaneous and full of life, and they are more likely to be the work of a lead animator.

secondary action. Secondary action is an action that occurs because of another action. Think of a jolly, fat man walking briskly down the street. The bouncing of his jowls and belly and any other loose bits could be described as secondary action. It creates interest and realism in the animation. In addition, secondary action should be staged such that it can be noticed but it still does not overpower the main action.

silhouette. *See also* staging, composition, and twins. From the camera's perspective, a silhouette is the shape of the subject as contrasted from the background. A "clear" silhouette is one in which you can not only distinguish where the character is in the shot, but what action is being portrayed as well. Keep in mind that as your camera moves in relation to the character, the character silhouette also changes. And in CG, it's usually not for the better.

simplicity. Don't unnecessarily overcomplicate your scene, character, or performance. Do just enough to tell the story. Too much secondary action and too many details can sometimes confuse the issue and render the idea unclear.

slow-in/slow-out. *See* ease-in/ease-out.

snap. Snap is action that happens quicker than the eye or frame rate. It's the kind of timing that is most associated with "snappy timing." If you watch your fingers as you snap them, you'll find that it's hard to see the finger in mid-snap. The most you might see is a blur between the snap positions. To animate something happening this fast effectively requires anticipation (antic) and follow-through to help convey the action.

Another way to think of this is the character who tends to move quickly from one pose to another in only a few frames. Computer animation has a tendency to look very flowing and mushy, and it is a good idea to work on timing and editing spline curves to add some snap to your animation.

A note of warning! There is another term that is sometimes used, which is "snap and drag." This refers to a quick change of direction due to a wavelike or whiplike motion. For example, with a whip there comes a point where the end of the whip is moving outward while the base mass moves the other way. The tip is essentially dragging behind until it suddenly snaps back the other way. This is known as "snap and drag."

staging. *See also* silhouette, composition, and twins. Staging is presenting an action or item so that it is easily understood. In general, action is presented one item at a time. If too much is going on, the audience will be unsure what to look at and the message you are trying to convey will be unclear. One important facet of staging is working in silhouette. This means that a pose of an object or character can be interpreted even in black-and-white silhouette. In most cases, if you cannot "read" the pose of a character in silhouette, it is not a strong pose and should probably be changed.

straight-ahead animation. *See also* pose-to-pose animation. There are two basic methods to creating animation. Straight-ahead animation is one in which the animator draws or sets up objects one frame at a time in order. For example, the animator draws the first frame of the animation, then draws the second, and so on until the sequence is complete. In this way there is one drawing or image per frame that the animator has set up. This approach tends to yield a more creative and fresh look, but can be difficult to time correctly as well as difficult to hit marks and follow layouts.

storyboard. *See also* animatic. Storyboards are drawings used to visualize the story and animation that is to be created. Typically, there is a drawing for any key point or change in camera angle. By looking at each image sequentially, one can plan out the shots that will be used in an animation. Drawings can be moved around to change the order or timing. The level of detail in acting and posing will vary due to production demands. Television storyboards are typically more detailed because the actual production of the animation is typically done overseas, demanding a much more focused approach.

story reel. *See* animatic.

successive breaking of joints. *See also* arcs and overlapping action. This refers the idea that a chain of objects linked together will move or rotate successively one after another, instead of all coming into position at the same time. This is similar to a whiplike motion in which the base moves, then middle section, and then the end. Imagine an arm reaching out to grab something. The base or upper arm would come to extension first, followed by the lower arm, and then slightly later by the hand. By offseting key frames instead of making each part of the arm have the same timing, the motion is more fluid and natural-looking.

Note that this is somewhat related to overlapping action in that many items animated for overlapping action will utilize a breaking joints–type motion. In the dog ears overlapping action example given for that definition, one would expect the ears to smoothly bend with the base reaching forward before the tips—in other words, each part of the ear "joint" is keyed slightly later working down the hierarchy. However, successive breaking of joints can be used for standard motion as well as in the arm reaching sample mentioned a moment ago.

squash and stretch. Squash and stretch is a way of deforming an object such that it shows how rigid and/or heavy an object is. For example, if a rubber ball bounces and hits the ground, it will tend to flatten at its base and distort in its general shape when it hits. This is the squash principle. As it starts to bounce up, it will stretch in the direction it is going. One important note about squash and stretch is that no matter how radically an object deforms, it should still appear to retain its volume.

timing. *See also* snap. Timing is the speed of an action. Timing is critical in animation because, among other things, it determines how characters are perceived. For example, a character who blinks his eyes quickly will appear awake and alert. The same motion done slowly will make the character seem sleepy or drowsy. This is obviously a very simplified explanation of timing. Its influences are all-encompassing and will have an effect on every piece of work you do. Timing—or rather, *good* timing—is critical to your scene's success. Bad timing will render even the most beautifully realized drawings a failure. To put it simply, a joke told with bad timing is not funny.

tweening. *See* in-betweens.

twins. *See also* staging and silhouette. When posing a character, one should pay attention to making sure the pose is not symmetrical—in other words, a character is not standing with his weight perfectly centered, both hands in the same position, shoulders and feet horizontal, and so on. When a pose is symmetrical and therefore unnatural (and boring), the problem is known as "twins." You should try to keep poses asymmetrical, and you can even do this for things such as eyes and blinks, mouth curves, other details, and actions. For example, for an action in which a character is jumping, you would animate one foot or leg hitting the ground before the other so they don't both hit at the same time. The point is that it is related to both the pose of the character and the timing of the actions of the parts of the character, or even multiple characters.

A good example of a natural standing pose without twins would be the contrapposto. This is an classic art term, particularly evident in ancient Greek sculpture. When standing, a human puts more weight on one foot than the other. On the side that has the most weight, the hip rotates up and the shoulder rotates down toward the hips, while the spine is shaped slightly like an arc. This makes the pose appear more natural and less stiff.

To maintain natural-looking performances, it is usually desirable to break up the motion of individual body parts so they are not doing the exact same thing at the exact same time. For example, when slapping your character's hands on a table, you might want the left hand to hit a frame or two before the right. A variation of the twinning concept is when members of a swarm or flock are exactly mimicking one another. Pay attention to the overall "texture" when animating groups of objects or characters. Consider a flock of birds or a field of grass reacting to the wind. What is the overall feel of the group? Is there enough variety in the trajectories of the individual elements? Is every bird flapping its wings at the exact same frequency? Is the wind affecting every blade of grass in exactly the same manner at exactly the same time? Are the individual elements supposed to be working together? If so, are you using an appropriate amount of variation between these individuals? Are your synchronized swimmers exactly synchronized? If so, is this intentional? Even when individual members of a group try to copy one another exactly, minor variations often occur.

weight. Demonstrating the implied mass of a character. This is a function of the proper application of squash and stretch, anticipation, follow-through, overlap, timing, exaggeration, and slow-in/slow-out. Whether or not a character looks especially heavy or especially light when getting up from a chair is dependent upon how these principles are applied. A heavier object requires more force to set it in motion. This is often demonstrated by increasing anticipation. Likewise, it requires more force to slow, stop, or reverse the direction of a heavier object. Placement of your character's center of gravity is an important aspect of weight. Physics dictate that a static object's center of gravity must be directly above or below the average of its point(s) of suspension. For instance, when you stand on one foot, your center of gravity needs to be directly above your support foot. Otherwise, you will begin to fall. Of course, this all changes if you are in motion. Pay attention to pivot/leverage points as well. Watch out for movements among isolated body parts. Even the simplest arm move often involves contributing motion from the shoulder and torso.

X-sheet. *See* exposure sheet.

These terms have been compiled from the following lists:

◆ The Fundamental Principles of Animation (updated 6/28/03)
Jeremy Cantor – Animation Supervisor – Sony Pictures Imageworks – May 4, 2002.
http://www.zayatz.com/text/twelve_principles_plus.htm.

◆ CG-CHAR Glossary.
http://www.comet-cartoons.com/3ddocs/cgfaq.html#section4.

◆ The ScratchPost Industry Definitions.
http://www.thescratchpost.com/resources/fx/vfx_dict_a.shtml.

Appendix G
Computer Animation Terms

aliasing. *See also* anti-aliasing. A form of image distortion caused by sampling frequencies being too low to faithfully reproduce image detail.

Examples include:

◆ Temporal aliasing (for example, rotating wagon wheel spokes apparently reversing direction)

◆ Raster scan aliasing (for example, twinkling or strobing effects on sharp horizontal lines)

◆ Stair-stepping: stepped or jagged edges of angled lines (for example, at the slanted edges of letters)

anti-aliasing. A form of interpolation used when combining images; pixels along the transitions between images are averaged to provide a smooth transition.

A/B roll. Video editing arrangement in which scenes are edited from two source VCRs (A and B) to a third (recording) VCR. Typically, a switcher or mixer is used to provide transition effects between sources. Control over the machines and process can be done manually or automatically using an edit controller.

aspect ratio. The relationship of width and height of a pixel. When an image is displayed on different screens, the aspect ratio must be kept the same to avoid stretching in either the vertical or horizontal direction. For standard TVs or monitors, the aspect ratio is 4:3, yielding 160×120, 320×240, and 640×480 sizes. The HDTV video format has an aspect ratio of 16 to 9 (16:9).

B-spline. *See also* spline. These are a type of spline in which the curve passes close to, but not through, the control points or knots. They are currently popular for use in spline-based modeling and are similar to NURBS. With these splines, you're dealing with the hull rather than the actual surface.

Bezier spline. Bezier splines and cardinal splines have their curves pass through the actual control points. Beziers have handles to achieve this. The handles control the tangent to the curve at each control point.

bitmap. Representation of characters or graphics by individual pixels arranged in row (horizontal) and column (vertical) order. Each pixel can be represented by one bit (simple black and white) or up to 32 bits (high-definition color). Also referred to as a raster image.

bluescreen. A film or video technique in which an object or performer is taped against a blue-colored background. In post-production, the blue color is electronically removed, allowing images to be combined. Also, the film industry's term for chroma key.

chatter. This is a term that can be used to describe jerkiness in motion. Typically it occurs when an object has too many key frames close together that are different. This makes the object appear to vibrate. This can occur when trying to manually key frame feet to appear locked to the ground without inverse kinematics. The legs may have many key frames that are slightly different, so they appear to have "chatter." This term can also be applied to digital paint. If an object is not painted consistently in film, it will "chatter."

clip. A continuous set of frames from a source tape or reel. Also called a scene or take.

D1/D2/D3/D5. Digital video recording and playback formats. The D1 and D5 systems use component video, while the D2 and D3 systems use composite video. By using fully digitized video in recording and playback, many problems such as generation loss and distortion are minimized or eliminated. The digital formats use mainly a 19mm wide magnetic tape (3/4").

- ◆ **D1.** A component digital video tape recording format that conforms to the specifications set in the CCIR 601 standard.
- ◆ **D2.** An 8-bit composite digital videotape recording format in which the composite video signal is digitized by sampling it at the rate of four times the frequency of the subcarrier.
- ◆ **D3.** An unofficial term for a composite digital videotape recording format invented by Panasonic.
- ◆ **D5.** A component digital videotape recording format that conforms to the specifications set in the CCIR 601 standard; Panasonic format.

DDR. Digital Disk Recorder. A high-performance disk recording device used for real-time random-access recording and playback of digital video.

edit. To assemble or modify the audio and video portions of a program, cutting out the bad parts; rearranging scenes; and adding effects, titles, and music.

forward kinematics. *See also* inverse kinematics. Forward kinematics, or FK, refers to how a basic hierarchy or chain of objects is animated. With FK, each joint in a chain is rotated individually. In order to pose or position a segment at the end of the chain, each previous link needs to be manually rotated into position. Many software packages in the past only had FK, which meant keeping a character's feet stationary or locked to the ground had to be done by manually rotating the legs when the character moved. Currently, many animators use inverse kinematics for feet locking.

Gimbal lock. With certain types of computer rotations, it is possible to lose an axis of rotation—in other words, you can rotate around, say, X and Y, but not Z. What happens is the object ends up aligned such that further rotations are about the same axis as before. One way to solve this problem is to add a dummy/null object as a parent of the object being rotated. Then you can rotate both the object and the dummy to get the desired orientation.

GUI. Graphical User Interface. An application, such as Microsoft Windows, that lays on top of other applications and provides a user interface based on graphical icons.

inverse kinematics. *See also* forward kinematics. Inverse kinematics, or IK, is a way to animate a hierarchy, or chain of objects, such that each link in the chain is automatically rotated so that a lower segment is at a specific position or orientation. For example, with an IK leg setup, an animator would position a foot. The legs would automatically bend to accommodate the position of the foot. As the character's main body moves, the IK chain (in this case, the legs) would rotate properly so the end chain, or foot, stays locked. This is one use of IK. Some animators prefer to use IK for the upper body, such as the spine or arms, as well.

matte. A solid color signal that may be adjusted for chrominance, hue, and luminance. Matte is used to fill areas of keys and borders.

model. In 3D computer animation, a model is an object represented inside of the computer. Essentially, it is a virtual object than can be colored, textured, and animated.

motion capture. Motion capture (mo-cap) in computer graphics is a way to digitally record position and motion information from the real world. A real actor can move, and that motion can be used inside of 3D animation software.

It is similar in idea to the rotoscope, a machine that projects a live actor on film to an animation disc. It is a device, patented in the 1920s by the Fleischer brothers, designed to allow animation to be matched to live action. It was later employed to create cheap but very humanlike animation, which is generally reviled by classic animators.

Motion capture is not without controversy, however. The goal of animation is not to create humanlike motion, but to impart unique personalities to animated characters, to give them the "illusion of life." Both the rotoscope and motion capture impose human motion on animated characters, which makes them seem flat and lifeless in comparison to those animated or hand-keyframed by skilled artists. In the case of the rotoscope, artists trace human motion but interpret it with the model of the animated character. In the case of motion capture, human motion is copied directly to the animated character. The temptation to use this captured motion and call it "animation" has led computer animators practiced in the art of traditional animation to call it "Satan's Rotoscope."

NURBS. *See also* spline. This acronym stands for Non-Uniform Rational B-Splines. These are a type of spline in which the curve passes close to but not through the control points or knots. They are currently popular for use in spline-based modeling and are similar to B-splines. With these splines, you're dealing with the hull rather than the actual surface. NURBS goes one step further than B-splines in that you can have different "weights" assigned to the hull-knots, giving you more control over the curves of your splines.

NTSC format. A color television format having 525 scan lines, a field frequency of 60 Hz, a broadcast bandwidth of 4 MHz, line frequency of 15.75 KHz, frame frequency of 1/30 of a second, and a color sub-carrier frequency of 3.58 MHz.

overlay. The ability to superimpose computer graphics over a live or recorded video signal and store the resulting video image on videotape. It is often used to add titles to videotape. In video, the overlay procedure requires synchronized sources for proper operation.

overscan. Video images generally exceed the size of the physical screen. The edge of the picture may or may not be displayed to allow variations in television sets. The extra area is called the overscan area. Video productions are planned so critical action only occurs in the center safe title area. Professional monitors are capable of displaying the entire video image, including the overscan area.

pixel. An abbreviation for picture element. The minimum raster display element, represented as a point with a specified color or intensity level. One way to measure picture resolution is by the number of pixels used to create the image.

polygon. *See also* spline. In computer graphics, models are typically created either with polygons or splines. A polygon is a 2D shape that exists inside of the 3D computer world. These are typically triangles or squares. By creating polygons in specific locations, 3D objects are made. For example, six square polygons can be arranged to create a cube object.

pre-visualization. A method used in feature film development that utilizes virtual sets by placing actors in scene mockups to test the viability of a set.

rendering. Rendering is the creation of images in the computer from the modeling, lighting, texturing, and animation information.

resolution. A measure of the ability to reproduce detail. Generally, referred to as horizontal resolution and evaluated by establishing the number of horizontal lines, which are clearly discernible on a test pattern. Resolution specifications are not very well standardized, especially as stated in connection with monitors. Using the rule of thumb of 80 lines per MHz of bandwidth, VHS and 8mm typically achieve 240 lines of resolution, S-VHS and Hi-8 achieve 400, and broadcast achieves 330.

RGB. Red-Green-Blue. A type of computer display output signal composed of separately controllable red, green, and blue signals. The other technique for output display is composite video, which typically offers less resolution than RGB. Using a color encoder in conjunction with sync information, a complete composite video signal composed of luminance, chrominance, and sync can be generated from RGB.

safe title area. Generally, the center 80 percent of the entire overscan video image area or the area that will display legible titles regardless of how a TV monitor is adjusted.

spline. *See also* B-spline, NURBS, Bezier spline, and cardinal spline. Splines are a way to describe curves with mathematical expressions. In computer graphics, splines are used to control motion as well as to create spline surfaces used for models.

technical director (TD). In large animation houses, jobs are typically broken down to specialists. Two main jobs are animator and technical director. While the animator deals with movement, the technical director tends to deal with modeling, texturing, lighting, setup, and rendering. In some houses the TD's job is further broken down to have people who only model, light scenes, and so on.

time code. A frame-by-frame address code time reference recorded on the spare track of a videotape or inserted in the vertical blanking interval for editing purposes. When decoded, the time code identifies every frame of a videotape using digits reading hours: minutes: seconds: and frames (for example, 02: 04: 48: 26). Each individual video frame is assigned a unique address, a must for accurate editing. The three time code systems used for video are VITC, LTC, and RC (consumer).

underscan. The opposite of overscan. In underscan, a video or computer image is reduced so that all four edges are visible onscreen, leaving it surrounded by black borders. Underscan is used to show what is happening in the blanking period and at the beginning and end of scan lines and frames. Underscanning can uncover latent image problems for identification and correction.

We would like to thank Michael Comet and Viviana Palacios for their industry definitions online. These terms have been compiled from the following lists:

◆ CG-CHAR Glossary:
http://www.comet-cartoons.com/3ddocs/cgfaq.html.

◆ The ScratchPost Industry Definitions:
http://www.thescratchpost.com/resources/fx/vfx_dict_a.shtml

Appendix H
Further Reading

Animation Magazine. http://www.animationmagazine.net.

Blair, Preston. *Cartoon Animation (The Collector's Series)*. Quayside Publishing Group, 1995.

Canemaker, John. *Walt Disney's Nine Old Men and the Art of Animation*. Disney Editions, 2001.

Caroselli, Henry M. *Cult of the Mouse: Can We Stop Corporate Greed from Killing Innovation in America?* Ten Speed Press, 2004.

Cantor, Jeremy. "The 12 (er...24) Fundamental Principles of Animation." http://www.zayatz.com/text/twelve_principles_plus.htm.

Cinefex Magazine. http://www.cineflex.com/store.html.

Culhane, Shamus. *Animation: From Script to Screen*. St. Martin's Griffin, 1990.

Egri, Lajos. *Art of Dramatic Writing: Its Basis in the Creative Interpretation of Human Motives*. Touchstone, 1972.

Ghez, Didier, Ed.*Walt's People: Talking Disney With the Artists Who Knew Him*. Xlibris Corporation, 2005.

Hooks, Ed. *Acting for Animators, Revised Edition: A Complete Guide to Performance Animation*. Heinemann Drama, 2003.

Johnston, Ollie and Frank Thomas. *The Illusion of Life: Disney Animation*. Disney Editions, 1995. Chapter three, paraphrased by Nataha Lightfoot. http://frankandollie.com/PhysicalAnimation.html.

Mascelli, Joseph V. *The Five C's of Cinematography: Motion Picture Filming Techniques*. Silman-James Press, 1998.

Muybridge. Eadweard. *Muybridge's Complete Human Animation and Animal Locomotion: New Volume 1*. Dover Publications, 1979.

Newlove, Jean. *Laban for Actors and Dancers: Putting Laban's Movement Theory into Practice: A Step-by-Step Guide*. A Theatre Arts Book, 1993.

Nierenberg, Gerard I. and Henry H. Calero. *How to Read a Person Like a Book*. Pocket, 1990.

Williams, Richard. *The Animator's Survival Kit: A Manual of Methods, Principles, and Formulas for Classical, Computer, Games, Stop Motion, and Internet Animators*. Faber & Faber, 2002.

Appendix I
Rigging Blog

Javier Solsona was kind enough to build the rig for our clown mascot. This appendix contains the blog he wrote during the process. Because there is no guarantee that the blog will remain online, we reprinted it here for posterity.

Sunday, July 24, 2005: First Steps

I've been asked by Angie Jones to rig a character for her upcoming book. The character I'll be rigging is the mascot for the book. I thought it would be nice to show how I go about developing the character, the R&D steps, etc., etc. I'll share as much as I can with everybody. Depending on what it is, I might share scripts, some test files, ideas, stills, etc. The character is very cartoony, so it'll be heavily based on squash and stretch, and the idea is to be able to do as much 2D-type animation on a 3D setup.

Here we go. This is the character.

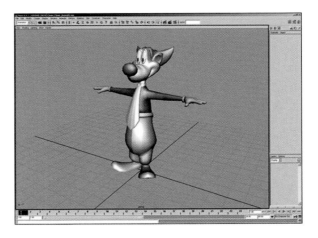

The model is being built by Dan Patterson. He'll take care of the mesh plus all the blend shapes (although those will probably be added on top of some kind of bone-driven setup). The model is great, and it'll be a blast to rig it. There is a lot of potential to do so many cool things. This particular file is a stand-in, and Dan will carry on working on it while I start the rig. I know things will change, but that's okay. This way I can get things going and when the final mesh is finally available, I'll just merge the two files together.

First of all, I like the character to be built in a relaxed pose. Something like 45 degrees, shoulders relaxed, and elbows bent slightly forward. But that's just what I prefer. I find that the deformation is better that way. However, having said that, this is a cartoony character, so we can get away with the arms being at 90 degrees.

The foot design is something that caught my attention. The way that they are right now it might cause a problem because the alignment will be a bit strange and off. But this depends on how it'll be animated. So we'll go with it for the time being. (We can also adjust things later on.)

The rig will be built procedurally. This means that if bones change position a bit, orientation, etc., all that is needed is to re-run the script and there is the new rig. This technique is very, very useful in production, where changes are constantly expected. I already know that there will be a few changes (for example, I know the hands will be touched up quite a bit), so having a procedural rig will be the way to go.

Sunday, July 24, 2005: My Workflow

I love to work with the biggest real estate possible. That's why I pretty much work using the hotbox. Once you get used to it, it's extremely fast. I also create my own custom marking menus. This allows a lot of flexibility, and I can change them according to what I'm working on. I also turn off as many things as I can. I don't use shelves. I don't use the toolbox and I turn off the help bar. This already gives me a much bigger screen to work with. On the side, I use the outliner quite a bit for selecting things and the hyper-graph to get in deep and see in and out connections, etc.

Monday, July 25, 2005: Bones

I got going today with the first pass at laying down the joints.

As a rigger, joint positioning is key, but with these types of character you have to be able to play with different things and see what works best. Because the rig will be built procedurally, it'll be easy to adjust a few bones and re-run the script to get the rig again.

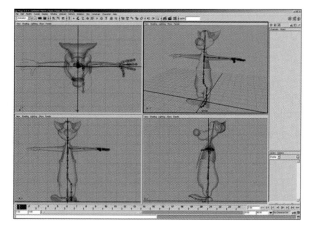

I often find laying out the bones a tricky one, especially on a cartoony character. In this case, the clown has a very long body and super-short legs. The legs—for now I'll treat them as any other leg. I'll deal with them later. The body is interesting. The hips are pretty low, but then the pants go all the way up high and it ends up having a fairly short chest.

I decided to start with some fairly loose ideas and see how things turn out. In the beginning I try not to limit myself too much. I try to work fairly loose and adjust as I go along. I'm also not bothering right now with the face. I'll just leave it as one main head bone. I'll add the whole facial setup later on, when I tackle that part. That's icing on the cake anyway.

I know the hands will change, but still I just put some joints there to help me get going. Even if I end up rigging them, I know it'll be super easy to adjust later on. The feet are also interesting. I'll end up doing a reverse foot lock. But the character has this 45-degree outward rotation on the legs. I brought in the foot and rotated it to be aligned with the world. This way it makes it a lot easier to align the bones to the foot. And I know my joint orientations will be a lot easier to manage. Once I'm happy with it, I'll rotate the foot back to its original position and rotate the joints to match the foot. Lastly, I always work on one side only, usually the left side. Once I'm happy with it I mirror the joints across to the right side.

Monday, July 25, 2005: Flexibility, Flexibility, Flexibility

One of the things I love about rigging is the initial stages, when I get to just think about what I should have on the rig, how I'm going to be doing and approaching things, etc. I don't really work that much on the computer. It's more of a mental exercise. I'll be walking down the street and trying to work out all these problems in my head. If I come up with something that I think might be cool to have, I'll go try it quickly in a fast setup and see how it goes. If it works that's great—I'll try to implement it. If it doesn't, I just move on. For this particular setup, the key is flexibility. The ideal is not to have any restrictions. I would like to be able to pull and push things as I desire. I'm sure there are a few animators out there who would like to be free of restrictions.

Tuesday, July 26, 2005: Mesh Update

I just got a quick little update from Dan (modeler). The clown is starting to get more and more personality.

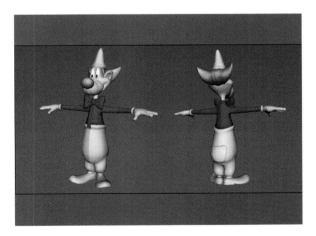

Wednesday, July 27, 2005: First Arm WIP

Okay. I did a little setup a month or so ago when I started thinking about a cartoony character. It still needs quite a bit of tweaking, but the main ideas are there. I wanted a setup where I could use a normal IK/FK setup, but also be able to run free with it. I wanted to have the ability to bend the elbow, so that I wouldn't get a sharp bend. I wanted to have the ability to smooth the curve out whenever I wanted. Something that would look more 2D.

Additionally, I wanted the setup to allow me to go into freeform. Not only should it stretch, but with the help of a few additional controllers the arm should be able to bend and be shaped in any way I want. This should free the animator to work more like a 2D character. The setup is still in the works. There are a lot of things that need to be worked out still. For starters, right now it's assuming that the elbow is halfway between the shoulder and the wrist. The IK/FK switching is a temporary one. And there is a lot of cleaning up to do. Ideally I would like to use the same principle for the legs (should be pretty similar to the arms), but I would also like to extend it to the neck and ultimately to the body. Being able to have this kind of freedom in the body should be the ideal and should free the animators from a lot of the 3D constraints.

Thursday, July 28, 2005: Stretchy IK

I've been doing some research on stretchy IK. Bonus Tools comes with one, but I'm not too convinced about it. For starters, I don't like the fact that it's using scale values to do the stretching. I would rather use translate values. I dug around a bit on the Web and found a great script by David Walden. He has some amazing tools, and the stretchy IK setup that he has going is pretty cool. So I figured I'd base mine off his. I would like to make a few minor modifications here and there. But I must admit, he has done all the hard work on this one.

Thursday, July 28, 2005: Stretchy IK Implemented

I played a bit with the stretchy IK setup and I got it to a level I'm happy enough with for the moment.

Right now it can:

◆ Stretch in IK mode
◆ The bones can have any length (they are not restricted to be halfway between the shoulder and the wrist)
◆ Have a limit set so that it doesn't stretch after a certain distance
◆ Be scaled per bone from the IK controller
◆ Be scaled in FK mode

In the future, I'd like to implement some more ideas I have and make it more robust with better control. But right now it's time to move on with the rest of the setup.

Monday, August 8, 2005: Bendy Leg Test

I've decided to do a quick test and see what would happen if I apply the stretch arm setup to the leg (since I'll be using pretty much the same setup). I was pretty glad to see that everything was working smoothly. Now that I know that the arm setup can be reused for the leg setup, I'll be ironing out a lot of the hard-coded stuff I put in the script.

Initially I like to take the easiest route and just see if things are going to work. Once I'm happy with it, I go back to the script and start making it generic so that I can run it on any bone with any bone name, etc. I try to hard-code the least possible stuff. Nothing should be name-dependent. I also check the code to see if I'm doing repetitive work and if I should be writing separate procedures to take care of certain things. So now it's time to get deep into the code and iron all those little details out.

Tuesday, August 9, 2005: The Ins and Outs of the Stretchy IK

Here is a bit of a high-level description of how the stretchy IK is implemented. Like I mentioned before, my script is heavily based on David Walden's script.

The way it works is as follows (let's assume that the Y axis runs down the bone).

There are two ways of "scaling" a bone. One way is to actually scale it in Y, and the other is to translate the child of the bone in Y (basically moving the position where the child starts). Now, even though it might visually look the same, we get different results in the skinned mesh. Personally, I think that translating the child bone is the way to go. So that's what the script does.

So, in order to scale an IK chain, we have to figure out what the maximum distance is when all the bones are straight. Once we hit this maximum distance, we want to start "scaling" the bones (i.e., translating the children in Y). So, the script goes through all the bones in the chain, checks the translation Y values, and adds them up into a variable that gets stored as the maximum distance.

Once that is done, the value is plugged into a condition node. (BTW, I never use expressions. I don't believe in them. They make Maya slow and I like working with nodes.) If the distance between the start of the chain and the end reaches the maximum length, then the condition node becomes true and a percentage value depending on the new distance that gets applied to the translate Y of each bone in the chain. (We can get this percentage value by dividing the new stretched distance by the original maximum distance we already had.) As simple as that.

On top of this, the script also allows for scaling each bone while in FK mode. This is just an additional layer put on top of what is already built, and it consists of an addition that is done (via a plusMinusAv node) before the new distance is actually plugged into the translate Y value. That's it. I still want to do a few minor modifications (like I need to update the new maximum distance when the bone is scaled in FK). Once that is done I'll post the script up for grabs.

Tuesday, August 9, 2005: Cleanup and Tests

Today I've just done a lot of cleaning up. The code was a mess for the cartoon arm so I wanted to optimize it a bit. I also had huge (and horrible) controllers and I wanted to make things a bit prettier. I also decided to run it through both arms and both legs. Initially it seemed to have worked out perfectly. But a quick skinning showed that the bones in the right side are twisting like crazy when I do the blend between straight and bent arm.

In a way it's strange because the left side works pretty good. So I'll have to do some debugging and maybe rework some areas to build it a bit differently. Once I know it's working properly, I'll write a high-end description on how the setup works. I am happy that things are slowly taking shape. It seems that the problem is that it's not liking the bones to be mirrored. So I might have to reorient them again on the right side. But that's a test for tomorrow.

Thursday, August 11, 2005: Bone Twist When Blending

As expected, the problem with the bones twisting when blending had to do with bone orientation when mirroring them.

The arms were easy to fix since they are in a T pose and orienting them is not a problem. I just ran an orient joint script on both arms and that was that. (It seems that everybody has an orient joint script these days. I end up using mostly Michael Comet's one since it's easy and fast. Somehow it wasn't working too well this time so I used Lluis Llobera's one that is even faster since it automatically picks the child bone so you can go through the whole hierarchy in seconds. Of course, props have to be given to Jason Schleifer, since I believe he is the mastermind behind the first joint orient script, which BTW is a script that I often use too.)

Anyhow, the feet were a bit different because the clown's feet are at a 45-degree angle. This causes problems with orientations. So I aligned them with the world and reoriented them and brought them back out to the 45 degrees. I thought this would do it, but still somehow I was getting weird results. A lot better than before, but still I was getting a lot of twisting.

So I decided to align them to the world again and orient the bones, but this time I didn't rotate them. I built the system this way, and later with the foot IK controller I rotated it to the correct place. This seems to have worked. I still get a small movement on the last joint. It's not too noticeable, but it bothers me so I'll dig in a bit deeper later on to see what could be the problem.

Thursday, August 11, 2005: Da Vinci or Relaxed Pose?

The topic of whether to model and rig a character in the Da Vinci (also known as the T pose) or a relaxed pose has always be a hot topic. Some people swear by one while others swear by the other.

This is my take on it: Both.

I strongly believe that modeling should be done on a relaxed pose. Arms bent at 45 degrees (or somewhere close to the body), elbows bent slightly, and fingers in a relaxed state. Also the legs should be slightly apart with a slight bend on the knees. Basically, a relaxed posed all around. This gives the best deformation. The shoulders are relaxed and there are no extreme poses.

While this is great for modeling, rigging is another matter. You get a lot of weird problems by trying to set up things that are not aligned to the world. So for rigging I like things to be in the standard T pose. Especially the arms, and the feet should be straight down, aligned straight with the world. Now this of course leaves the rig at a different position to the mesh.

There are two approaches that can be taken:

1.) Have two different skeletons: one that is used for skinning and is in the relaxed pose and the other that is in the T pose and used for rigging. Once both the mesh and the rigs are approved, all that needs to be done is to bring both into a new scene and constrain the skinning bones to the rig bones.

2.) Use only one rig. Once the rig is done it can be repositioned to fit inside the mesh, and then you can skin the character from there.

I personally like the first one. It does mean that you get a lot more bones in the scene and there are all the extra connections. But it gives a lot of freedom. Two people can be working on the character at the same time. One could be modeling and skinning and the other rigging. Also, if there is a need to do any changes on either the rig or the model, it can easily be done without having to redo a lot of work since things have become modular.

Saturday, August 13, 2005: Feet

After some tweaking here and there I managed to finally get the leg to act the same way as the arms.

So now with just one script procedure I can quickly not just build the arms, but also build the legs. This helps a lot since I don't have to be writing a different script for different parts of the body. Also it allows for a common language when it comes to the controllers and how the rig will be used.

I originally started building a standard reverse foot lock for the feet. In the beginning I decided to have an extra bone in the feet since they are so long and I thought it would be a nice extra bone. After playing with the idea and building a reverse foot lock, I realized that it wasn't going to work and I had to go back and rethink the approach.

So I decided to reuse once again the arm setup. This time I didn't need to have IK/FK switching since I knew I was going to implement a reverse foot lock to it. So I stripped the IK and the stretchy IK part of the arms (and legs) script and ran it through.

Now I found myself with the bendy setup on the legs (with IK/FK switching) and then another bendy setup on the feet (just FK). So I treated this as if it had no special bend setup on it. After all, the main controllers for the bend setup were just the original bones (foot > ball > toes). So I built the super standard reverse foot lock to it and that was it.

This gave me the freedom to have a normal setup for the feet, and if I wanted I could turn (just like in the arms) the bend option on. By doing this I got a huge amount of freedom in the feet—and one that is very nice to have when you have to deal with those huge cartoony feet.

Sunday, August 14, 2005: Scale Bone (in FK)

I wanted to have a quick way to scale bones while in FK mode.

As I mentioned earlier, I don't like to use the scale values of the bone, I'd rather use the translate values of the child bone. So I decided that the easiest way would be to connect the translate (depending on the orientation of the bone it would be X, Y, or Z) of the child to a custom Scale attribute of the bone. For this I wrote a quick script.

```
global proc gScaleBone(string $bone, string $translateAttribute)
{
    // get the children. We'll add the value in the scale to the translate attribute
    //    in the first child bone
    string $children[] = `listRelatives -children $bone`;
    // add the scale attribute
    addAttr -ln "Scale" -at double -keyable true $bone;

    // create the plusMinusAv node to where we'll add the current length of the bone
    //    plus the new scale attribute
    createNode plusMinusAverage -name ("nodePlusMinusAv_" + $bone);

    // get the current translate attribute of the child
    float $currentTranslate = `getAttr ($children[0] + "." + $translateAttribute)`;
    // puts the current translate value into the plusMinus node
    setAttr ("nodePlusMinusAv_" + $bone + ".input1D[0]") $currentTranslate;
    // connects the scale value to the second input attribute in the plusMinus node
    connectAttr ($bone + ".Scale") ("nodePlusMinusAv_" + $bone + ".input1D[1]");
    // connects the output to the scale of the bone
    connectAttr ("nodePlusMinusAv_" + $bone + ".output1D") ($children[0] + "." +
        $translateAttribute);
}
```

If you want to scale a bone all you have to do is type **gScaleBone("joint1", "translateX");**

Assuming the joint you want to scale is joint1 and the attribute that needs to be connected to it the X translate.

Monday, August 15, 2005: Cartoon Spine

I decided to tackle the area that was worrying me a bit: the spine. I ended up building a system that is mainly controlled by FK but can be overwritten by an IK system with an IK spline connected to it. It sounds a lot more complicated than it really is.

Building it directly in Maya was okay. Not too hard. But that was a controlled environment. The problem right now is building the setup procedurally. There are a lot of different scenarios that can happen, and I want it to be pretty modular so that I could apply it to any number of bones, etc. It has been a real challenge. Once it's finally built I'll do a screen cap to show how it works.

Tuesday, August 16, 2005: Spine Setup

I took a step back today and started thinking about the spine all over again. I knew the result I wanted to get, but it seemed that I was trying to get there in a very complicated way. So I started rethinking about each step and sure enough, there were things that were totally obsolete. So I got rid of them.

In the end, the setup is a fairly simple one: FK spine that drives the CVs of a stretchy spine. The CVs in turn can be overwritten by locators so that we can get the cartoony feel of breaking the rig wherever we want.

Wednesday, August 17, 2005: Clown Update

Here is the latest update from Dan.

He has done an amazing job! I love the hair, and the new reshaped face gives him a lot more personality! Love it.

Thursday, August 18, 2005: Uh Oh

Yesterday was one of those days that just nothing worked.

I decided to expand the arm setup a bit. I wanted to have even greater control. I wanted to make it look like the foot spline IK system that I had implemented already. Things are a bit more complicated on the arms because you have the hands to worry about. After a lot of tries I ended with something I was happy with, and the IK spline arm was looking good. But when I tried to use the FK arms or attach it to the body, things got all crazy. So I decided to pull back to what I had before. It so happens that I didn't keep a backup copy of my setup script and I had made tons of little changes here and there. So it took me a while to get back to what I originally had.

Since I had seen a bit of an explosion when I connected the full arm setup to the spine setup, I decided to also do a quick test on the whole setup. And sure enough, things did not work together. The problem lay on the fact that I had the stretchy IK built onto the arms. And the arms have an IK blend on them to switch between IK and FK. This just didn't work together very well when I moved the spine around. (My FK arms were scaling whenever I moved the spine because the distance between the clavicle and the IK controller was getting bigger. I thought instead of using a distance node I would use Michael Comet's technique to find the distance of the arm, but I wasn't ready to abandon all hope just yet.) Early in the morning, before coming to work, I thought I'd try something different, and I built the good, old, trusted 3-chain IK/FK setup. What I gained with this was isolating the stretchy IK to the normal FK arm. With this I can apply the stretch IK setup to the IK bones and have a completely different setup for the FK arms. Then I just blend from one to the other. So now things work the way they should. I think.

I also took Morgan's advice and I isolated the arms from the spine. I'm still not sure the approach I took is the best. I'll want to work a bit more on it. The way it works is that I've parented the clavicle joints not to the bendy spine nor to the FK controllers, but to a separate one that follows the FK control but can be manipulated whichever way I want. This allows me to overwrite and adjust the clavicle arms if the body and the arms don't align too well. But it still needs some work. I might add a slider to be able to follow either the FK or the bendy spine and still have the option to overwrite. We'll see.

Tuesday, August 23, 2005: A Bit of Cleaning Up

I spent a bit of the time today cleaning up the rig. In a complex rig like this (even in a simple rig), things can get pretty messy; a lot of things are built behind the scenes—IK handles, extra bones, clusters, locators, etc., etc. Before a rig is released to the animators it should be cleaned up of all these things. Only the controllers or bones that are animatable should be visible, and even then some of these can be hidden depending on things like whether IK or FK are active, if the bend option has been turned on or not, etc.

Attributes in the channel box should be hidden and only the ones that can be animated should be available to the animator. Also, if possible, an intuitive pick walking system should be built so that animators can easily select the controllers. On the hypergraph, things should be grouped together accordingly and end up on just one node so it's easy to find all the different parts.

Thursday, August 25, 2005: Slow Progress

It's been rather slow recently.

I'm currently waiting for the latest assets so that I can carry on with the last stages of the rig. I'm waiting to have final geometry so that I can start weighting and testing how the character will deform and see if I have to make any modifications. I'm also waiting for the facial shapes. This will probably be done in a few stages since it has to get done quickly for the book. Once it's done, we'll go back and revise the shapes and make them a lot more robust. Until then I'll carry on cleaning the rig and start making things as bulletproof as a cartoony rig can be made.

Tuesday, August 30, 2005: Still Waiting

I'm still waiting for more updates.

I was hoping to have everything done by the end of the month, but it looks like it won't happen. Since I was waiting, I started thinking on what else I could add, and I thought it might be cool to get each finger a bendy setup. I'm not sure if it'll be a bit of overkill or not. This would pretty much work the same as the foot, where you can go freeform. I'm a bit worried that with so many bones, etc., it'll slow down the setup a bit for not a huge gain since they are already pretty small. I'll play with it a bit and see.

Tuesday, September 6, 2005: Back at It

So, I'm back working on the clown at full speed after a week of taking it easy. I still haven't got the final mesh, but I'm hoping that will happen during this week. In the meantime, I've decided to expand on the hand setup. I want each finger to be able to go into "bend" mode so that the animator has total freedom over the fingers. I realize that this will mean a lot more bones and extra setup since for each "bend" system a lot of things happen underneath. I'm hoping it won't slow down the setup too much. I'll run tests later on to see if it's worth the hopefully minor performance issues compared to the added control. The setup should work similar to how the foot setup works right now, but on individual fingers.

I'll post some updates on it soon.

Tuesday, September 6, 2005: Flexible Fingers

I borrowed from the already bendy setup for the feet and modified it slightly to make it work with the hands. The idea behind this is to give maximum control to the animator. Now they can go into flexible (bendy) mode in each finger. This should help with adding that extra layer of cartoony-ness and flexibility needed with maximum control. Additionally, the animator can scale each individual finger joint.

I divided the setup into two. The main is the finger control that controls the curl of the fingers, spread and twist. The main controller also has a child where the additional controllers are located (scale for each finger and the option to go in and out of bend mode). Once in bend mode, the same controllers as always appear where the animator is free to place them wherever they want.

Thursday, September 8, 2005: Time Is Running Out

I was hoping to have the setup by the end of last month; that didn't happen so I'm setting a new deadline for the end of this month. Now this has to be a hard deadline 'cause poses need to be created for the book and they need to be done and submitted soon. So there isn't too much time left.

That means that I'll probably have to cut a few corners for the time being and get it out the door. I'll come back to it later (next month I'm sure) and finish the facial off properly. That's the problem with deadlines: You sometimes don't have all the time you would like to do all the things you want to do. Oh well. The good thing is that after this first deadline, there will be no more deadlines, so I'll have a lot of time to tweak and improve the rig.

Wednesday, September 21, 2005: Back on the Clown

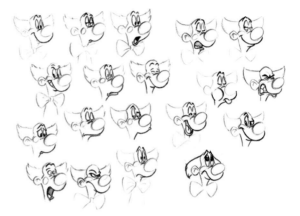

Ok, I'm back on the clown.

Dan sent me yesterday a lot of blend shapes, and today Angie sent me a very useful facial sheet (drawn by Jamie). This will help a lot to try to get the proper shapes needed for the book. Right now, because of time constraints, I'll be doing a very quick facial setup. I might not even put everything up on a nice GUI. That and a lot more shapes will have to come later on.

I'll have to rework a lot of the shapes so that we can achieve the look that we want. For the time being I'll go for a frown, sad, and raise for the eyebrows and a normal, happy, and sad for the mouth. They'll all have a left and right. I'll keep on adding to them as time goes by.

Tuesday, October 4, 2005: Facial Shapes

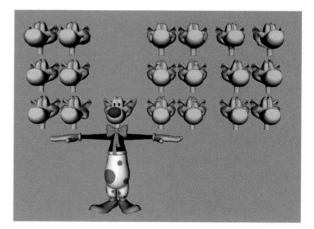

I know it's been a while. But things have slowly been progressing. Now I'm in the last stages of development. Paul Tanner, one of the great modelers at Propaganda Games, reworked the shapes a bit to get them ready for animation. I'll build a bigger, more robust system later on. But we need to get this book done, and time is of the essence.

I'll be working on a GUI the next couple of days to link all the shapes together. I'll be using something similar to what it is now known as the "Osipa Style." Though most of my learning has been from Mike Ferraro, whom I consider the silent partner in the "Osipa Style," since they developed a lot of the techniques in Jason's great book, *Stop Staring*, while at Mainframe. Mike has been key in my development as a TD, especially in the facial setup/animation area.

The shapes that are currently built are:

Mouth:

- ◆ E (wide)
- ◆ O (narrow)
- ◆ Smile L & R
- ◆ Sad L & R
- ◆ Sneer L & R
- ◆ Puff L & R

Eyes:

- ◆ Mad L & R
- ◆ Sad L & R
- ◆ Raise L & R
- ◆ Squint L & R

Wednesday, October 5, 2005: Facial GUI

I'm trying to keep it very simple and fast.

This is what the core GUI will look like. I've taken out the squint and the sneer because I didn't feel the shapes were as good as the rest. Once I tweak them a bit, I'll add them back in. The eyes for the moment will be controlled by a simple aim constraint, and the eyelids will be by custom attributes in

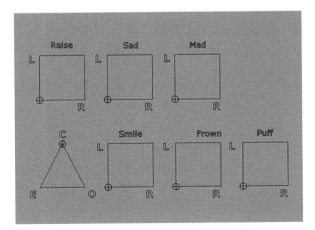

the aim controller. The rest of the deformation will come from bones. There will eventually be two types of bone deformation.

1. Structural. Things like the jaw, the nose (which has 3 bones), the cheeks, etc.
2. Deformation. These bones will be attached to the skin and will be used to deform the shapes further.

Friday, October 7, 2005: CEO Triangle

I figured the CEO triangle needed a bit more explanation, so here it goes.

This is one of the tricks I learned from Mike Ferraro. The idea behind it is that you have the C (for close), E (for wide), and O (for narrow). Now, the problem with having, say, one bar that goes horizontal (or vertical, makes no difference) from narrow to wide is that you have to go through close to get there.

```
|----|----|
```

```
E----C----O
```

But you might want to go directly from E to O without having to hit the close shape. It's a different transition; it feels more organic and smoother. Having the triangle eliminates this. Because now I can go from E to C or C to O, but also directly from E to O.

Wednesday, October 12, 2005: Painting Weights

I'm in the boring process of painting weights right now.

I'm doing a quick test to see if everything is in place and if there should be any mayor changes. The initial weighting is quick, something to see big movements. Once I'm happy that bones are in the right location, I'll start doing a more detailed pass.

Monday, October 17, 2005: Clown Rig Done

The clown rig is complete!

This last week I spent most of the time skinning and fixing little things here and there. As it usually happens, I came across a lot of little problems while skinning that I hadn't caught before. I dealt with most of them as I went along. I still would like to fix a lot of things. But time is up and the clown has to move on. I'll probably carry on working on it on my spare time—making the rig more robust, making sure that all the pieces are there and they work properly. For the time being, I'm happy. At least, happy enough. The facial is the area that needs more work. I would like to take on a completely different approach. I'll see how things work out and if I can improve on it.

After working on a rig I would pass it on to the animators and let them play with it for a while and get some feedback from them. (I would have done it before I spent all this time on the skinning. We usually use proxies or parented geometry, which makes the rigs fast to animate with and we don't have to worry about skinning.) Once the animators have had time to work with the rig, I would talk to them and see what they liked, what they didn't, where I need to improve it, etc. I would compile a list of notes, and then the rig would come back to me, I would work on it, and once again it would go back to the animators. This process would go back and forth a few times until both the animators and myself are happy with the rig. (Of course, deadlines sometimes get in the way, but usually estimates allocate for these kinds of multiple revisions.)

Appendix J
Timeline Bibliography

To create such a comprehensive timeline, multiple sources had to be used. The need to cross-check facts created quite a list of source material for the timeline in this book. We would like to thank Jerry Beck of Cartoon Research and Cartoon Brew, Wayne Carlson of the Advanced Computing Center for the Arts and Design, Joshua Mosley at the School of Design at the University of Pennsylvania, Nancy Pollard of Brown University, the ACM SIGGRAPH Education Committee, the Academy of Motion Pictures and Sciences, Wikipedia: The Free Encyclopedia, Dan McLaughlin of the UCLA Animation Workshop, Michael Morrison, Terrence Masson, Patrick Prince, Robert Holzman, Daniel Sevo, William Shoaf, Matthew Ward of Worcester Polytechnic Institute, David Winter, and Tom Sito for their help piecing together the history for the animation timeline and other historical facts throughout this book.

The following sites provided information used in the timeline:

- The Academy of Motion Picture Arts and Sciences. The Academy Awards Database. http://academy.org.
- Beck, Jerry. Cartoon Research. "The Animated Movie Guide." http://cartoonresearch.com.
- Carlson, Wayne. "A Critical History of Computer Graphics and Animation." http://accad.osu.edu/~waynec/history/lesson6.html.
- McLaughlin, Dan. "A Rather Incomplete but Still Fascinating History of Animation." http://animation.filmtv.ucla.edu/program/anihist.html.
- Masson, Terrence. *CG 101: A Computer Graphics Industry Reference*. New Riders Press, 1999. Excerpt. "Brief History of the New York Institute of Technology Computer Graphics Lab." http://www.cs.cmu.edu/~ph/nyit/masson/nyit.html.
- Morrison, Michael. *Becoming a Computer Animator*. Sams, 1994. Excerpt. "Advances of the 1970s." http://www.cs.cmu.edu/afs/cs/usr/ph/www/nyit/morrison/1970s.txt.
- Mosely, Joshua. Compiled History of Animation. http://www.joshuamosley.com/UPenn/courses/Ani/AnimationHistory.html.
- Pollard, Nancy. Animation Timeline. http://www.cs.brown.edu/courses/cs229/animTimeline.html.
- Prince, Patrick and Robert Holzman. SIGGRAPH paper. "John Whitney: 'The Problem: How Shall Motion Pattern Time?'" http://www.siggraph.org/education/stuff/spacef95/john.html.

◆ Sevo, Daniel. History of Computer Graphics. http://hem.passagen.se/des/hocg/hocg_intro.htm.

◆ Shoaff, William. A Short History of Computer Graphics.
http://www.cs.fit.edu/~wds/classes/graphics/History/history/history.html.

◆ Sito, Tom. The Animation Guild. "Cartoonists Unions: A Legacy of Artists Helping Artists."
http://www.animationguild.org.

◆ Ward, Matthew. "A (Spotty) History and Who's Who of Computer Graphics."
http://web.cs.wpi.edu/~matt/courses/cs563/talks/history.html.

◆ Wikipedia: The Free Encyclopedia. http://en.wikipedia.org.

◆ Winter, David. PONG-Story. http://www.pong-story.com/intro.htm.

Index

Numbers
180-degree rule
defined, 295
camera cuts, 51

A
A/B roll, 307
Abel (& Associates), Robert 7, 9, 11, 84, 129, 146, 149, 206
acting out (scenes), animation strategy, 105–109
acting, 295
addictions, character bio element, 73
aesthetic appeal, 2D versus 3D animation, 4
age, character bio element, 71
aliasing, 307
angle views, CG tools advantage, 153, 155–156
animal voiceovers, moral/social concept delivery method, 36–37
animatics
choreography pass, 32
defined, 295
layout finalling, 32
pre-viz step, 32, 46–47
storyboard presentations, 44–48
workbook pass, 31–32
animating on 1s/2s, 295
animation cels, 296
Animation Mentor, learning opportunity, 210
animation principles, 289–293
animation strategies
acting out (scenes), 105–109
gesture drawings, 109–111
idea sharing, 113

reference footage, 103–106
thinking and planning, 101–103
thumbnails, 111–112
animations
computer-generated versus traditional, 3–4
defined, 295
ever-evolving art form, 5–6
medium and not the story, 25
silhouette importance, 181–182
anti-aliasing, 307
anticipation
animation principles, 289
defined, 296
appeal
animation principles, 292
defined, 296
approval layers, multiple art direction, 204–207
archetypes
character development, 63–66, 73–74
defined, 63
arcs
animation principles, 290
defined, 296
art direction
computer-generated (CG) animation revolution, 20
studio politics, 204–207
artistic integrity, outsourcing issues, 228
aspect ratio
defined, 307
film versus television storyboards, 55
at will contracts, freelancers, 223
atmosphere
character bio element, 73
role in emotions, 191

attentiveness, psychological gestures, 192–193

audiences

CG (computer-generated) animation appeal, 4, 13

visual-effects appeal, 16–18

author's biographies, 241–257

Avery, Tex, 22, 28, 33, 39, 115, 125, 206, 210

B

Babbitt, Art 92, 167

back story, character development, 40–42

background paintings, 296

Bakshi, Ralph, 61, 72, 84, 91, 101, 106, 120, 126, 129, 169

belief systems, memorable villains, 82

believability

lines of tension, 188

memorable characters, 74–76

storytelling element, 34–35

Bezier handles, curve shape control, 135

Bezier spline, 307

bitmap, 307

Blair, Preston 23, 179, 214

Blanc, Mel, 23, 159

blend shapes, dialogue development, 162

blocking, 296–297

blogs, rigging, 315–329

bluescreen, 308

Bluth, Don, 9, 12, 25, 106, 121, 128, 175, 177, 189, 218

Bluth Studios, second Golden Age of Animation, 9

body structure, character development element, 72, 78–80, 191–192

books, suggested reading, 313

Bosustow, Steve, 117, 211

Bray, John, 6

breakdowns, motion definition, 147–149

brevity, e-mail communications, 220–221

B-spline, 307

C

camera cuts, storytelling element, 49–51

camera staging

motion-capture advantages, 179

shot construction element, 50–51

shot pacing, 53

Cameron, James 156, 165, 173

CAPS (Computer Animation Production System), 2D production aid, 20

Catmull, Ed, 9, 20, 90, 94, 101, 113, 134

cels, 297

CG productions (1994-2005), 259–265

character animation terms, 295–305

character bios, development questions, 71–73

character development. *See also* memorable characters

2D to 3D translation, 86–90

back story, 40–42

body structures, 191–192

character bios, 71–73

design guidelines, 84–85

emotions, 69–70, 188–191

empathy, 61, 68–69

empathy versus sympathy, 191

flaws, 69–70

high versus low status conduct, 184

Laban techniques, 185–186

memorable villains, 80–84

power centers, 183–184

psychological gestures, 192–193

real-life inspiration, 67–69

rule of threes, 79

situational reaction, 186–188

space occupation, 184–185

stereotype versus archetype, 63–66, 73–74

subtext, 192–193

texture handling, 90–92

character growth, storytelling element, 38–40

character model sheets, 297
character posing
  key frame layering, 143–144
  layering method, 143–144
  motion offsets, 142–143
character rules, storytelling element, 36
character voices, scratch track development, 44
character-driven movies, 2D/3D combination successes, 12–13
chatter, 308
choreo animators, on set feedback, 46–47
choreography, animatic pass, 32
cinematic storytelling, character development decisions, 78–80
Clampett, Bob, 17, 22, 131
clarity, storytelling element, 33
cleanup, 297
clichés, character development, 63–66
clip, 308
clown mascot, rigging blog, 315–329
color model cels, 297
comments, director/supervisor, 283–287
commercials, storyboard development, 56
competition, studio politics, 212–213
composition, 297
Computer Animation Production System (CAPS), 2D production aid, 20
computer animation terms, 307–311
computer-generated (CG) animation
  approval process, 169–170
  art direction revolution, 20
  camera angle advantages, 153, 155–156
  cleanup process, 173–174
  crossover from 2D, 21–23, 27–28
  dialogue development, 161–162
  digital artistry development, 18–21
  dollar-return advantages, 16
  drawing skill benefits, 167–169
  floaty motion, 155
  instant feedback benefits, 153

  learning from the past, 235–236
  mass-production approach, 226–227
  mentoring structure, 207–210
  multiple-animator-per-shot pipeline, 211–212
  outsourcing reactions, 227–229
  revision process, 171–173
  rig development, 154
  rig principles, 92–93
  software "jockey" classification, 215–216
  software revision issues, 131–132
  technology advancements, 7–13
  texture handling, 90–92
  versus traditional (2D), 3–4
  visual-effects appeal, 16–18
  workflow development issues, 131–132
computery motion, avoiding, 133–138
concept art, 297
confusion, psychological gestures, 192–193
continuity
  camera cuts, 49–51
  defined, 299
core skills, animator development element, 215–216
creditability, memorable characters, 74–76
culture, character bio element, 72
curves
  avoiding motion defect, 135–138
  graph editor display, 138–139
  motion carving, 140–142
cuts
  180-degree rule, 51
  defined, 297
  shot pacing, 52–54

D
D1/D2/D3/D5, 308
dailies
  defined, 297
  studio politics, 203–204
departmental communications, studio politics, 218–222

details
defined, 298
importance of, 164–165
dialogue
Henson method, 161
Digital Age of animation, studios and movies, 277–280
digital artistry, development history, 18–21
Digital Disk Recorder (DDR), 308
Digital Effects (DE), CGI development role, 7
dimensions, Laban elements, 185–186
directive, storytelling importance, 32–33
directors
motion-capture interaction advantages, 178–179
multiple art direction, 204–207
true comments, 283–287
Disney, Walt, 5, 8–9, 11, 16, 20, 25, 28, 31, 42–43, 47–48, 68, 75, 79, 83, 160, 165, 167
Disney Studios
animated film abandonment, 8, 9
switch to computer-generated (CG) animation, 15–16, 23
drawing skills, CG benefits, 167–169
dreams, character bio element, 73
DreamWorks Animation
switch to computer-generated (CG) animation, 15–16
traditional (2D) animation role, 12

E
ease-in/ease-out, 298
edit, 308
education, character bio element, 71–72
ego, psychological gestures, 192–193
e-mail, department communications, 220–221

emotions
atmosphere's role, 191
attitude changes, 162
character development, 69–70, 188–191
storytelling element, 37–38
empathy
camera placement guidelines, 53
memorable villains, 81
storytelling element, 37–38
versus sympathy, 191
ethnicity, character bio element, 71
event orchestration, storytelling element, 41–42
evolutionary cycle, character bio element, 72
exaggeration
animation principles, 291
defined, 298
exposure sheet, 298
eyebrows, dialogue development, 162
eyes
moving-hold importance, 163

F
facial shapes
dialogue development, 161–162
moving holds, 163
family, character bio element, 72
field, 12, 298
field, 16, 298
fielding, 298
fielding: panning shots, 299
Final Cut, storyboard presentations, 45
flaws (fatal)
character bio element, 72
character development, 69–70
memorable villains, 80–84
Fleischer, Dave, 7, 112
Fleischer, Max, 7–8, 89, 112, 153, 183
floaty motion, techniques, 133–138
flow, Laban technique, 185–186

follow-through
  animation principles, 290
  defined, 296, 299
food/eating, character bio element, 72
forces, 299
forward kinematics, 308
FPS (frames per second), 295, 299
frames
  breakdown motions, 147–149
  defined, 299
  in-betweens, 149–150
  motion blurs, 165–167
  motion clarity, 135
  motion defect techniques, 133–138
  motion overlap, 150–152
  on-the-twos animation, 149
  secondary motion, 150–152
  timing offsets, 137
frames per second (FPS), 295, 299
freelancers, pros/cons, 223–225
Freleng, Friz, 9, 13, 17, 23, 62, 131, 178

G
game playing, visual-effects movie role, 17
gender, character bio element, 71
gesture drawings, animation strategy,
    109–111
Gimbal lock, 308–309
glitz skills, animator development element,
    215–216
goal-seeking, memorable characters, 76–78
goals, character bio element, 73
Golden Age of animation, studios and
    movies, 267–269
gooey motion, avoiding, 133–138
graph editors
  2D motion representation, 138
  curve display, 138–139
  floaty motion techniques, 133–138
  linear curves, 140–142
  stepped key pose test, 140

growth, character arcs, 39–40
GUI (Graphical User Interface), 309

H
Hanna-Barbera, CGI development role, 7–8
health, character bio element, 71
Hearst Studio, storyboard development, 43
height, character bio element, 71
Henson method, dialogue development, 161
hold, 299
hookups, 299
Hubley, Faith, 56, 64, 209
Hubley, John, 56, 64, 211
humanity, memorable villains, 80

I
idea sharing
  animation strategy, 113
  storytelling element, 35–36
idiosyncrasies, character bio element, 73
improvisational actors
  high versus low status conduct, 184
  Laban technique, 185–186
  power center (lead), 183–184
  situational reaction, 186–188
  space occupation, 184–185
improvisational classes, acting education
    opportunity, 182–183
in-betweens, 300
indifference, psychological gestures,
    192–193
Industrial Light and Magic, CGI develop-
    ment role, 9
Information International Inc. (III), CGI
    development role, 7
intelligence, character bio element, 71
inverse kinematics, 309
Ising, Rudy, 17
Iwerks, Ub, 8–9, 14–15, 19, 85, 141

J

job market, competition issues, 212–213

joints, successive breaking, 303

Johnston, Ollie, 8, 68, 93, 109, 119, 138, 142

Jones, Chuck, 17, 39, 52, 56, 73, 77, 92, 166, 178, 217

judgmental, psychological gestures, 192–193

K

Kahl, Milt, 8, 41–42, 51, 68, 93

key frames
    defined, 300
    layering techniques, 143–144
    motion-capture technology, 178–182
    motion clarity, 135–138
    weight redistribution, 156–159

L

Laban technique, improvisational actors, 185–186

Lantz, Walter 10, 12–13, 175

Lasseter, John, 9–12, 114, 125, 134–136, 143, 152, 155, 178, 214

layering, character posing, 143–144

layout drawing, 300

layout finalling, animatic process, 32

lead (power center), improvisational actor tool, 183–184

leica reel, 300

linear curves, graph editors, 140–142

lines of tension, acting believability, 188

listening (dialogue/soundtrack), animation strategy, 102

live-action directors, animation transition difficulty, 45

live-action films, traditional (2D) animation combination successes, 12–13

Lucas, George, 9, 87, 95, 113, 143

Lucasfilm, CGI development role, 9–10

M

MAGI Synthavision, CGI development role, 7

mass-production approach, studio politics, 226–227

matte, 309

McLaren, Norman, 21, 147

memorable characters. *See also* character development
    believability, 74–76
    bio development questions, 71–73
    credibility, 74–76
    motivation, 76–78
    narrative versus cinematic storytelling, 78–80
    qualities, 62–66
    real-life inspiration, 67–69
    stereotype versus archetype, 63–66, 73–74
    villains, 80–84

mentorship
    educational opportunities, 210–212
    studio politics, 207–210

Messmer, Otto, 8, 127

model, 309

money, character bio element, 72

moral concepts, talking animals, 36–37

motion blurs, techniques, 165–167

motion capture
    actor-animator bridge, 178–182
    camera staging, 179
    defined, 309
    performance input opportunity, 179–180
    realistic animation, 179
    silhouette importance, 181–182

motion defects, techniques, 133–138

motivation, memorable characters, 76–78

mouths, dialogue development, 161–162

movement
    timing contrasts, 159–160
    weight redistribution, 156–159

movies, by animation era and studio, 267–281

moving hold
  defined, 299, 300
  development techniques, 162–164
multiple art direction, studio politics,
    204–207
multiple characters, primary/secondary
    motion contrast, 152

N

naiveté, weak character flaw, 70
narrative storytelling, character develop-
    ment decisions, 78–80
nervousness, psychological gestures,
    192–193
networking, reputation building, 225–226
New York Institute of Technology (NYIT),
    CGI development role, 7
nocturnal, character bio element, 72
Non-Uniform Rational B-Splines (NURBS),
    309
Norman, Floyd, 11, 15, 21, 24, 34–35, 42,
    53, 64, 81, 106, 133–134, 180, 187,
    190, 209, 213, 217, 222, 231
NTSC format, 310
NYIT, CAPS (Computer Animation
    Production System), 20

O

One-On-One Animation, hands-on mentor-
    ing, 210–211
orchestration, storytelling element, 41–42
outsourcing, reaction to, 227–229
overlap
  floaty motion, 138
  motion techniques, 150–152
overlapping action
  animation principles, 290
  defined, 300
overlay, 310
overscan, 310

P

pencil test, 301
persona, character development element,
    78–80
personality, 301
photo-realistic effects, CG (computer-gener-
    ated) animation appeal, 4
pigeonholing, studio politics, 214–215
pipeline structures, multiple-animator-per-
    shot, 211–212
Pixar
  CGI development role, 9, 12–13
  crossover from 2D animation, 22
pixel, 310
planning ahead, 301
planning, animation strategy, 101–103
play acting, animation strategy, 105–109
Playblast, CG tools advantages, 153
plot development, storytelling element,
    32–36
point of view (POV), storytelling element,
    49
pointers, storyboard presentations, 44
posing, 301
polygon, 310
pose test, stepped mode, 140
poses
  breakdowns, 147–149
  breaking rig constraints, 145–147
  in-between frames, 149–150
  layering techniques, 143–144
  motion offsets, 142–143
  power center (lead), 183–184
  psychological gestures, 192–193
pose-to-pose animation, 290, 301
Post-War era (animated television influ-
    ence), studios and movies, 271–275
POV (point of view), storytelling element,
    49
power center (lead), improvisational actor
    tool, 183–184

Premiere, storyboard presentations, 45
premise, plot importance, 32–33, 48
presentations, storyboards, 44–48
pre-visualization
    animatics element, 32, 46–47
    defined, 310
problem-solving, studio politics, 222–223
production schedules, studio politics,
    229–231
productions, traditional and CG
    (1994–2005), 259–265
profession, character bio element, 72
projects
    approval, 169–170
    cleanup, 173–174
    revision, 171–173
psychological gestures
    character development, 192–193

Q
qualities, memorable characters, 62–66
questions, character bios, 71–73

R
Ranft, Joe, 237
real-world situations, character develop-
    ment, 67–69
reality, versus entertainment exaggeration,
    160–161
Red-Green-Blue (RGB), 310
reference footage, animation strategy,
    103–106
Reitherman, Wolfgang "Woolie," 8, 68, 119
rendering, 310
reproduction/sex, character bio element, 71
resolution, 310
responsibility, studio politics, 216–218
revisions, CG tools advantage, 153
RGB (Red-Green-Blue), 310
rhythm
    timing contrasts, 159–160

rigging, clown mascot blog, 315–329
rigs
    breaking constraints, 145–147
    CG development, 154
    solid drawing principles, 92–93
Robert Abel & Associates Studio, CGI devel-
    opment role, 7, 9–10
rotoscope, 301
rough, 301–302
rule of threes, character development, 79

S
safe title area, 310
savoring the moment, storytelling element,
    52–54
scale, CG advantages, 155–156
scene development, storytelling element,
    33–34
scene flow, camera cuts, 49–51
scene referencing, animation strategy,
    103–106
scenes, acting out, 105–109
schedules, studio politics, 229–231
Schlesinger, Leon, 13, 22, 23, 33
scratch tracks, character voice development,
    44
Second Golden Age of animation, 275–277
secondary action
    animation principles, 291
    defined, 302
    floaty motion, 138
    techniques, 150–152
sex/reproduction, character bio element, 71
shading levels, CAPS (Computer Animation
    Production System), 20
shared ideas, animation strategy, 113
shot pacing, storytelling element, 52–54
silhouette, 297, 302
simplicity
    2D to 3D character translation, 86–88
    defined, 302
    storytelling element, 33

slow-in/slow-out
  animation principles, 290
  defined, 302
snap, 302
snapshots, thumbnail images, 111–112
social concepts, talking animals, 36–37
software
  "jockey" classification, 215–216
  revision issues, 131–132
solid drawing
  animation principles, 291
  rig principles, 92–93
space
  character interaction, 184–185
  Laban technique, 185–186
spacing, in-between frames, 149–150
Spielberg, Steven 171, 178, 180, 205
spline, 311
spliney motion
  avoiding, 133–138
squash
  animation principles, 289
  defined, 303
staging (cameras)
  animation principles, 289–290
  defined, 297, 302–303
  shot construction, 50–51
Stalling, Carl, 14, 88
status, high versus low conduct, 184
stepped mode, pose test, 140
stereotypes
  character development, 63–66, 73–74
  defined, 63
story reel, 303
storyboards
  animatic process, 31–32
  commercials, 56
  defined, 295, 303
  development history, 43
  film versus television, 54–56
  pointer presentations, 44

storytelling
  2D (traditional) animation downfall, 4, 13–14, 16
  back story orchestration, 40–42
  believability, 34–35
  camera cuts, 49–51
  character growth, 38–40
  character rules, 36
  clarity, 33
  emotion, 37–38
  empathy, 37–38
  event orchestration, 41–42
  idea sharing, 35–36
  narrative versus cinematic stories, 78–80
  plot development, 32–36
  POV (point of view), 49
  premise (directive) importance, 32–33, 48
  savoring the moment, 52–54
  scene development, 33–34
  scratch track development, 44
  shot pacing, 52–54
  simplicity, 33
  talking animals, 36–37
  thumbnail sketching, 43
straight-ahead animation
  defined, 301, 303
  principles, 290
stretch
  animation principles, 289
  defined, 303
studio politics
  competition, 212–213
  dailies, 203–204
  departmental communications, 218–222
  freelancers, 223–225
  mass-production approach, 226–227
  mentoring structure, 207–210
  multiple art direction, 204–207
  networking, 225–226
  outsourcing issues, 227–229
  pigeonholing, 214–215

responsibility acceptance, 216–218
schedules, 229–231
software "jockey", 215–216
workflow, 202–203
studios, movies by animation era, 267–281
stuffy, shot framing uses, 46
subtext
character development, 192–193
successive breaking of joints, 303
superiority, psychological gestures, 192–193
supervisors
approval process, 169–170
multiple art direction, 204–207
problem-solving, 222–223
true comments, 283–287
workflow requirements, 202–203
sympathy, versus empathy, 191

T
talent, character bio element, 73
talking animals, moral/social concept delivery method, 36–37
Tashlin, Frank, 89
technical director (TD), 311
television, storyboard development, 54–56
tension lines, acting believability, 188
Terry, Paul, 11, 14, 34, 55
texture handling, CG characters, 90–92
textures
moving-hold development, 162
think and plan, animation strategy, 101–103
Thomas, Frank, 8, 68, 93, 138 142
thumbnails
animation strategy, 111–112
storyboard development, 43
time code, 311
time, Laban technique, 185–186

timing
animation principles, 291
defined, 304
timing contrasts
moving holds, 163–164
natural-looking motion, 159–160
timing offsets, floaty motion, 137
traditional (2D) animation
antiquated medium, 14–16
CAPS (Computer Animation Production System), 20
caricaturing reality, 13
CG animation crossover, 21–23, 27–28
CG translation, 86–90
character posing, 142–143
dollar-return disadvantages, 16
live-action combination successes, 12–13
mentoring structure, 208
pencil and paper medium, 6, 7
second Golden Age of Animation, 8–9
storytelling downfall, 4, 13–14, 16
versus computer-generated (CG/3D), 3–4
traditional productions (1994-2005), 259–265
trauma, character bio element, 73
tweening, 304
twins, 304
Tytla, Bill, 36

U
underscan, 311
underwater characters, floaty motion advantage, 155
Undo button, CG tools advantage, 153
United Film Production (UPA), production contributions, 210–212

V

villains, memorable characters, 80–84
visual effects
audience appeal, 16–18
CG (computer-generated) animation appeal, 4
visualization, animation strategy, 101–103

W

Walt Disney Feature Animation, storyboard
development, 43
Wartime era (propaganda), studios and
movies, 270–271
watery motion, avoiding, 133–138
waveforms, dialogue development, 161
weariness, psychological gestures, 192–193
weight
character bio element, 71
defined, 304–305
Laban technique, 185–186
motion hierarchy element, 156–159
moving-hold role, 163

Whitney, John Jr., 7, 94
Whitney, John Sr., 7, 23, 36, 44, 65, 75,
118, 134, 177
Williams, Richard, 62, 92, 104, 107, 154,
160, 208
workbooks, animatic pass, 31–32
workflow
CG tools advantage, 153
revision process, 171–173
studio politics, 202–203

X

x-sheet, 305

Z

Z-axis, multiple character scene handling,
152

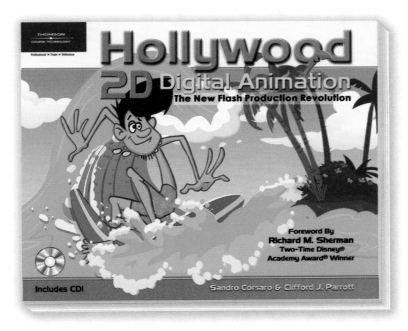